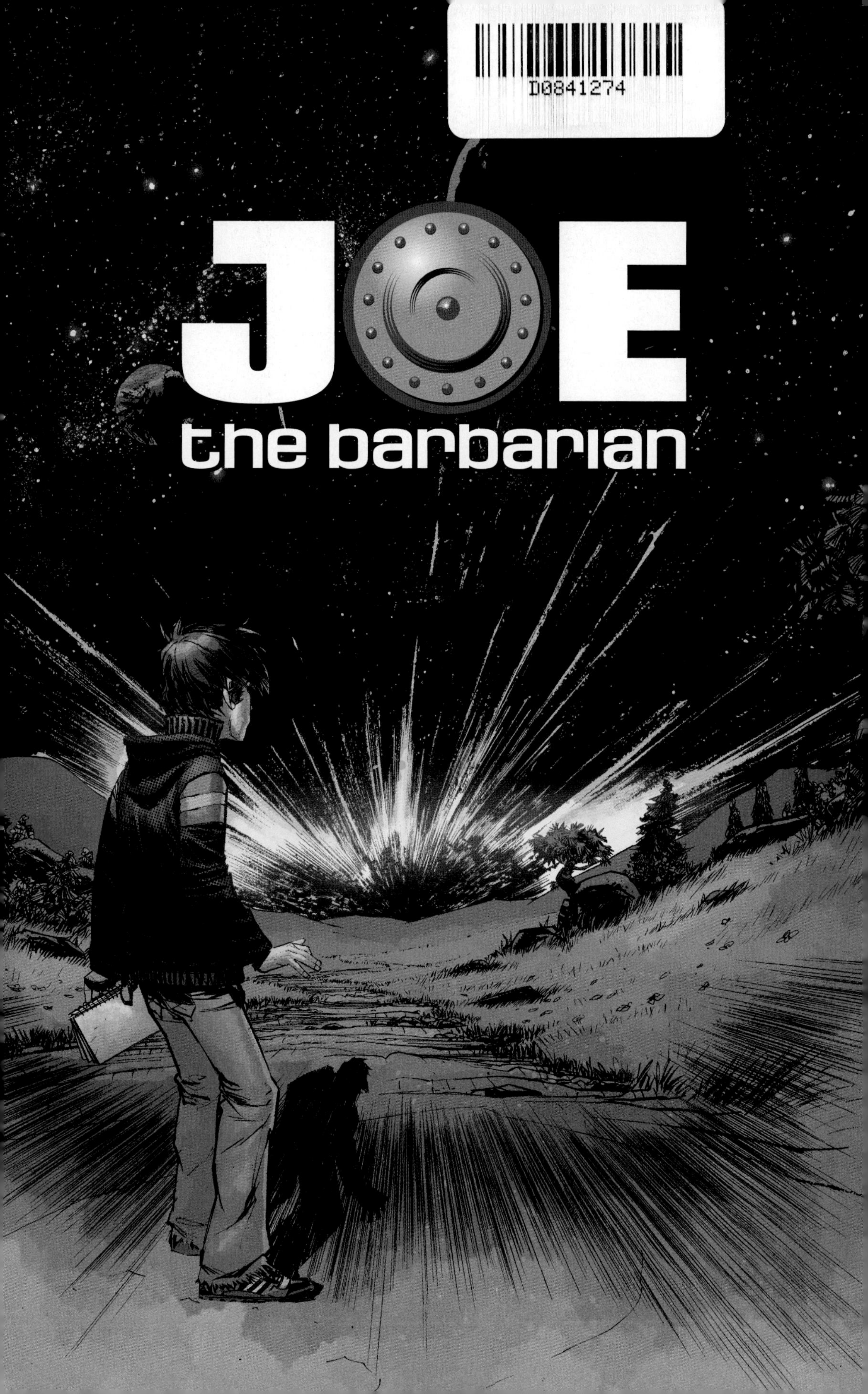
JOE
the barbarian

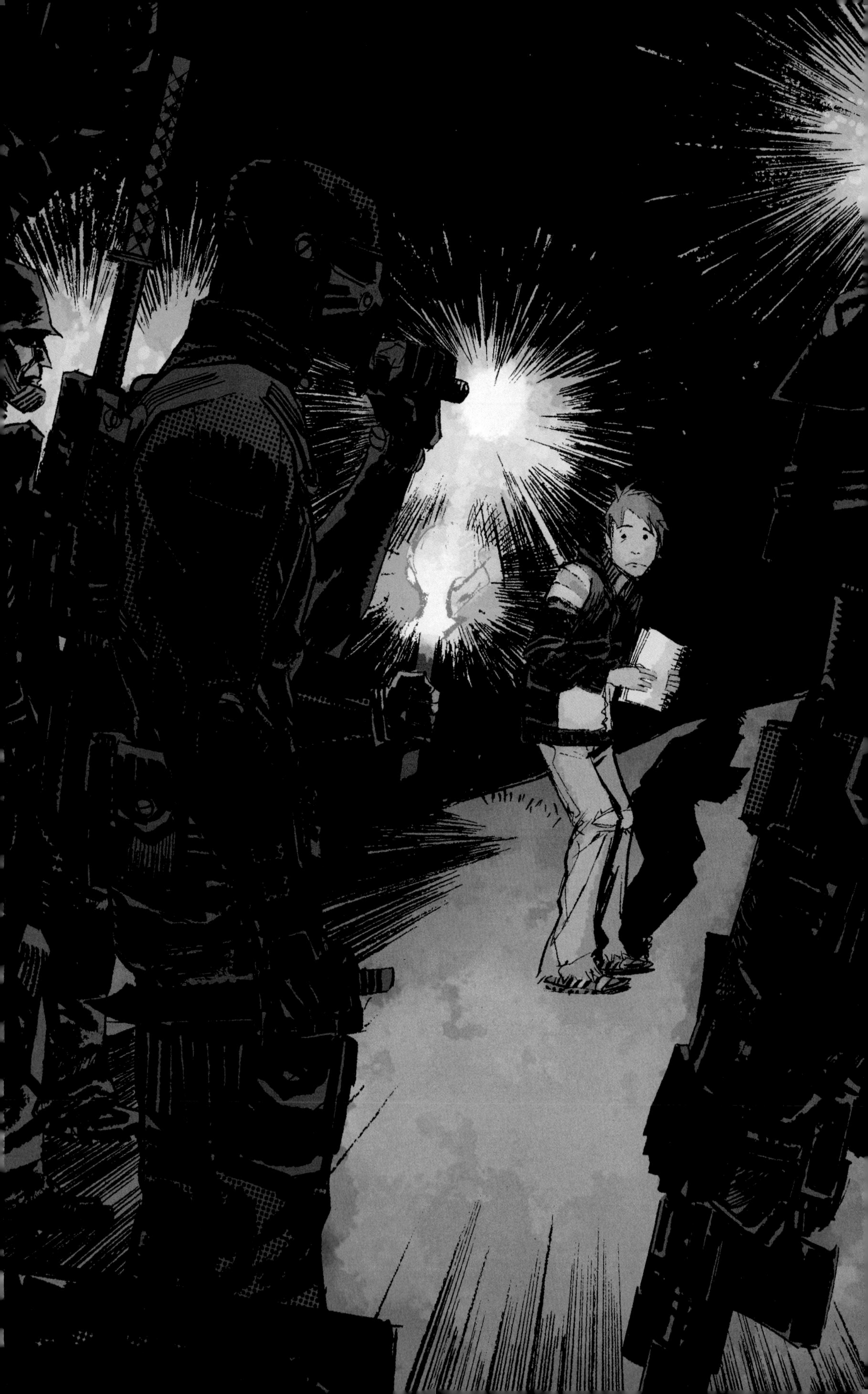

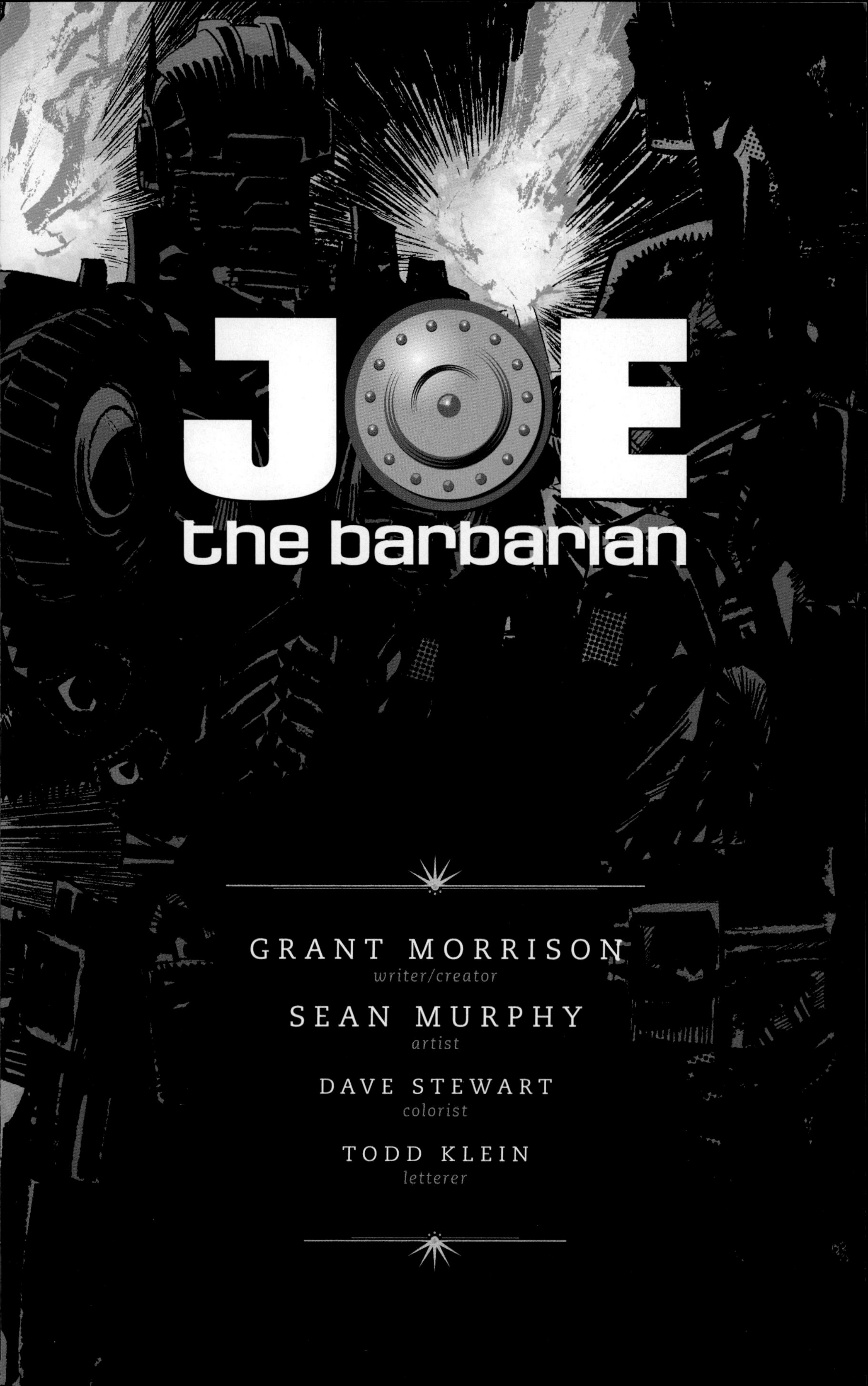

JOE
the barbarian

GRANT MORRISON
writer/creator

SEAN MURPHY
artist

DAVE STEWART
colorist

TODD KLEIN
letterer

Karen Berger
Editor – Original Series

Pornsak Pichetshote
Associate Editor – Original Series

Jeb Woodard
Group Editor – Collected Editions

Scott Nybakken
Editor – Collected Edition

Brainchild Studios/NYC
Publication Design

Shelly Bond
VP & Executive Editor – Vertigo

Diane Nelson
President

Dan DiDio and Jim Lee
Co-Publishers

Geoff Johns
Chief Creative Officer

Amit Desai
Senior VP – Marketing & Global Franchise
Management

Nairi Gardiner
Senior VP – Finance

Sam Ades
VP – Digital Marketing

Bobbie Chase
VP – Talent Development

Mark Chiarello
Senior VP – Art, Design & Collected Editions

John Cunningham
VP – Content Strategy

Anne DePies
VP – Strategy Planning & Reporting

Don Falletti
VP – Manufacturing Operations

Lawrence Ganem
VP – Editorial Administration & Talent
Relations

Alison Gill
Senior VP – Manufacturing
& Operations

Hank Kanalz
Senior VP – Editorial Strategy &
Administration

Jay Kogan
VP – Legal Affairs

Derek Maddalena
Senior VP – Sales & Business Development

Jack Mahan
VP – Business Affairs

Dan Miron
VP – Sales Planning & Trade Development

Nick Napolitano
VP – Manufacturing Administration

Carol Roeder
VP – Marketing

Eddie Scannell
VP – Mass Account & Digital Sales

Courtney Simmons
Senior VP – Publicity & Communications

Jim (Ski) Sokolowski
VP – Comic Book Specialty & Newsstand Sales

Sandy Yi
Senior VP – Global Franchise Management

JOE THE BARBARIAN

Published by DC Comics. Cover and compilation Copyright © 2011 Grant Morrison and DC Comics. All Rights Reserved.
Originally published in single magazine form in JOE THE BARBARIAN 1-8. Copyright © 2010, 2011 Grant Morrison and DC Comics. All Rights
Reserved. All characters, their distinctive likenesses and related elements featured in this publication are trademarks of Grant Morrison. VERTIGO is
a trademark of DC Comics. The stories, characters and incidents featured in this publication are entirely fictional. DC Comics does not read or accept
unsolicited submissions of ideas, stories or artwork.

DC Comics, 4000 Warner Blvd., Burbank, CA 91522
A Warner Bros. Entertainment Company
Printed in the USA. Third Printing.
ISBN: 978-1-4012-3747-9

Library of Congress Cataloging-in-Publication Data

Morrison, Grant, author
Joe the Barbarian / Grant Morrison, Sean Murphy.
pages cm
"Originally published in single magazine form in Joe the Barbarian 1-8."
ISBN 978-1-4012-3747-9
1. Graphic novels. I. Murphy, Sean Gordon, 1980- illustrator. II. Title
PN6727.M67J63 2013
741.5'9411--dc23
2012047802

PEFC Certified

Printed on paper from
sustainably managed
forests and controlled
sources

PEFC/29-31-75   www.pefc.org

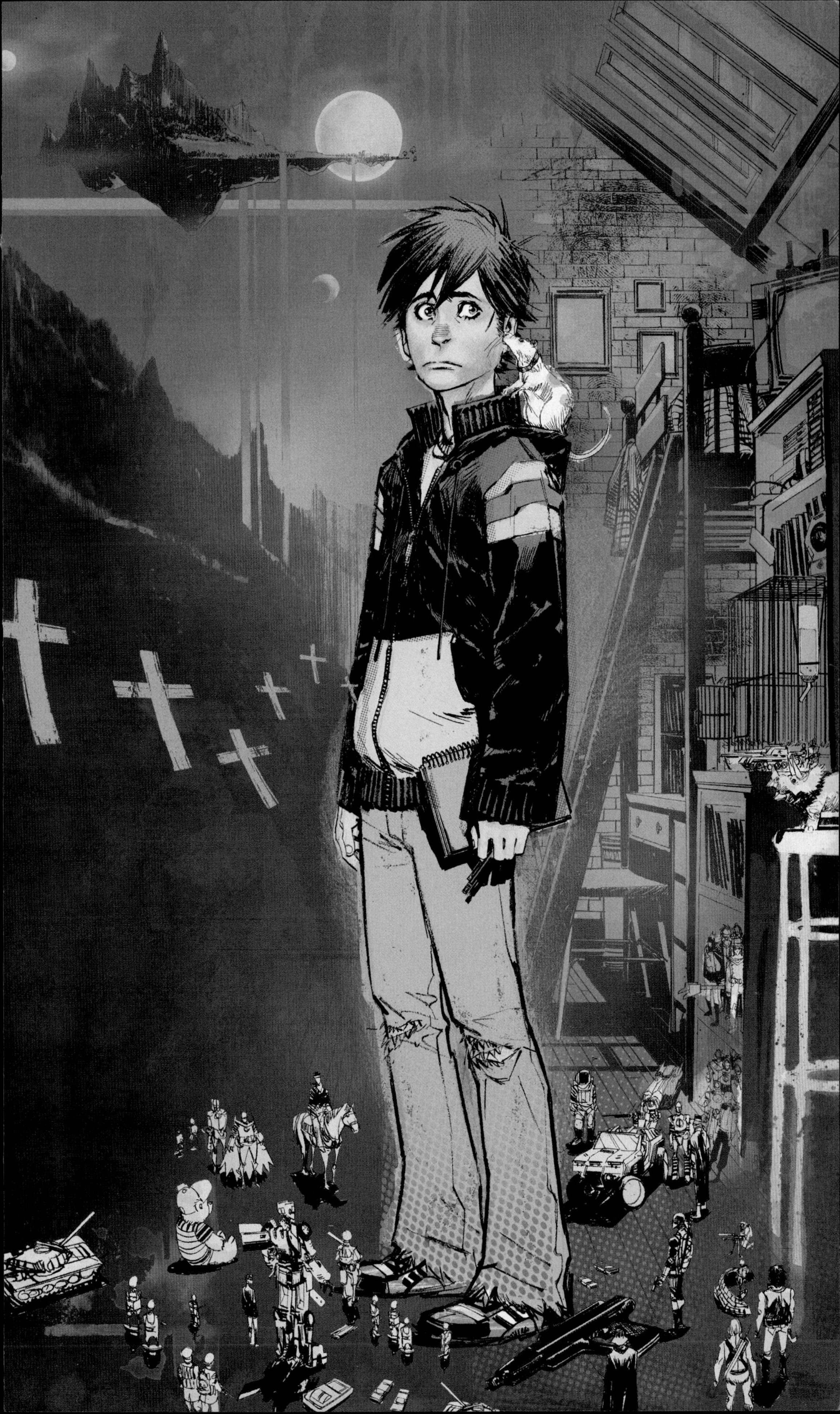

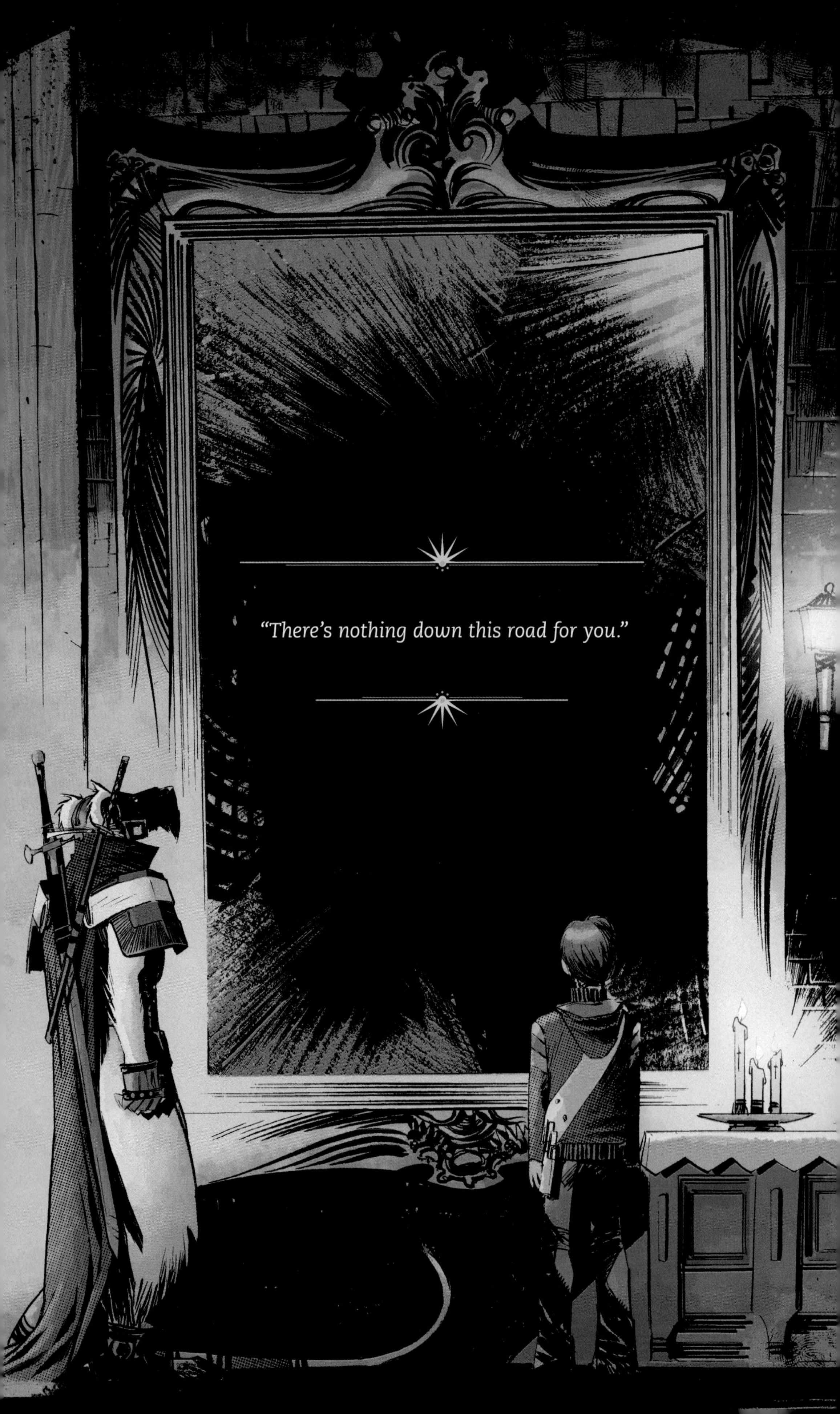
"There's nothing down this road for you."

chapter 1:
hypo

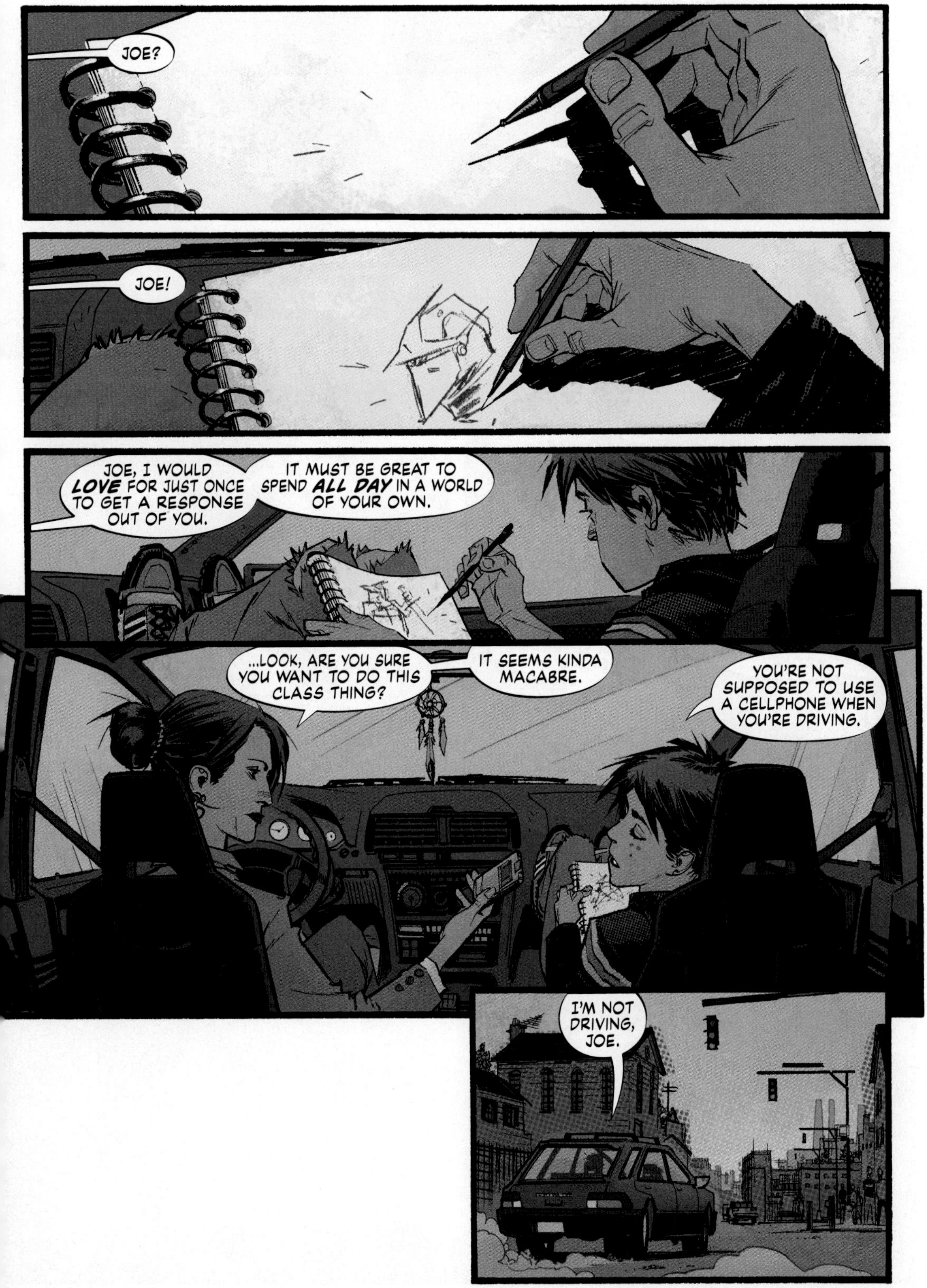
JOE?
JOE!
JOE, I WOULD LOVE FOR JUST ONCE TO GET A RESPONSE OUT OF YOU.
IT MUST BE GREAT TO SPEND ALL DAY IN A WORLD OF YOUR OWN.
...LOOK, ARE YOU SURE YOU WANT TO DO THIS CLASS THING?
IT SEEMS KINDA MACABRE.
YOU'RE NOT SUPPOSED TO USE A CELLPHONE WHEN YOU'RE DRIVING.
I'M NOT DRIVING, JOE.

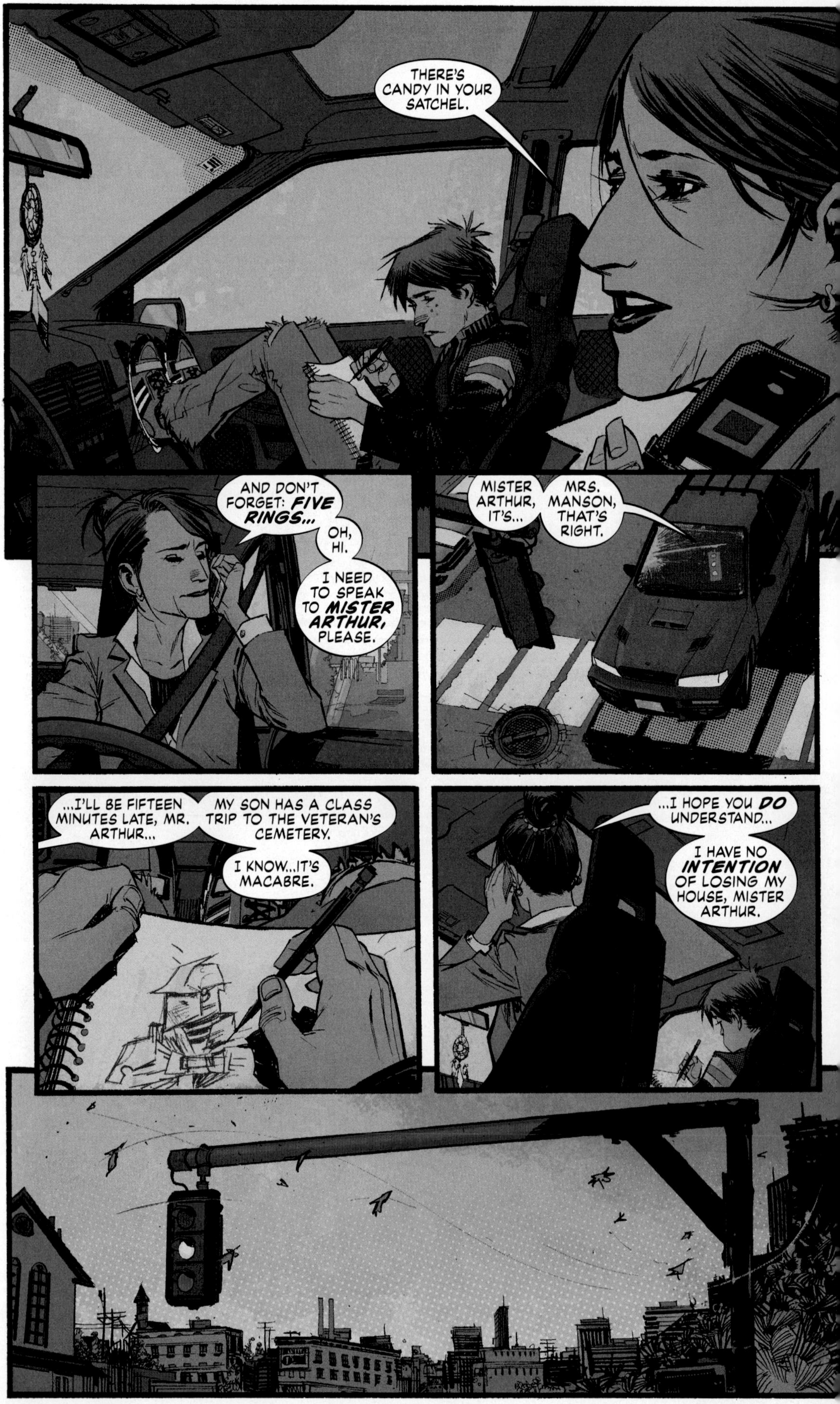
THERE'S CANDY IN YOUR SATCHEL.
AND DON'T FORGET: FIVE RINGS...
OH, HI.
I NEED TO SPEAK TO MISTER ARTHUR, PLEASE.
MISTER ARTHUR, IT'S...
MRS. MANSON, THAT'S RIGHT.
...I'LL BE FIFTEEN MINUTES LATE, MR. ARTHUR...
MY SON HAS A CLASS TRIP TO THE VETERAN'S CEMETERY.
I KNOW...IT'S MACABRE.
...I HOPE YOU DO UNDERSTAND...
I HAVE NO INTENTION OF LOSING MY HOUSE, MISTER ARTHUR.

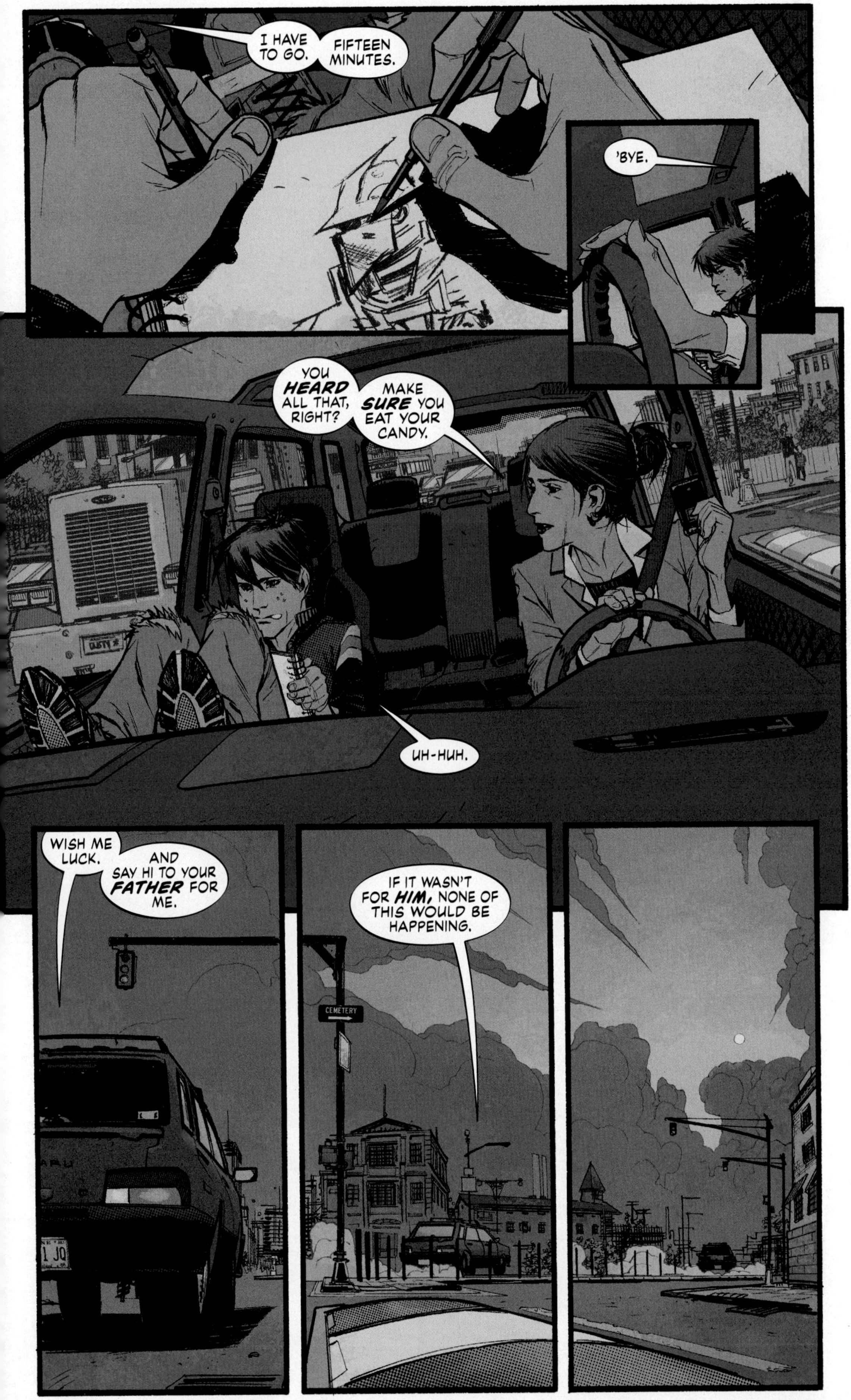

I HAVE TO GO.
FIFTEEN MINUTES.
'BYE.
YOU HEARD ALL THAT, RIGHT?
MAKE SURE YOU EAT YOUR CANDY.
UH-HUH.
WISH ME LUCK.
AND SAY HI TO YOUR FATHER FOR ME.
IF IT WASN'T FOR HIM, NONE OF THIS WOULD BE HAPPENING.
CEMETERY

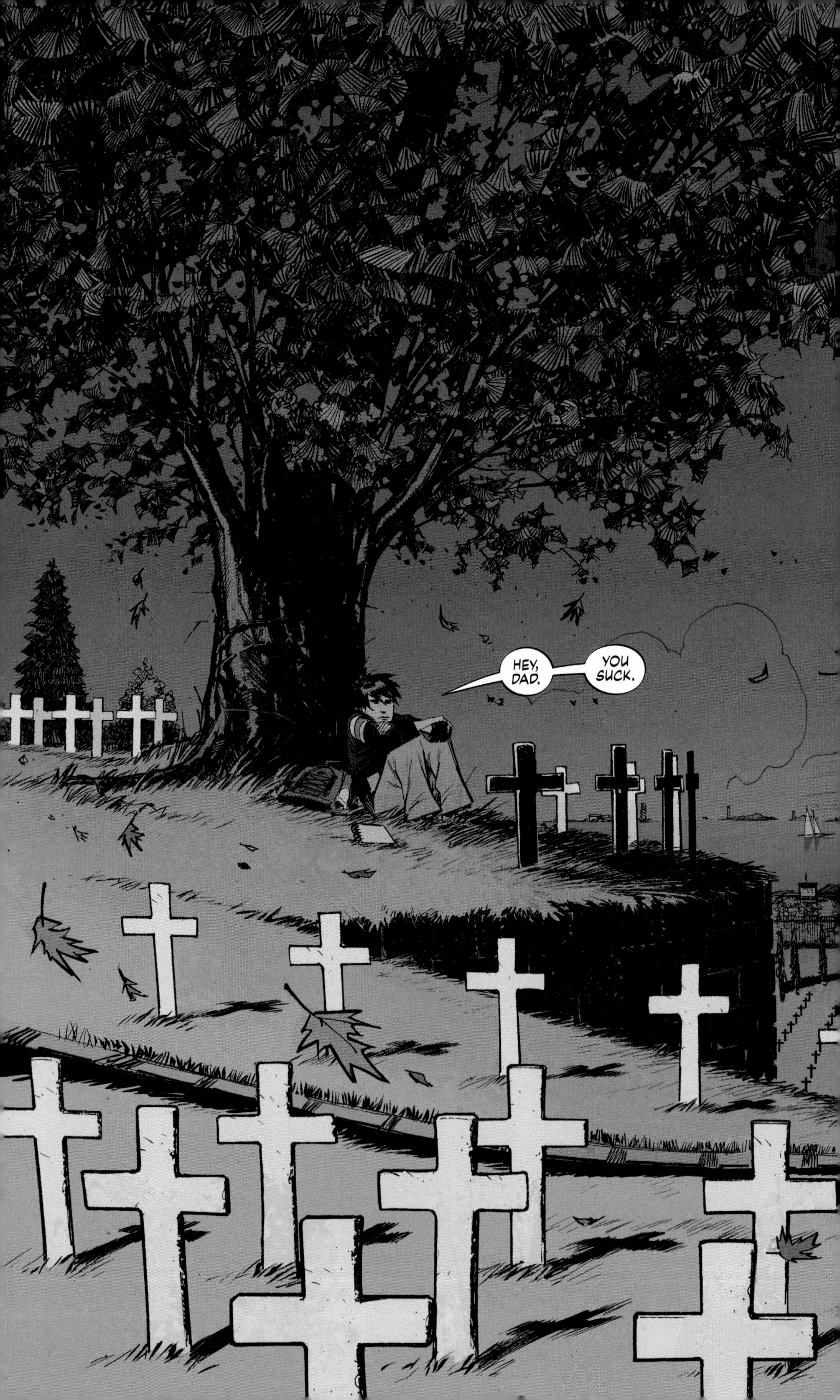
HEY, DAD.
YOU SUCK.

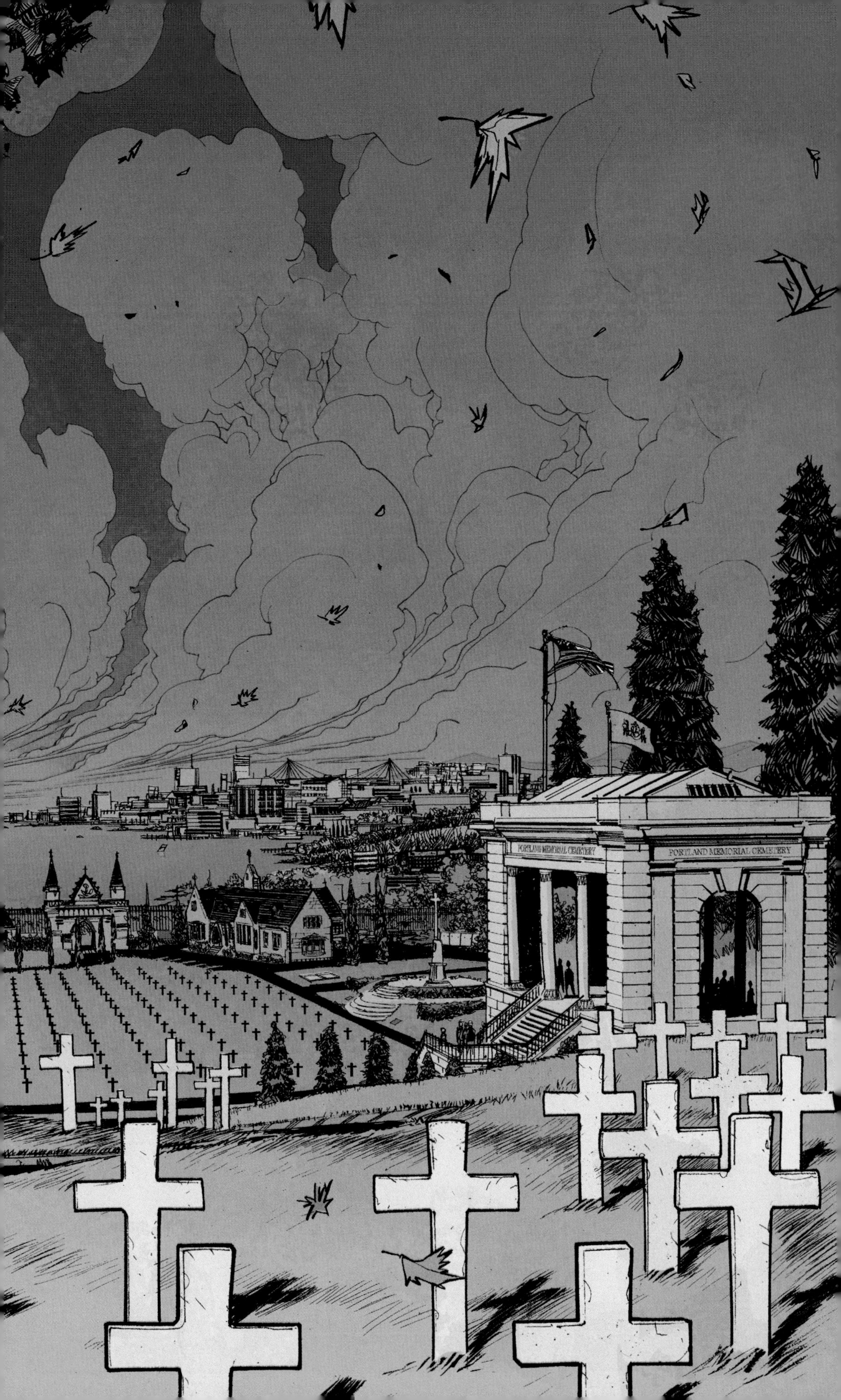
PORTLAND MEMORIAL CEMETERY
PORTLAND MEMORIAL CEMETERY

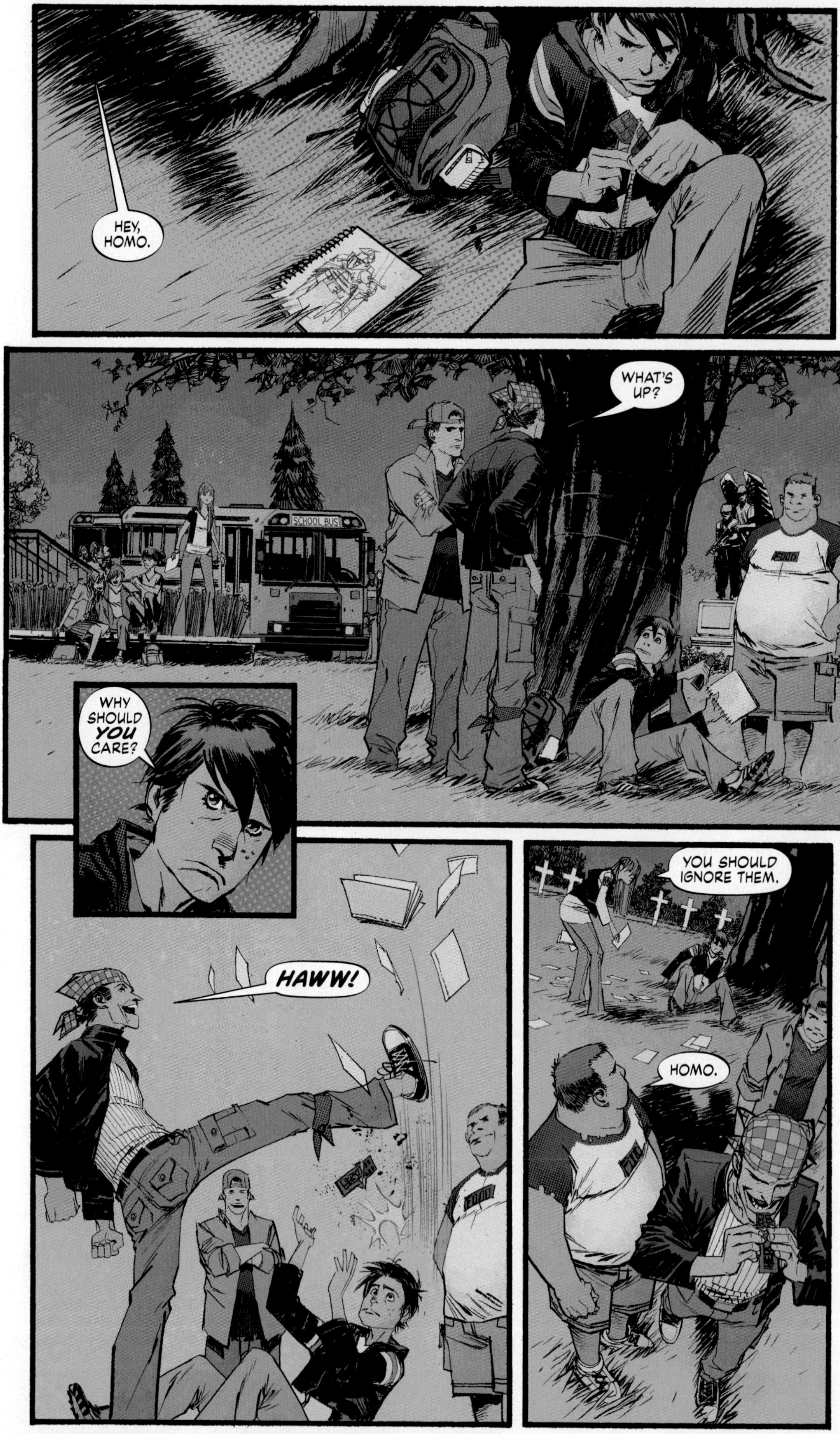
HEY, HOMO.
WHAT'S UP?
SCHOOL BUS
WHY SHOULD YOU CARE?
HAWW!
YOU SHOULD IGNORE THEM.
HOMO.

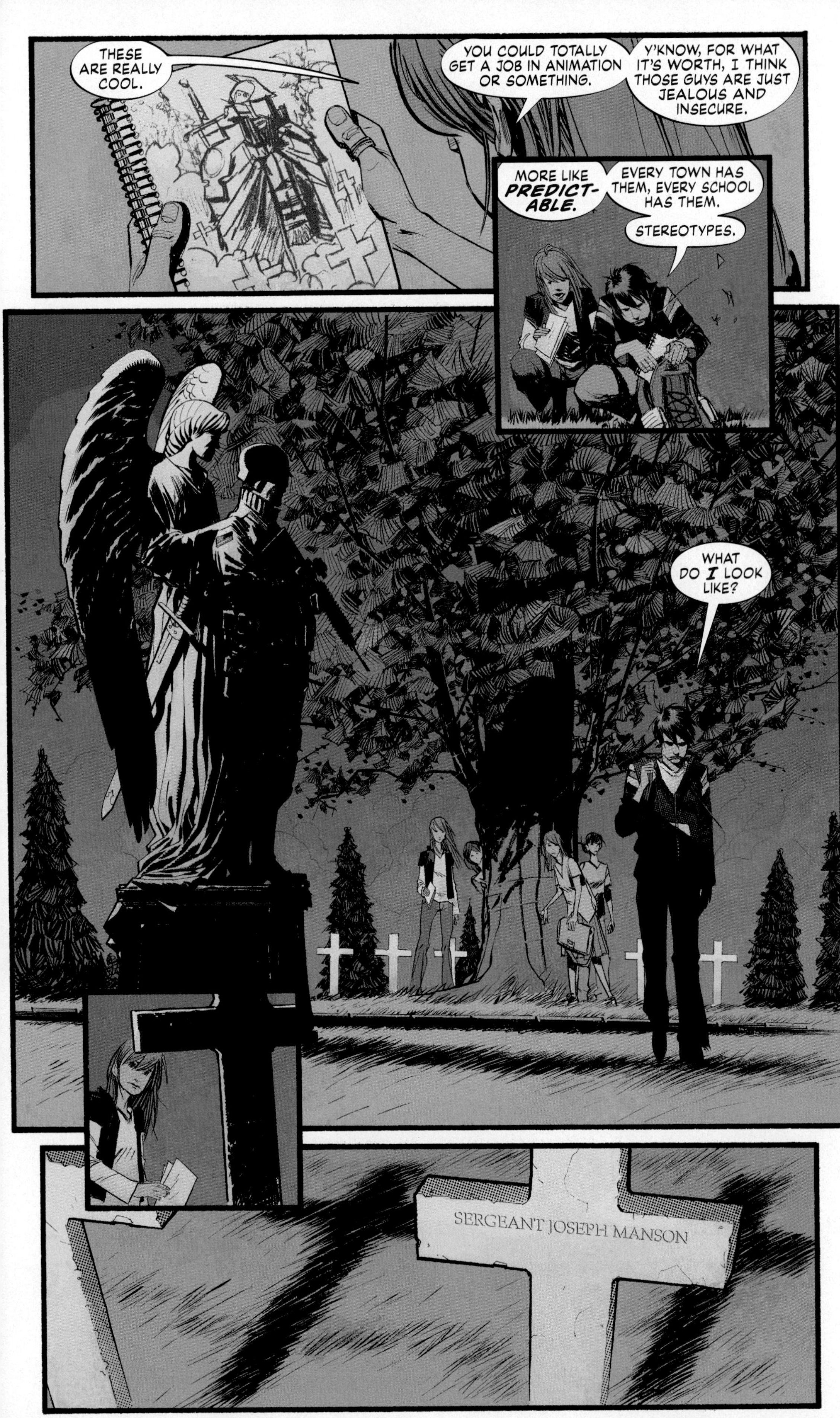
THESE ARE REALLY COOL.
YOU COULD TOTALLY GET A JOB IN ANIMATION OR SOMETHING.
Y'KNOW, FOR WHAT IT'S WORTH, I THINK THOSE GUYS ARE JUST JEALOUS AND INSECURE.
MORE LIKE PREDICT-ABLE.
EVERY TOWN HAS THEM, EVERY SCHOOL HAS THEM.
STEREOTYPES.
WHAT DO I LOOK LIKE?
SERGEANT JOSEPH MANSON

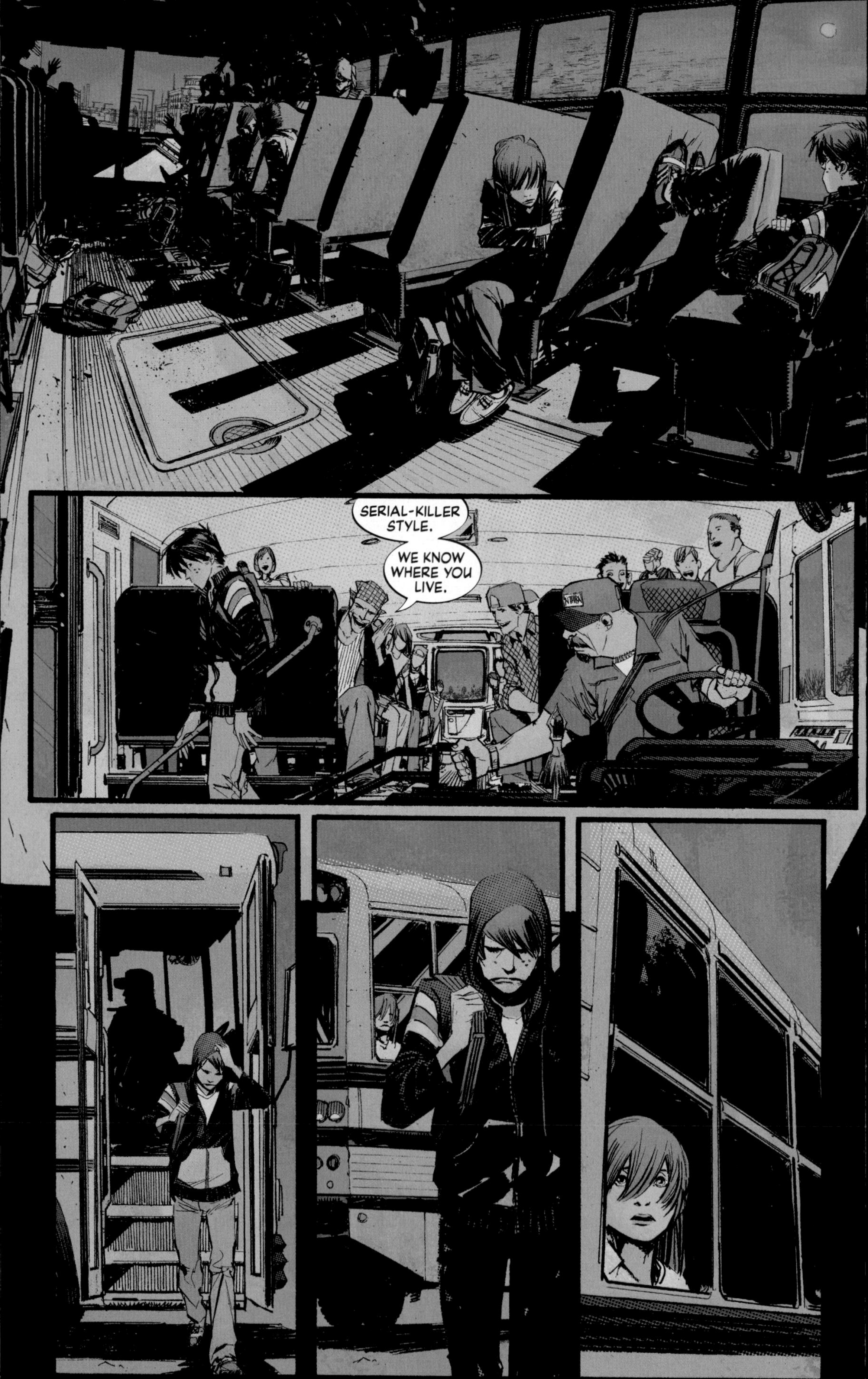
SERIAL-KILLER STYLE.
WE KNOW WHERE YOU LIVE.

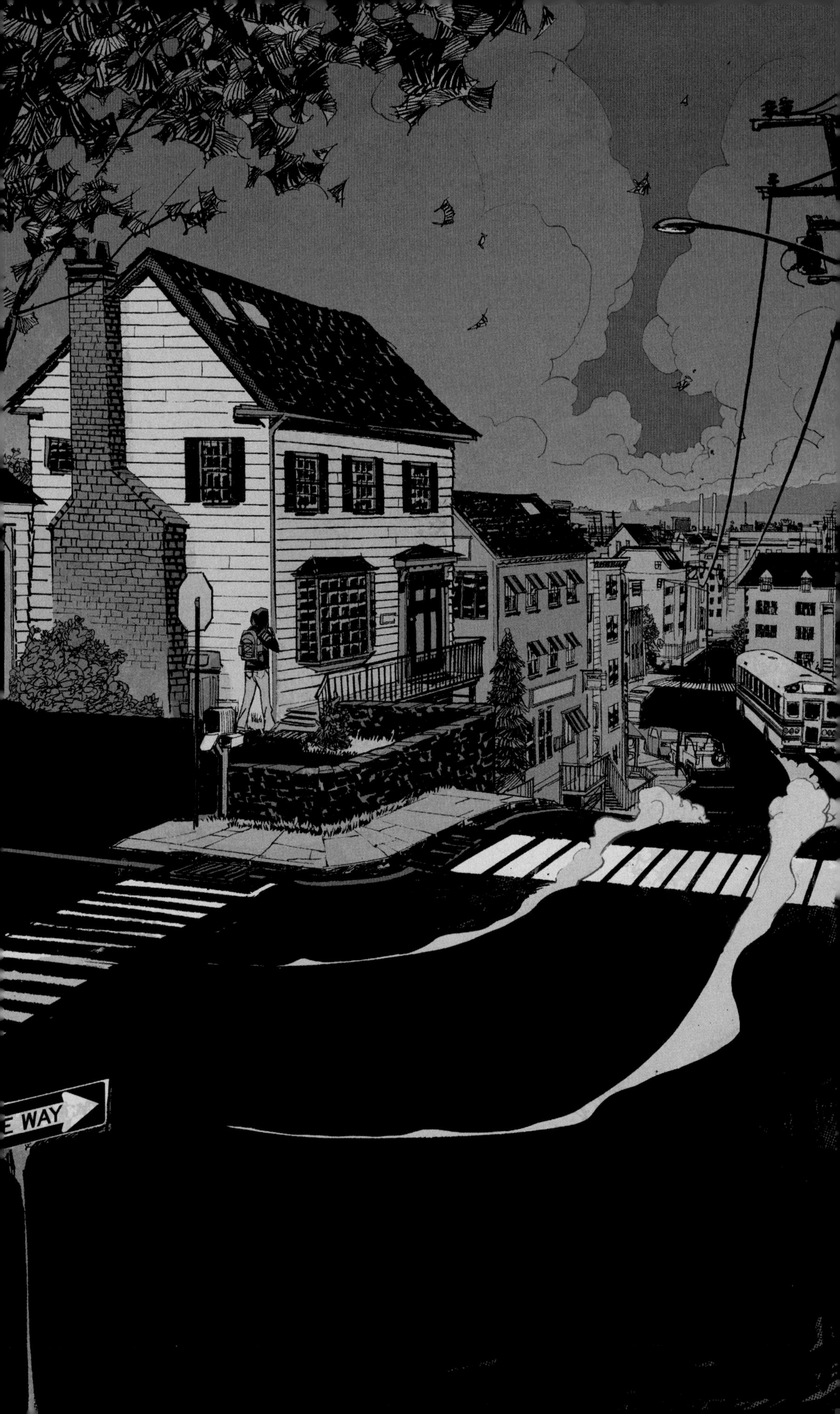
E WAY

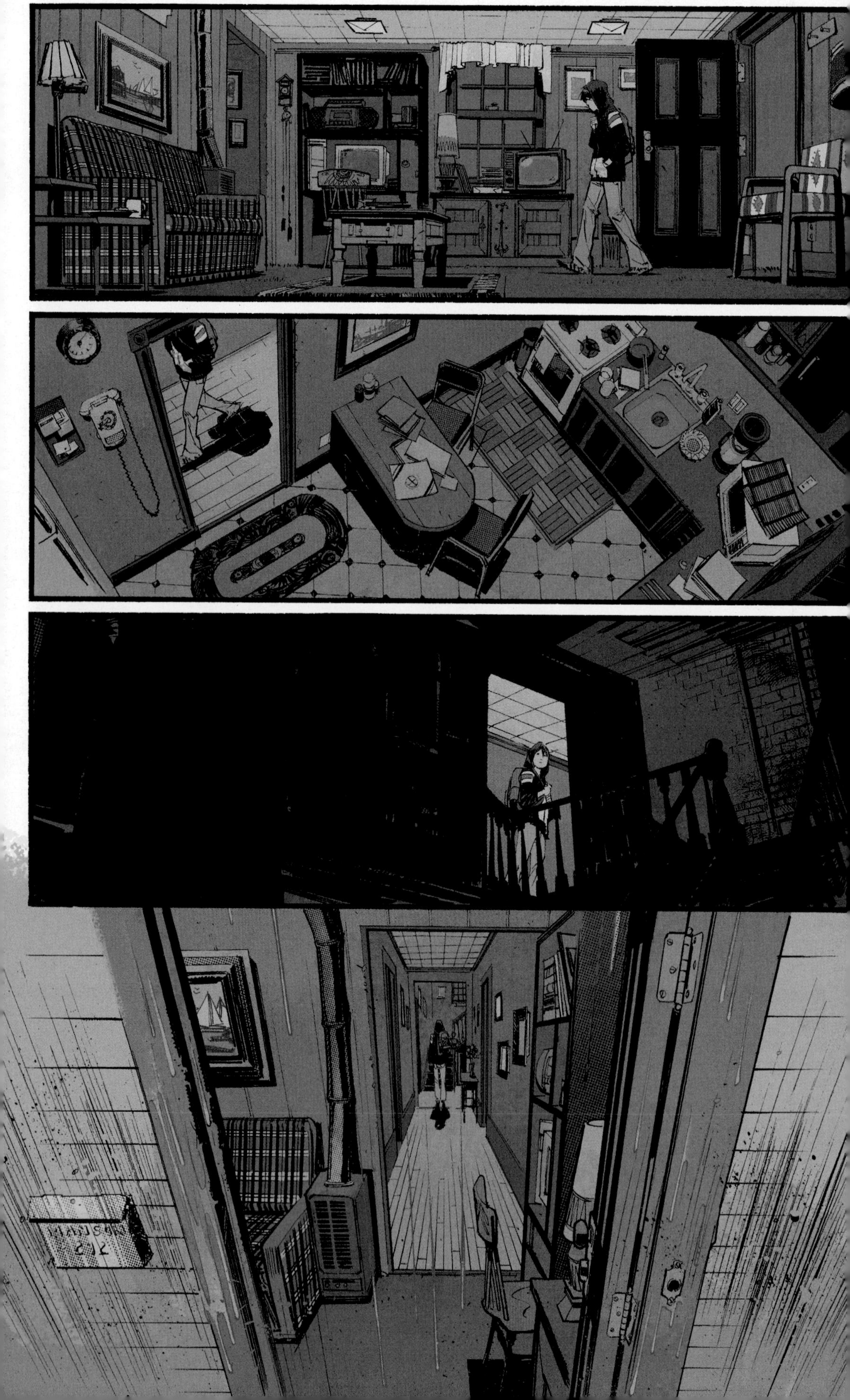

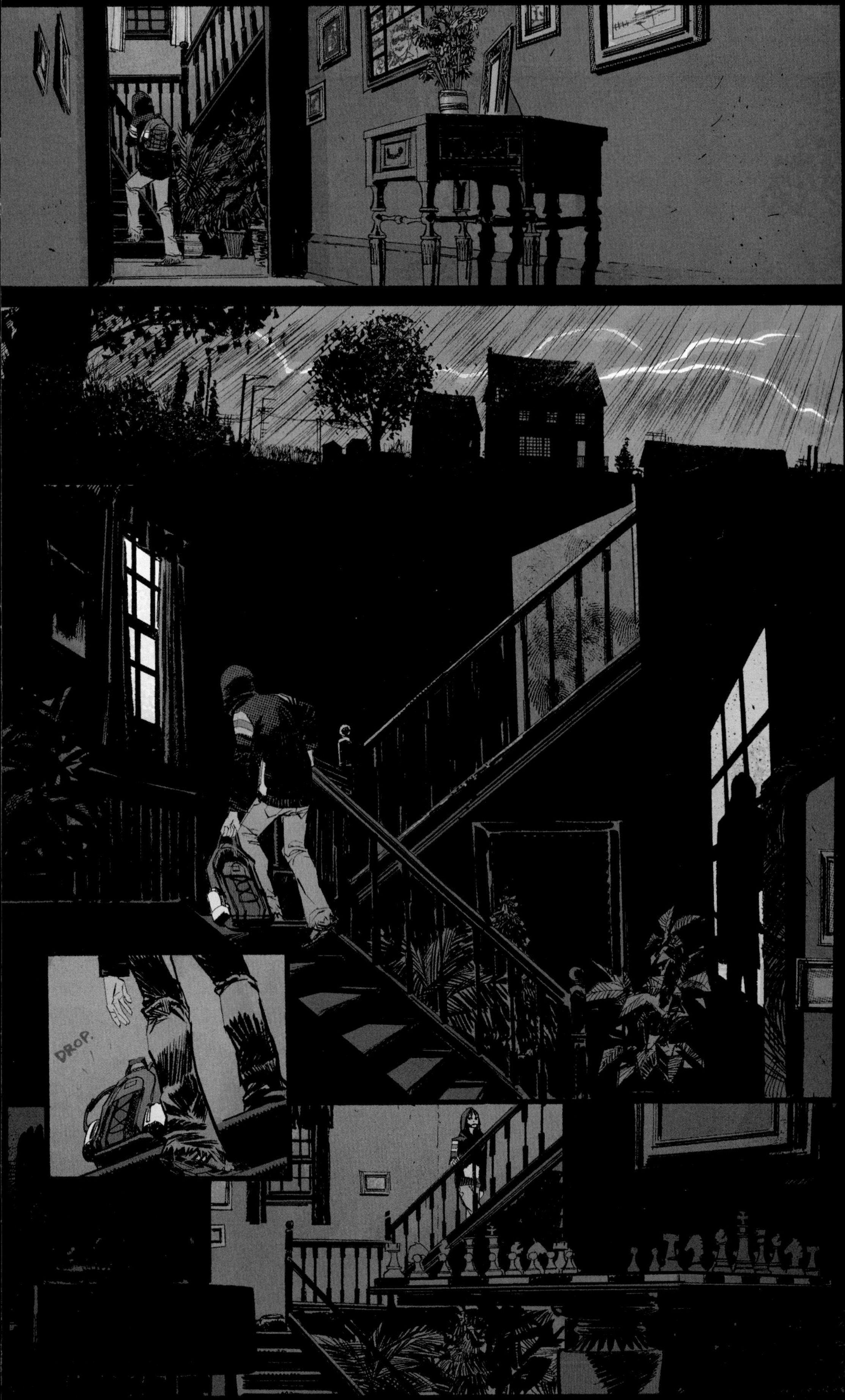
DROP.

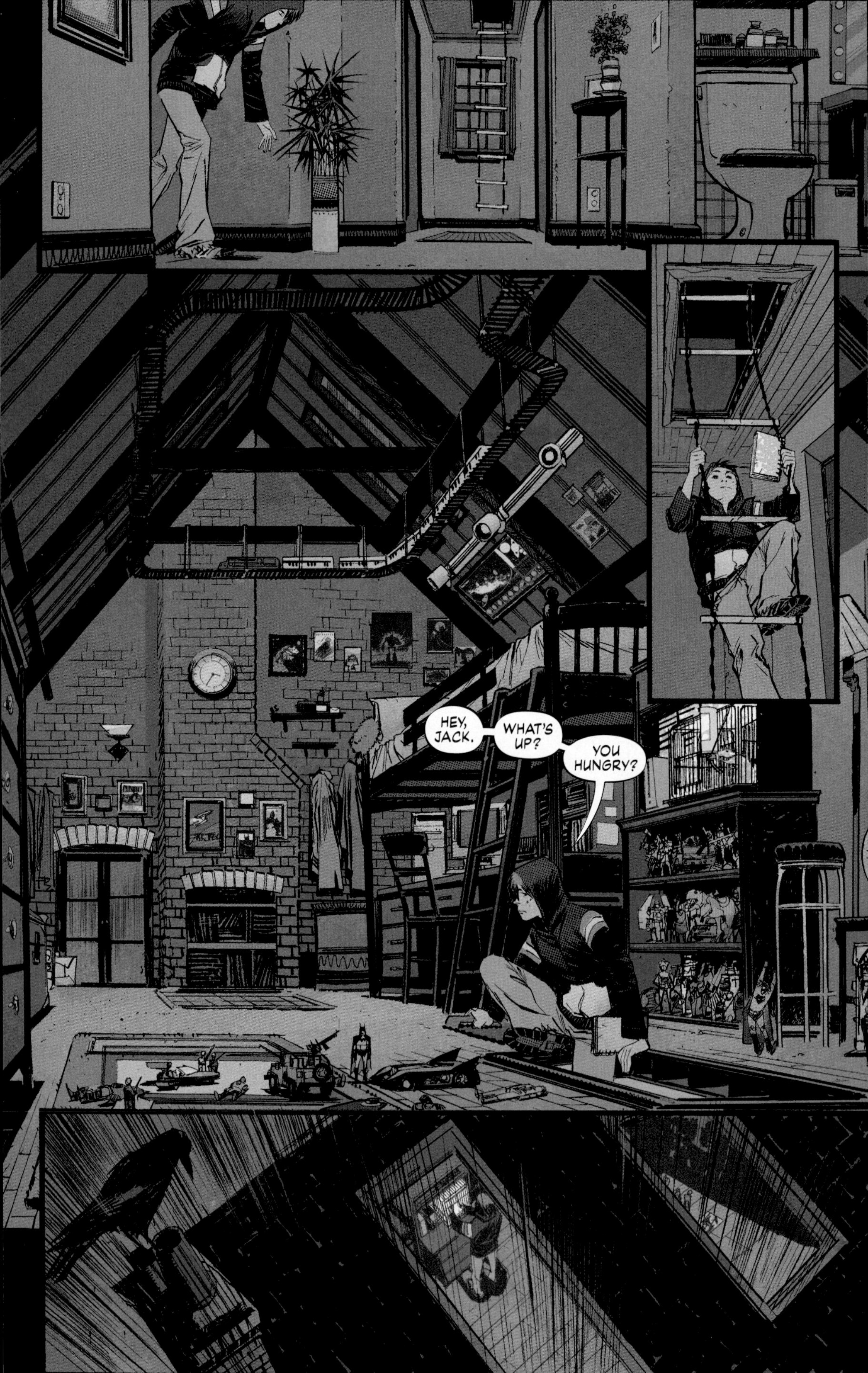
HEY, JACK.
WHAT'S UP?
YOU HUNGRY?

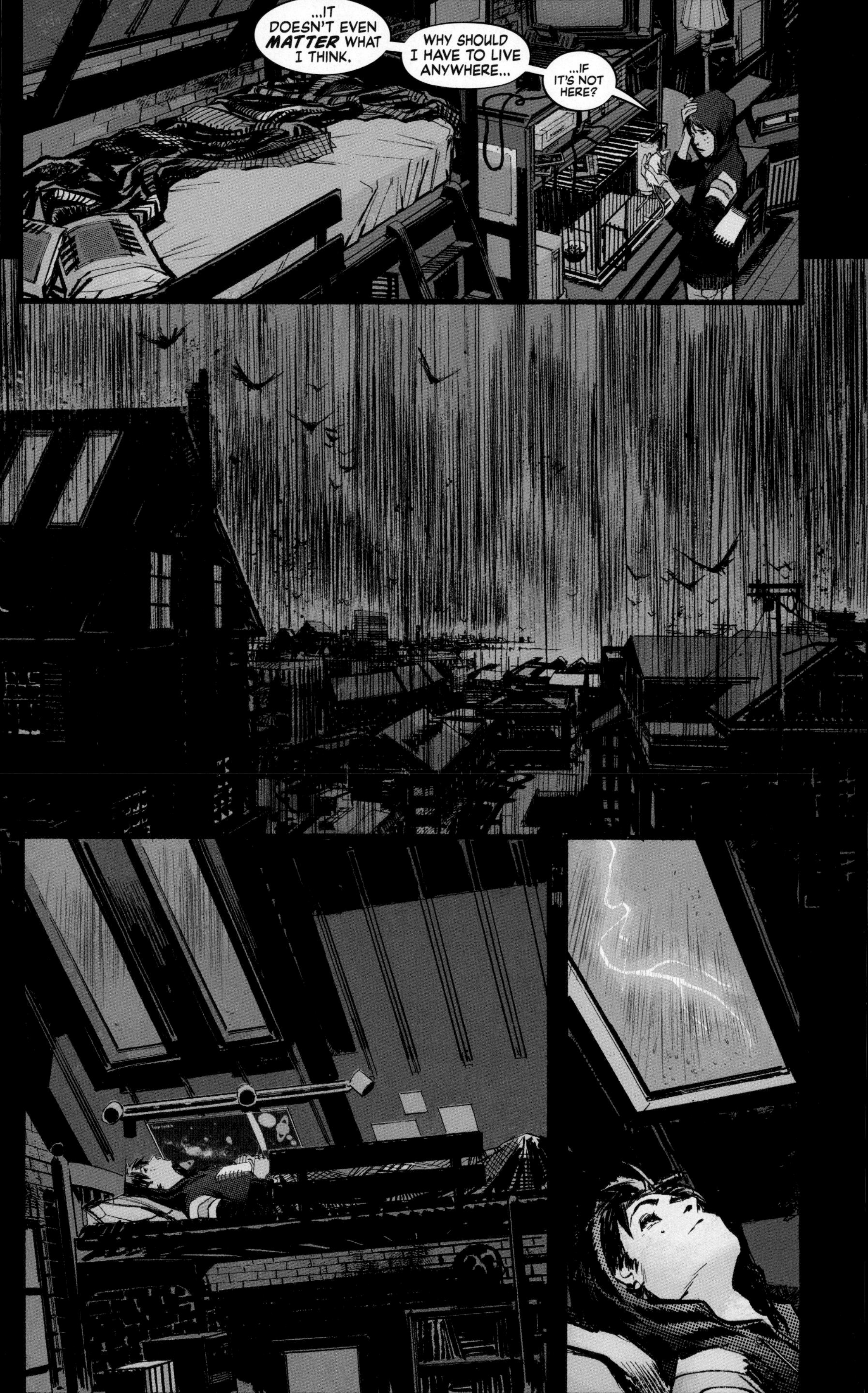
...IT DOESN'T EVEN MATTER WHAT I THINK.
WHY SHOULD I HAVE TO LIVE ANYWHERE...
...IF IT'S NOT HERE?

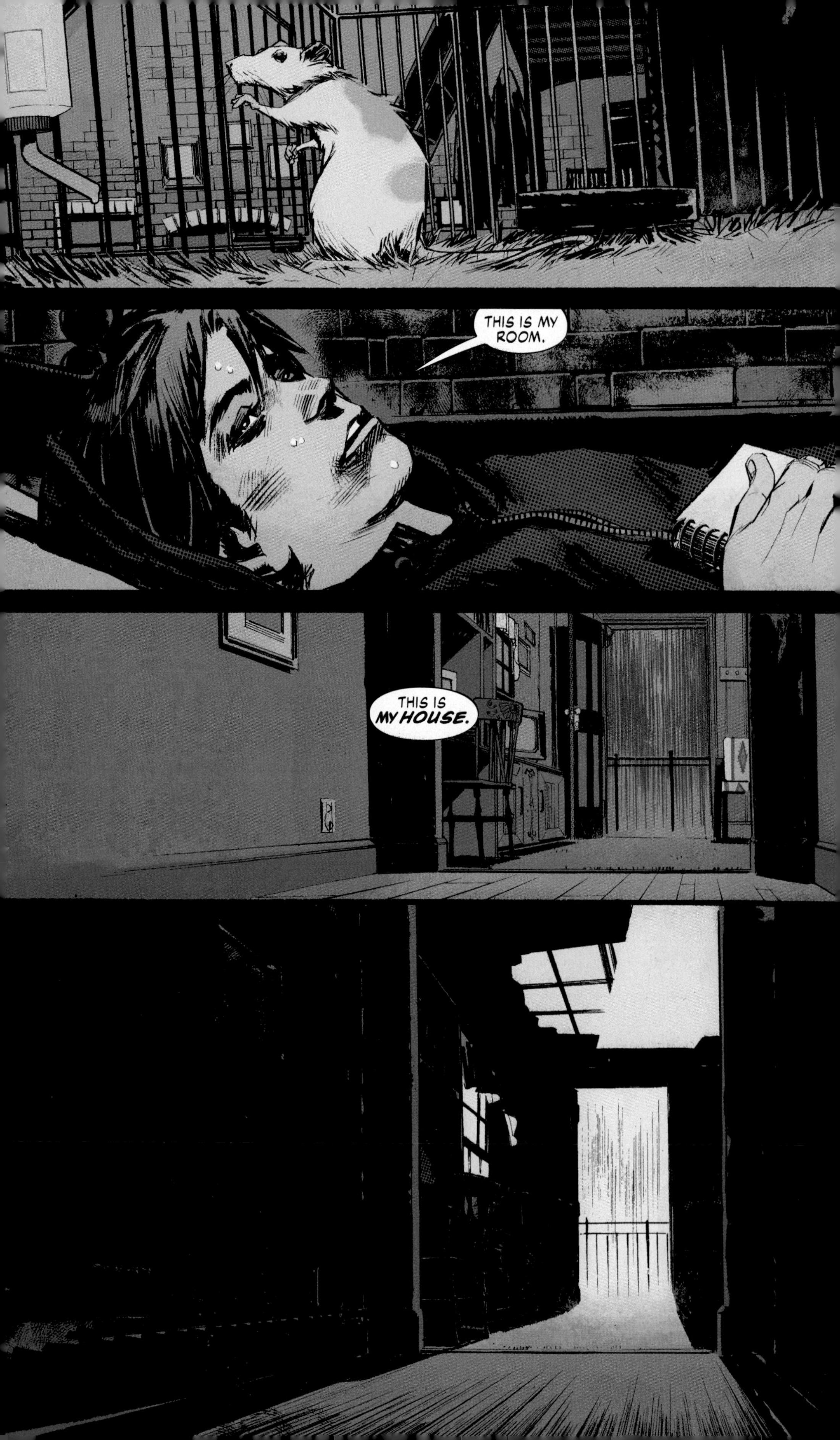
THIS IS MY ROOM.
THIS IS MY HOUSE.

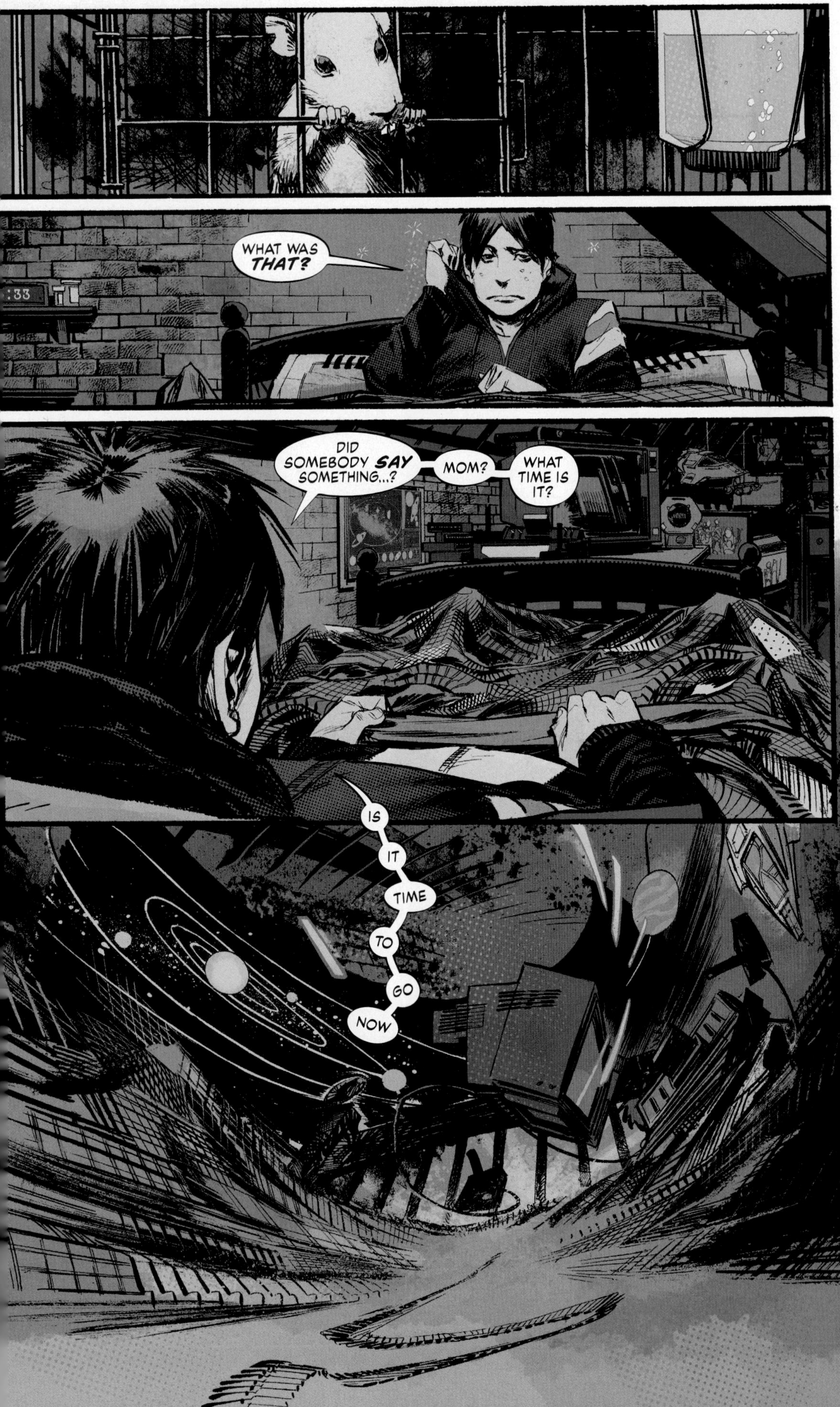

:33
WHAT WAS THAT?
DID SOMEBODY SAY SOMETHING...?
MOM?
WHAT TIME IS IT?
IS IT TIME TO GO NOW

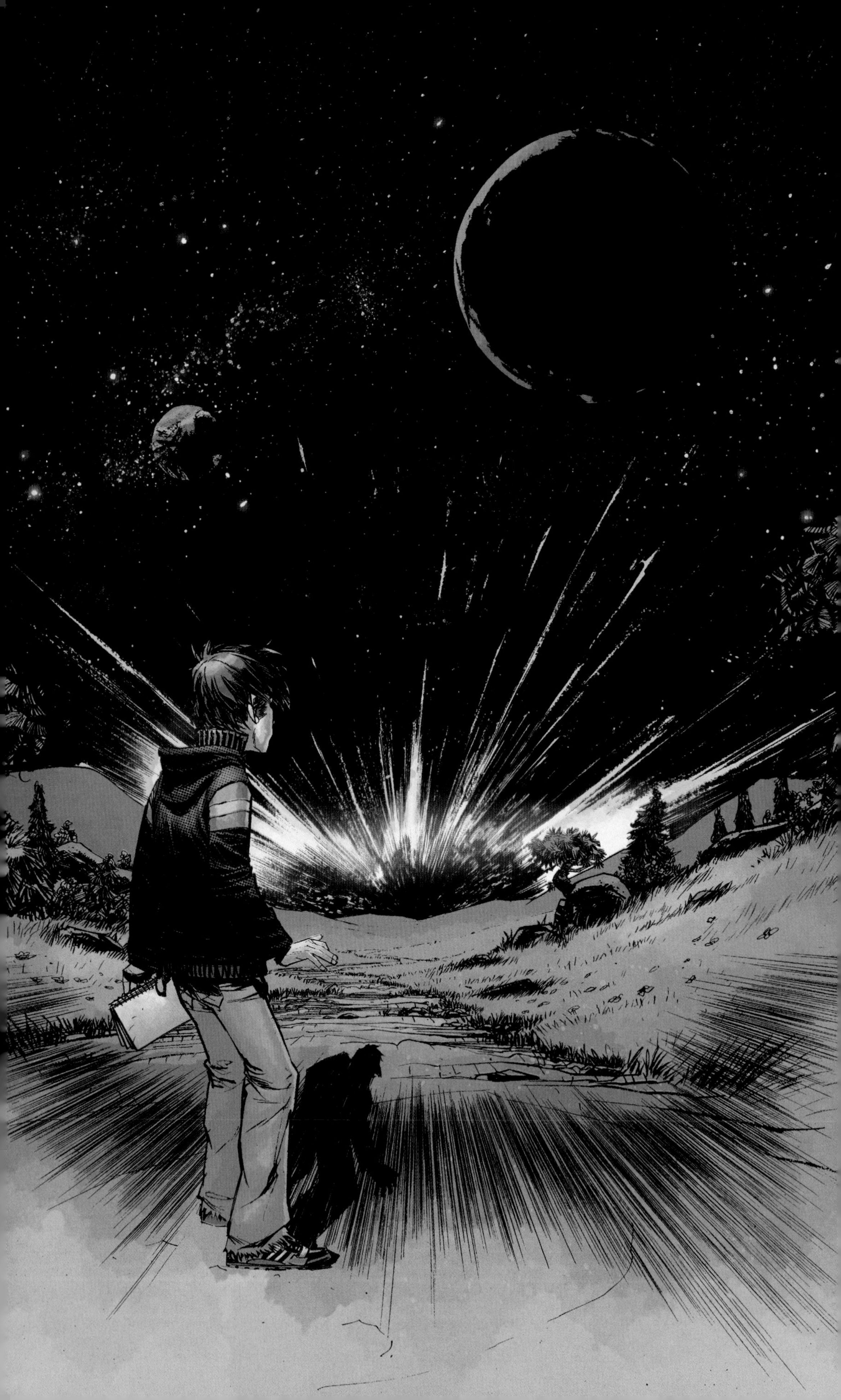

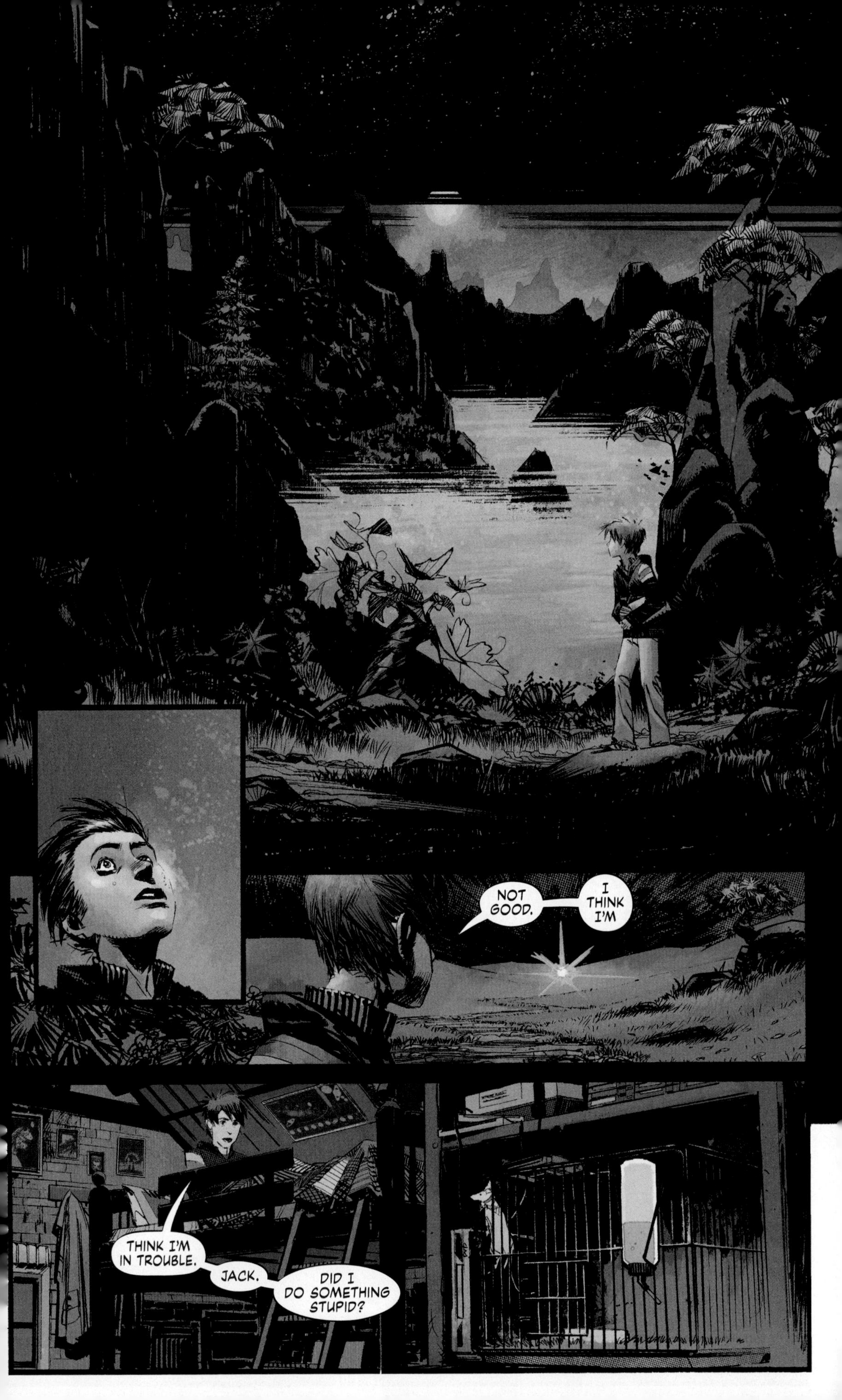

NOT GOOD.
I THINK I'M
THINK I'M IN TROUBLE.
JACK.
DID I DO SOMETHING STUPID?

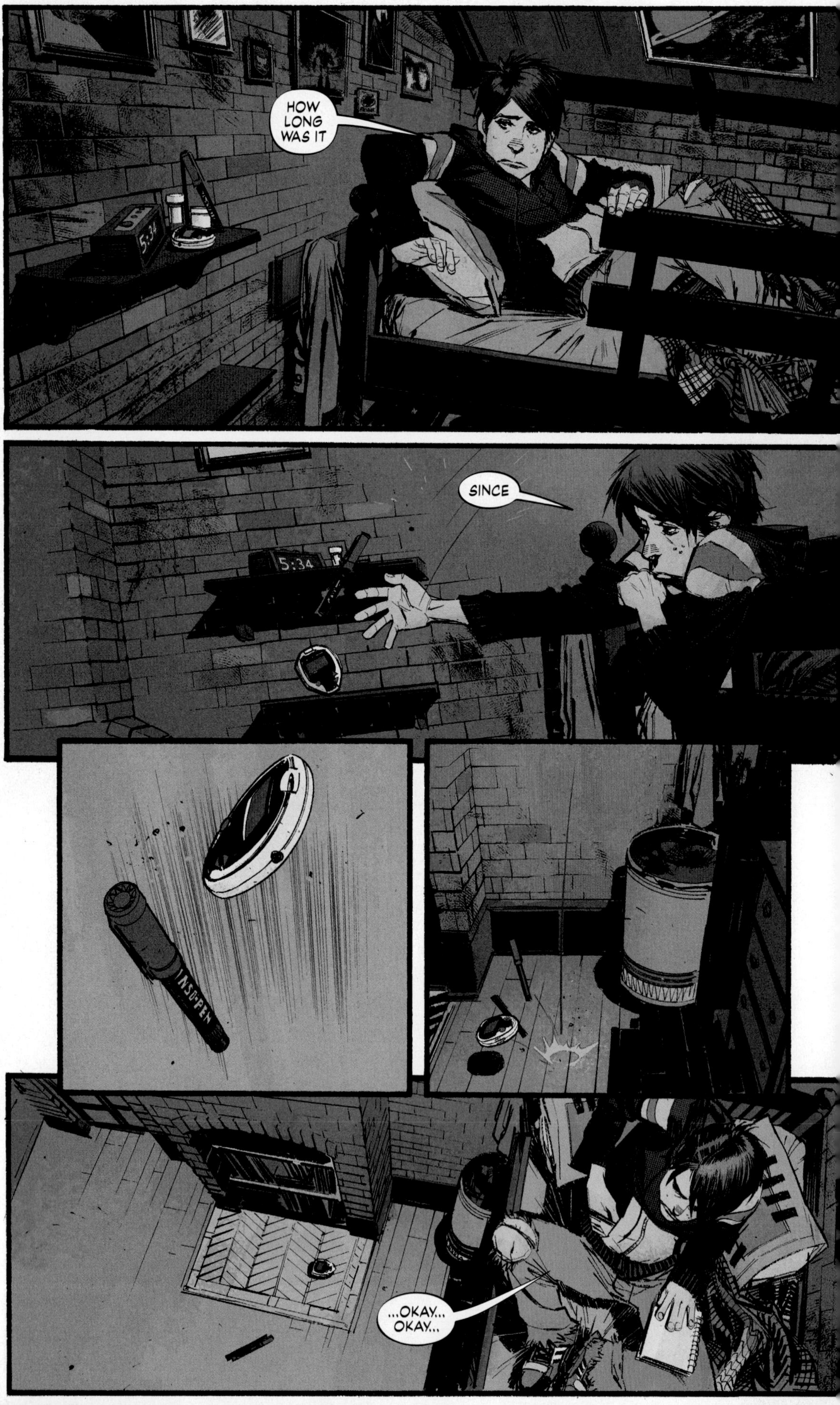
HOW LONG WAS IT
5:34
SINCE
5:34
INSU-PEN
...OKAY... OKAY...

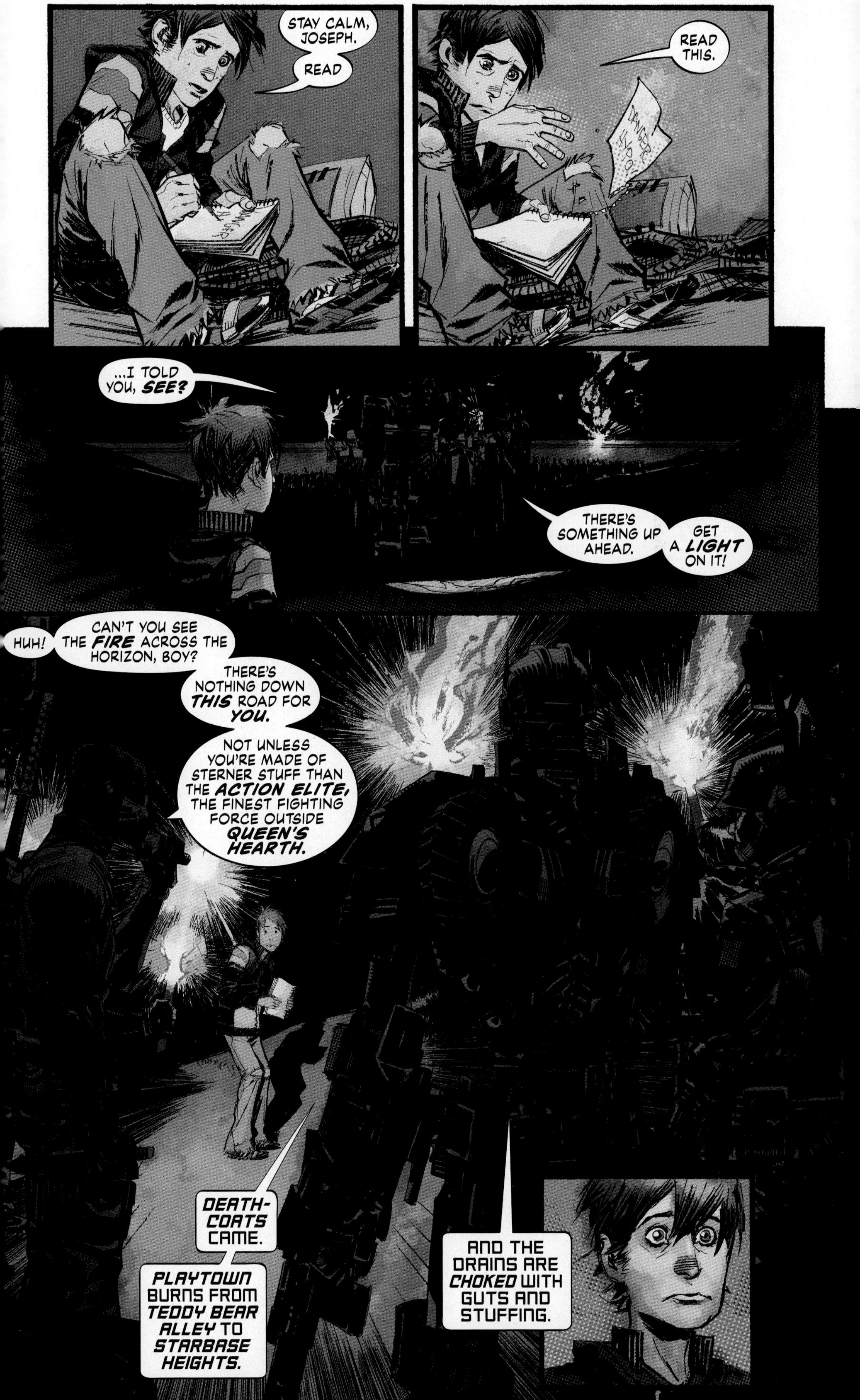
STAY CALM, JOSEPH.
READ
READ THIS.
...I TOLD YOU, SEE?
THERE'S SOMETHING UP AHEAD.
GET A LIGHT ON IT!
HUH!
CAN'T YOU SEE THE FIRE ACROSS THE HORIZON, BOY?
THERE'S NOTHING DOWN THIS ROAD FOR YOU.
NOT UNLESS YOU'RE MADE OF STERNER STUFF THAN THE ACTION ELITE, THE FINEST FIGHTING FORCE OUTSIDE QUEEN'S HEARTH.
DEATH-COATS CAME.
PLAYTOWN BURNS FROM TEDDY BEAR ALLEY TO STARBASE HEIGHTS.
AND THE DRAINS ARE CHOKED WITH GUTS AND STUFFING.

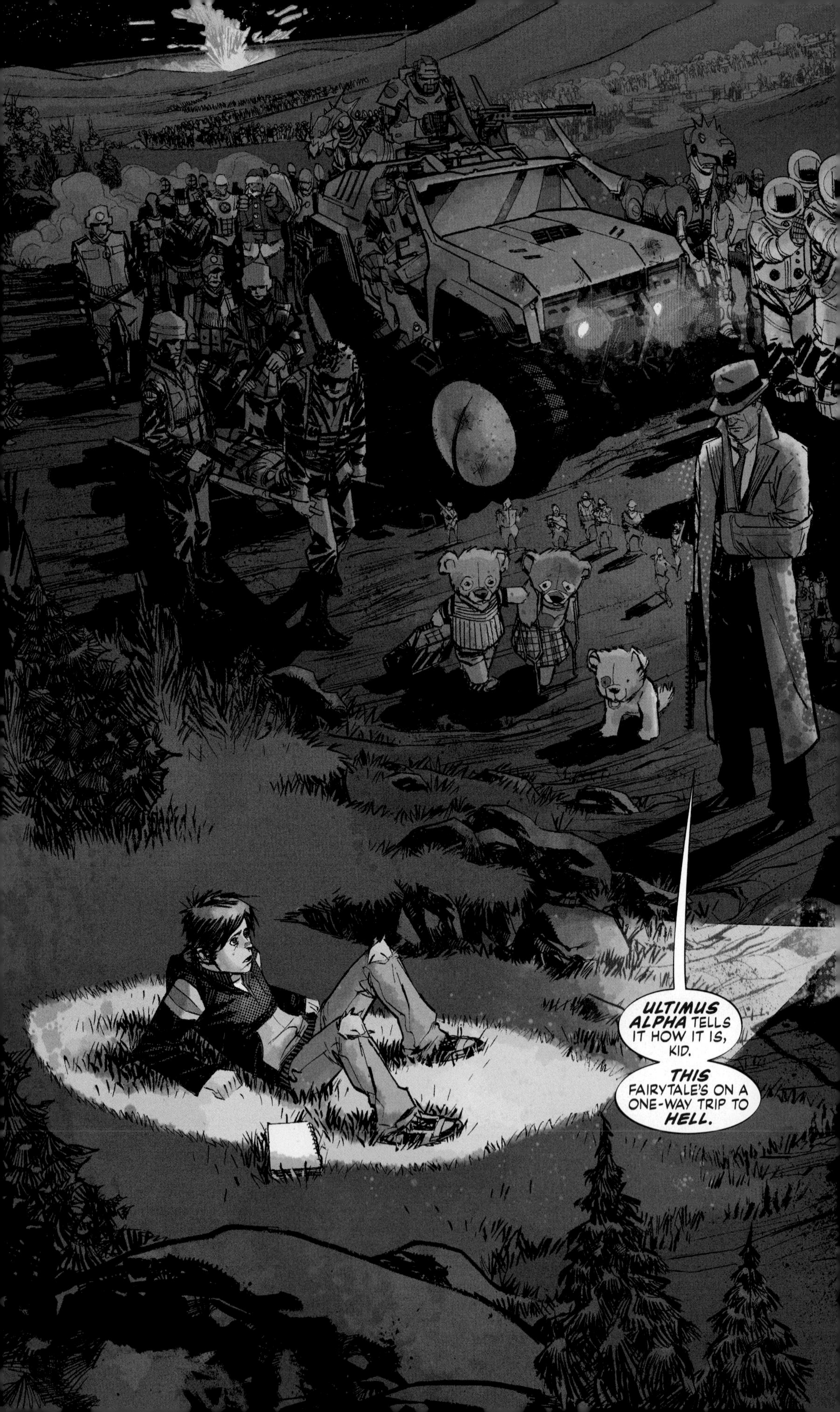
ULTIMUS ALPHA TELLS IT HOW IT IS, KID.
THIS FAIRYTALE'S ON A ONE-WAY TRIP TO HELL.

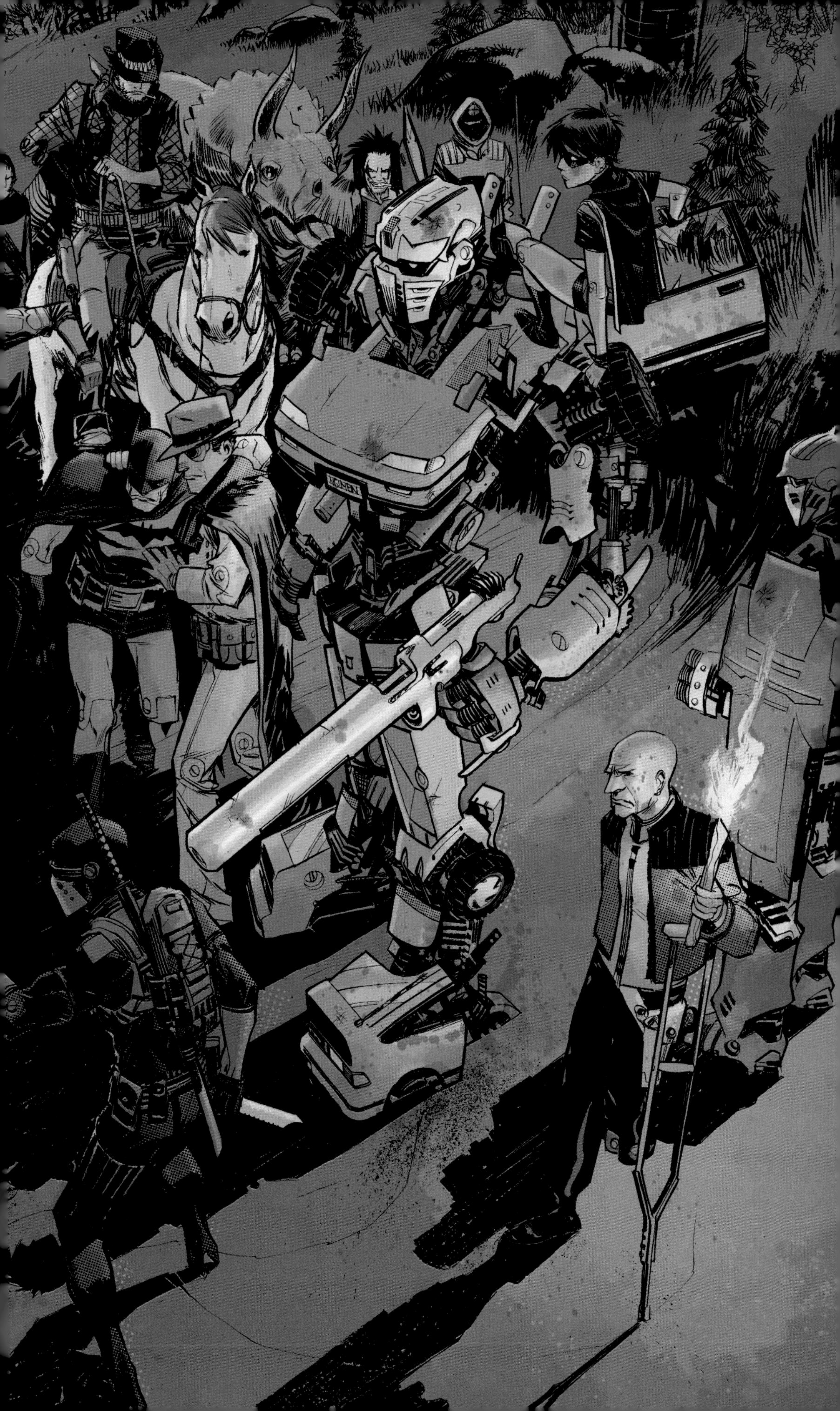

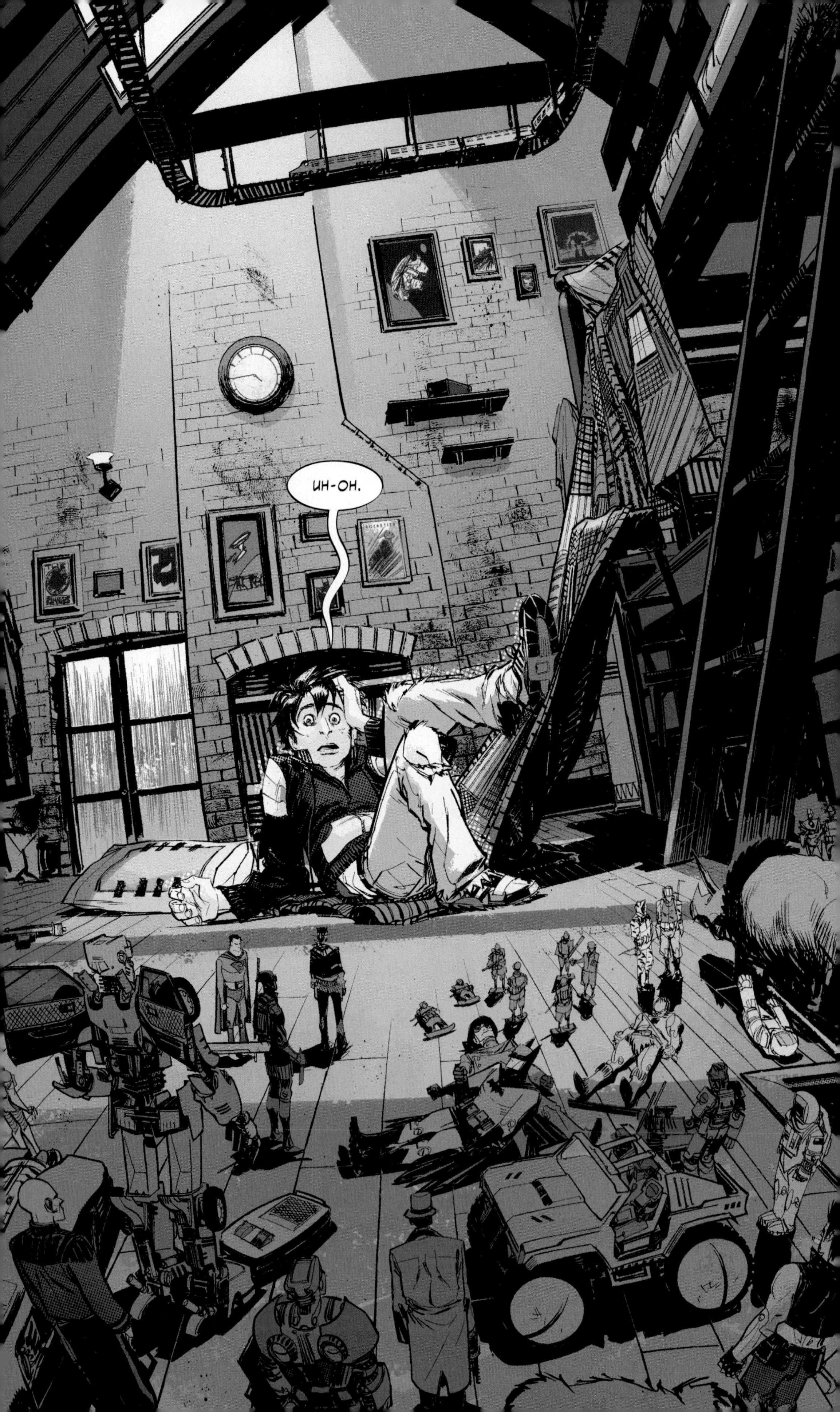
UH-OH.

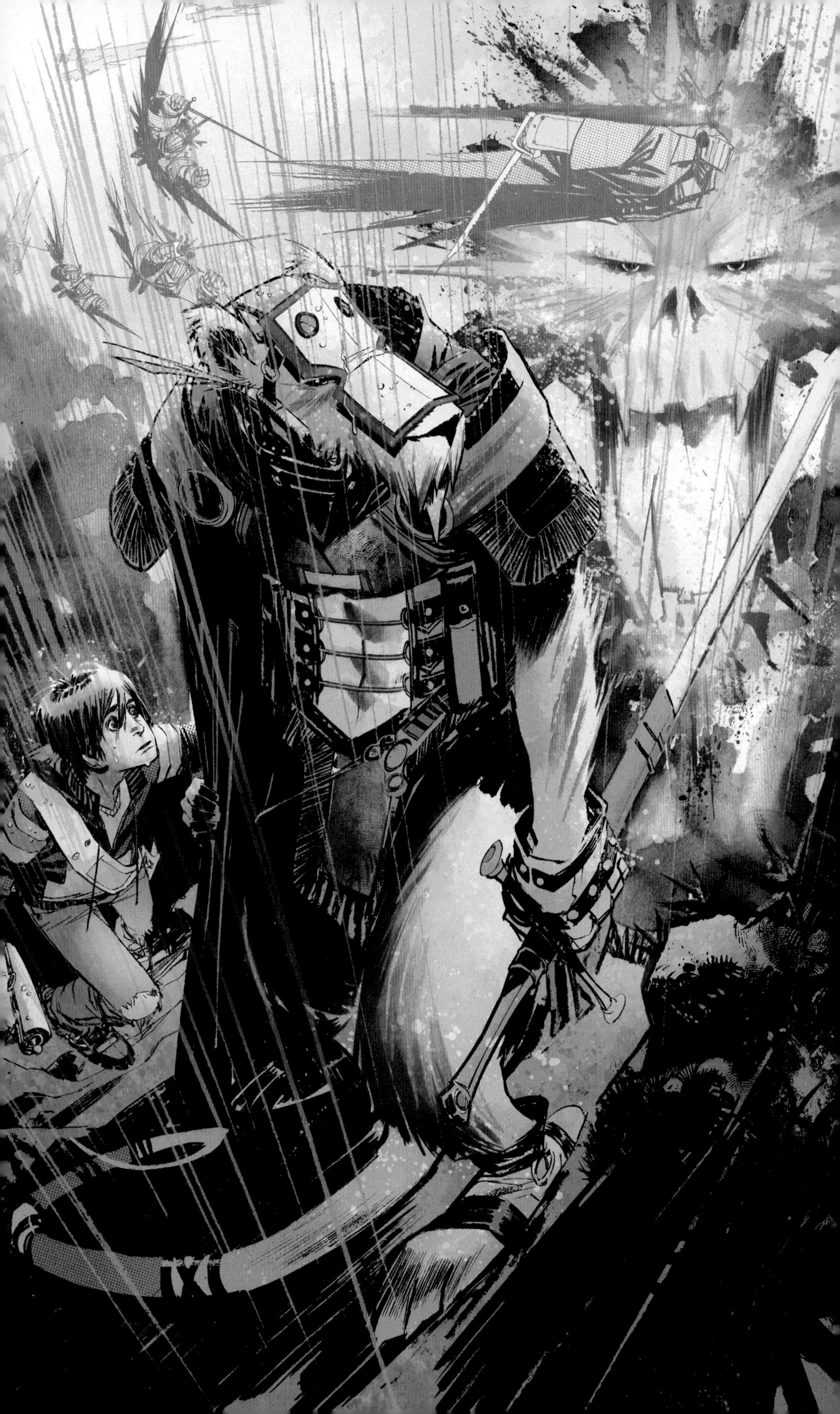

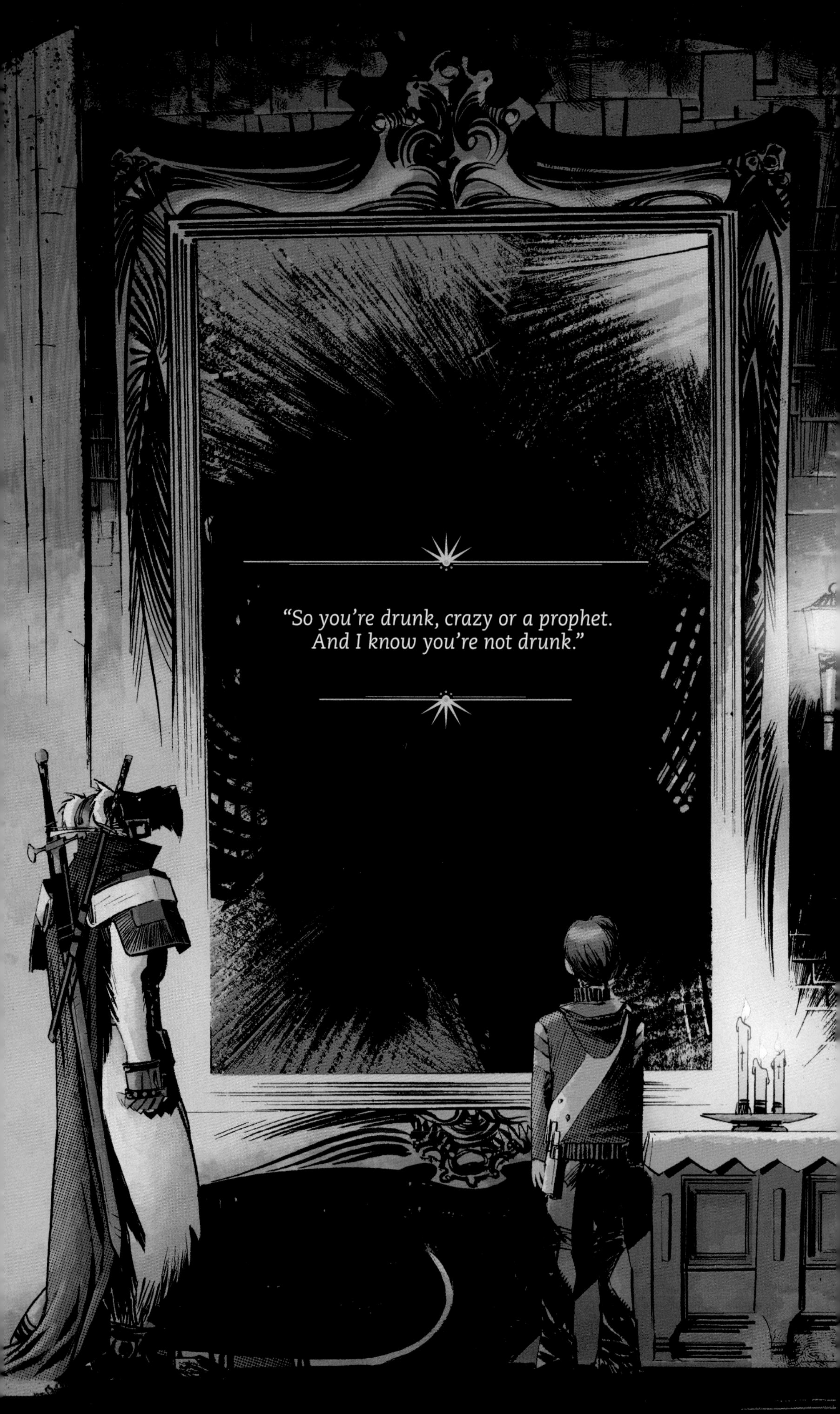
"So you're drunk, crazy or a prophet.
And I know you're not drunk."

:hapter 2: cloud quay to feather forest falls

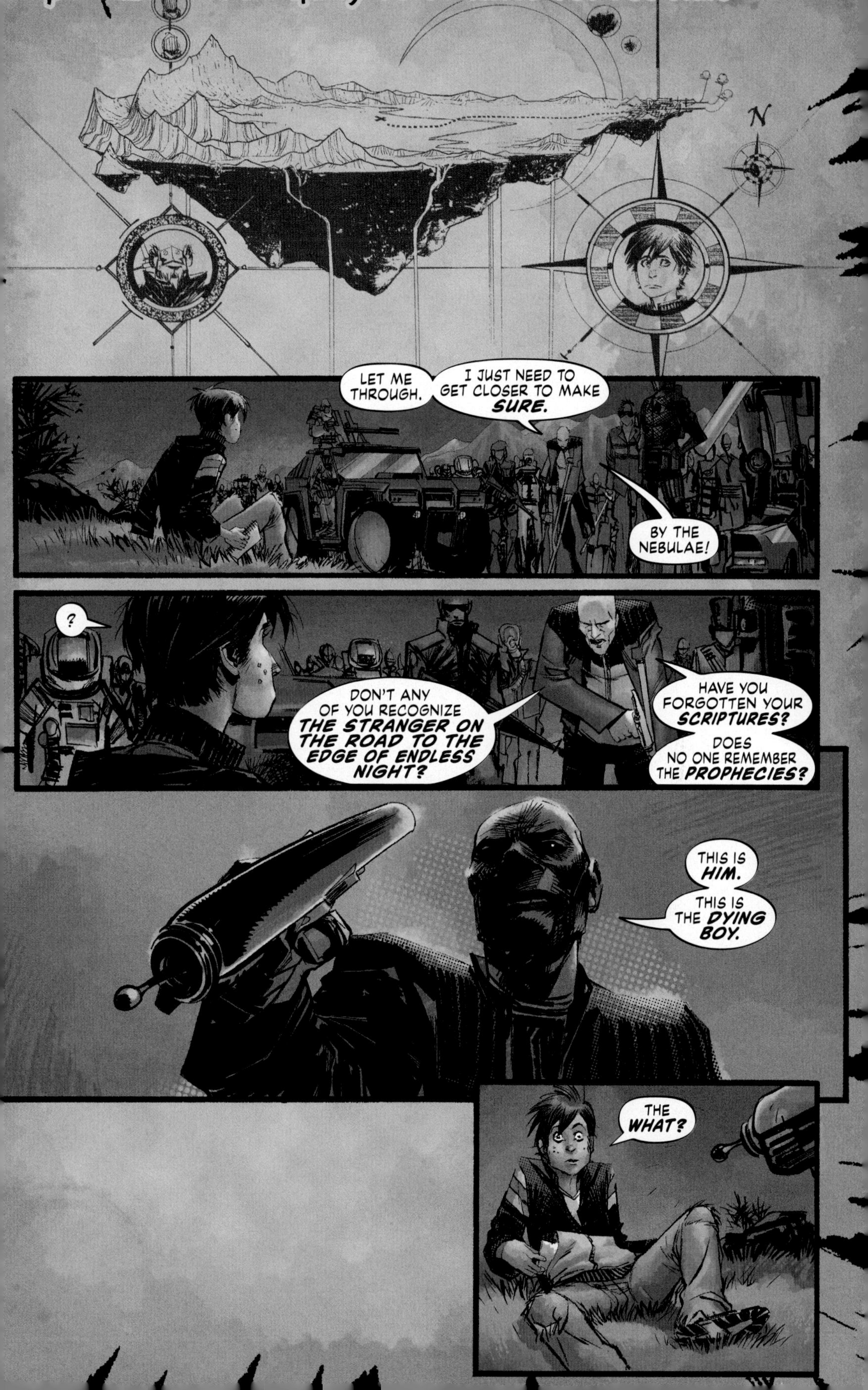
LET ME THROUGH.
I JUST NEED TO GET CLOSER TO MAKE SURE.
BY THE NEBULAE!
?
DON'T ANY OF YOU RECOGNIZE THE STRANGER ON THE ROAD TO THE EDGE OF ENDLESS NIGHT?
HAVE YOU FORGOTTEN YOUR SCRIPTURES?
DOES NO ONE REMEMBER THE PROPHECIES?
THIS IS HIM.
THIS IS THE DYING BOY.
THE WHAT?

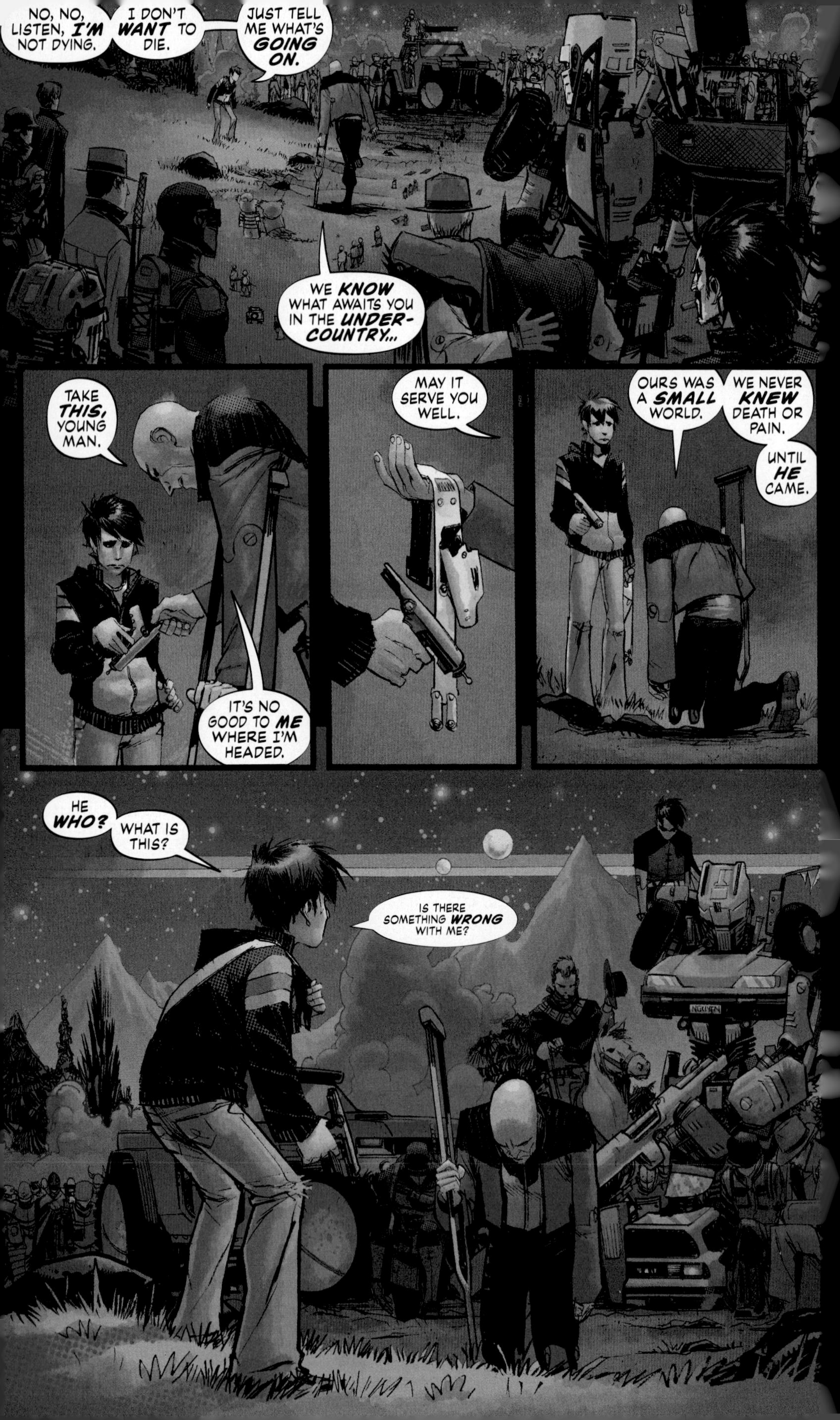
NO, NO, LISTEN, I'M NOT DYING.
I DON'T WANT TO DIE.
JUST TELL ME WHAT'S GOING ON.
WE KNOW WHAT AWAITS YOU IN THE UNDER-COUNTRY...
TAKE THIS, YOUNG MAN.
IT'S NO GOOD TO ME WHERE I'M HEADED.
MAY IT SERVE YOU WELL.
OURS WAS A SMALL WORLD.
WE NEVER KNEW DEATH OR PAIN.
UNTIL HE CAME.
HE WHO?
WHAT IS THIS?
IS THERE SOMETHING WRONG WITH ME?

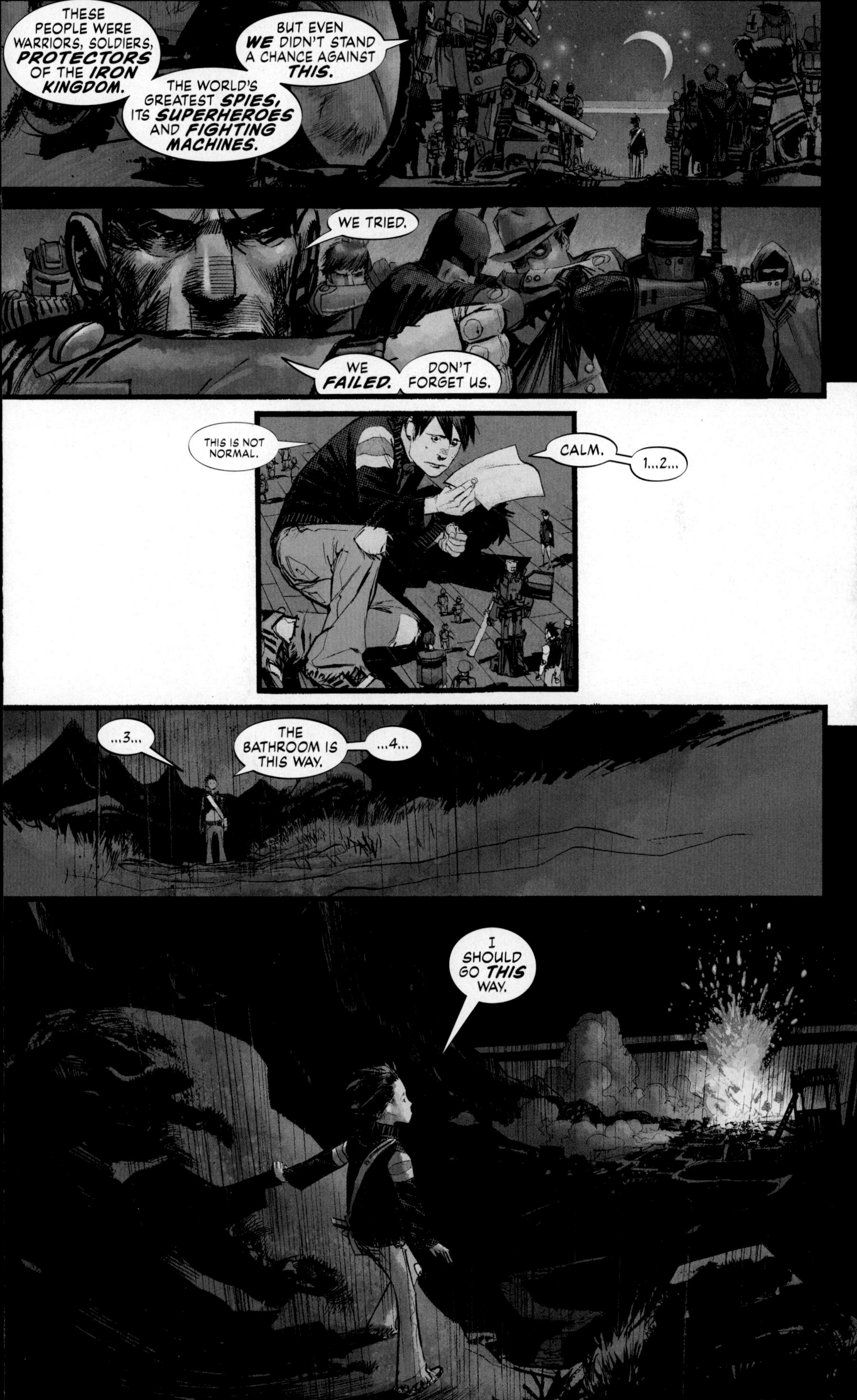
THESE PEOPLE WERE WARRIORS, SOLDIERS, PROTECTORS OF THE IRON KINGDOM.
THE WORLD'S GREATEST SPIES, ITS SUPERHEROES AND FIGHTING MACHINES.
BUT EVEN WE DIDN'T STAND A CHANCE AGAINST THIS.
WE TRIED.
WE FAILED.
DON'T FORGET US.
THIS IS NOT NORMAL.
CALM.
1...2...
...3...
THE BATHROOM IS THIS WAY.
...4...
I SHOULD GO THIS WAY.

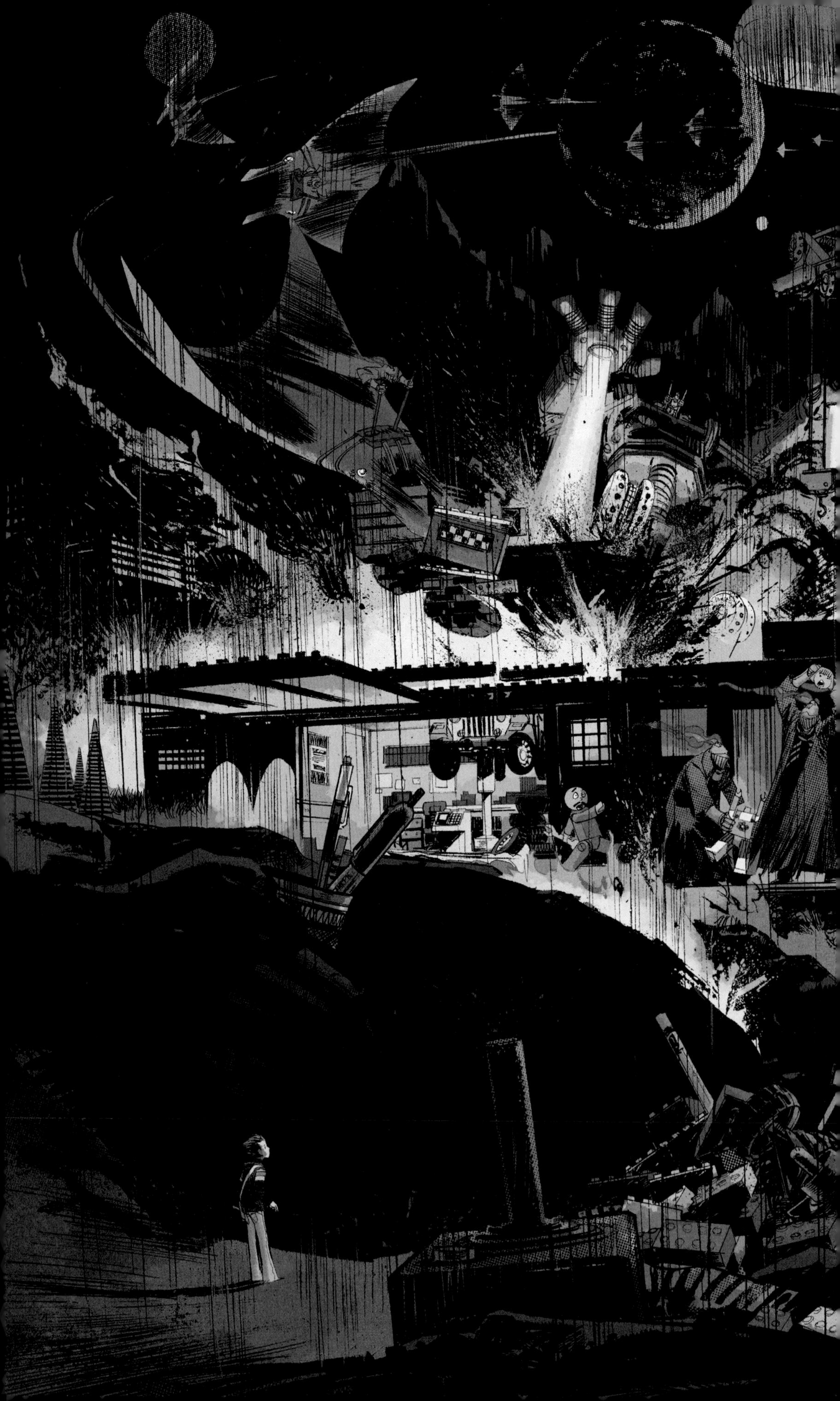

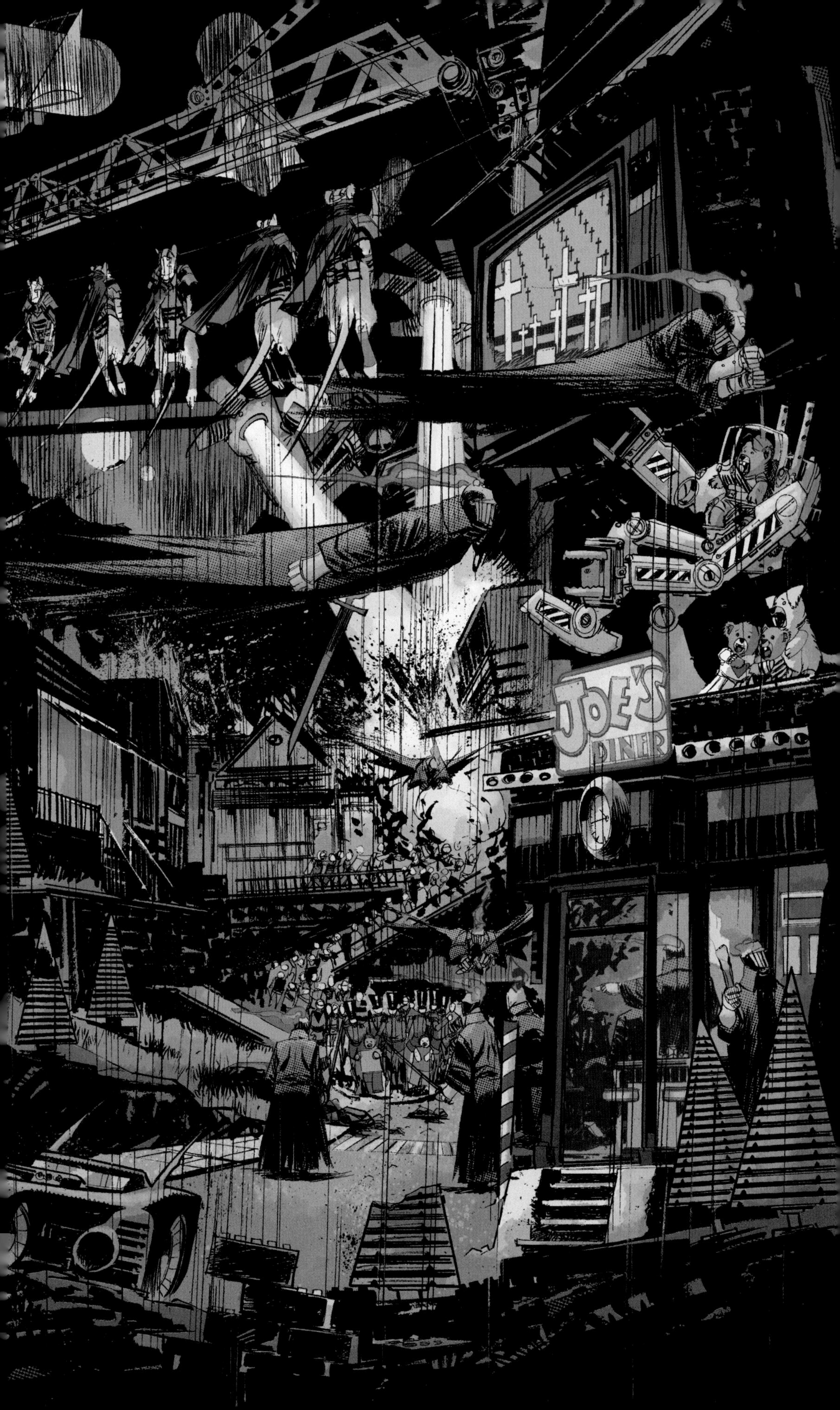
JOE'S
DINER

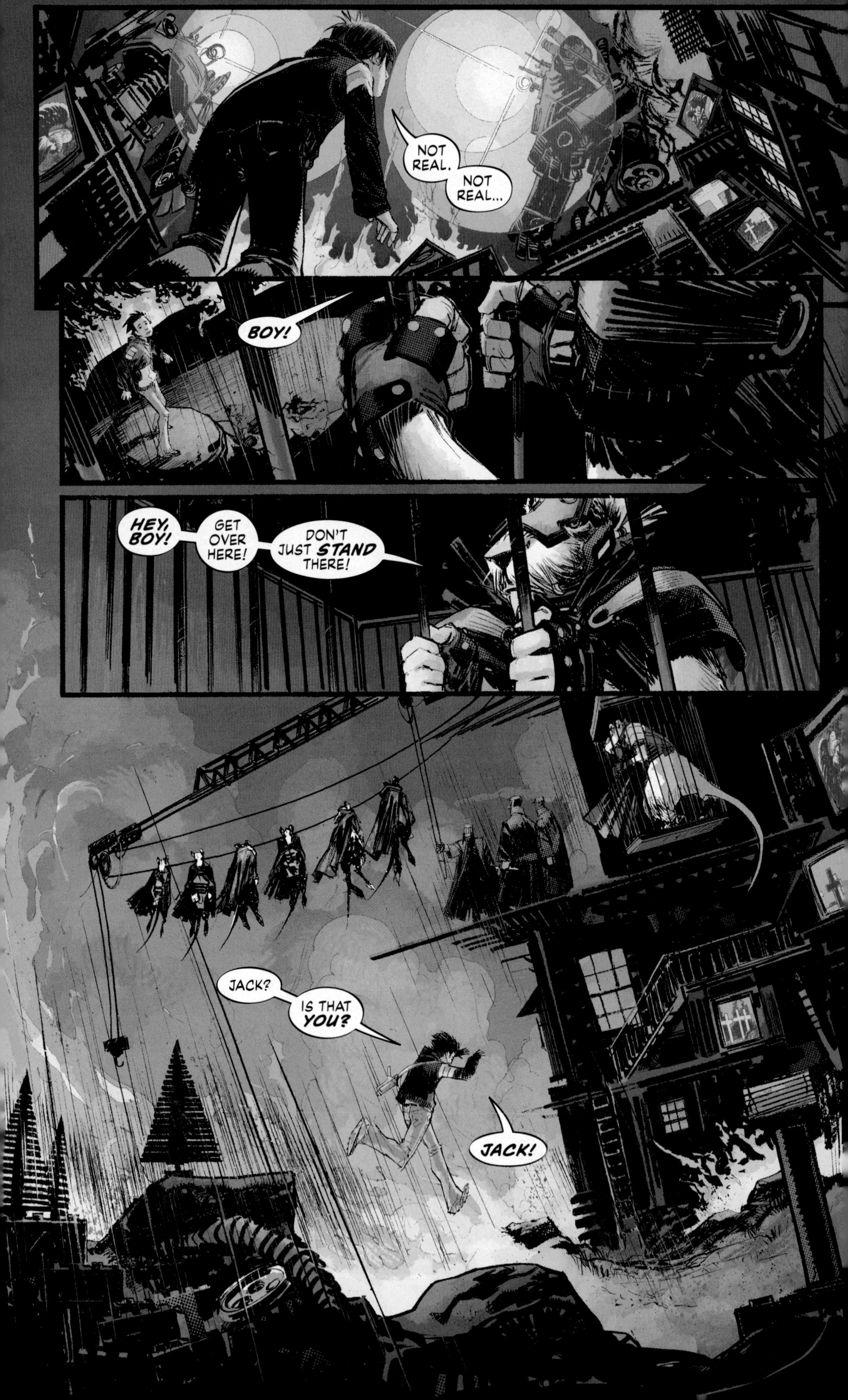
NOT REAL.
NOT REAL...
BOY!
HEY, BOY!
GET OVER HERE!
DON'T JUST STAND THERE!
JACK?
IS THAT YOU?
JACK!

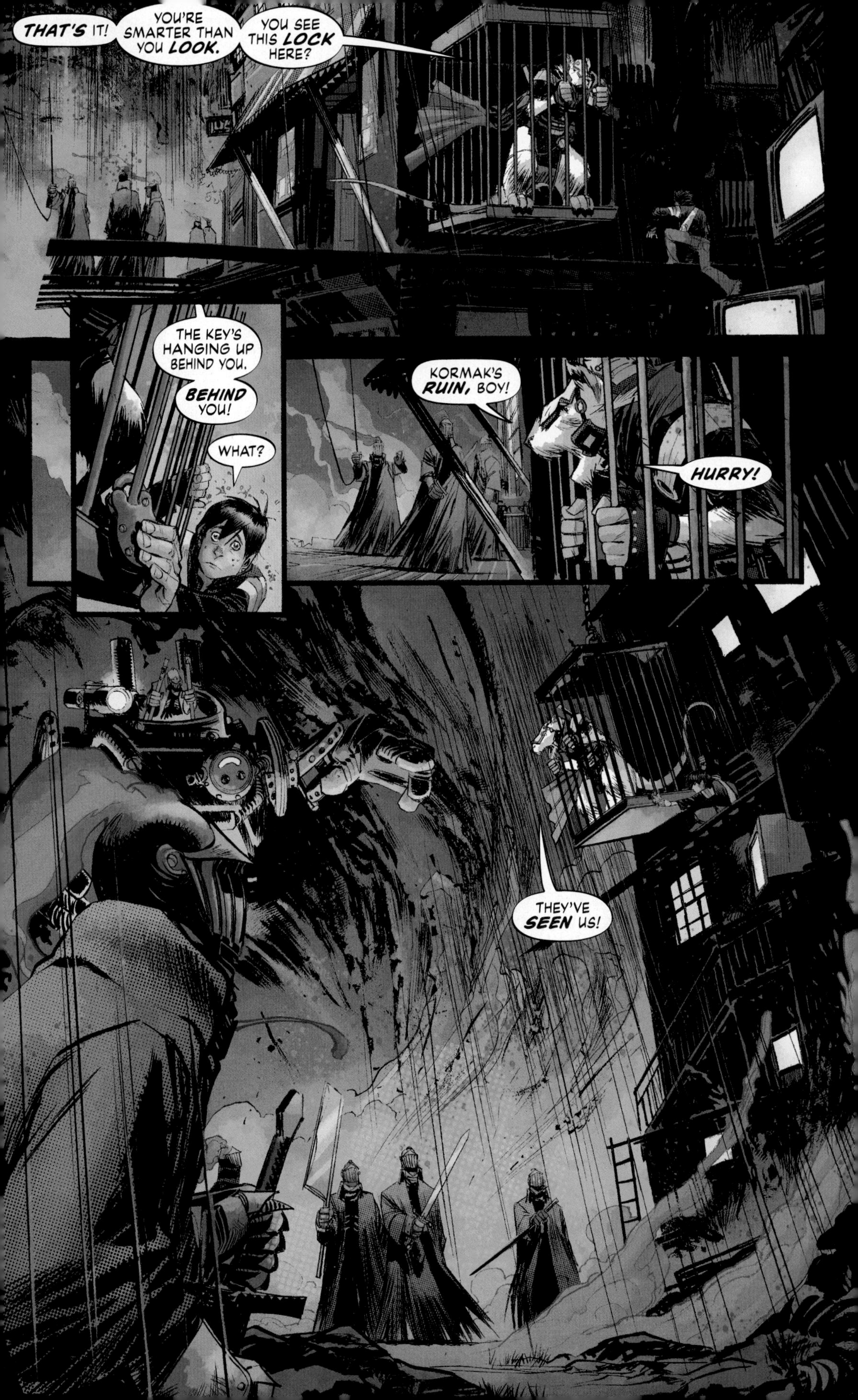
THAT'S IT!
YOU'RE SMARTER THAN YOU LOOK.
YOU SEE THIS LOCK HERE?
THE KEY'S HANGING UP BEHIND YOU. BEHIND YOU!
WHAT?
KORMAK'S RUIN, BOY!
HURRY!
THEY'VE SEEN US!

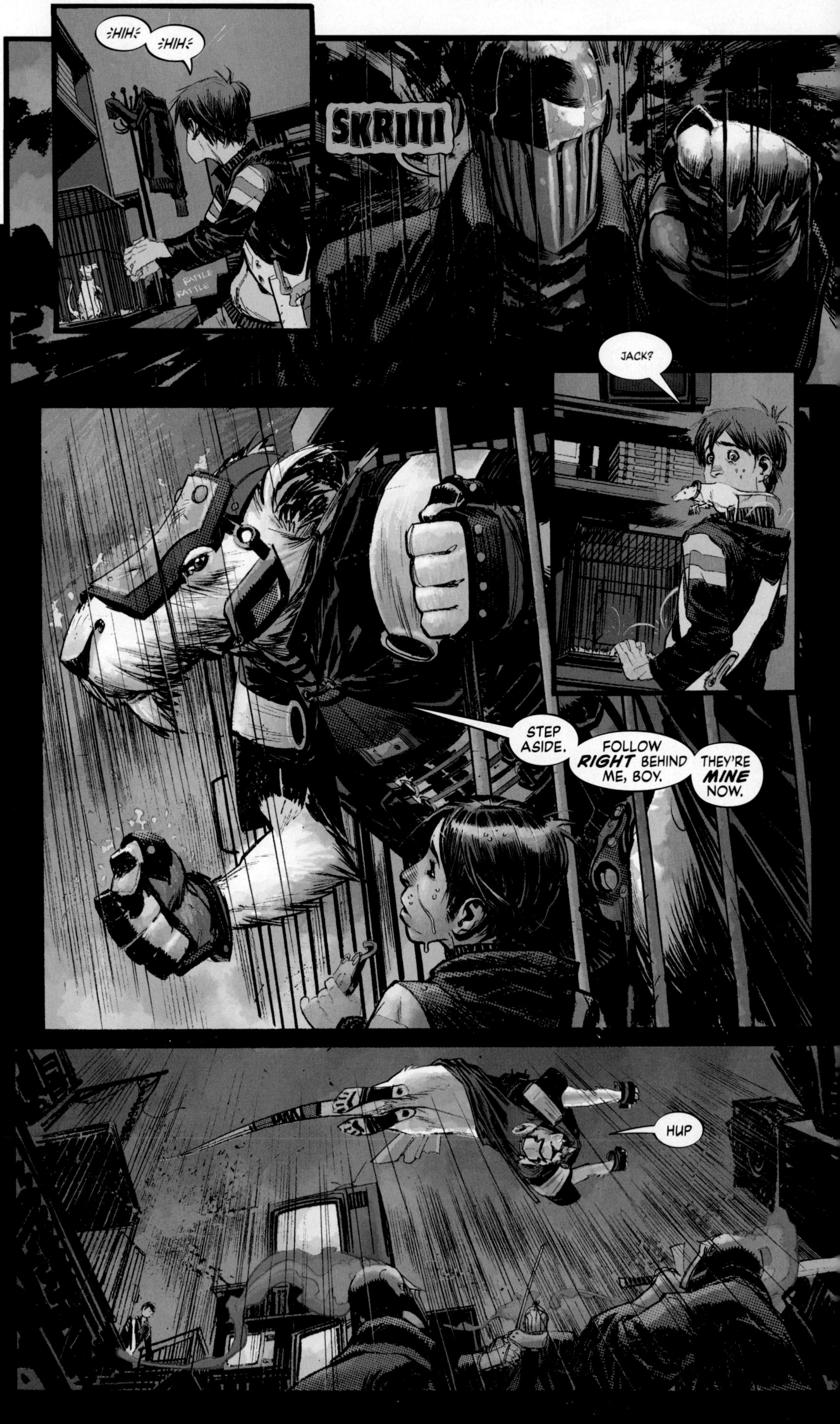

HIH
HIH
RATTLE RATTLE
SKRIIII
JACK?
STEP ASIDE.
FOLLOW RIGHT BEHIND ME, BOY.
THEY'RE MINE NOW.
HUP

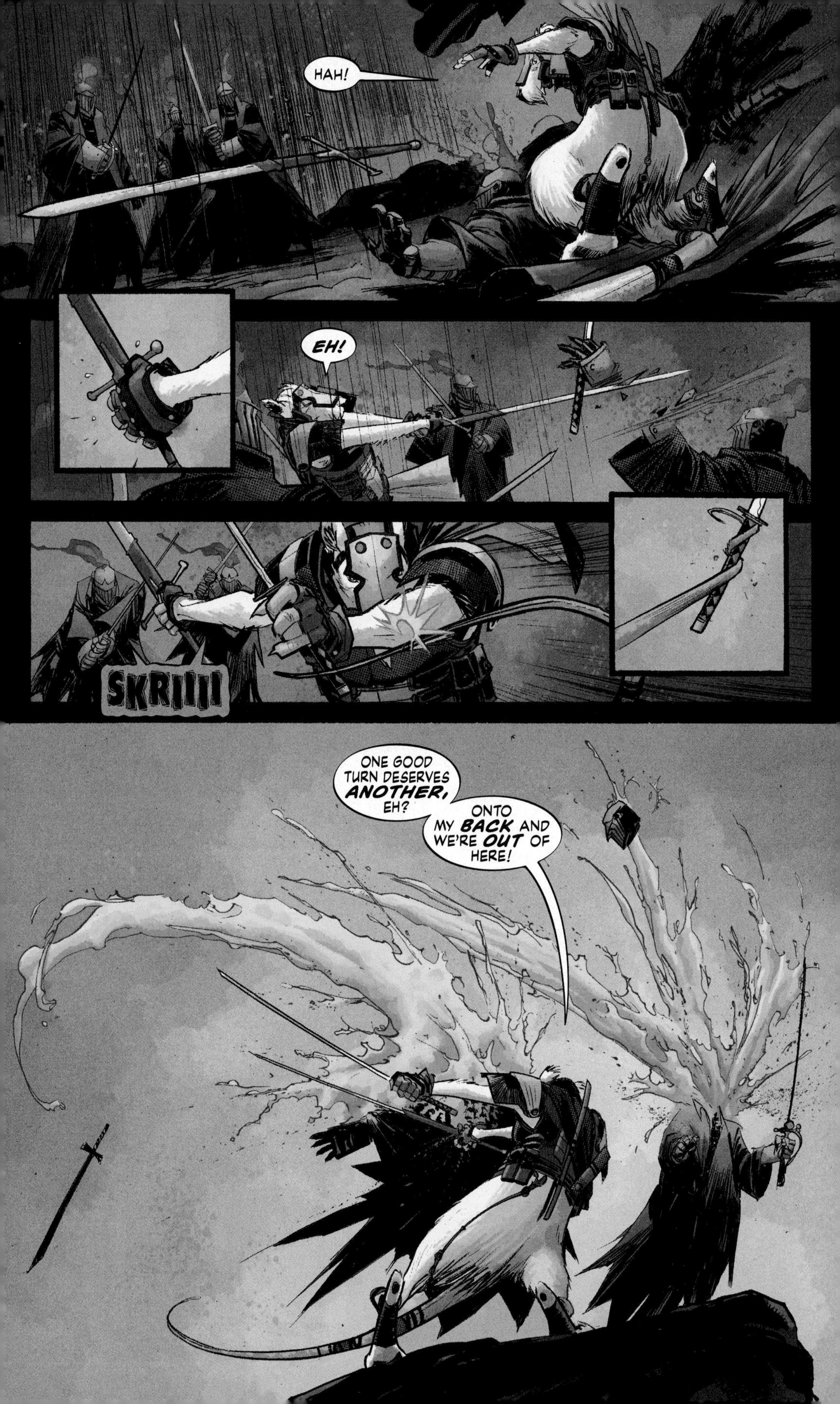
HAH!
EH!
SKRIIII
ONE GOOD TURN DESERVES ANOTHER, EH?
ONTO MY BACK AND WE'RE OUT OF HERE!

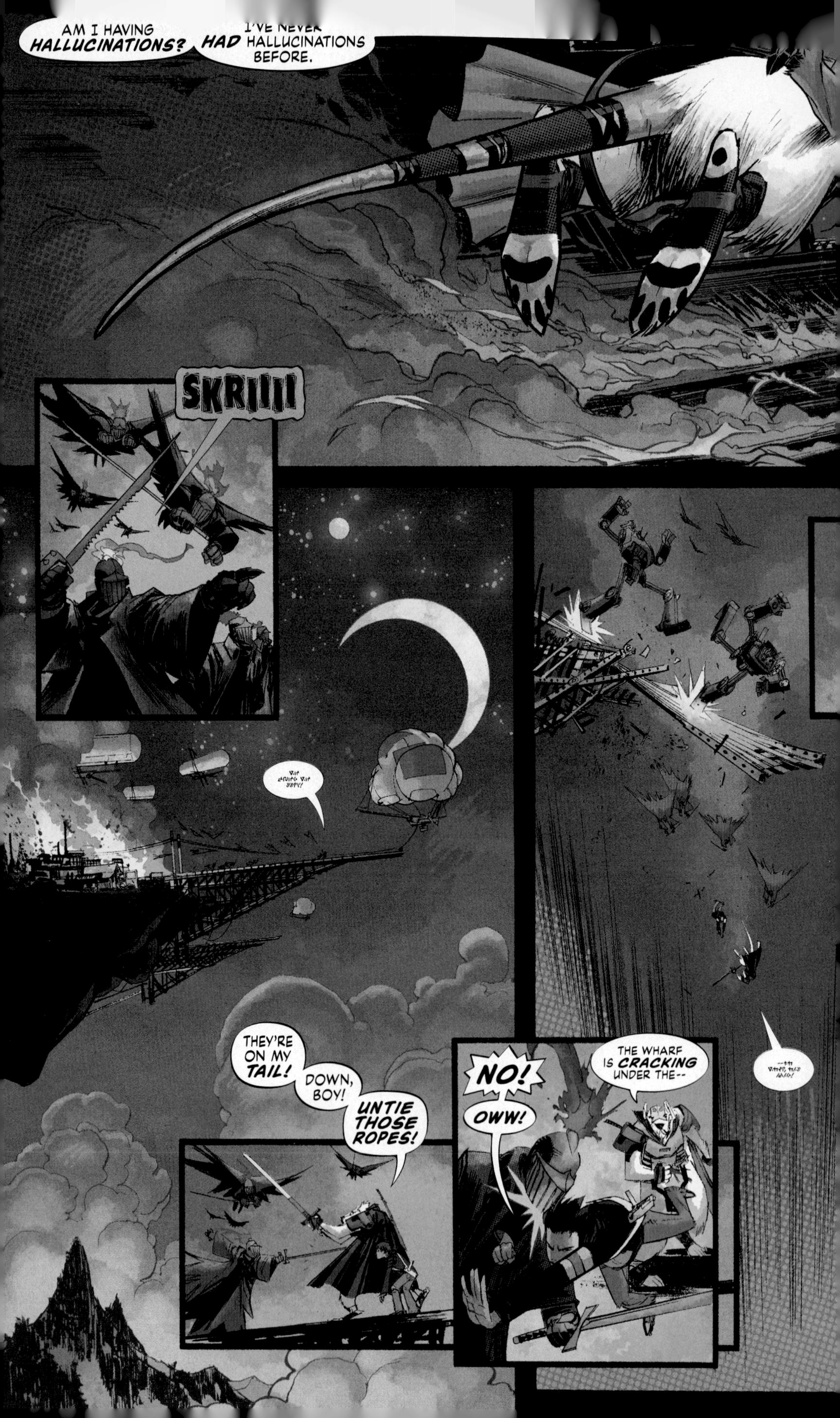
AM I HAVING HALLUCINATIONS?
I'VE NEVER HAD HALLUCINATIONS BEFORE.
SKRIIII
THEY'RE ON MY TAIL!
DOWN, BOY!
UNTIE THOSE ROPES!
NO!
OWW!
THE WHARF IS CRACKING UNDER THE--

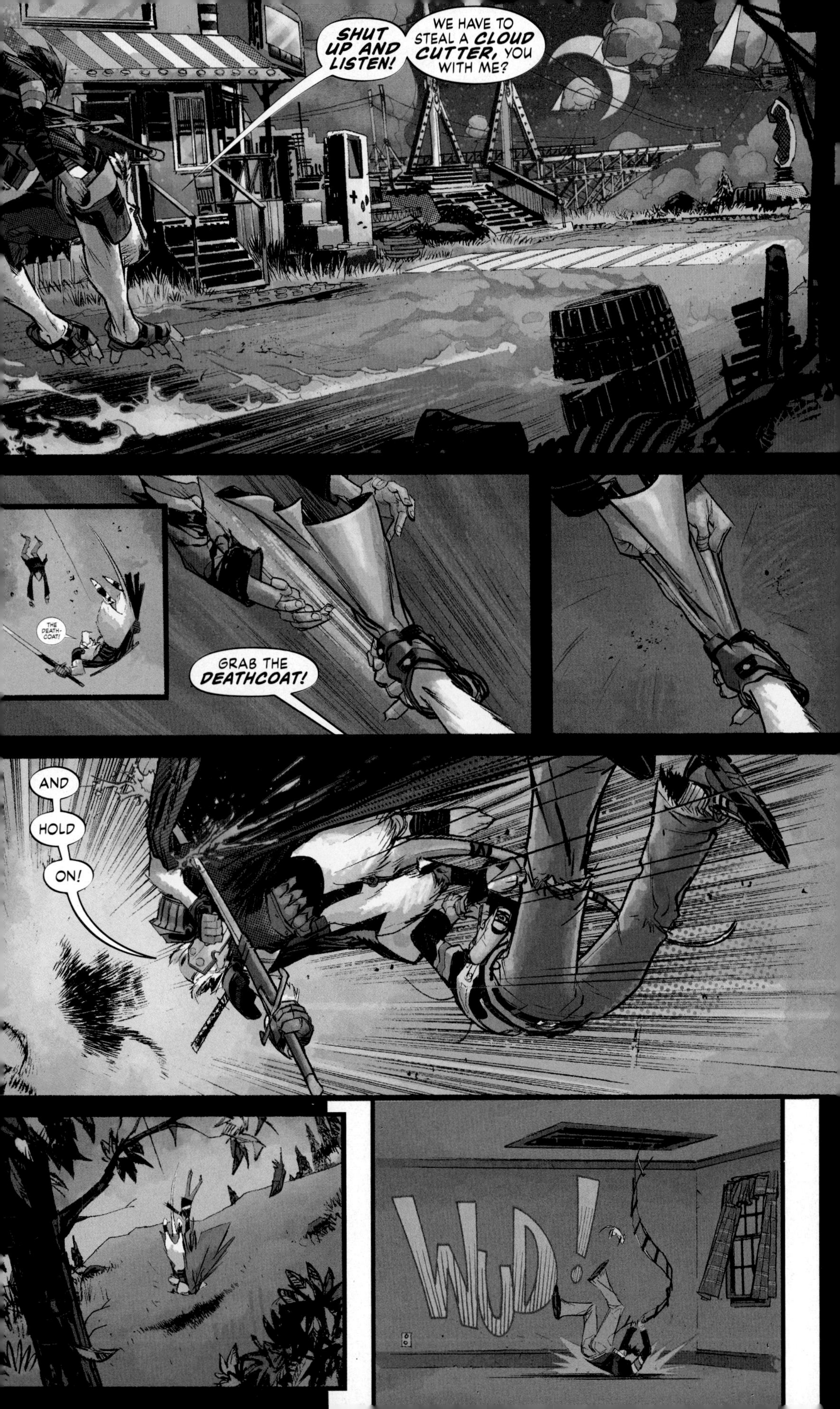
SHUT UP AND LISTEN!
WE HAVE TO STEAL A CLOUD CUTTER, YOU WITH ME?
THE DEATH-COAT!
GRAB THE DEATHCOAT!
AND
HOLD
ON!
WUD!

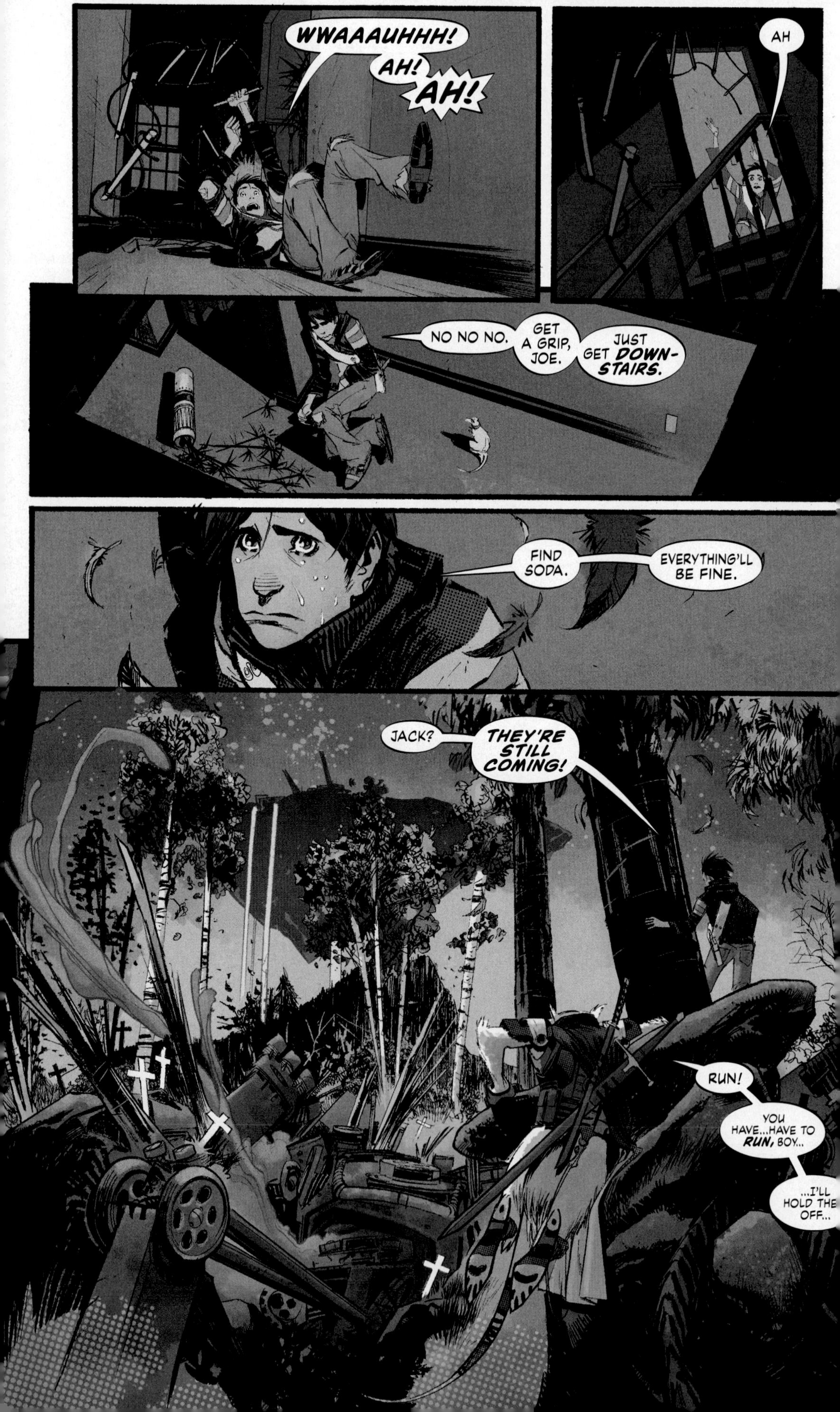
WWAAAUHHH!
AH!
AH!
AH
NO NO NO.
GET A GRIP, JOE.
JUST GET DOWN-STAIRS.
FIND SODA.
EVERYTHING'LL BE FINE.
JACK?
THEY'RE STILL COMING!
RUN!
YOU HAVE...HAVE TO RUN, BOY...
...I'LL HOLD THE OFF...

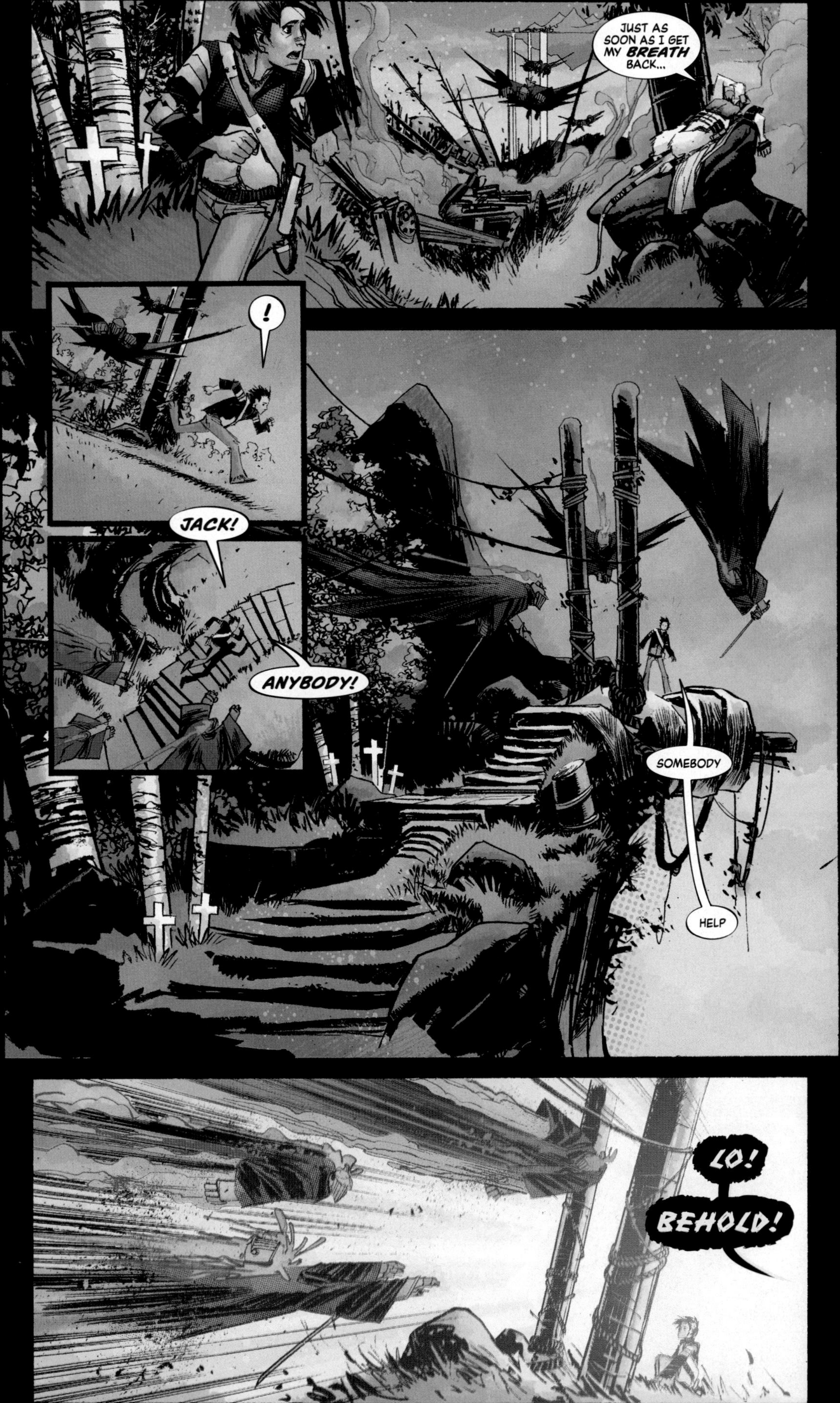

JUST AS SOON AS I GET MY **BREATH** BACK...
!
JACK!
ANYBODY!
SOMEBODY
HELP
LO!
BEHOLD!

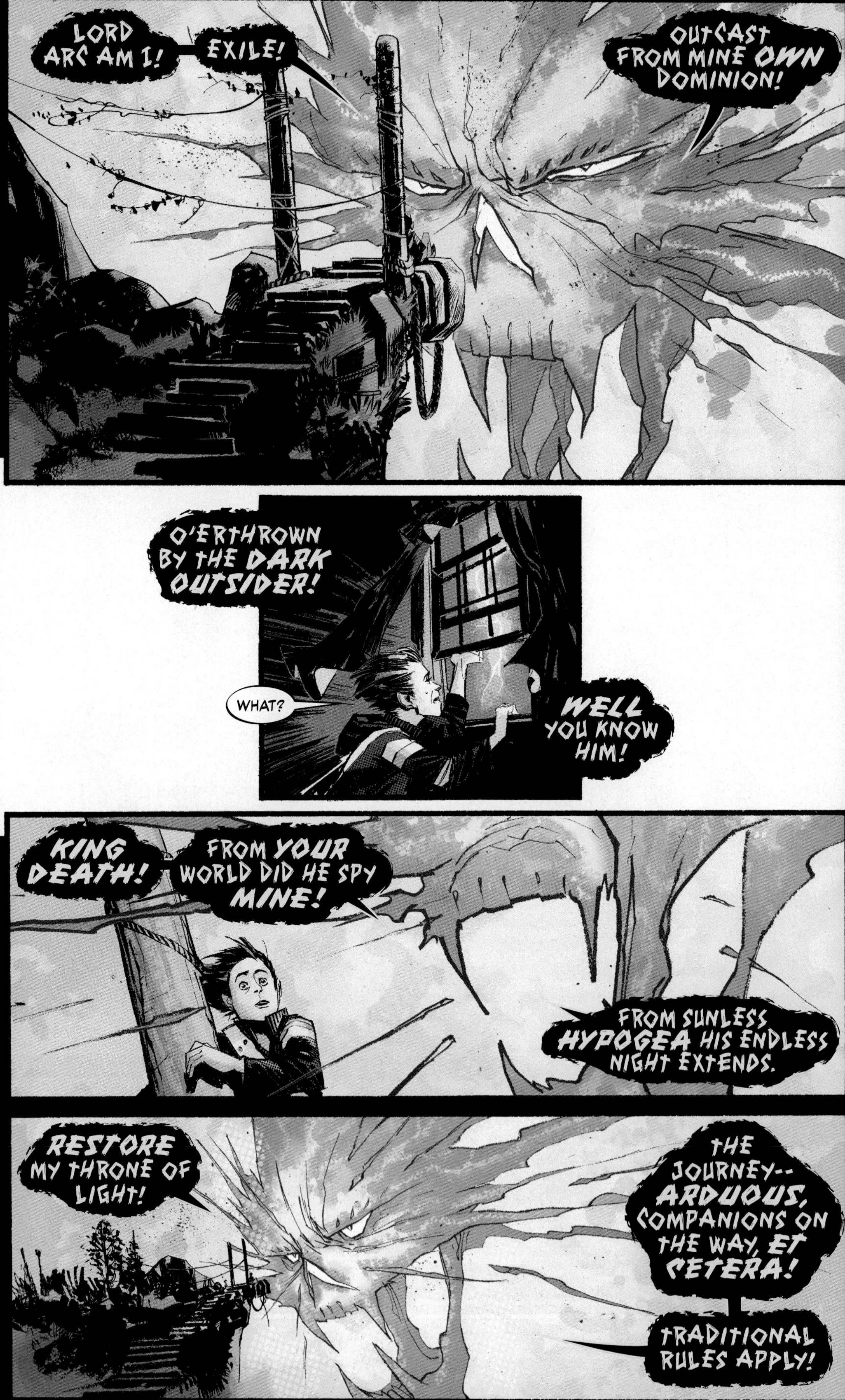
LORD ARC AM I!
EXILE!
OUTCAST FROM MINE OWN DOMINION!
O'ERTHROWN BY THE DARK OUTSIDER!
WHAT?
WELL YOU KNOW HIM!
KING DEATH!
FROM YOUR WORLD DID HE SPY MINE!
FROM SUNLESS HYPOGEA HIS ENDLESS NIGHT EXTENDS.
RESTORE MY THRONE OF LIGHT!
THE JOURNEY-- ARDUOUS, COMPANIONS ON THE WAY, ET CETERA!
TRADITIONAL RULES APPLY!

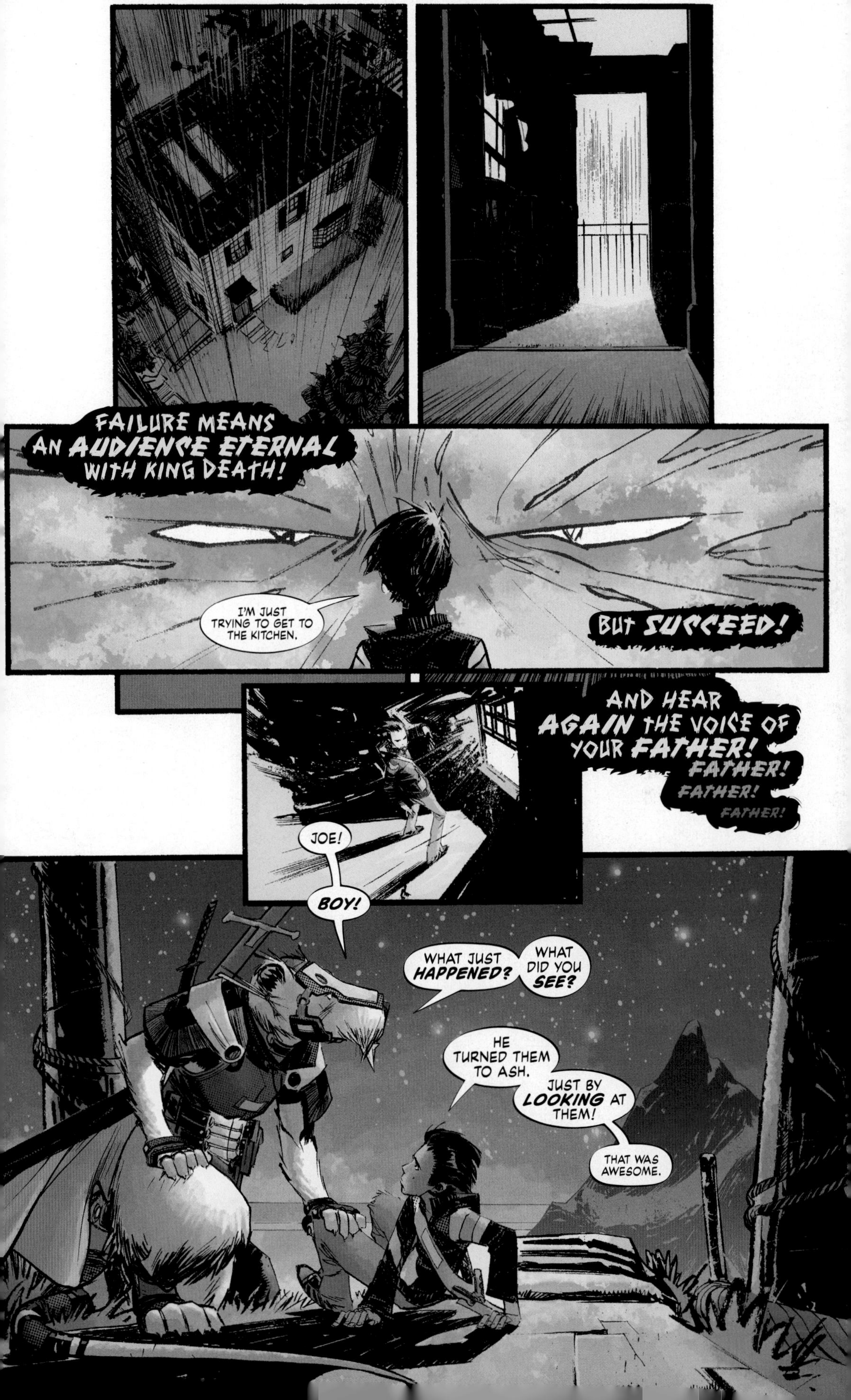
FAILURE MEANS AN AUDIENCE ETERNAL WITH KING DEATH!
I'M JUST TRYING TO GET TO THE KITCHEN.
BUT SUCCEED!
AND HEAR AGAIN THE VOICE OF YOUR FATHER!
FATHER!
FATHER!
FATHER!
JOE!
BOY!
WHAT JUST HAPPENED?
WHAT DID YOU SEE?
HE TURNED THEM TO ASH.
JUST BY LOOKING AT THEM!
THAT WAS AWESOME.

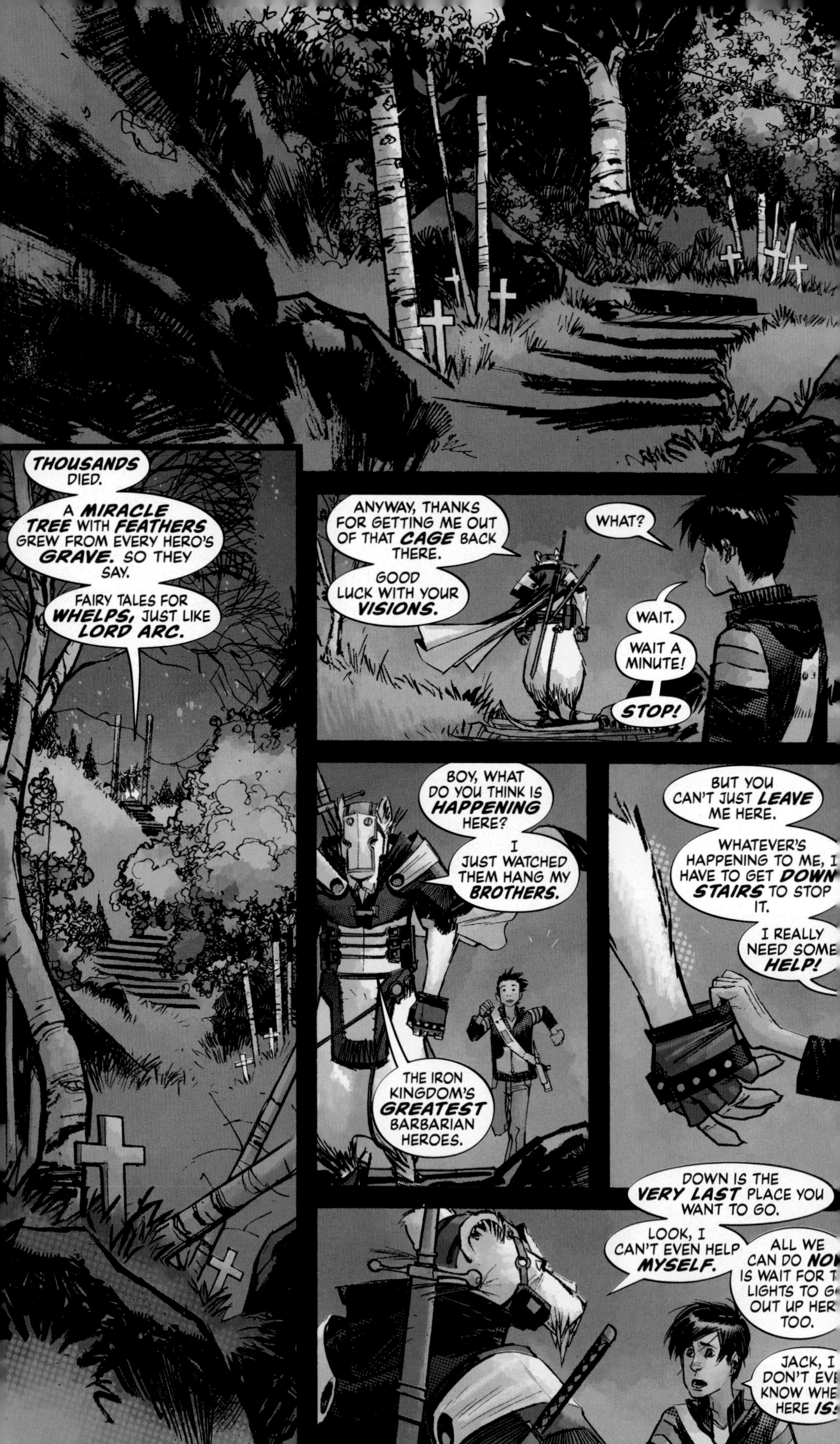
THOUSANDS DIED.
A MIRACLE TREE WITH FEATHERS GREW FROM EVERY HERO'S GRAVE. SO THEY SAY.
FAIRY TALES FOR WHELPS, JUST LIKE LORD ARC.
ANYWAY, THANKS FOR GETTING ME OUT OF THAT CAGE BACK THERE.
GOOD LUCK WITH YOUR VISIONS.
WHAT?
WAIT.
WAIT A MINUTE!
STOP!
BOY, WHAT DO YOU THINK IS HAPPENING HERE?
I JUST WATCHED THEM HANG MY BROTHERS.
THE IRON KINGDOM'S GREATEST BARBARIAN HEROES.
BUT YOU CAN'T JUST LEAVE ME HERE.
WHATEVER'S HAPPENING TO ME, I HAVE TO GET DOWN STAIRS TO STOP IT.
I REALLY NEED SOME HELP!
DOWN IS THE VERY LAST PLACE YOU WANT TO GO.
LOOK, I CAN'T EVEN HELP MYSELF.
ALL WE CAN DO NO IS WAIT FOR T LIGHTS TO G OUT UP HER TOO.
JACK, I DON'T EVE KNOW WHE HERE IS!

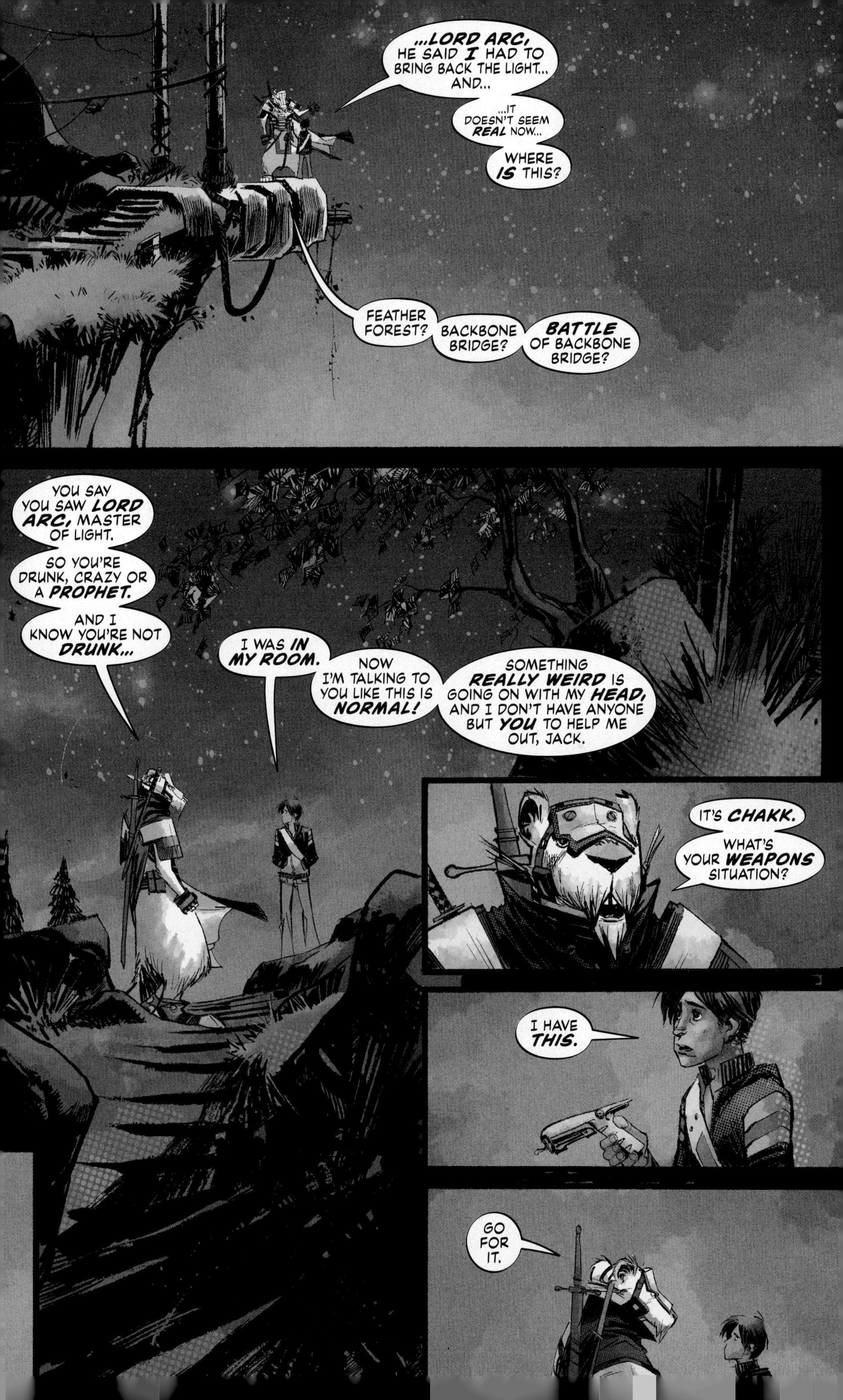
...LORD ARC, HE SAID I HAD TO BRING BACK THE LIGHT... AND...
...IT DOESN'T SEEM REAL NOW...
WHERE IS THIS?
FEATHER FOREST?
BACKBONE BRIDGE?
BATTLE OF BACKBONE BRIDGE?
YOU SAY YOU SAW LORD ARC, MASTER OF LIGHT.
SO YOU'RE DRUNK, CRAZY OR A PROPHET.
AND I KNOW YOU'RE NOT DRUNK...
I WAS IN MY ROOM.
NOW I'M TALKING TO YOU LIKE THIS IS NORMAL!
SOMETHING REALLY WEIRD IS GOING ON WITH MY HEAD, AND I DON'T HAVE ANYONE BUT YOU TO HELP ME OUT, JACK.
IT'S CHAKK.
WHAT'S YOUR WEAPONS SITUATION?
I HAVE THIS.
GO FOR IT.

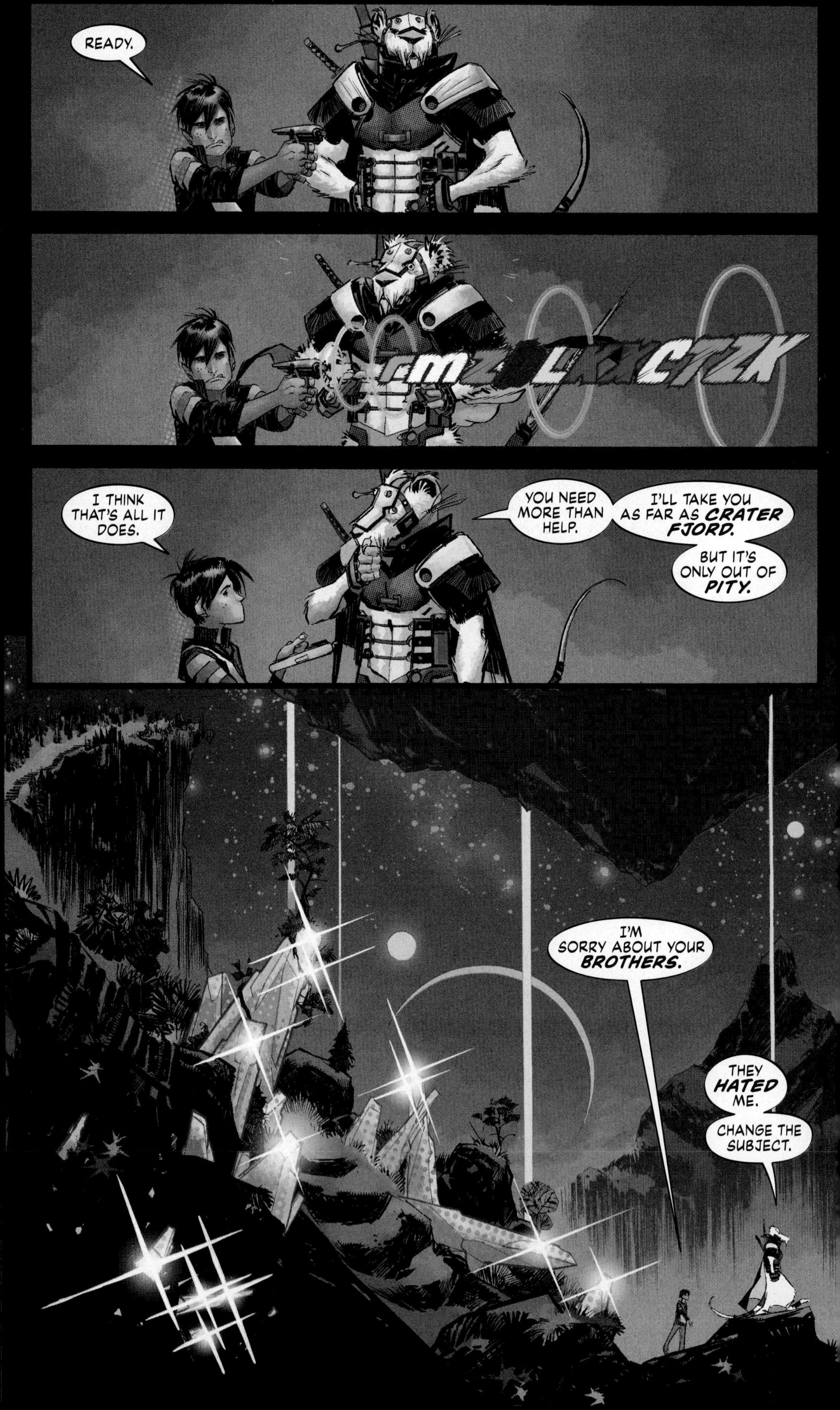
READY.
I THINK THAT'S ALL IT DOES.
YOU NEED MORE THAN HELP.
I'LL TAKE YOU AS FAR AS **CRATER FJORD.**
BUT IT'S ONLY OUT OF **PITY.**
I'M SORRY ABOUT YOUR **BROTHERS.**
THEY **HATED** ME.
CHANGE THE SUBJECT.

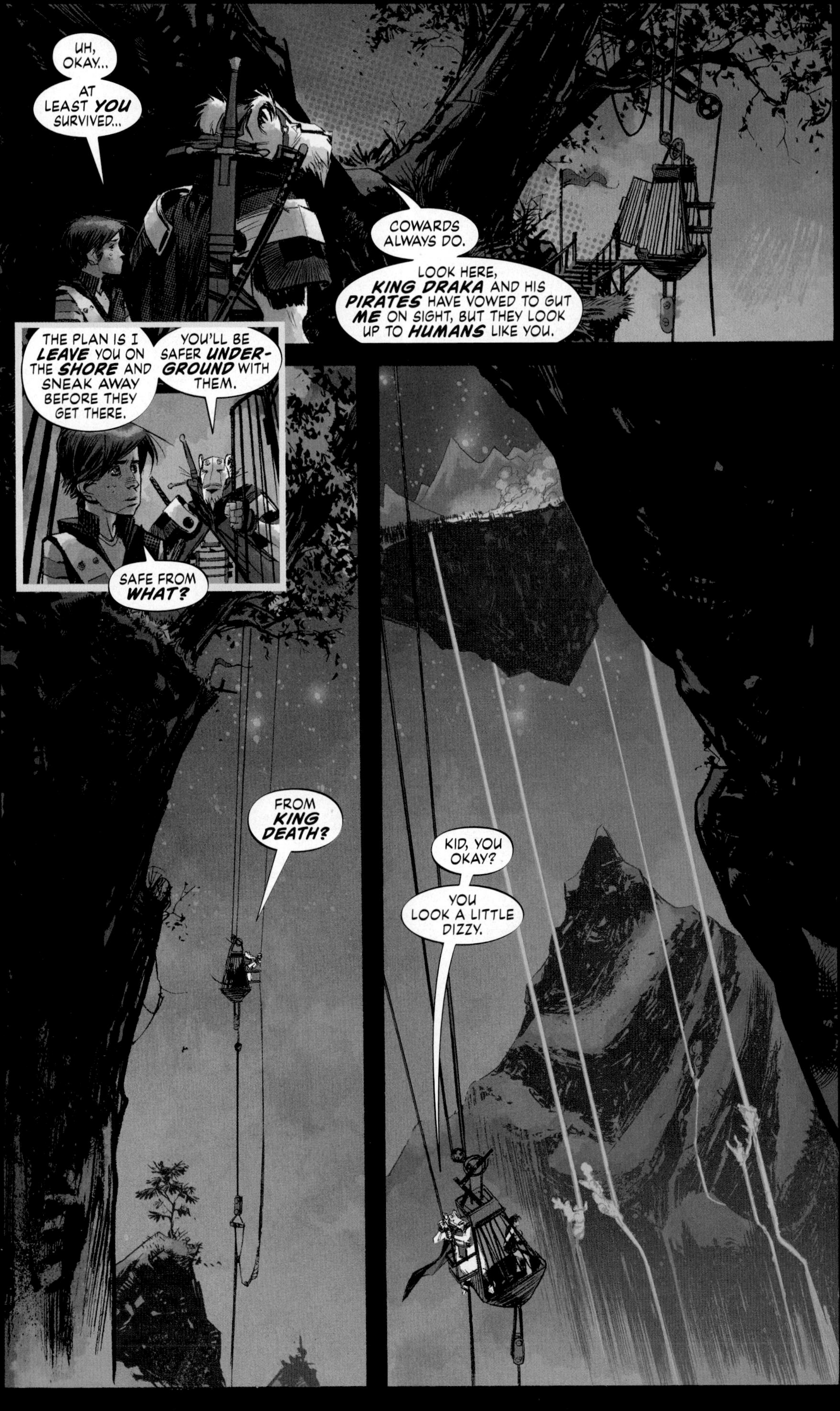
UH, OKAY...
AT LEAST YOU SURVIVED...
COWARDS ALWAYS DO.
LOOK HERE, KING DRAKA AND HIS PIRATES HAVE VOWED TO GUT ME ON SIGHT, BUT THEY LOOK UP TO HUMANS LIKE YOU.
THE PLAN IS I LEAVE YOU ON THE SHORE AND SNEAK AWAY BEFORE THEY GET THERE.
YOU'LL BE SAFER UNDER-GROUND WITH THEM.
SAFE FROM WHAT?
FROM KING DEATH?
KID, YOU OKAY?
YOU LOOK A LITTLE DIZZY.

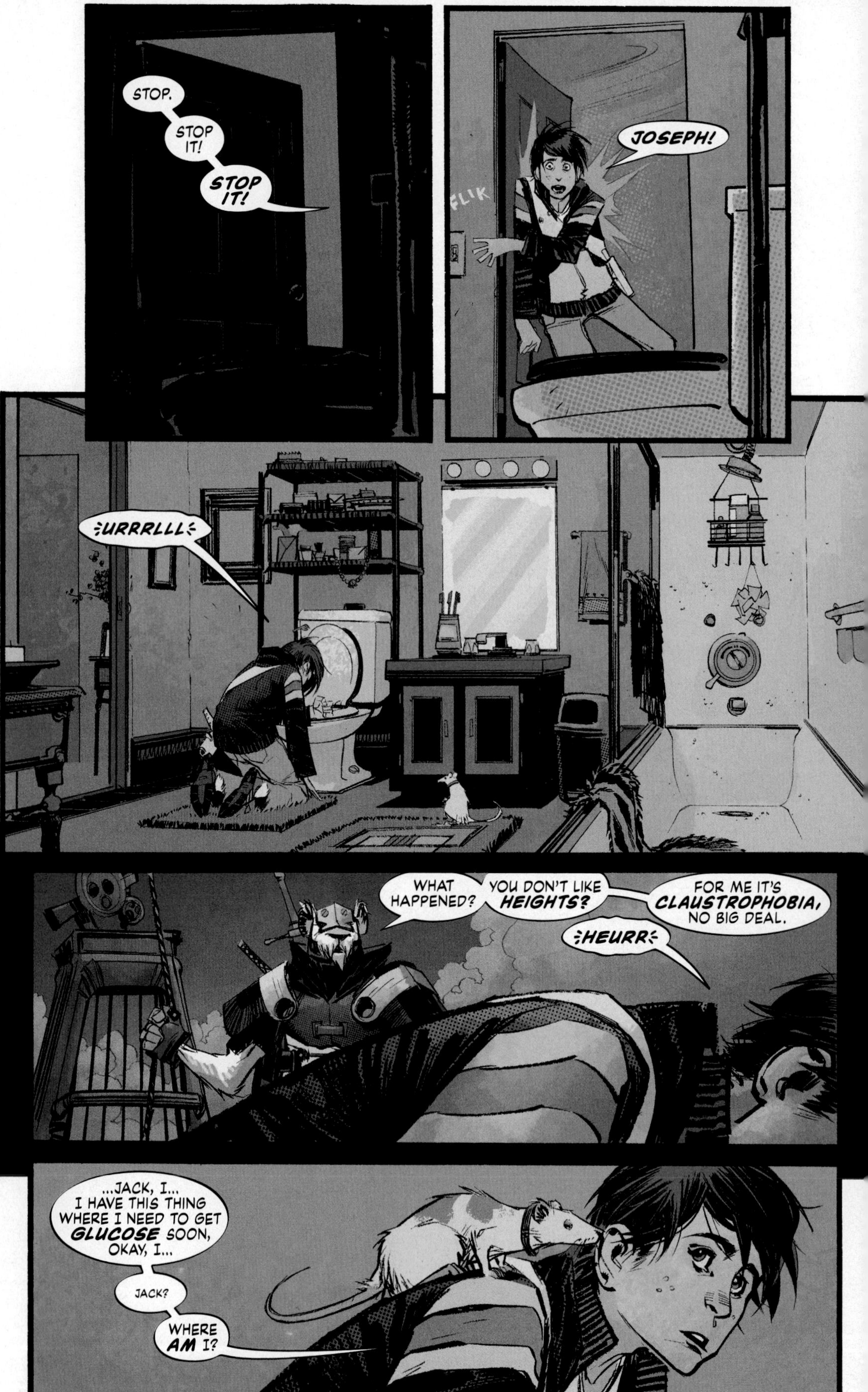
STOP.
STOP IT!
STOP IT!
FLIK
JOSEPH!
URRRLLL
WHAT HAPPENED?
YOU DON'T LIKE HEIGHTS?
FOR ME IT'S CLAUSTROPHOBIA, NO BIG DEAL.
HEURR
...JACK, I... I HAVE THIS THING WHERE I NEED TO GET GLUCOSE SOON, OKAY, I...
JACK?
WHERE AM I?

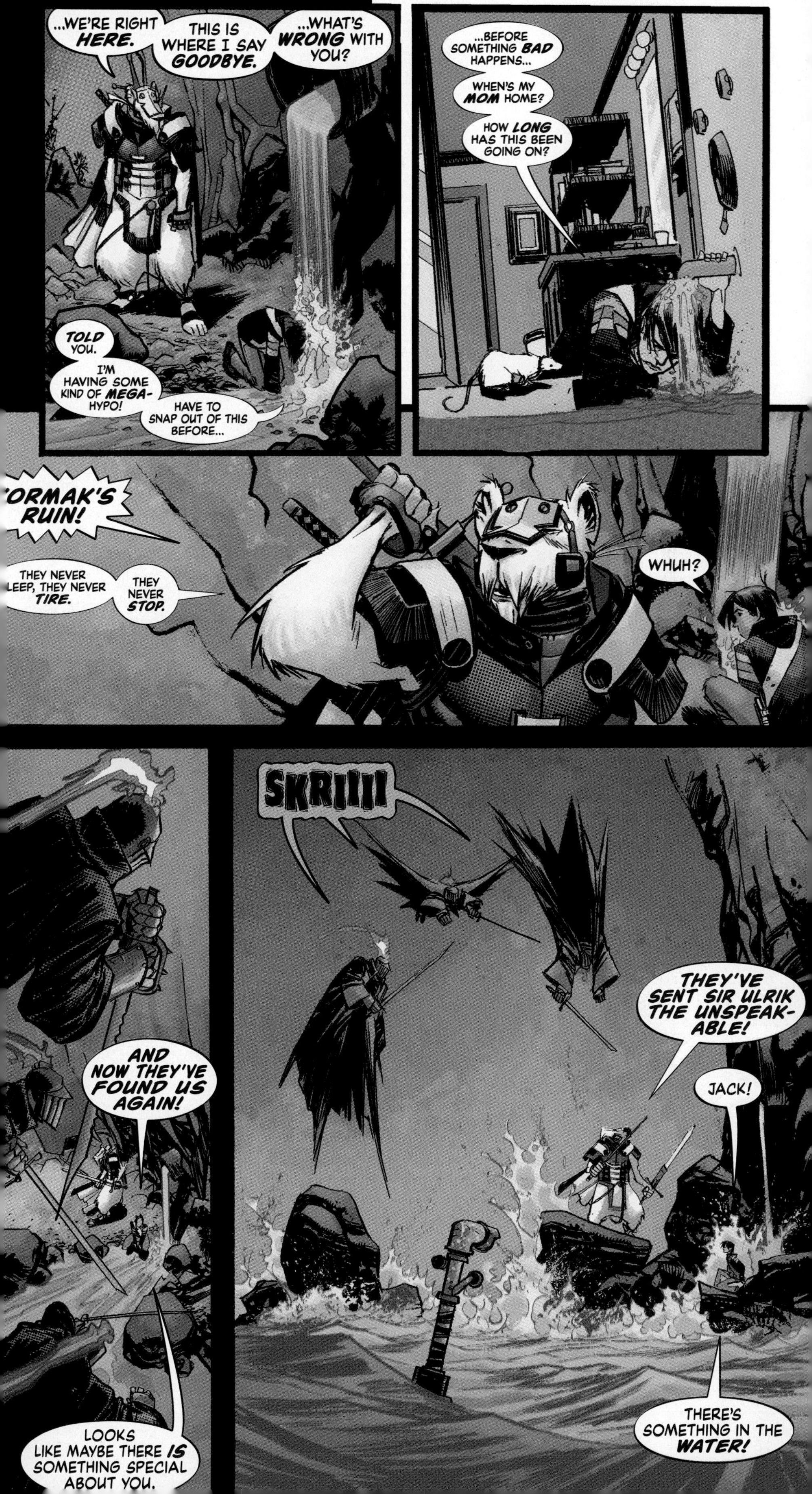
...WE'RE RIGHT HERE.
THIS IS WHERE I SAY GOODBYE.
...WHAT'S WRONG WITH YOU?
TOLD YOU.
I'M HAVING SOME KIND OF MEGA-HYPO!
HAVE TO SNAP OUT OF THIS BEFORE...
...BEFORE SOMETHING BAD HAPPENS...
WHEN'S MY MOM HOME?
HOW LONG HAS THIS BEEN GOING ON?
ORMAK'S RUIN!
THEY NEVER LEEP, THEY NEVER TIRE.
THEY NEVER STOP.
WHUH?
AND NOW THEY'VE FOUND US AGAIN!
LOOKS LIKE MAYBE THERE IS SOMETHING SPECIAL ABOUT YOU.
SKRIIII
THEY'VE SENT SIR ULRIK THE UNSPEAKABLE!
JACK!
THERE'S SOMETHING IN THE WATER!

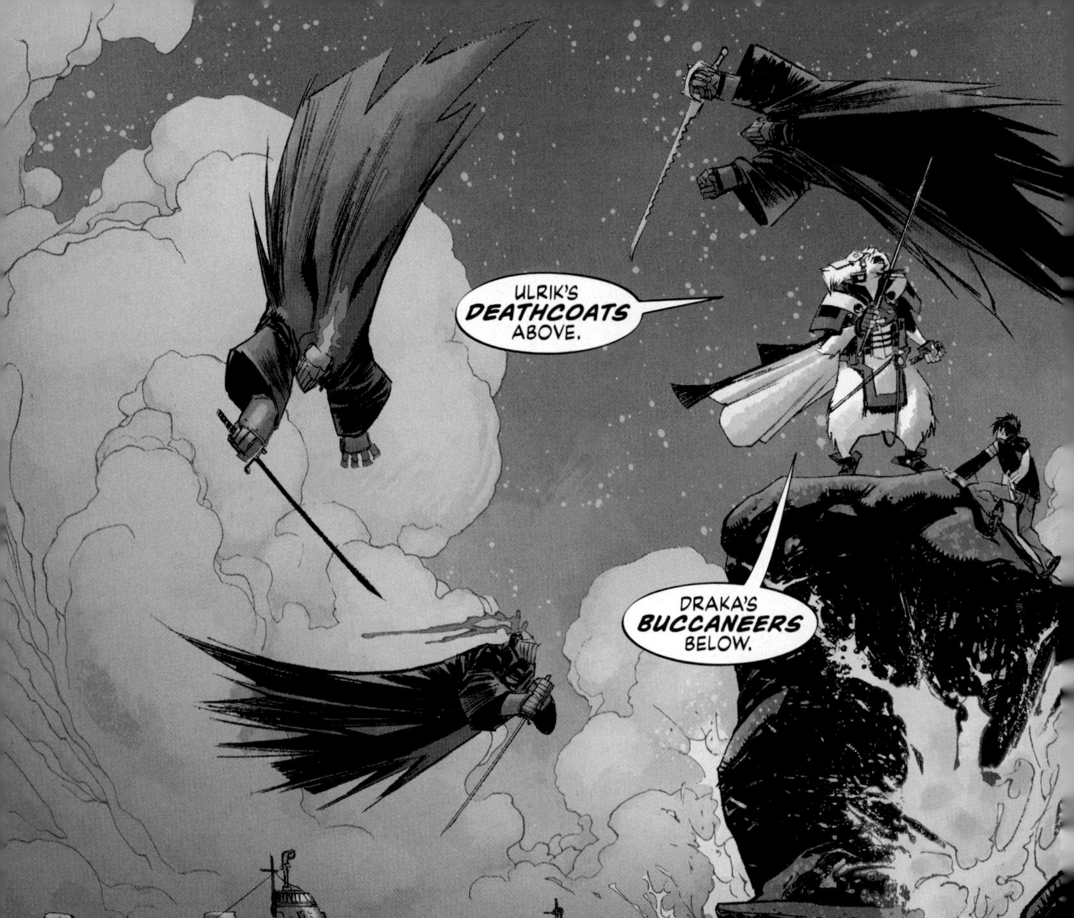
ULRIK'S DEATHCOATS ABOVE.
DRAKA'S BUCCANEERS BELOW.

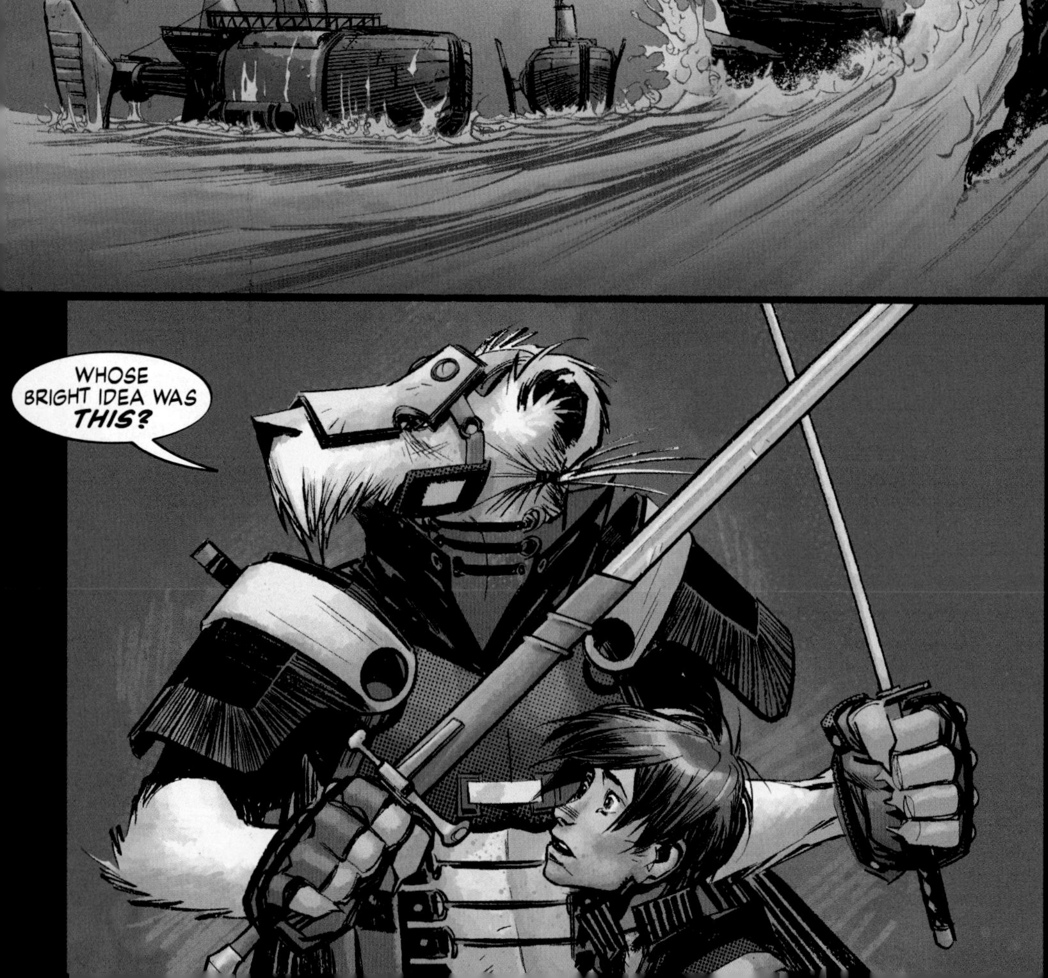
WHOSE BRIGHT IDEA WAS THIS?

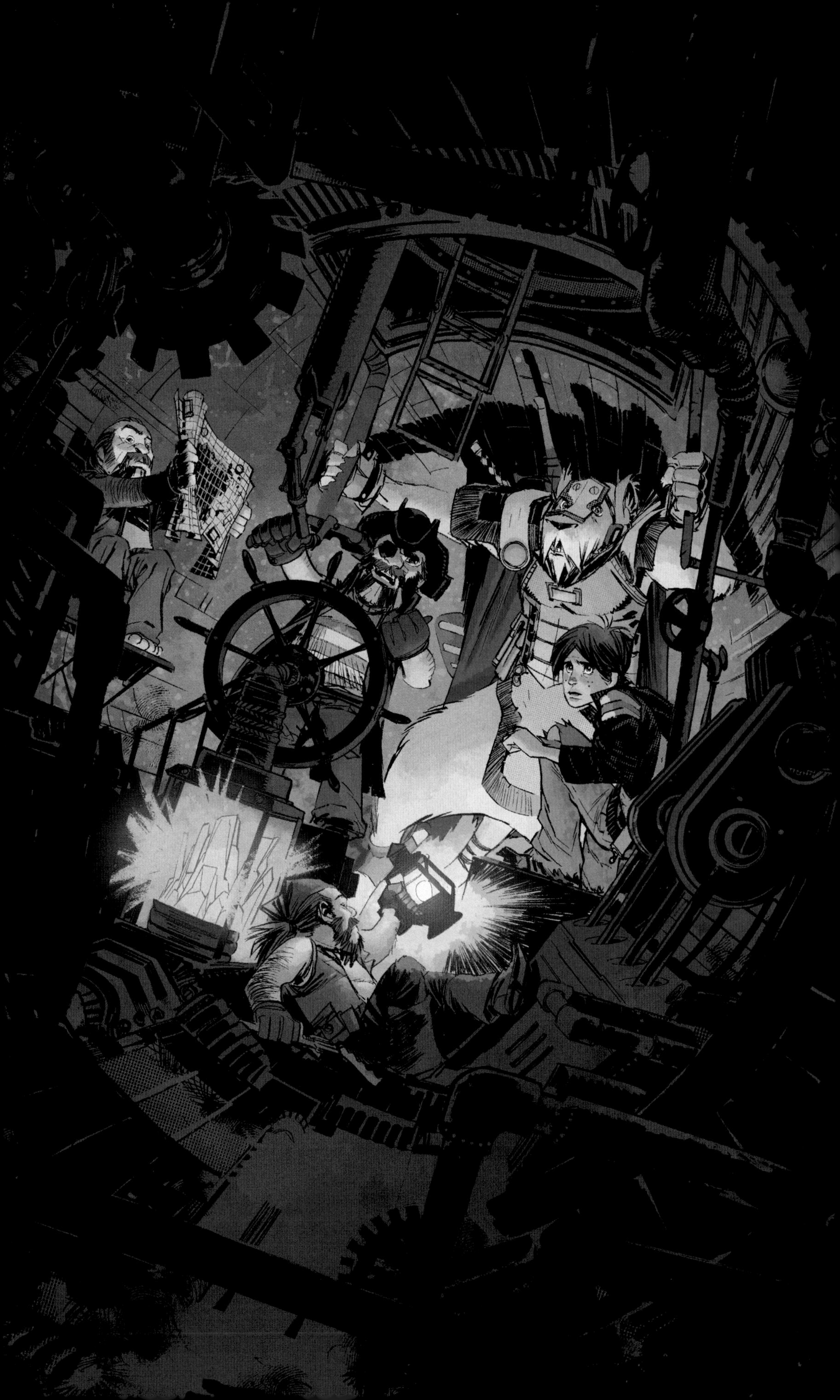

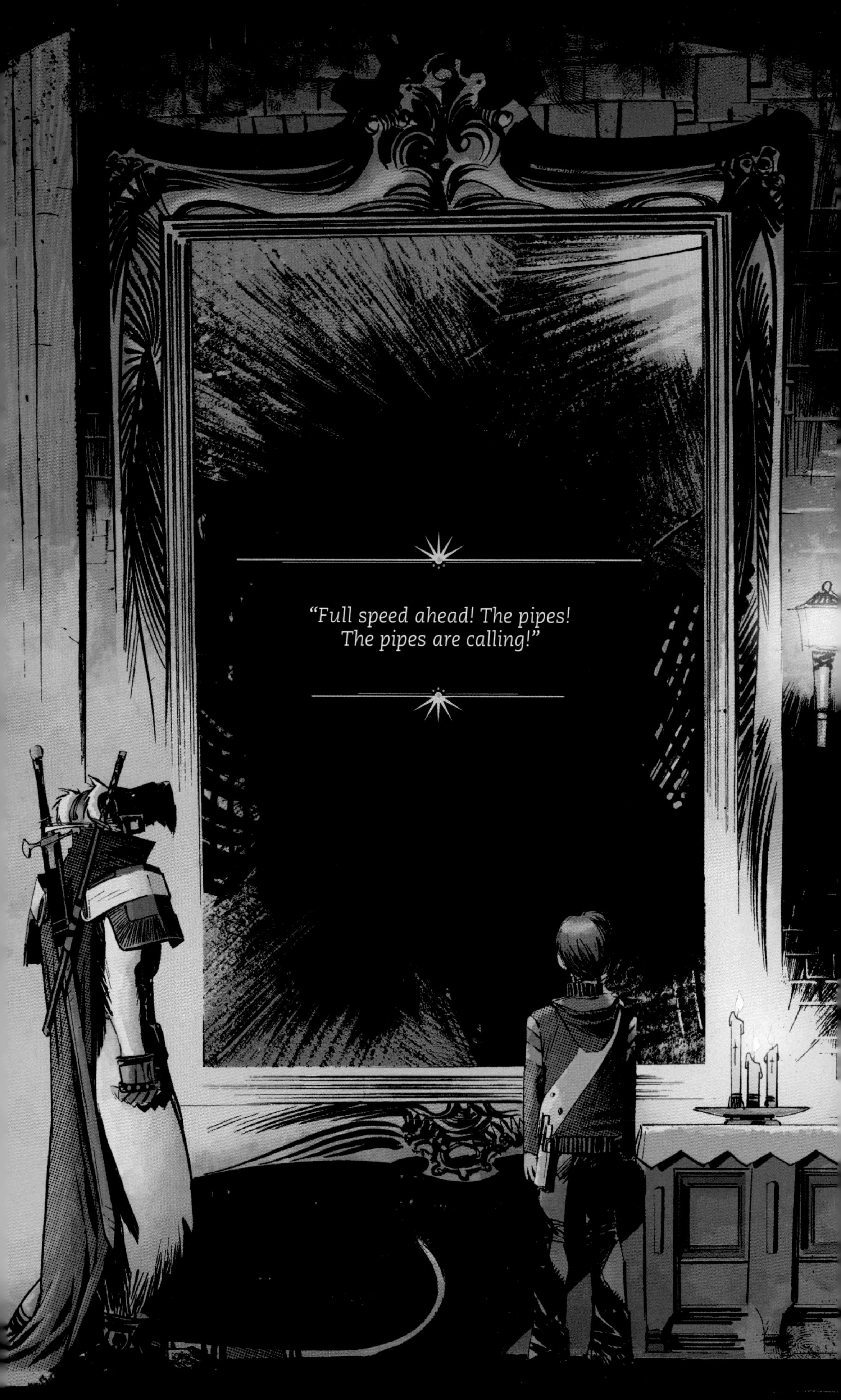
"Full speed ahead! The pipes!
The pipes are calling!"

chapter 3: the dying boy

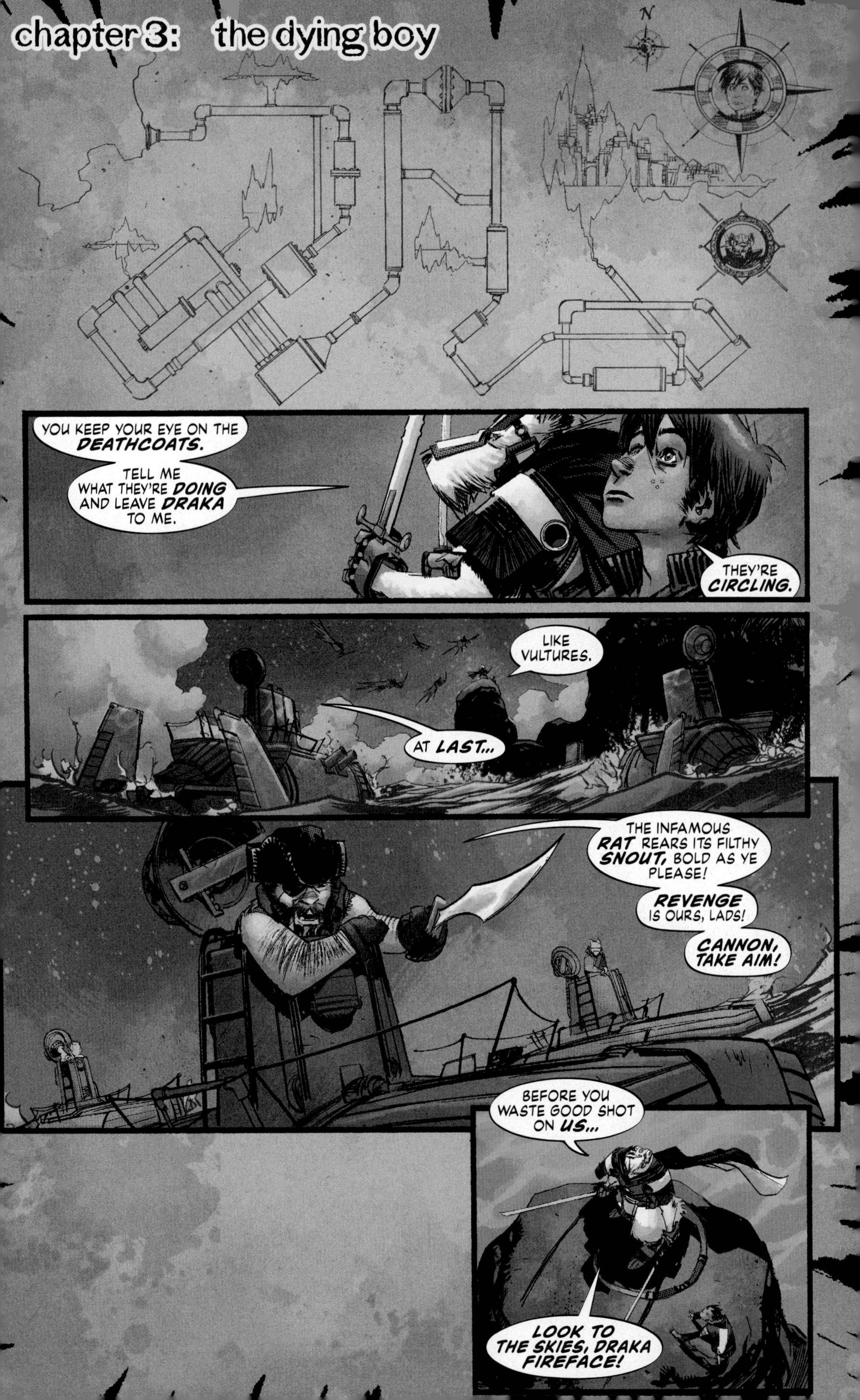
N
YOU KEEP YOUR EYE ON THE DEATHCOATS.
TELL ME WHAT THEY'RE DOING AND LEAVE DRAKA TO ME.
THEY'RE CIRCLING.
LIKE VULTURES.
AT LAST...
THE INFAMOUS RAT REARS ITS FILTHY SNOUT, BOLD AS YE PLEASE!
REVENGE IS OURS, LADS!
CANNON, TAKE AIM!
BEFORE YOU WASTE GOOD SHOT ON US...
LOOK TO THE SKIES, DRAKA FIREFACE!

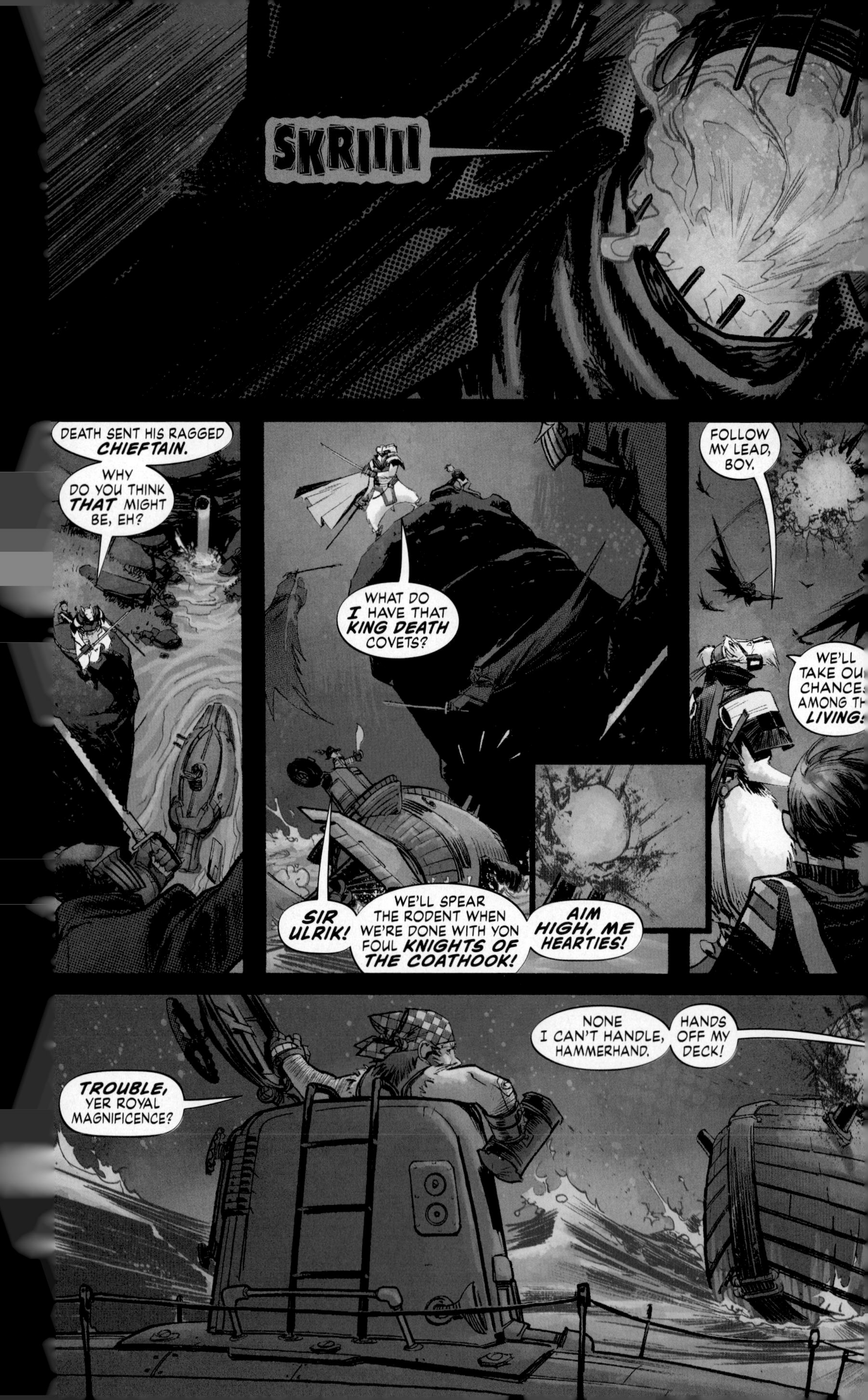
SKRIIII
DEATH SENT HIS RAGGED CHIEFTAIN.
WHY DO YOU THINK THAT MIGHT BE, EH?
WHAT DO I HAVE THAT KING DEATH COVETS?
SIR ULRIK!
WE'LL SPEAR THE RODENT WHEN WE'RE DONE WITH YON FOUL KNIGHTS OF THE COATHOOK!
AIM HIGH, ME HEARTIES!
FOLLOW MY LEAD, BOY.
WE'LL TAKE OU CHANCE AMONG T LIVING!
TROUBLE, YER ROYAL MAGNIFICENCE?
NONE I CAN'T HANDLE, HAMMERHAND.
HANDS OFF MY DECK!

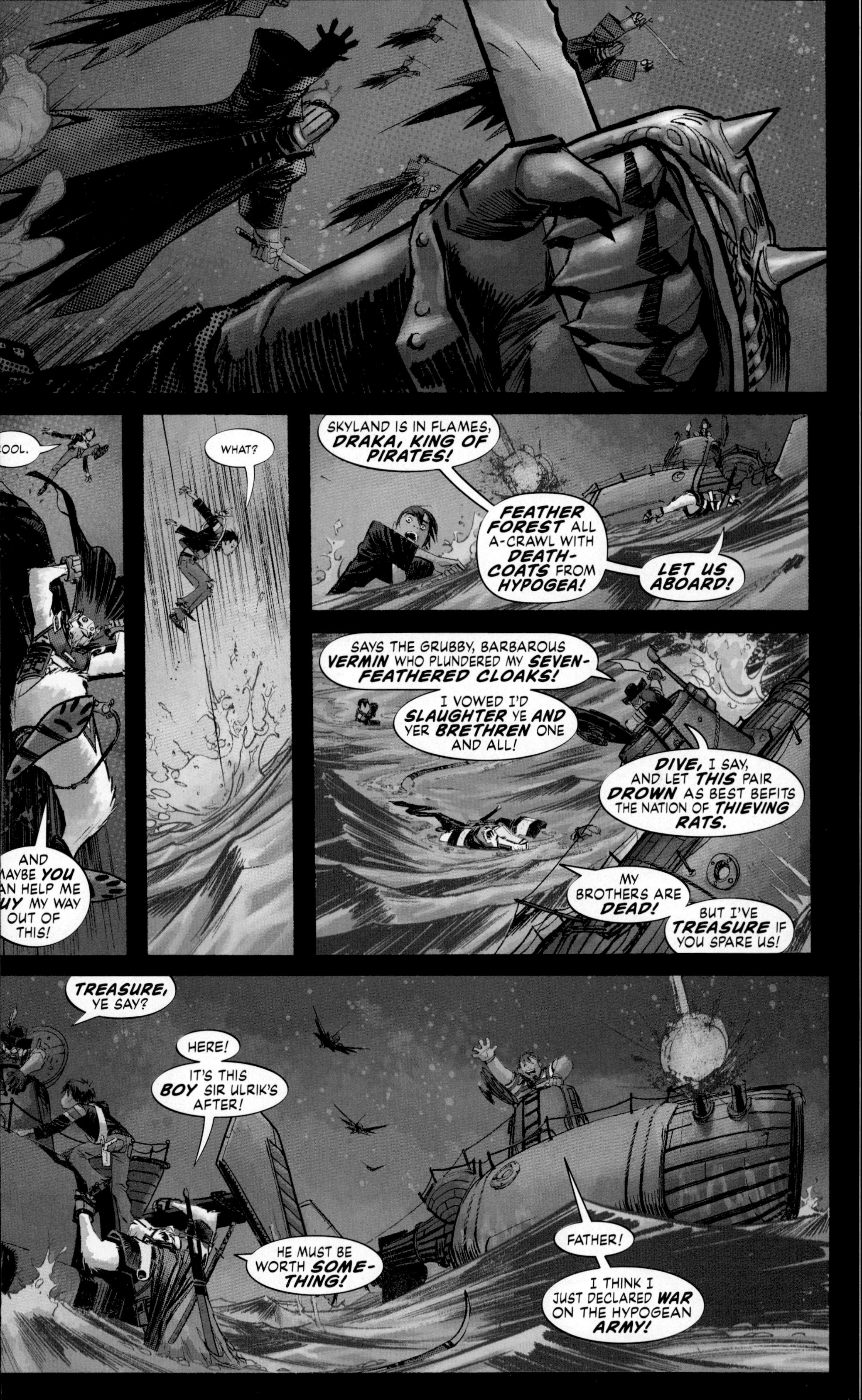
OOL.
AND MAYBE YOU AN HELP ME UY MY WAY OUT OF THIS!
WHAT?
SKYLAND IS IN FLAMES, DRAKA, KING OF PIRATES!
FEATHER FOREST ALL A-CRAWL WITH DEATH-COATS FROM HYPOGEA!
LET US ABOARD!
SAYS THE GRUBBY, BARBAROUS VERMIN WHO PLUNDERED MY SEVEN-FEATHERED CLOAKS!
I VOWED I'D SLAUGHTER YE AND YER BRETHREN ONE AND ALL!
DIVE, I SAY, AND LET THIS PAIR DROWN AS BEST BEFITS THE NATION OF THIEVING RATS.
MY BROTHERS ARE DEAD!
BUT I'VE TREASURE IF YOU SPARE US!
TREASURE, YE SAY?
HERE!
IT'S THIS BOY SIR ULRIK'S AFTER!
HE MUST BE WORTH SOME-THING!
FATHER!
I THINK I JUST DECLARED WAR ON THE HYPOGEAN ARMY!

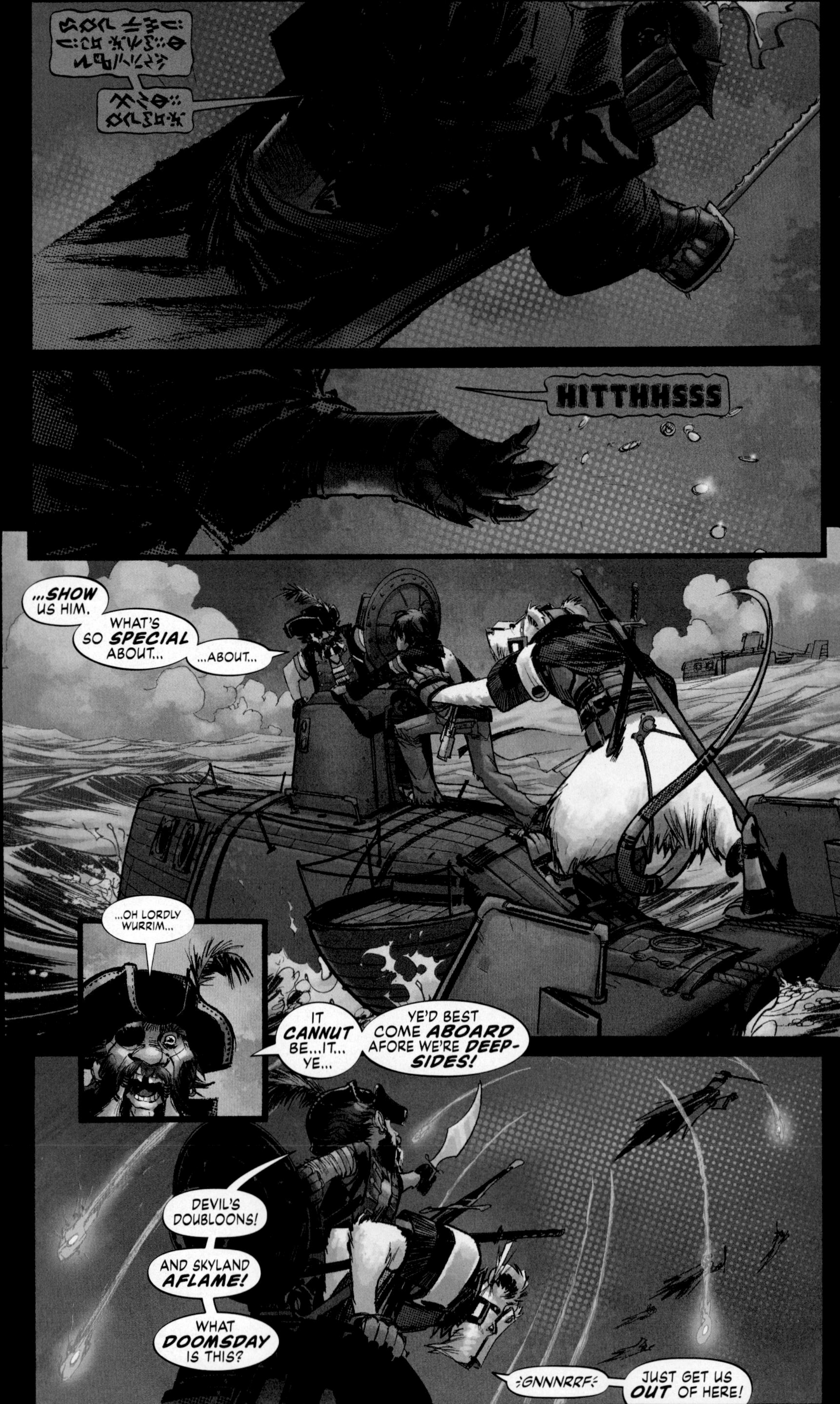
HITTHHSSS
...SHOW US HIM.
WHAT'S SO SPECIAL ABOUT...
...ABOUT...
...OH LORDLY WURRIM...
IT CANNUT BE...IT... YE...
YE'D BEST COME ABOARD AFORE WE'RE DEEP-SIDES!
DEVIL'S DOUBLOONS!
AND SKYLAND AFLAME!
WHAT DOOMSDAY IS THIS?
GNNNRRF
JUST GET US OUT OF HERE!

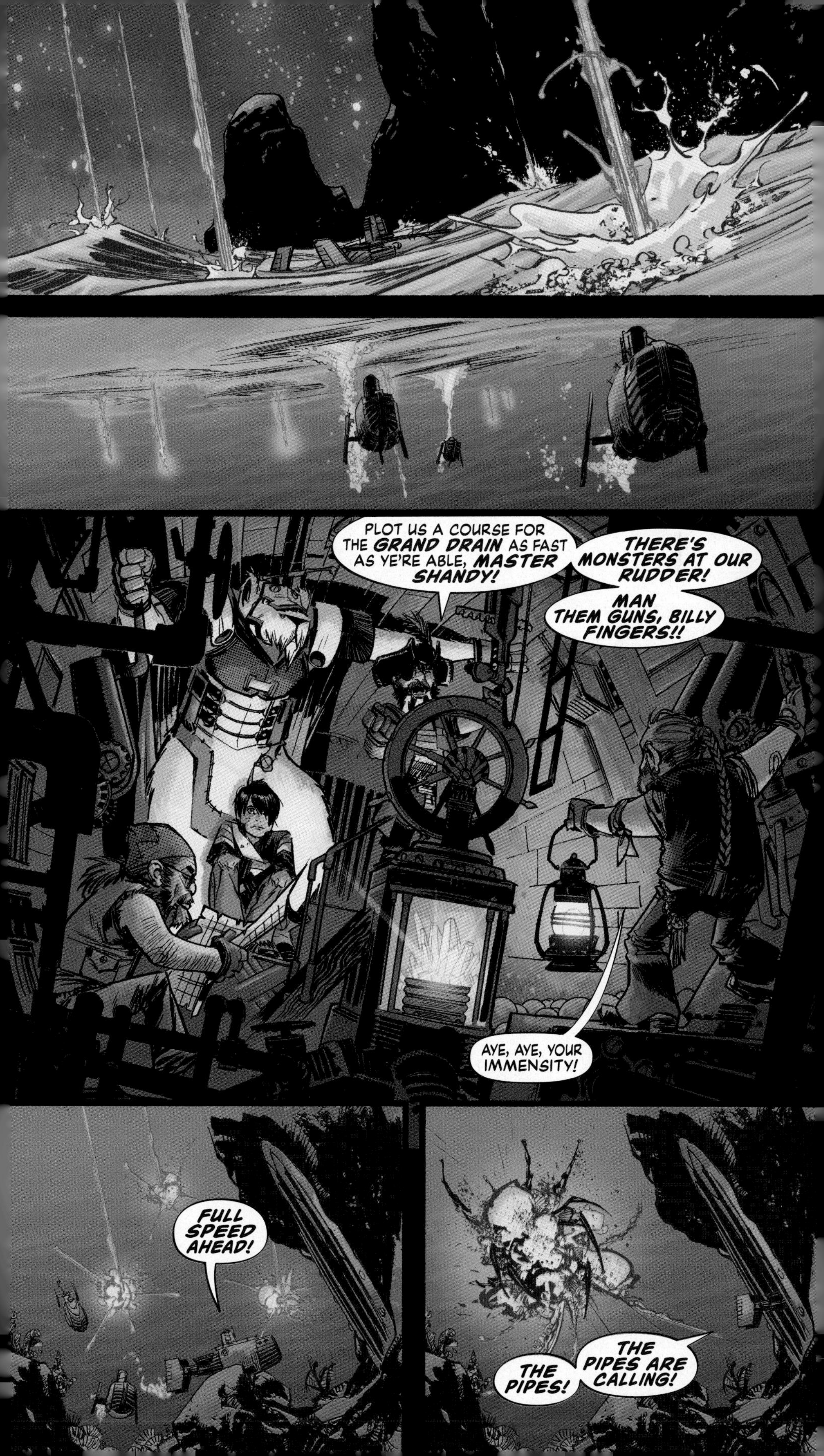
PLOT US A COURSE FOR THE GRAND DRAIN AS FAST AS YE'RE ABLE, MASTER SHANDY!
THERE'S MONSTERS AT OUR RUDDER!
MAN THEM GUNS, BILLY FINGERS!!
AYE, AYE, YOUR IMMENSITY!
FULL SPEED AHEAD!
THE PIPES!
THE PIPES ARE CALLING!

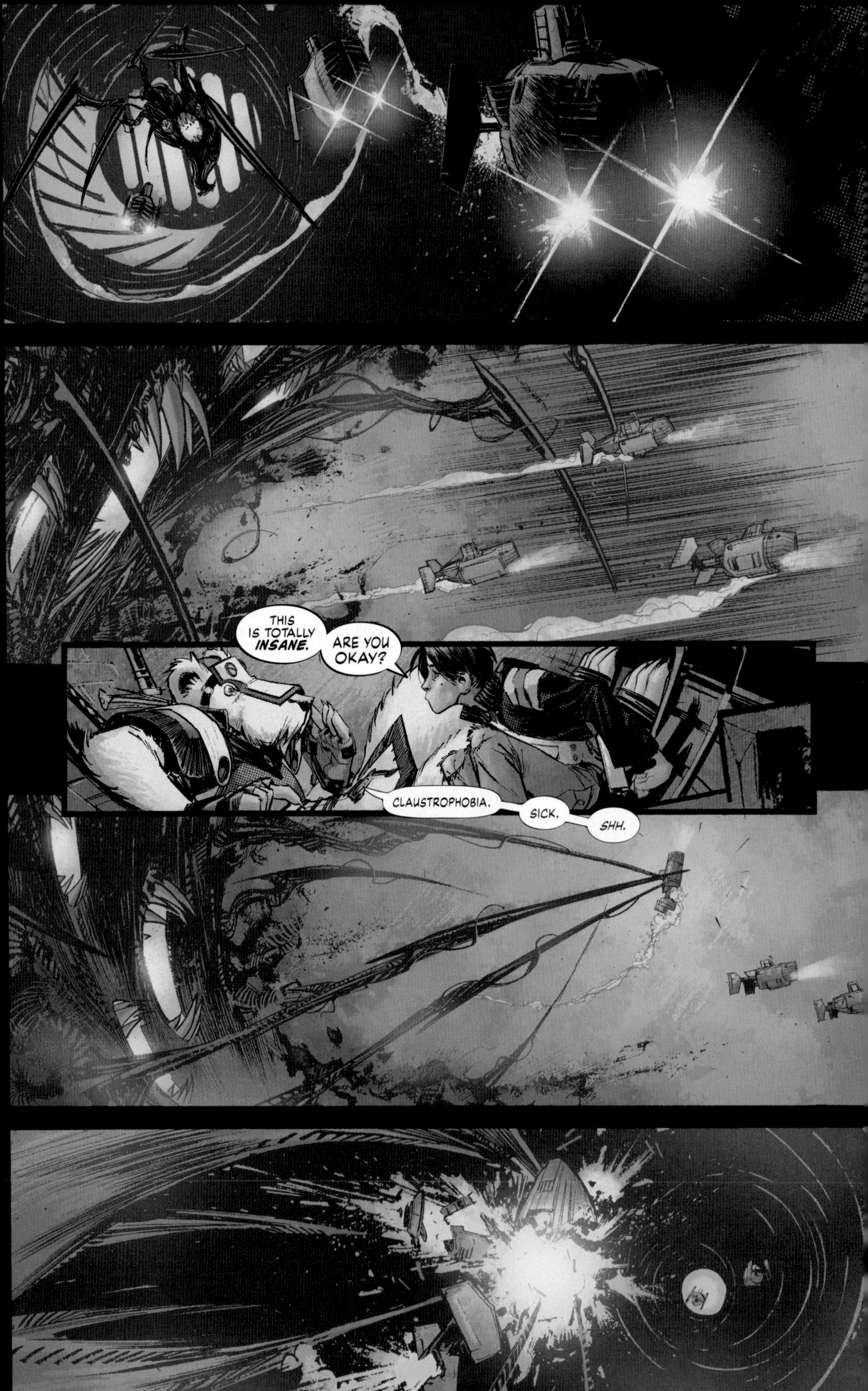
THIS IS TOTALLY *INSANE.*
ARE YOU OKAY?
CLAUSTROPHOBIA.
SICK.
SHH.

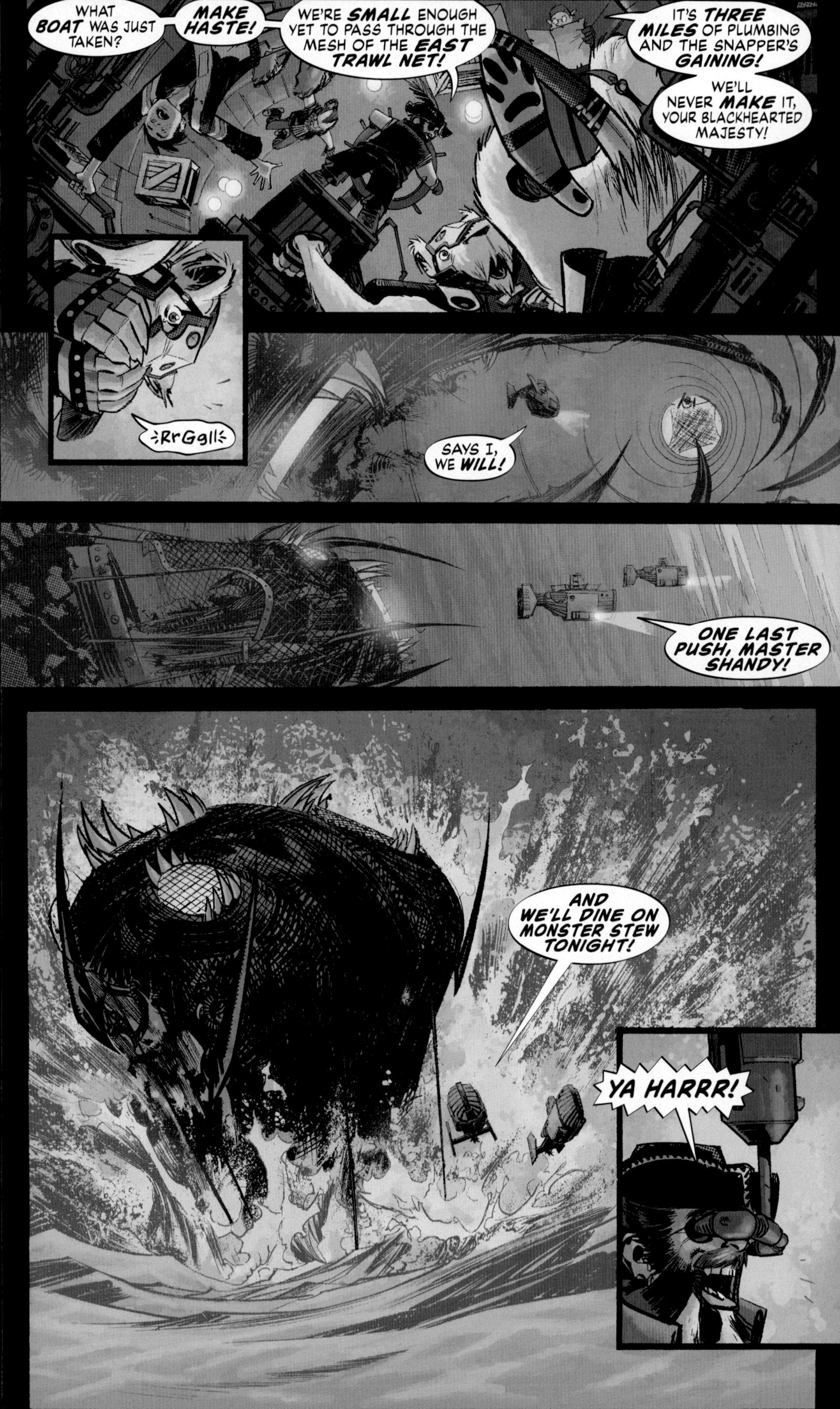
WHAT BOAT WAS JUST TAKEN?
MAKE HASTE!
WE'RE SMALL ENOUGH YET TO PASS THROUGH THE MESH OF THE EAST TRAWL NET!
IT'S THREE MILES OF PLUMBING AND THE SNAPPER'S GAINING!
WE'LL NEVER MAKE IT, YOUR BLACKHEARTED MAJESTY!
RrGgll
SAYS I, WE WILL!
ONE LAST PUSH, MASTER SHANDY!
AND WE'LL DINE ON MONSTER STEW TONIGHT!
YA HARRR!

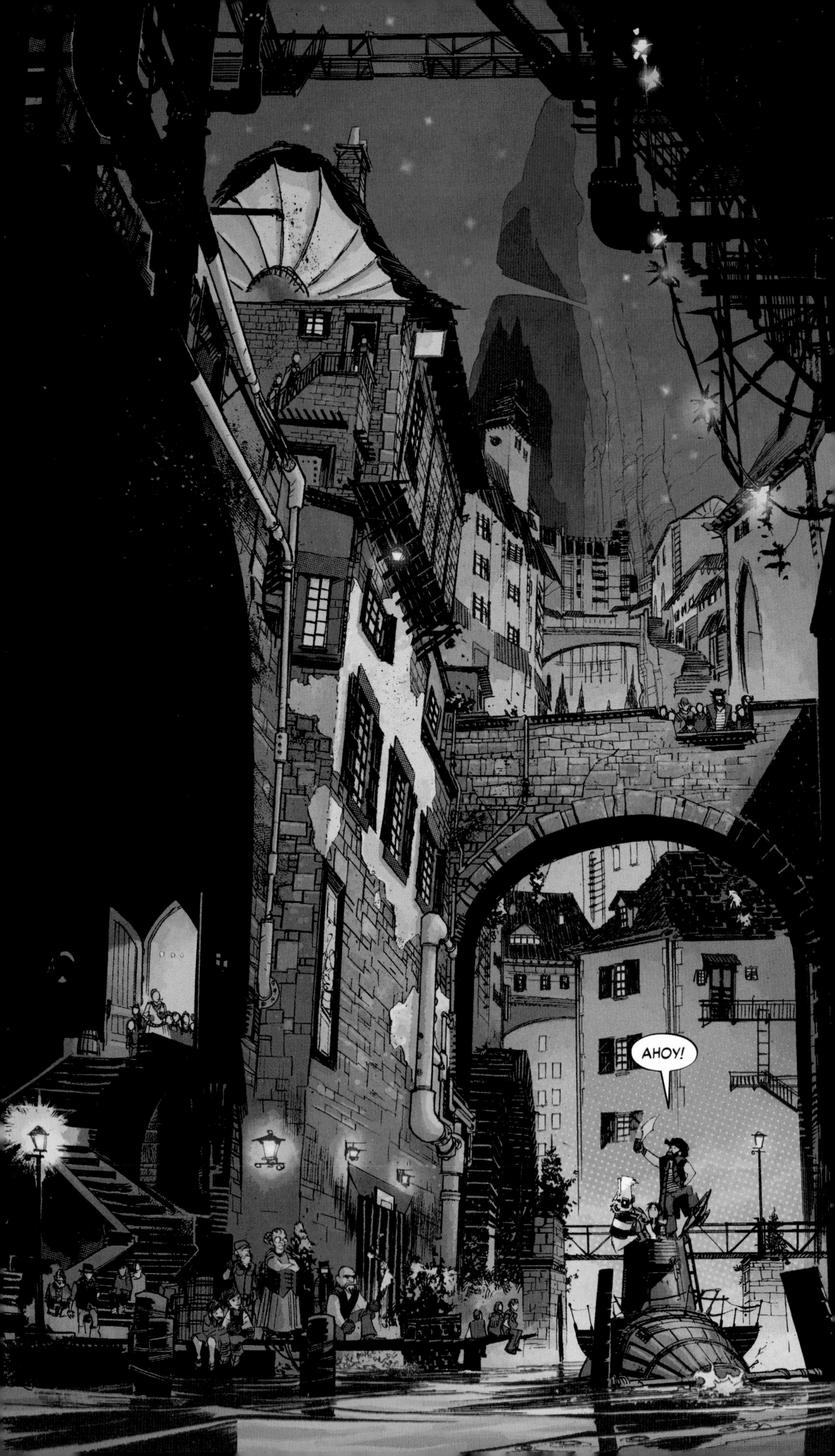
AHOY!

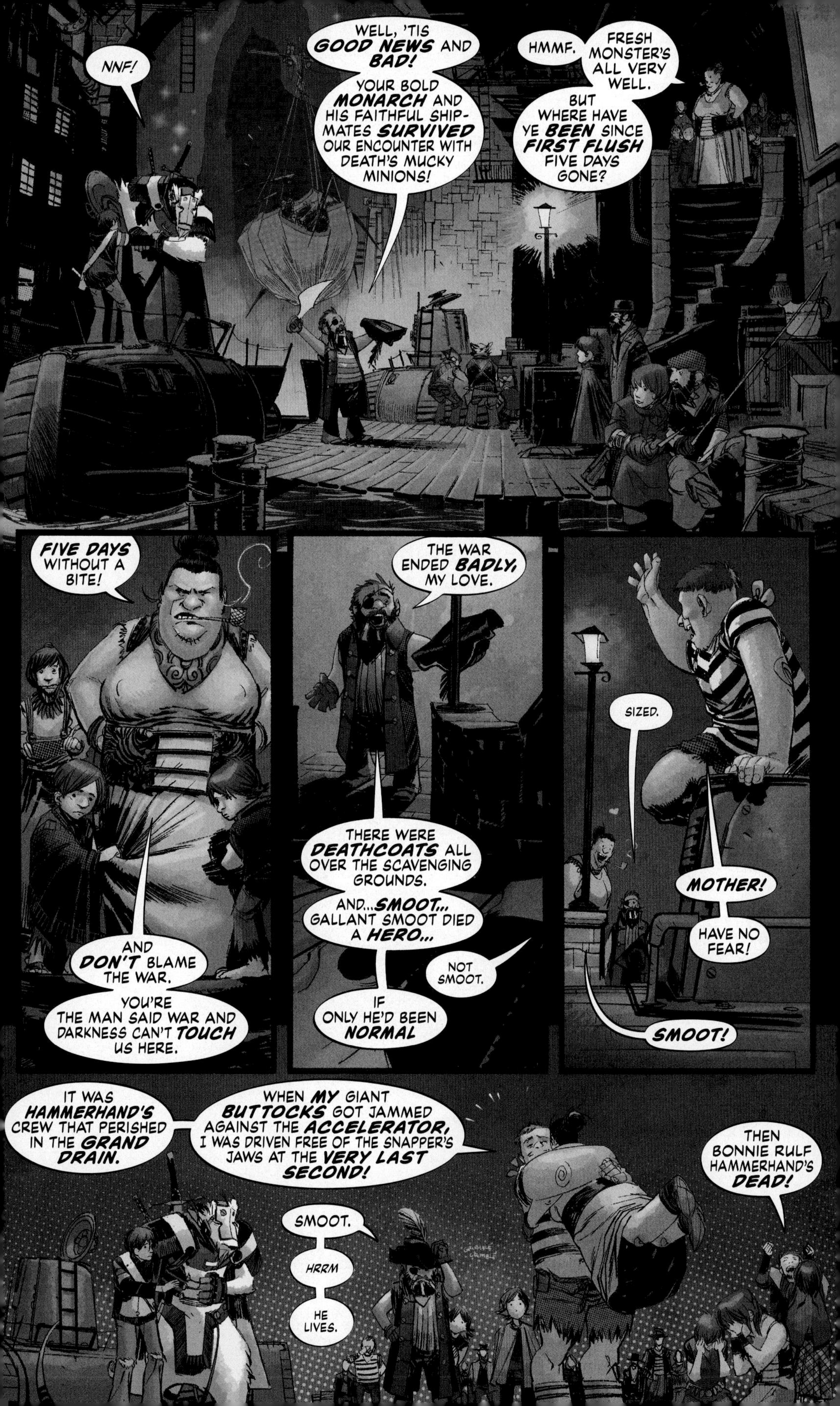
NNF!
WELL, 'TIS GOOD NEWS AND BAD!
YOUR BOLD MONARCH AND HIS FAITHFUL SHIP-MATES SURVIVED OUR ENCOUNTER WITH DEATH'S MUCKY MINIONS!
HMMF.
FRESH MONSTER'S ALL VERY WELL.
BUT WHERE HAVE YE BEEN SINCE FIRST FLUSH FIVE DAYS GONE?
FIVE DAYS WITHOUT A BITE!
AND DON'T BLAME THE WAR.
YOU'RE THE MAN SAID WAR AND DARKNESS CAN'T TOUCH US HERE.
THE WAR ENDED BADLY, MY LOVE.
THERE WERE DEATHCOATS ALL OVER THE SCAVENGING GROUNDS.
AND...SMOOT... GALLANT SMOOT DIED A HERO...
NOT SMOOT.
IF ONLY HE'D BEEN NORMAL
SIZED.
MOTHER!
HAVE NO FEAR!
SMOOT!
IT WAS HAMMERHAND'S CREW THAT PERISHED IN THE GRAND DRAIN.
WHEN MY GIANT BUTTOCKS GOT JAMMED AGAINST THE ACCELERATOR, I WAS DRIVEN FREE OF THE SNAPPER'S JAWS AT THE VERY LAST SECOND!
SMOOT.
HRRM
HE LIVES.
THEN BONNIE RULF HAMMERHAND'S DEAD!

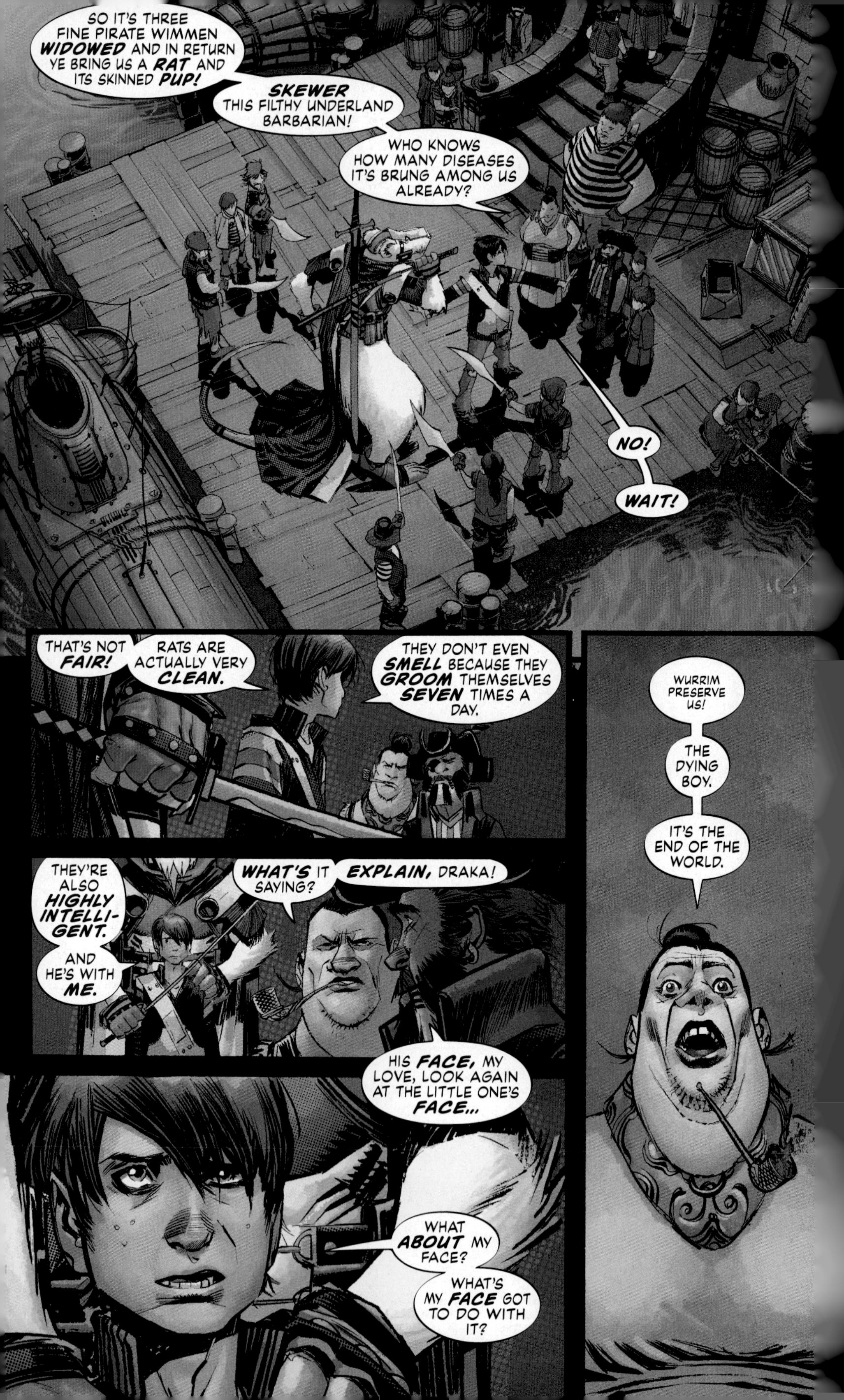

SO IT'S THREE FINE PIRATE WIMMEN WIDOWED AND IN RETURN YE BRING US A RAT AND ITS SKINNED PUP!
SKEWER THIS FILTHY UNDERLAND BARBARIAN!
WHO KNOWS HOW MANY DISEASES IT'S BRUNG AMONG US ALREADY?
NO!
WAIT!
THAT'S NOT FAIR!
RATS ARE ACTUALLY VERY CLEAN.
THEY DON'T EVEN SMELL BECAUSE THEY GROOM THEMSELVES SEVEN TIMES A DAY.
THEY'RE ALSO HIGHLY INTELLI-GENT.
AND HE'S WITH ME.
WHAT'S IT SAYING?
EXPLAIN, DRAKA!
HIS FACE, MY LOVE, LOOK AGAIN AT THE LITTLE ONE'S FACE...
WHAT ABOUT MY FACE?
WHAT'S MY FACE GOT TO DO WITH IT?
WURRIM PRESERVE US!
THE DYING BOY.
IT'S THE END OF THE WORLD.

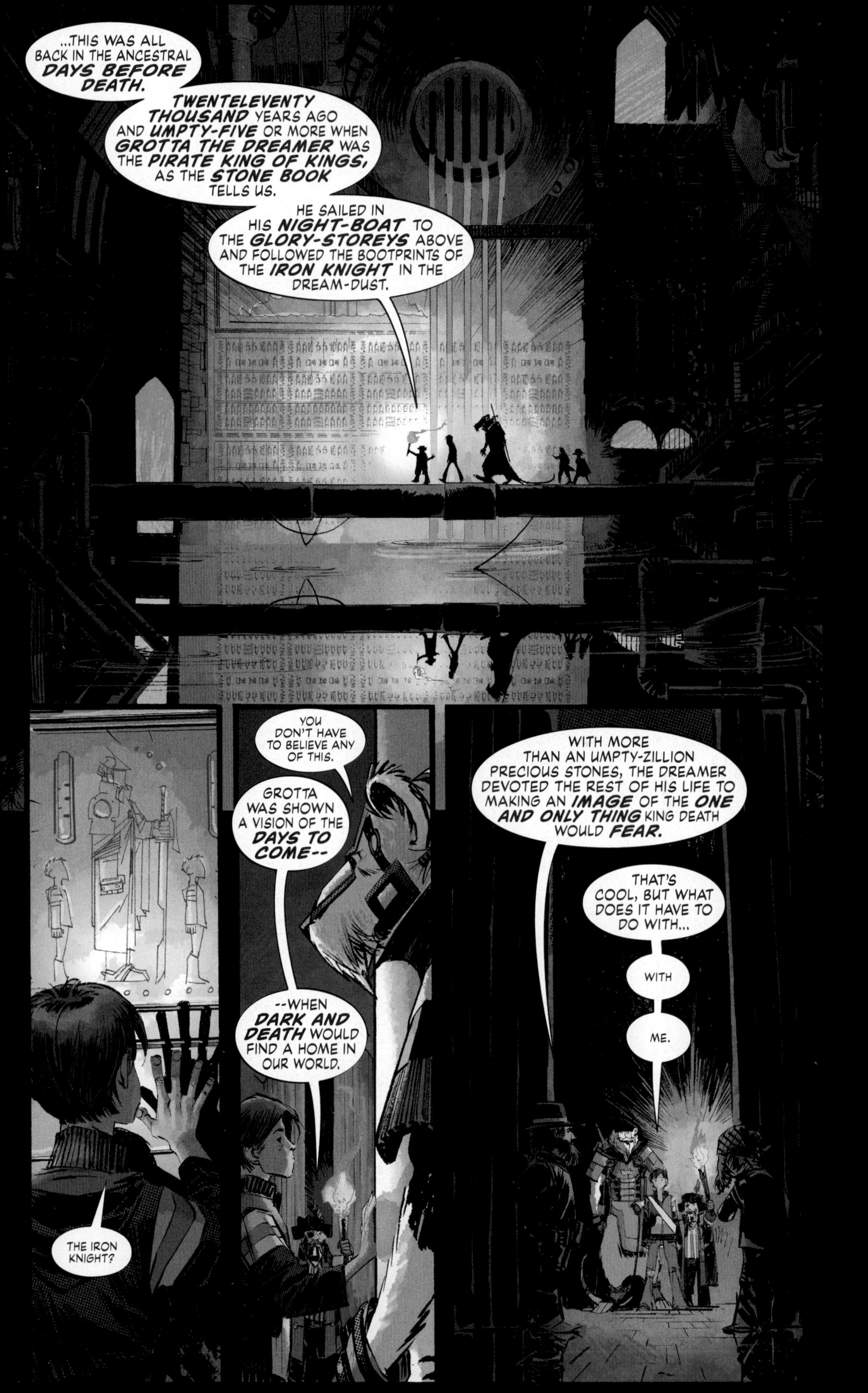
...THIS WAS ALL BACK IN THE ANCESTRAL DAYS BEFORE DEATH.
TWENTELEVENTY THOUSAND YEARS AGO AND UMPTY-FIVE OR MORE WHEN GROTTA THE DREAMER WAS THE PIRATE KING OF KINGS, AS THE STONE BOOK TELLS US.
HE SAILED IN HIS NIGHT-BOAT TO THE GLORY-STOREYS ABOVE AND FOLLOWED THE BOOTPRINTS OF THE IRON KNIGHT IN THE DREAM-DUST.
THE IRON KNIGHT?
YOU DON'T HAVE TO BELIEVE ANY OF THIS.
GROTTA WAS SHOWN A VISION OF THE DAYS TO COME--
--WHEN DARK AND DEATH WOULD FIND A HOME IN OUR WORLD.
WITH MORE THAN AN UMPTY-ZILLION PRECIOUS STONES, THE DREAMER DEVOTED THE REST OF HIS LIFE TO MAKING AN IMAGE OF THE ONE AND ONLY THING KING DEATH WOULD FEAR.
THAT'S COOL, BUT WHAT DOES IT HAVE TO DO WITH...
WITH
ME.

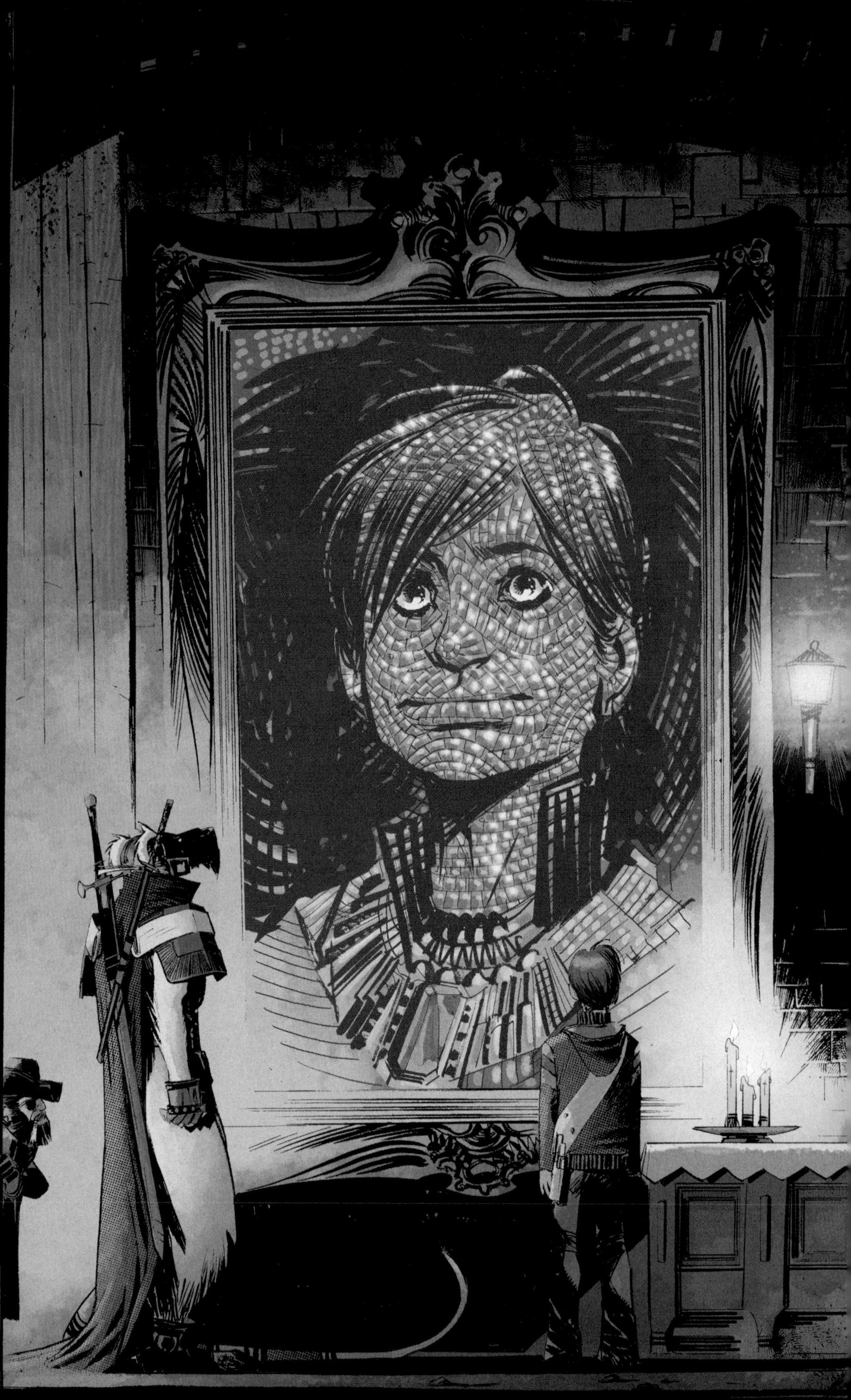

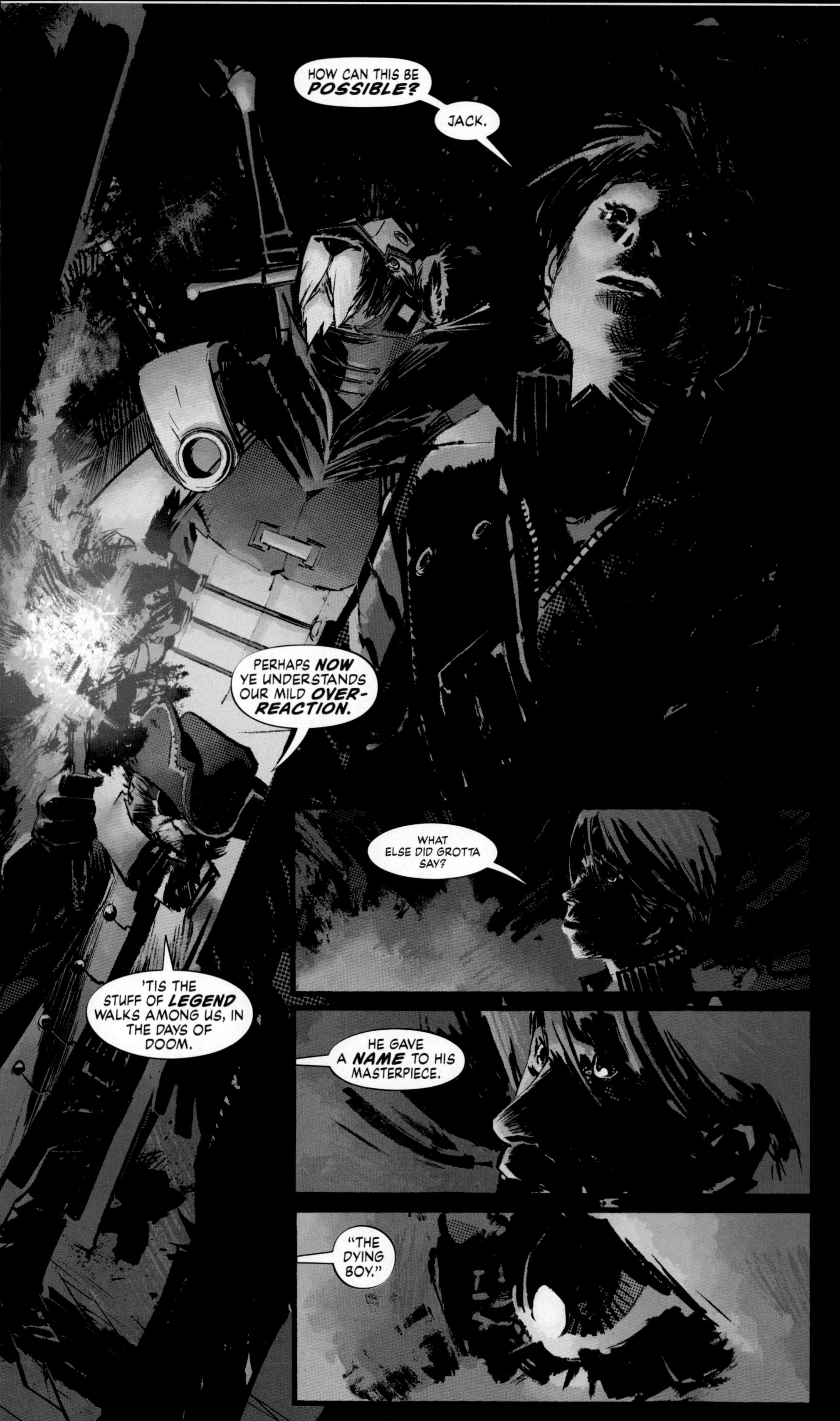

HOW CAN THIS BE **POSSIBLE?**
JACK.
PERHAPS **NOW** YE UNDERSTANDS OUR MILD **OVER-REACTION.**
'TIS THE STUFF OF **LEGEND** WALKS AMONG US, IN THE DAYS OF DOOM.
WHAT ELSE DID GROTTA SAY?
HE GAVE A **NAME** TO HIS MASTERPIECE.
"THE DYING BOY."

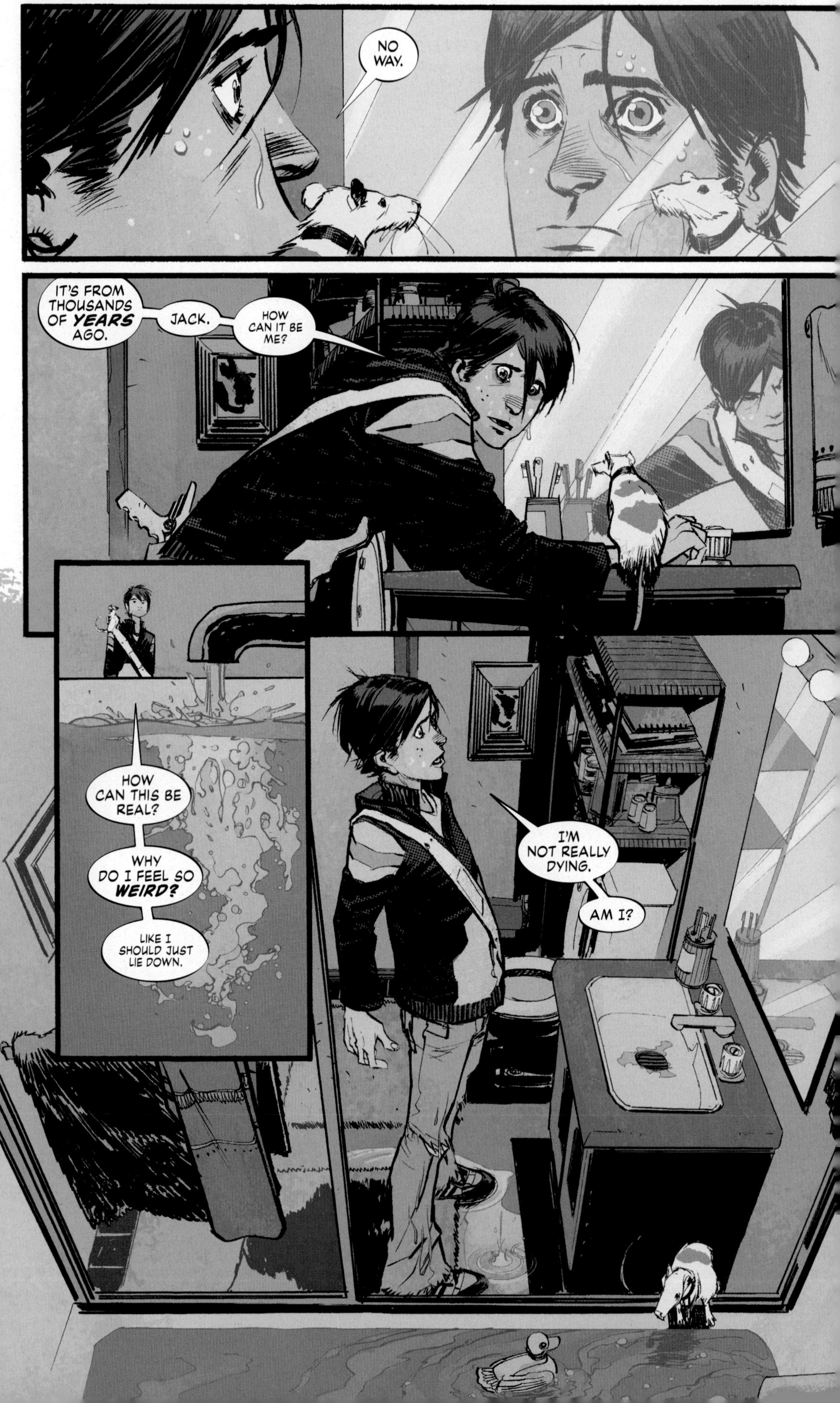
NO WAY.
IT'S FROM THOUSANDS OF **YEARS** AGO.
JACK.
HOW CAN IT BE ME?
HOW CAN THIS BE REAL?
WHY DO I FEEL SO **WEIRD?**
LIKE I SHOULD JUST LIE DOWN.
I'M NOT REALLY DYING.
AM I?

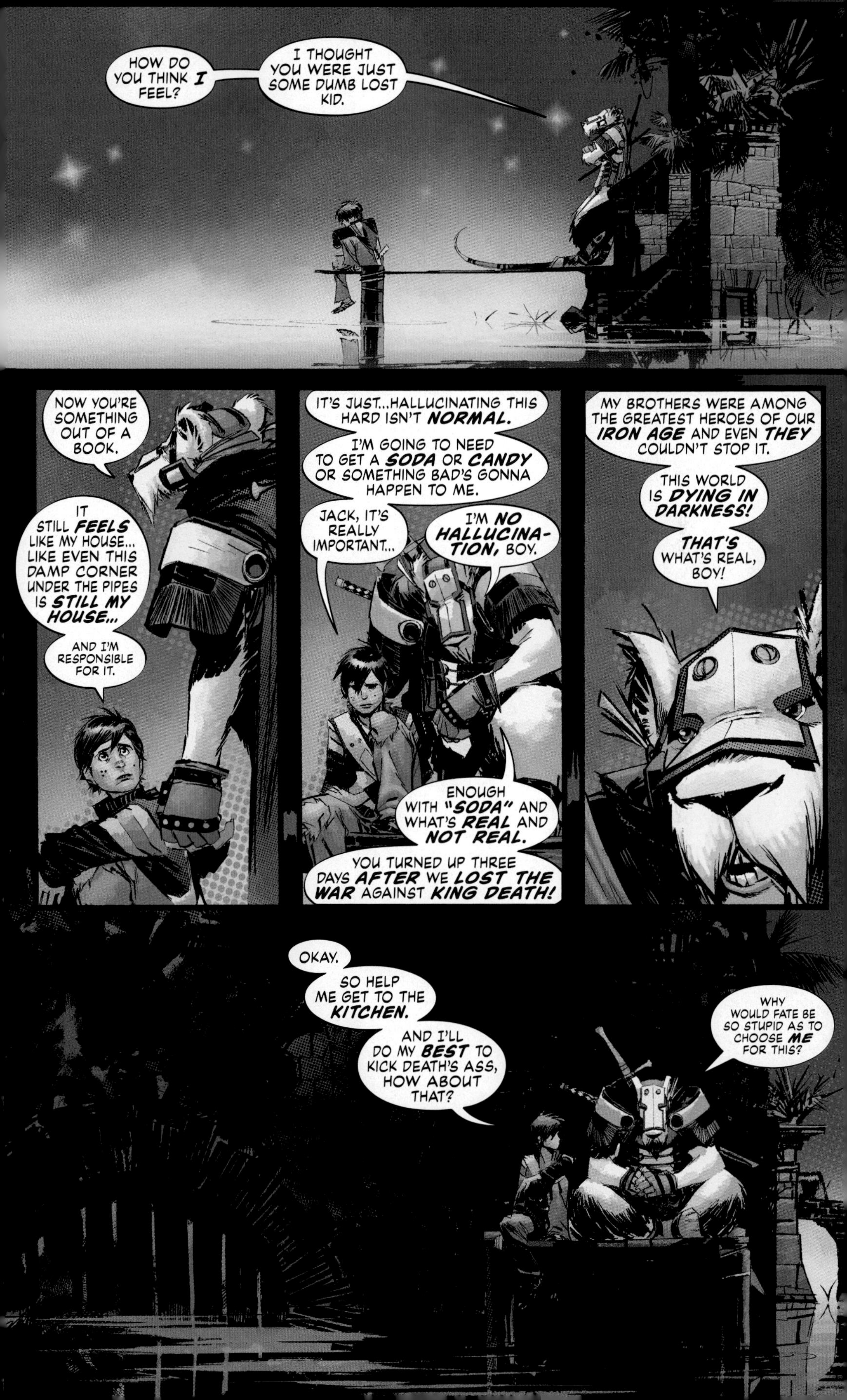
HOW DO YOU THINK *I* FEEL?
I THOUGHT YOU WERE JUST SOME DUMB LOST KID.
NOW YOU'RE SOMETHING OUT OF A BOOK.
IT STILL *FEELS* LIKE MY HOUSE... LIKE EVEN THIS DAMP CORNER UNDER THE PIPES IS *STILL MY HOUSE...*
AND I'M RESPONSIBLE FOR IT.
IT'S JUST...HALLUCINATING THIS HARD ISN'T *NORMAL.*
I'M GOING TO NEED TO GET A *SODA* OR *CANDY* OR SOMETHING BAD'S GONNA HAPPEN TO ME.
JACK, IT'S REALLY IMPORTANT...
I'M *NO HALLUCINATION,* BOY.
ENOUGH WITH *"SODA"* AND WHAT'S *REAL* AND *NOT REAL.*
YOU TURNED UP THREE DAYS *AFTER* WE *LOST THE WAR* AGAINST *KING DEATH!*
MY BROTHERS WERE AMONG THE GREATEST HEROES OF OUR *IRON AGE* AND EVEN *THEY* COULDN'T STOP IT.
THIS WORLD IS *DYING IN DARKNESS!*
THAT'S WHAT'S REAL, BOY!
OKAY.
SO HELP ME GET TO THE *KITCHEN.*
AND I'LL DO MY *BEST* TO KICK DEATH'S ASS, HOW ABOUT THAT?
WHY WOULD FATE BE SO STUPID AS TO CHOOSE *ME* FOR THIS?

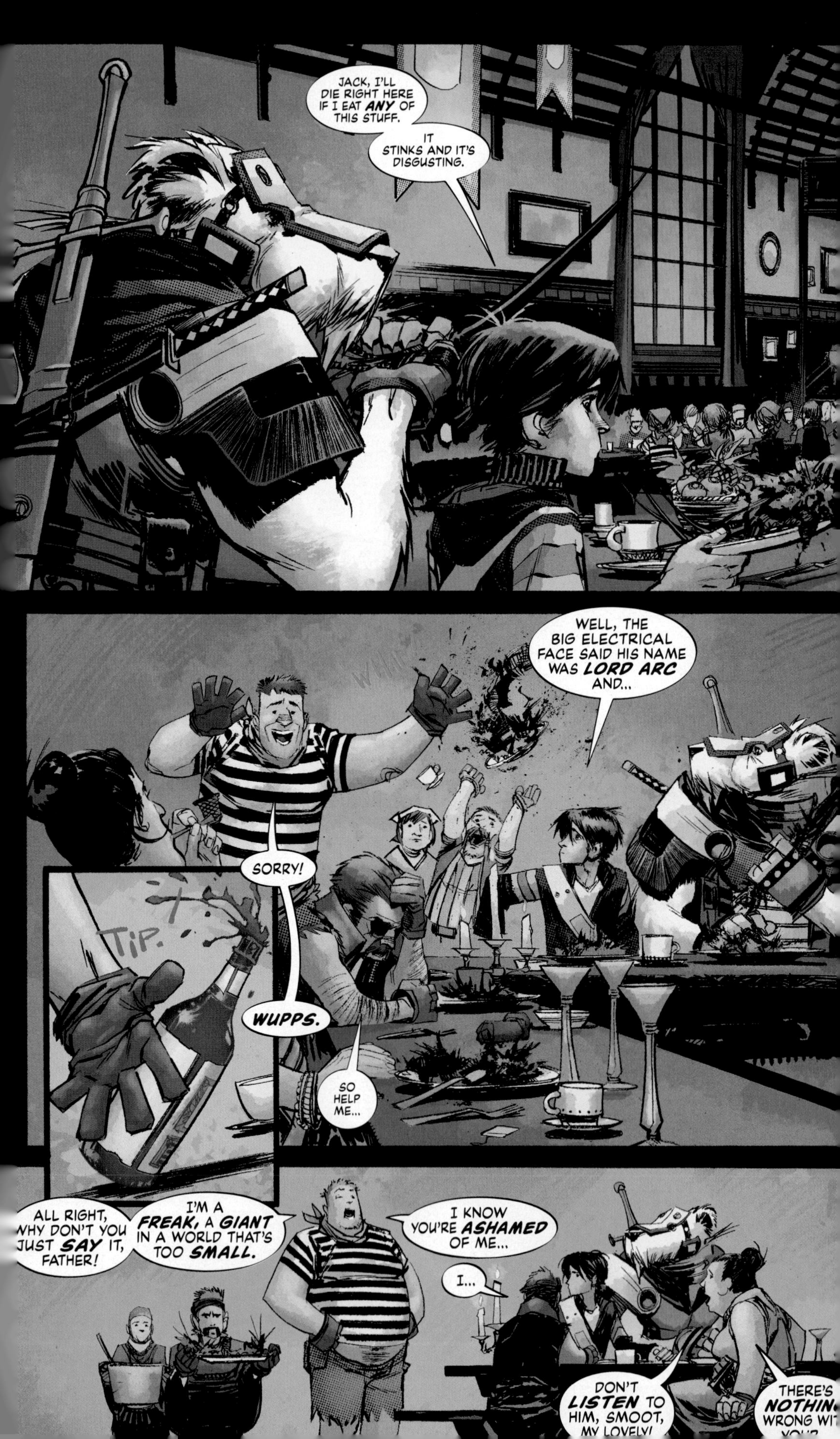
JACK, I'LL DIE RIGHT HERE IF I EAT ANY OF THIS STUFF.
IT STINKS AND IT'S DISGUSTING.
WELL, THE BIG ELECTRICAL FACE SAID HIS NAME WAS LORD ARC AND...
SORRY!
TIP.
WUPPS.
SO HELP ME...
ALL RIGHT, WHY DON'T YOU JUST SAY IT, FATHER!
I'M A FREAK, A GIANT IN A WORLD THAT'S TOO SMALL.
I KNOW YOU'RE ASHAMED OF ME...
I...
DON'T LISTEN TO HIM, SMOOT, MY LOVELY!
THERE'S NOTHIN WRONG WIT

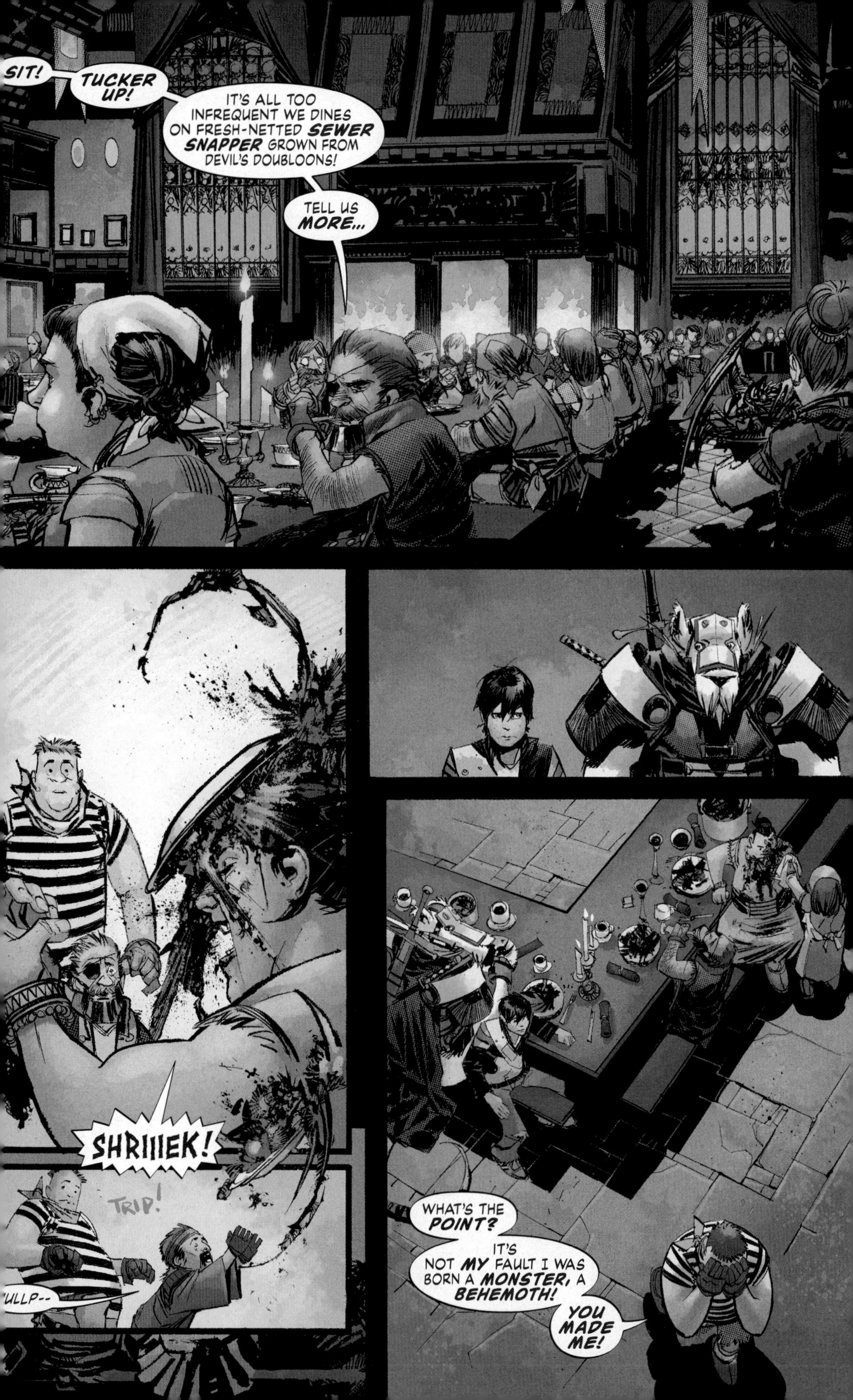
SIT!
TUCKER UP!
IT'S ALL TOO INFREQUENT WE DINES ON FRESH-NETTED SEWER SNAPPER GROWN FROM DEVIL'S DOUBLOONS!
TELL US MORE...
SHRIIIEK!
TRIP!
ULLP--
WHAT'S THE POINT?
IT'S NOT MY FAULT I WAS BORN A MONSTER, A BEHEMOTH!
YOU MADE ME!

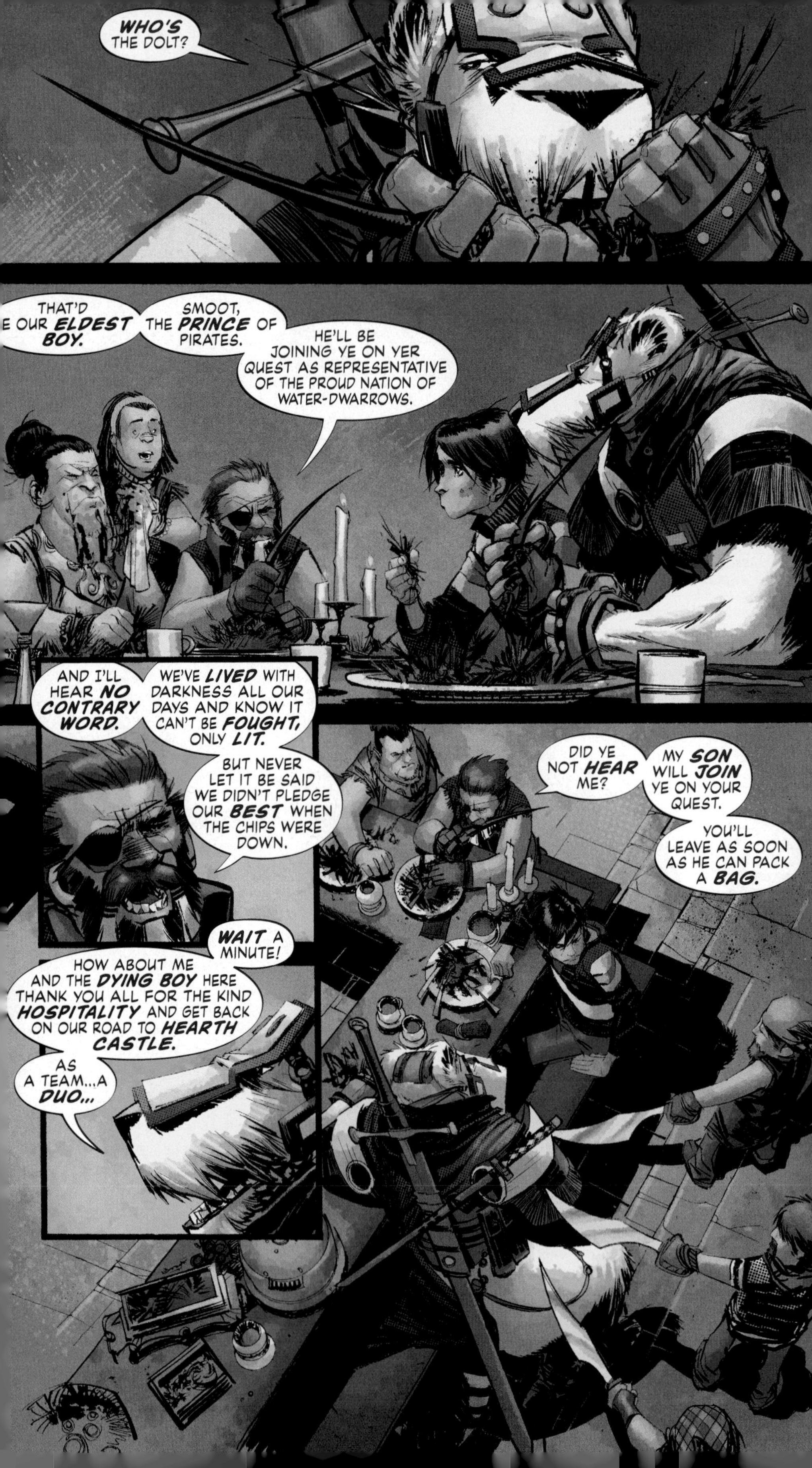
WHO'S THE DOLT?
THAT'D BE OUR ELDEST BOY.
SMOOT, THE PRINCE OF PIRATES.
HE'LL BE JOINING YE ON YER QUEST AS REPRESENTATIVE OF THE PROUD NATION OF WATER-DWARROWS.
AND I'LL HEAR NO CONTRARY WORD.
WE'VE LIVED WITH DARKNESS ALL OUR DAYS AND KNOW IT CAN'T BE FOUGHT, ONLY LIT.
BUT NEVER LET IT BE SAID WE DIDN'T PLEDGE OUR BEST WHEN THE CHIPS WERE DOWN.
WAIT A MINUTE!
HOW ABOUT ME AND THE DYING BOY HERE THANK YOU ALL FOR THE KIND HOSPITALITY AND GET BACK ON OUR ROAD TO HEARTH CASTLE.
AS A TEAM...A DUO...
DID YE NOT HEAR ME?
MY SON WILL JOIN YE ON YOUR QUEST.
YOU'LL LEAVE AS SOON AS HE CAN PACK A BAG.

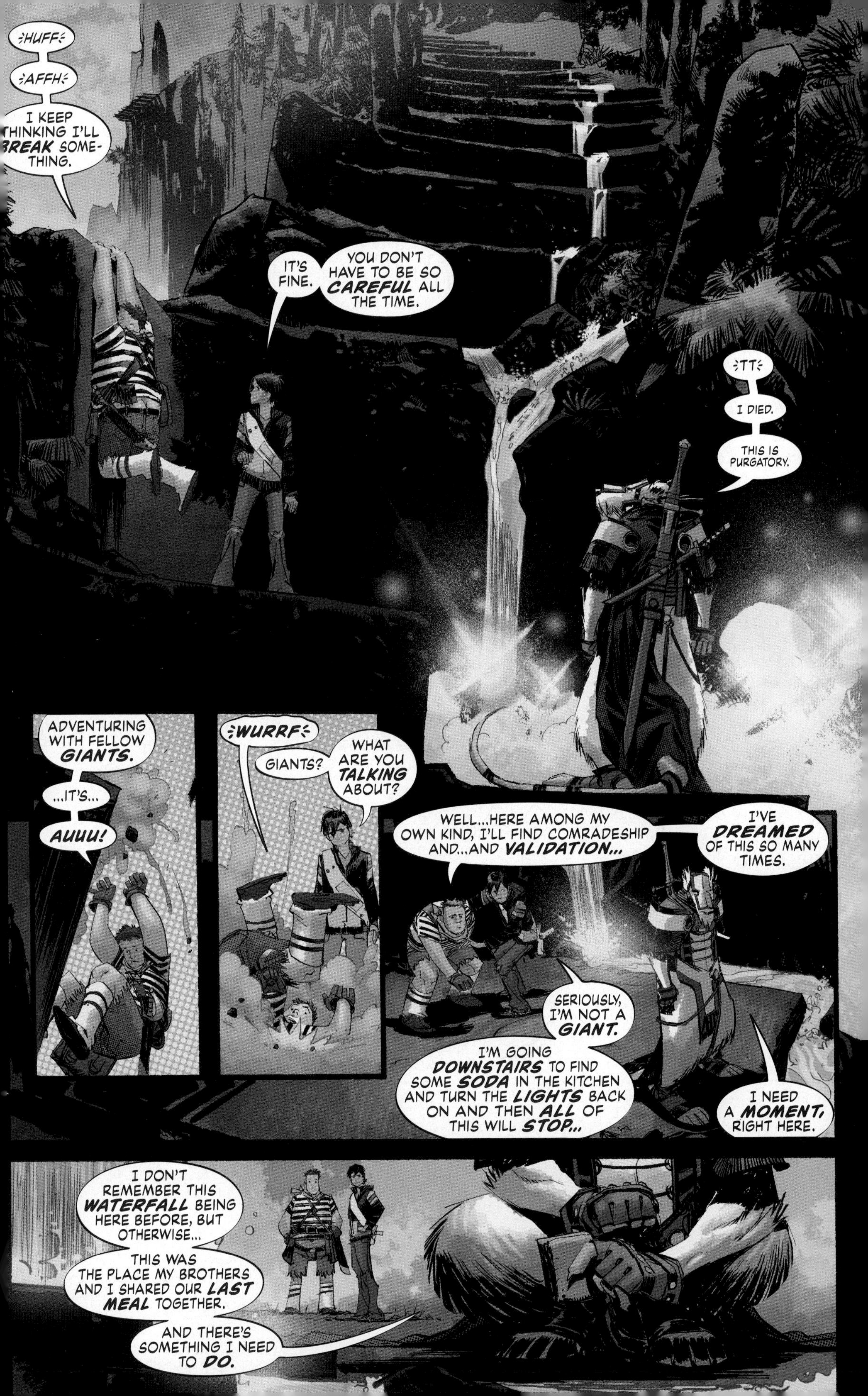

HUFF
AFFH
I KEEP THINKING I'LL BREAK SOMETHING.
IT'S FINE.
YOU DON'T HAVE TO BE SO CAREFUL ALL THE TIME.
TT
I DIED.
THIS IS PURGATORY.
ADVENTURING WITH FELLOW GIANTS.
...IT'S...
AUUU!
WURRF
GIANTS?
WHAT ARE YOU TALKING ABOUT?
WELL...HERE AMONG MY OWN KIND, I'LL FIND COMRADESHIP AND...AND VALIDATION...
I'VE DREAMED OF THIS SO MANY TIMES.
SERIOUSLY, I'M NOT A GIANT.
I'M GOING DOWNSTAIRS TO FIND SOME SODA IN THE KITCHEN AND TURN THE LIGHTS BACK ON AND THEN ALL OF THIS WILL STOP...
I NEED A MOMENT, RIGHT HERE.
I DON'T REMEMBER THIS WATERFALL BEING HERE BEFORE, BUT OTHERWISE...
THIS WAS THE PLACE MY BROTHERS AND I SHARED OUR LAST MEAL TOGETHER.
AND THERE'S SOMETHING I NEED TO DO.

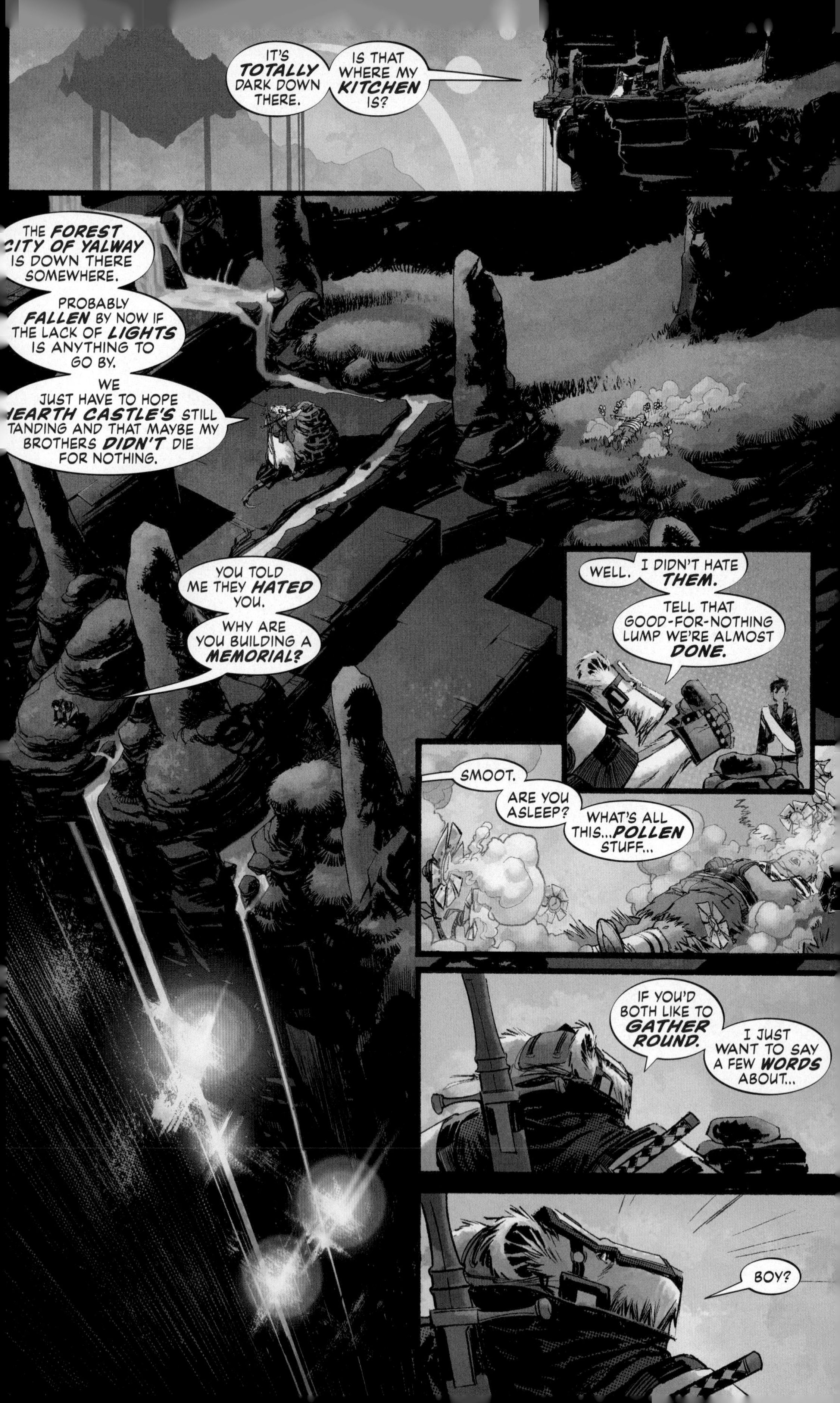

IT'S TOTALLY DARK DOWN THERE.
IS THAT WHERE MY KITCHEN IS?
THE FOREST CITY OF YALWAY IS DOWN THERE SOMEWHERE.
PROBABLY FALLEN BY NOW IF THE LACK OF LIGHTS IS ANYTHING TO GO BY.
WE JUST HAVE TO HOPE HEARTH CASTLE'S STILL STANDING AND THAT MAYBE MY BROTHERS DIDN'T DIE FOR NOTHING.
YOU TOLD ME THEY HATED YOU.
WHY ARE YOU BUILDING A MEMORIAL?
WELL.
I DIDN'T HATE THEM.
TELL THAT GOOD-FOR-NOTHING LUMP WE'RE ALMOST DONE.
SMOOT.
ARE YOU ASLEEP?
WHAT'S ALL THIS...POLLEN STUFF...
IF YOU'D BOTH LIKE TO GATHER ROUND.
I JUST WANT TO SAY A FEW WORDS ABOUT...
BOY?

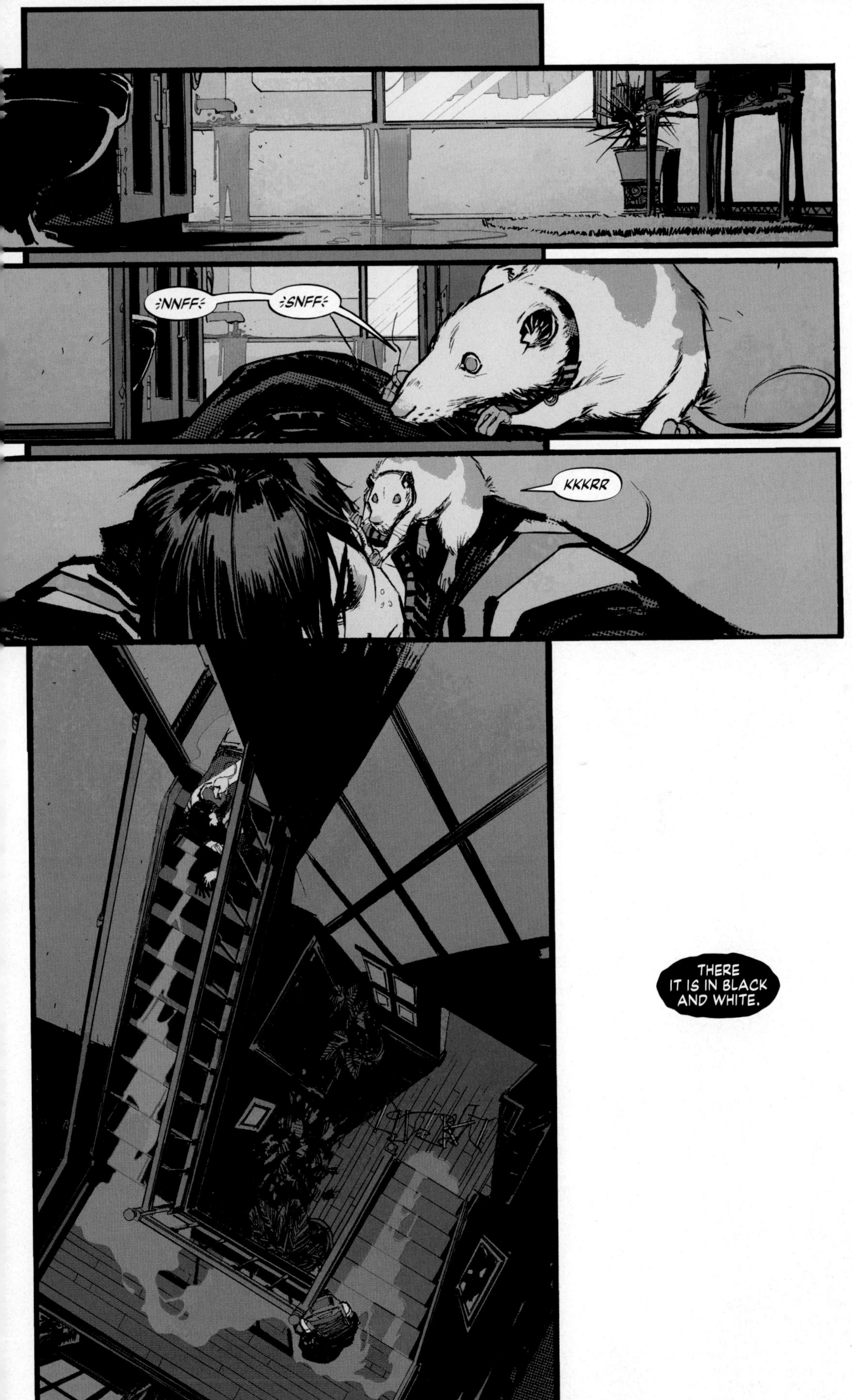
NNFF
SNFF
KKKRR
THERE IT IS IN BLACK AND WHITE.

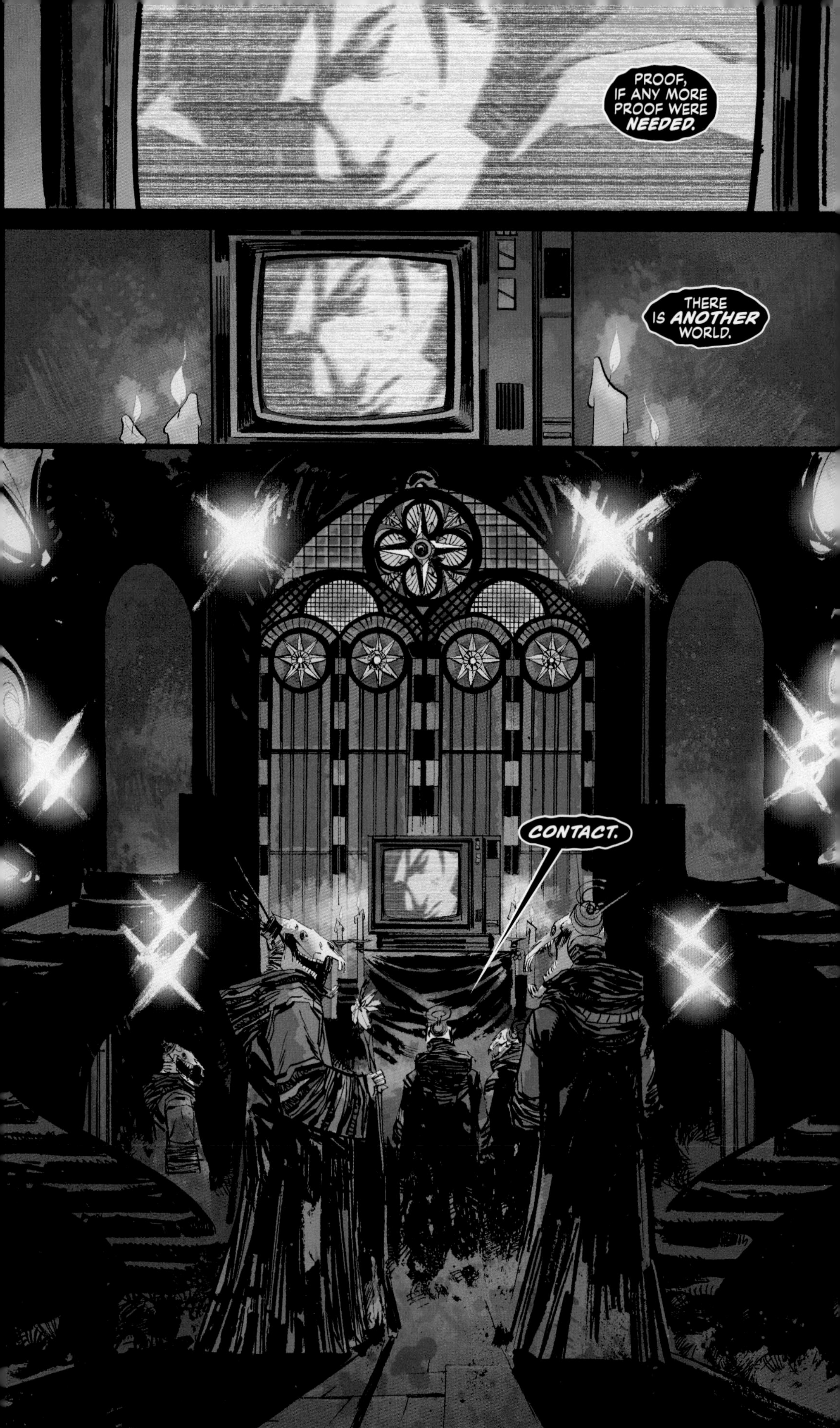
PROOF, IF ANY MORE PROOF WERE NEEDED.
THERE IS ANOTHER WORLD.
CONTACT.

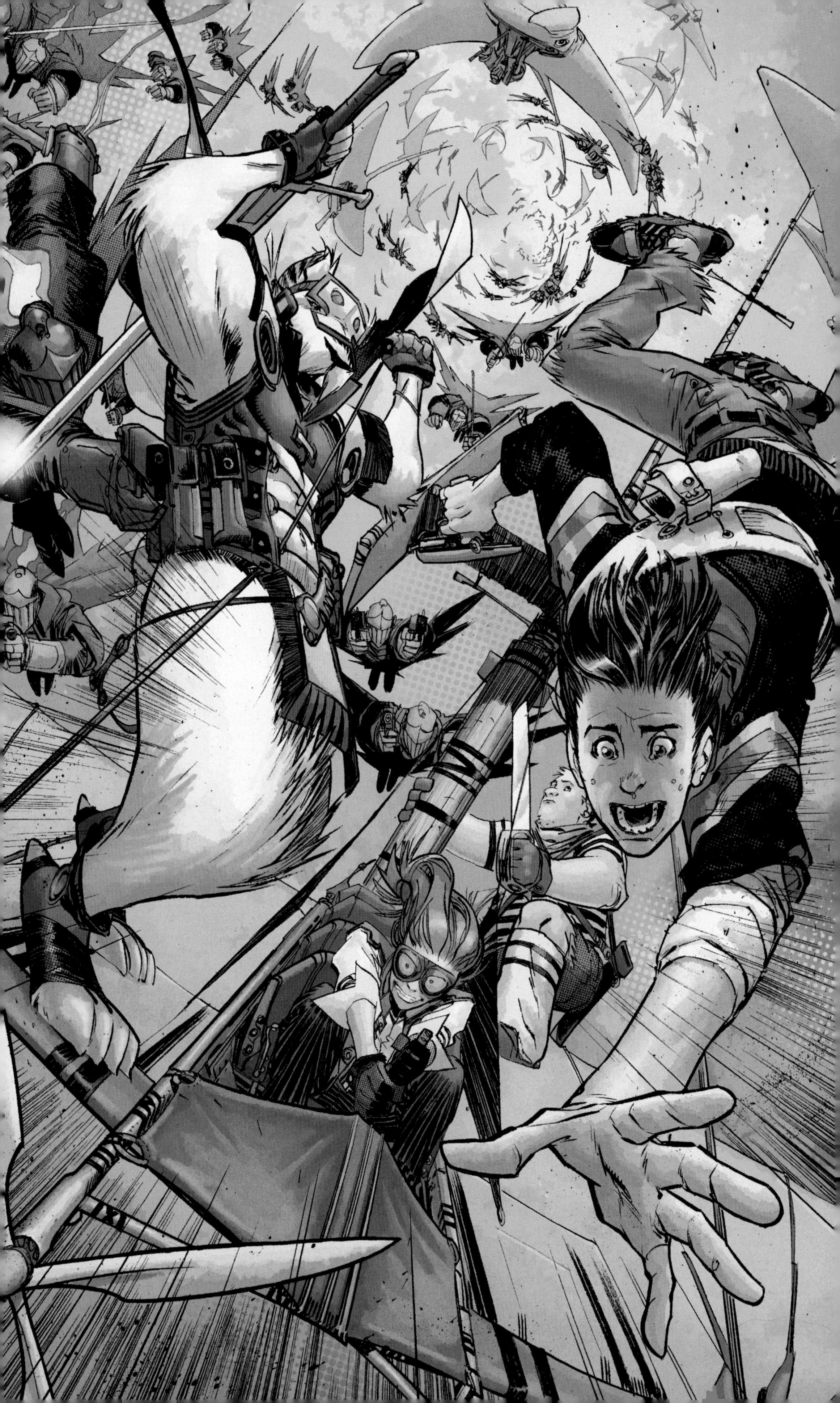

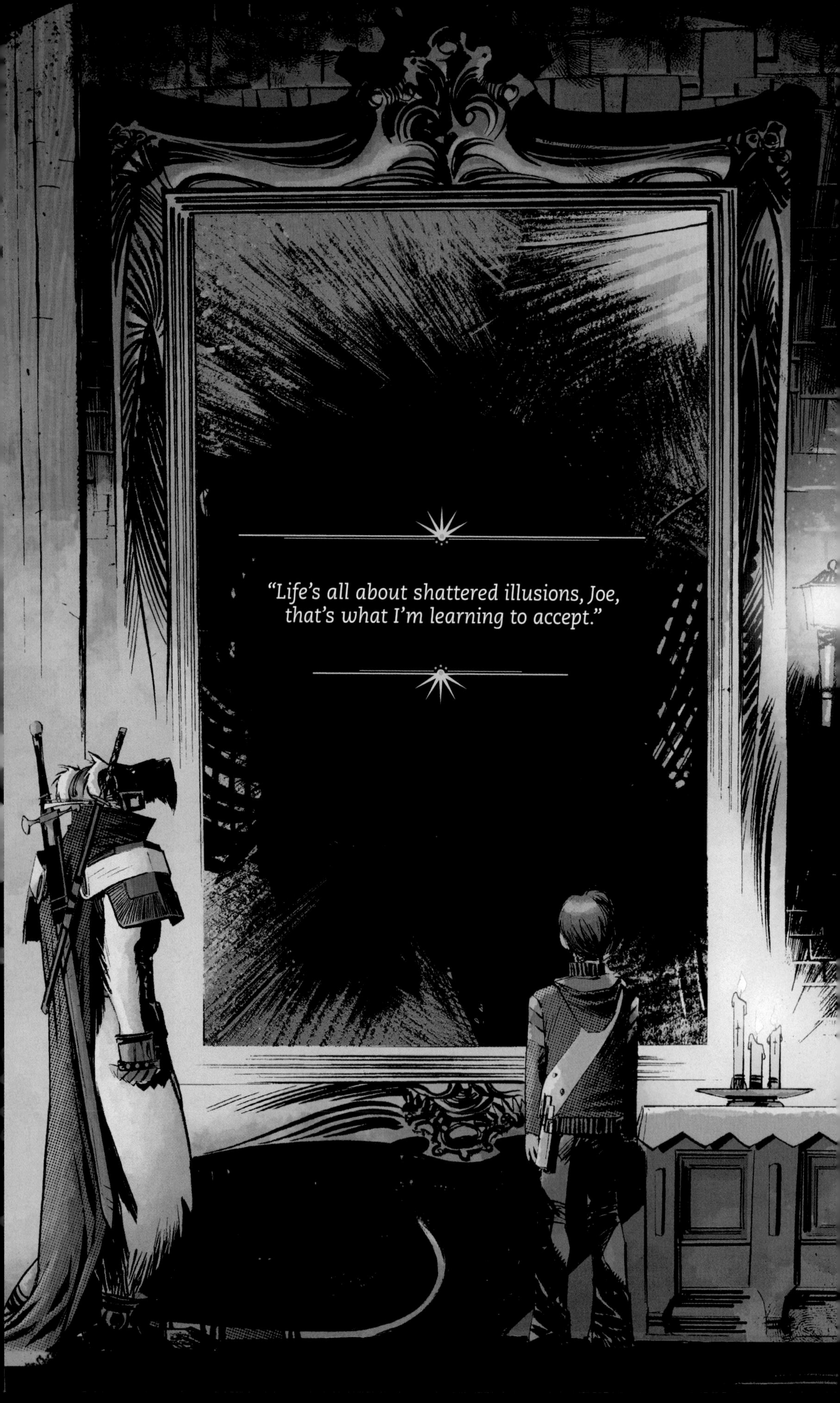
"Life's all about shattered illusions, Joe, that's what I'm learning to accept."

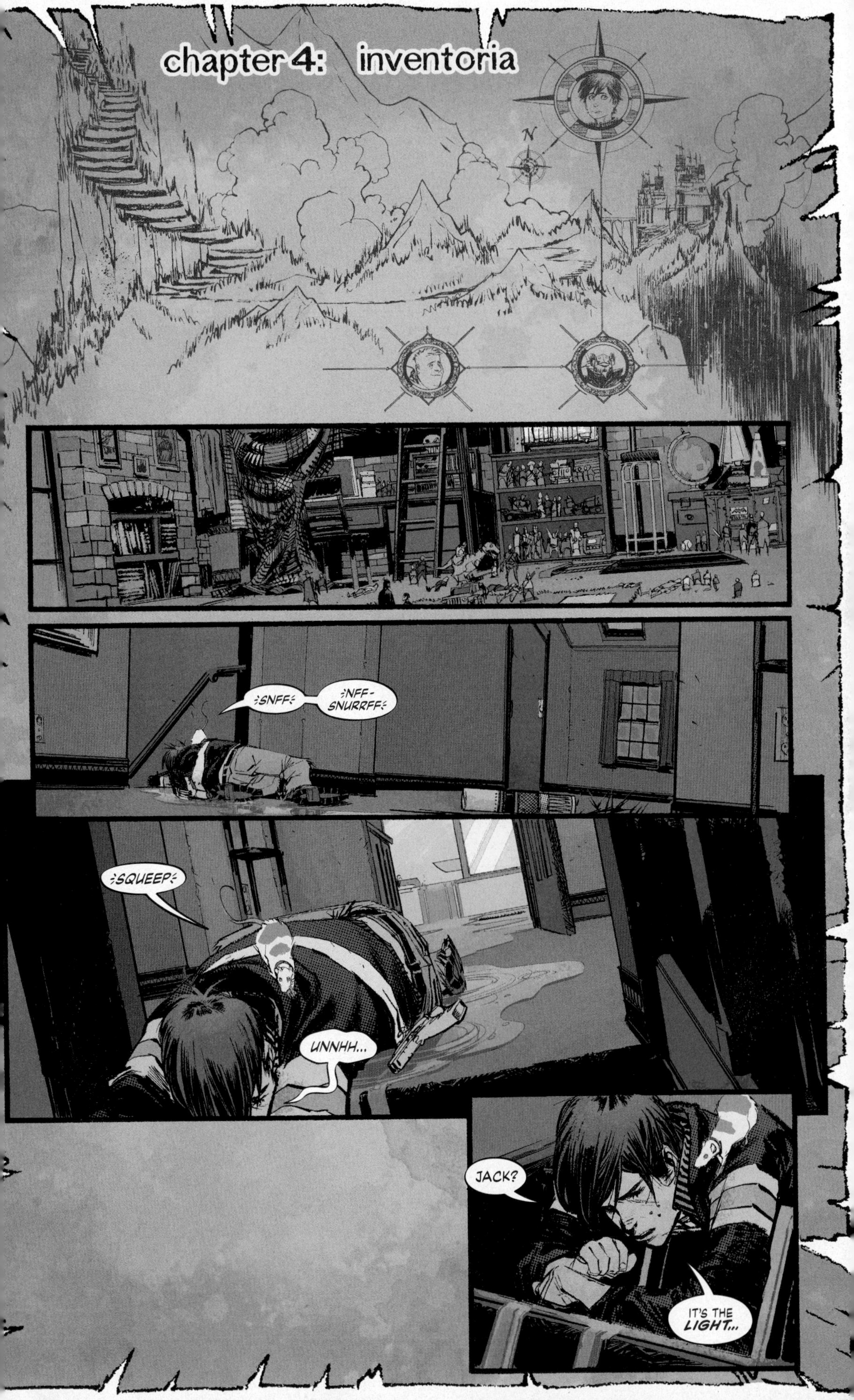

chapter 4: inventoria
SNFF
NFF-SNURRFF
SQUEEP
UNNHH...
JACK?
IT'S THE LIGHT...

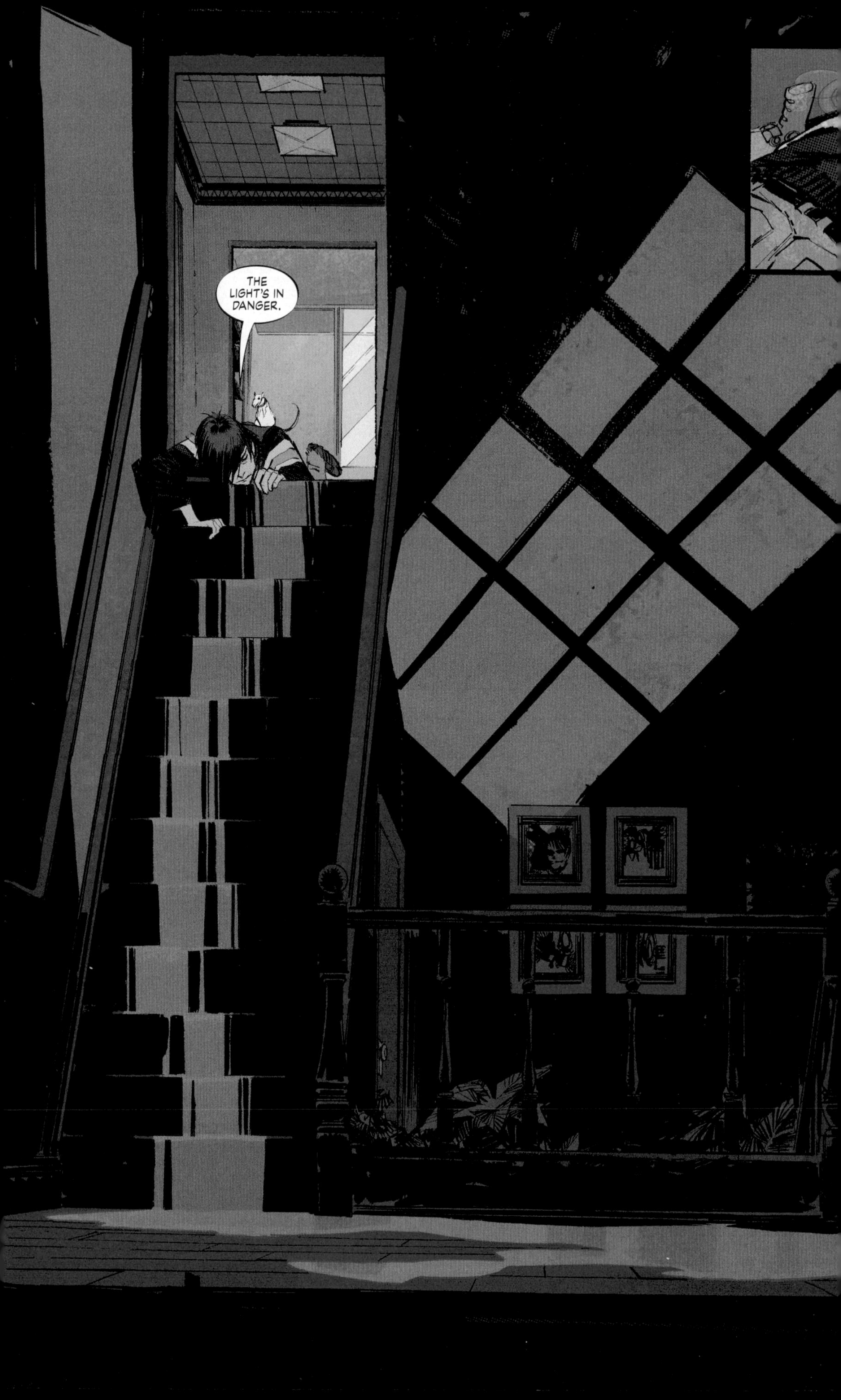
THE LIGHT'S IN DANGER.

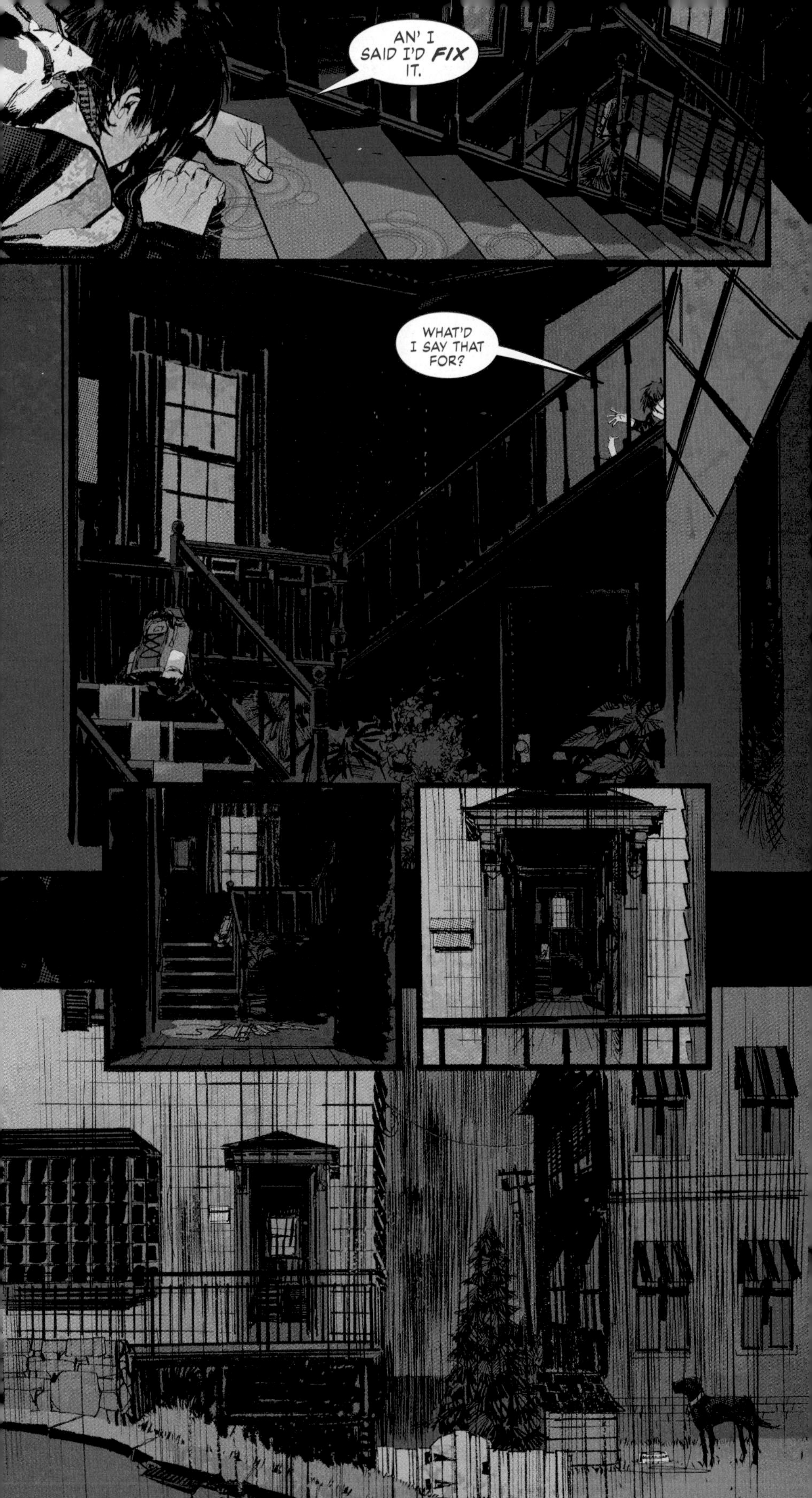
AN' I SAID I'D FIX IT.
WHAT'D I SAY THAT FOR?

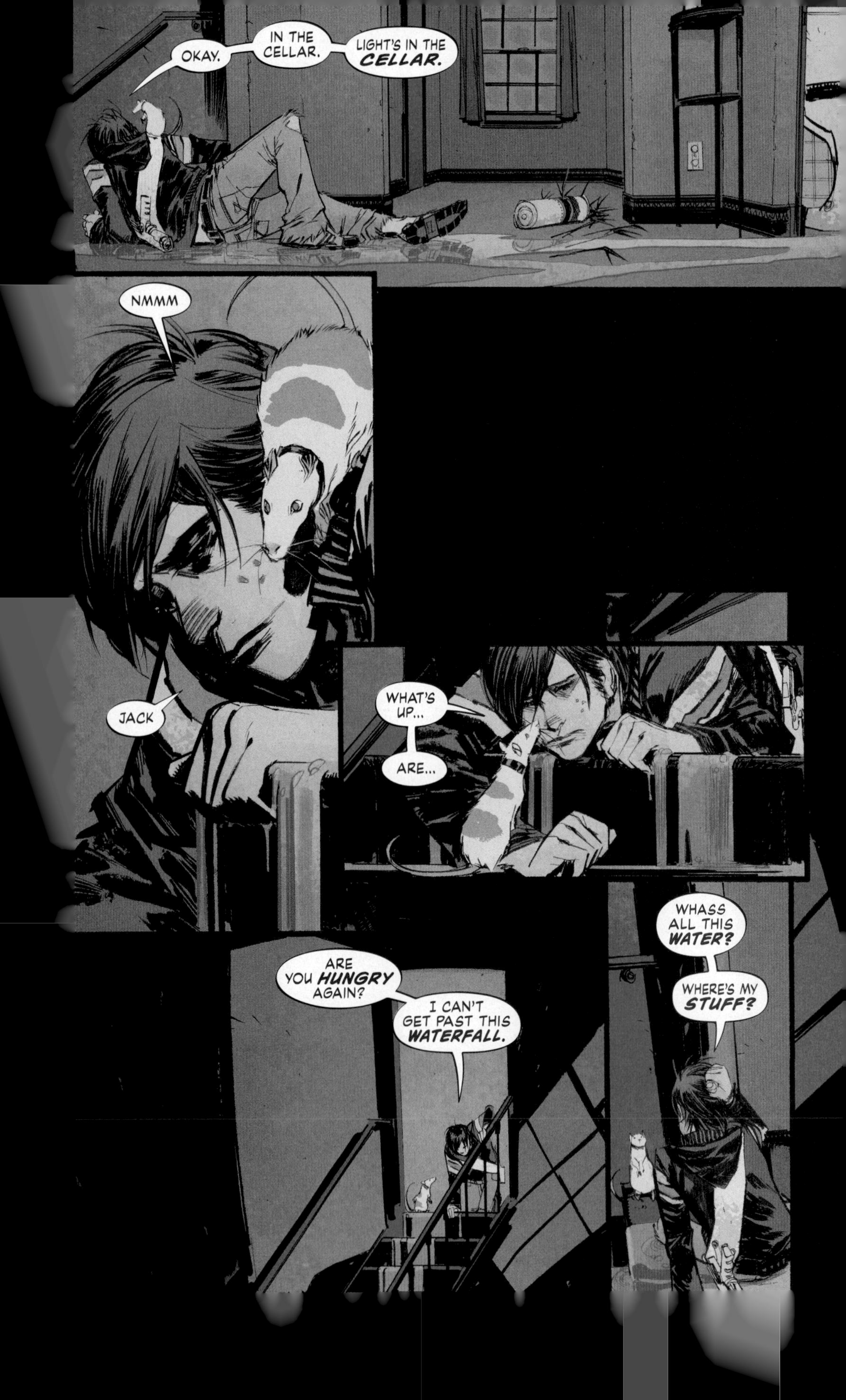
OKAY.
IN THE CELLAR.
LIGHT'S IN THE CELLAR.
NMMM
JACK
WHAT'S UP...
ARE...
WHASS ALL THIS WATER?
WHERE'S MY STUFF?
ARE YOU HUNGRY AGAIN?
I CAN'T GET PAST THIS WATERFALL.

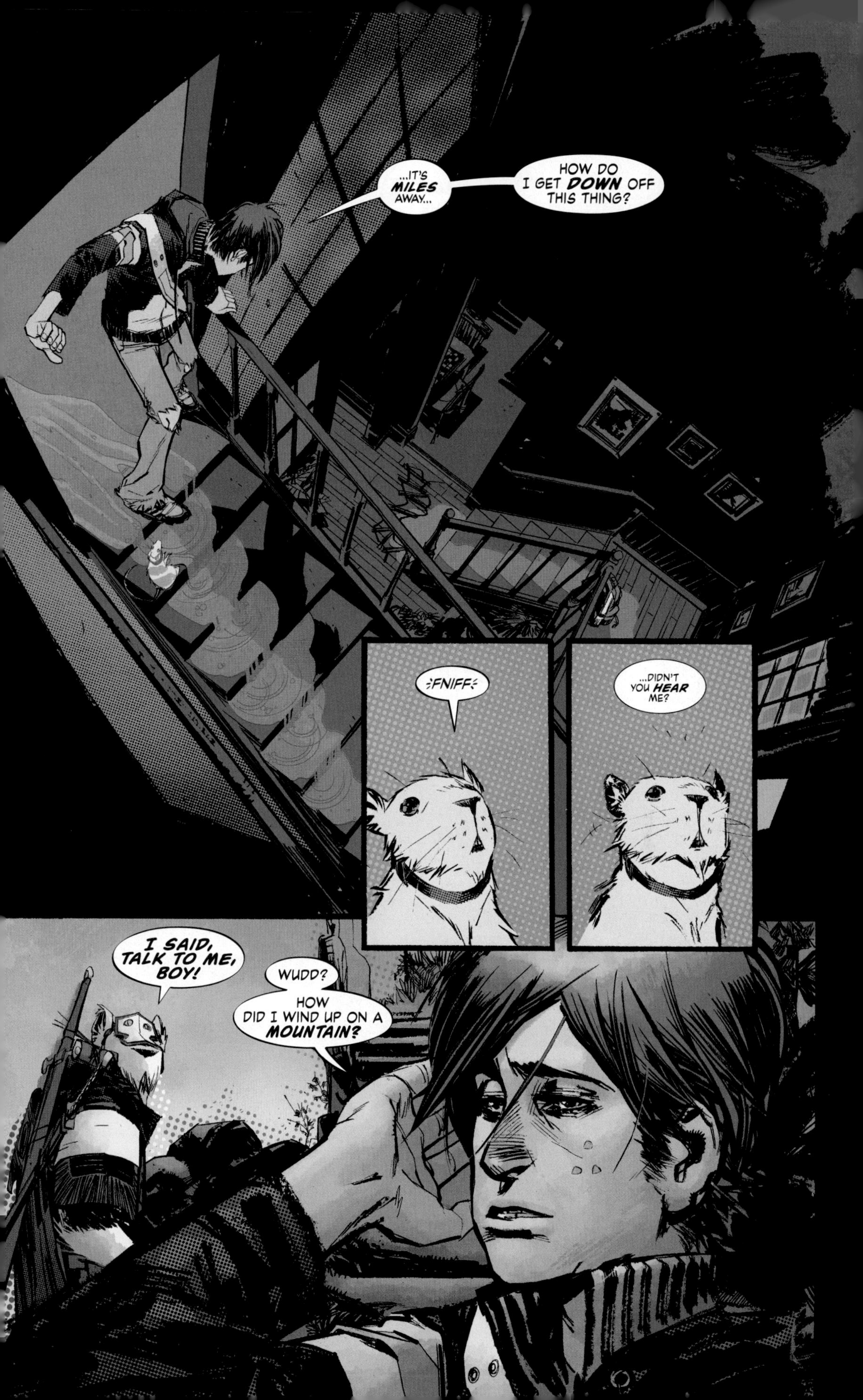
...IT'S MILES AWAY...
HOW DO I GET DOWN OFF THIS THING?
FNIFF
...DIDN'T YOU HEAR ME?
I SAID, TALK TO ME, BOY!
WUDD?
HOW DID I WIND UP ON A MOUNTAIN?

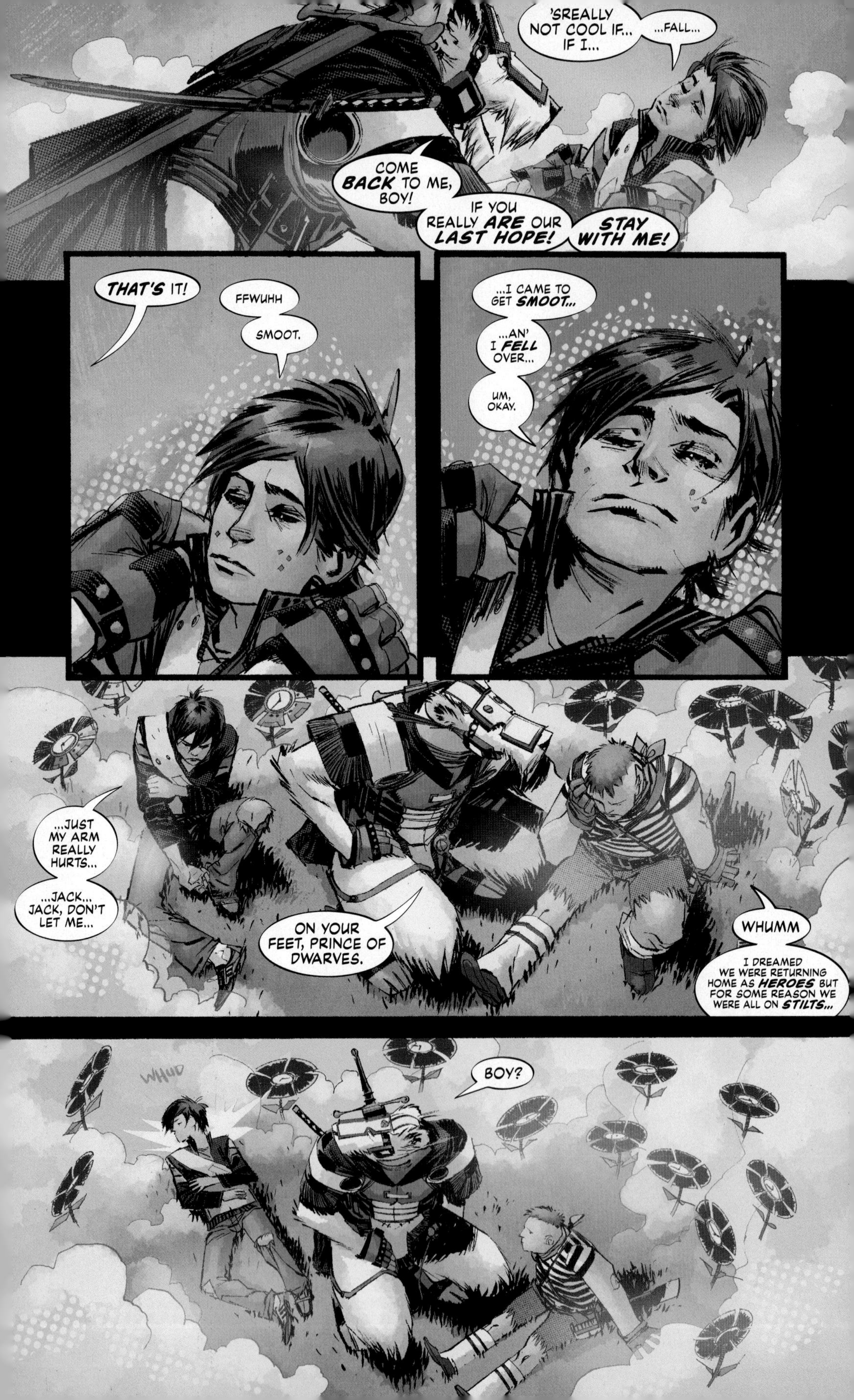
'SREALLY NOT COOL IF... IF I...
...FALL...
COME BACK TO ME, BOY!
IF YOU REALLY ARE OUR LAST HOPE!
STAY WITH ME!
THAT'S IT!
FFWUHH
SMOOT.
...I CAME TO GET SMOOT...
...AN' I FELL OVER...
UM, OKAY.
...JUST MY ARM REALLY HURTS...
...JACK... JACK, DON'T LET ME...
ON YOUR FEET, PRINCE OF DWARVES.
WHUMM
I DREAMED WE WERE RETURNING HOME AS HEROES BUT FOR SOME REASON WE WERE ALL ON STILTS...
WHUD
BOY?

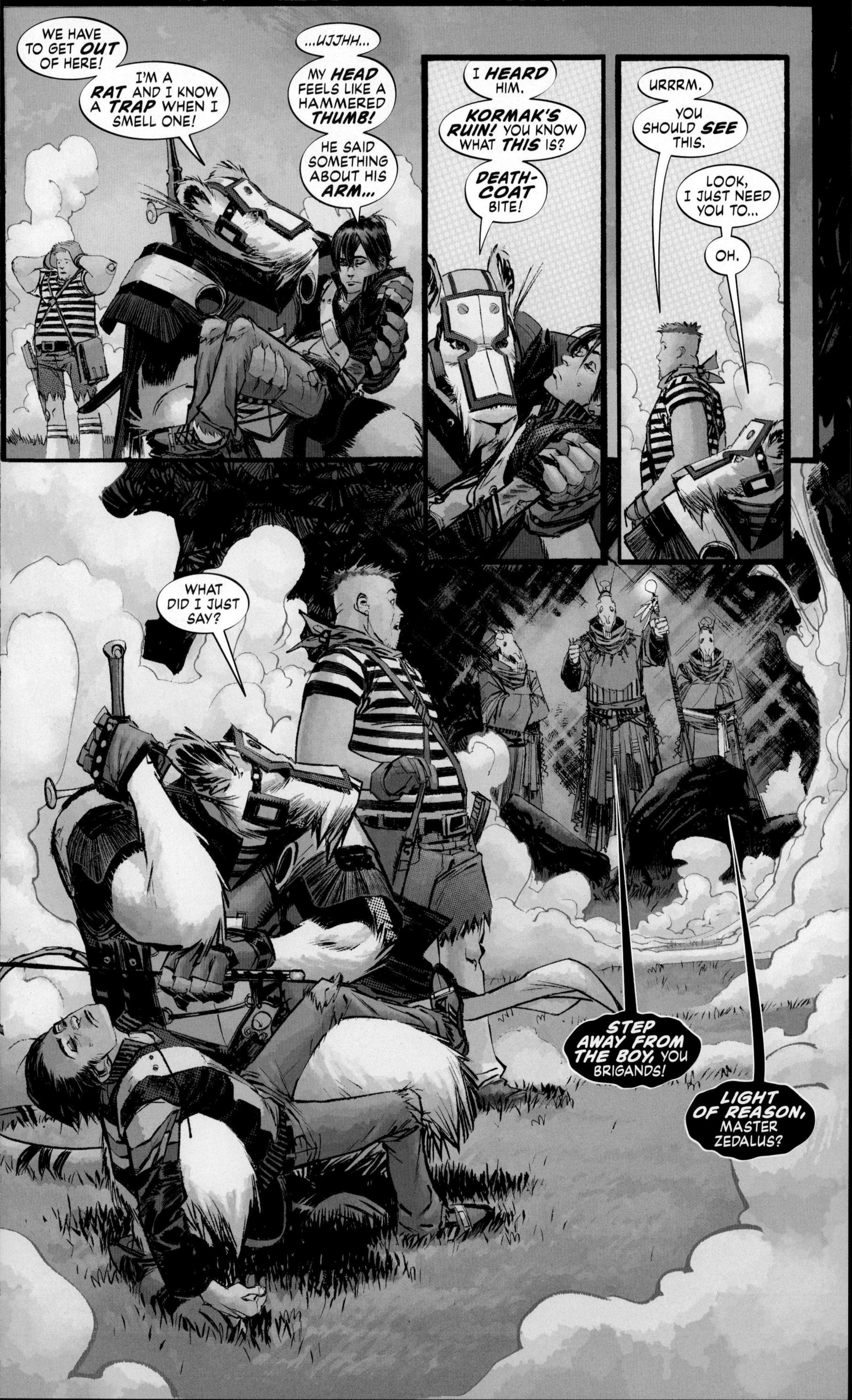

WE HAVE TO GET OUT OF HERE!
I'M A RAT AND I KNOW A TRAP WHEN I SMELL ONE!
...UJJHH...
MY HEAD FEELS LIKE A HAMMERED THUMB!
HE SAID SOMETHING ABOUT HIS ARM...
I HEARD HIM.
KORMAK'S RUIN! YOU KNOW WHAT THIS IS?
DEATH-COAT BITE!
URRRM.
YOU SHOULD SEE THIS.
LOOK, I JUST NEED YOU TO...
OH.
WHAT DID I JUST SAY?
STEP AWAY FROM THE BOY, YOU BRIGANDS!
LIGHT OF REASON, MASTER ZEDALUS?

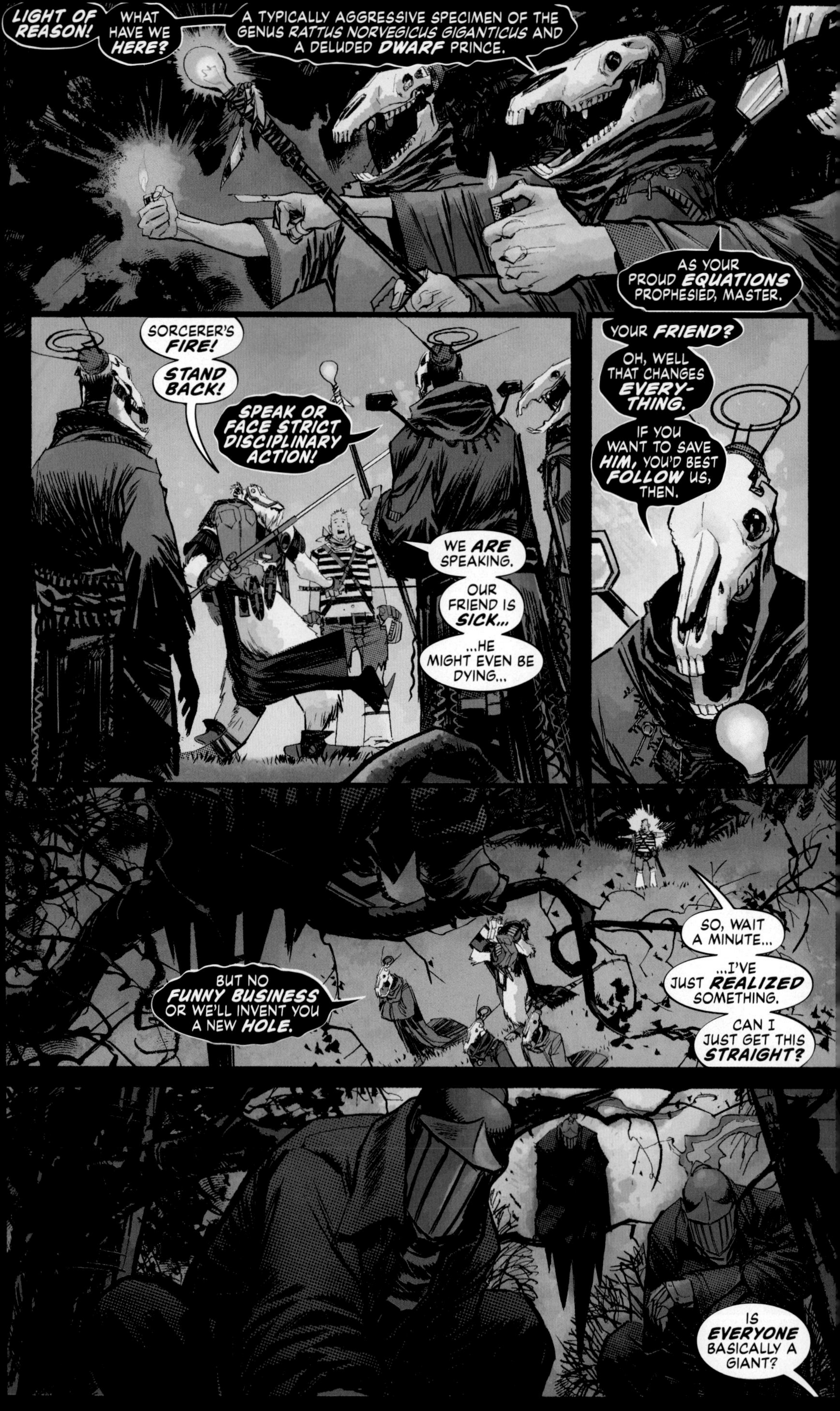
LIGHT OF REASON!
WHAT HAVE WE HERE?
A TYPICALLY AGGRESSIVE SPECIMEN OF THE GENUS RATTUS NORVEGICUS GIGANTICUS AND A DELUDED DWARF PRINCE.
AS YOUR PROUD EQUATIONS PROPHESIED, MASTER.
SORCERER'S FIRE!
STAND BACK!
SPEAK OR FACE STRICT DISCIPLINARY ACTION!
WE ARE SPEAKING.
OUR FRIEND IS SICK...
...HE MIGHT EVEN BE DYING...
YOUR FRIEND?
OH, WELL THAT CHANGES EVERY-THING.
IF YOU WANT TO SAVE HIM, YOU'D BEST FOLLOW US, THEN.
BUT NO FUNNY BUSINESS OR WE'LL INVENT YOU A NEW HOLE.
SO, WAIT A MINUTE...
...I'VE JUST REALIZED SOMETHING.
CAN I JUST GET THIS STRAIGHT?
IS EVERYONE BASICALLY A GIANT?

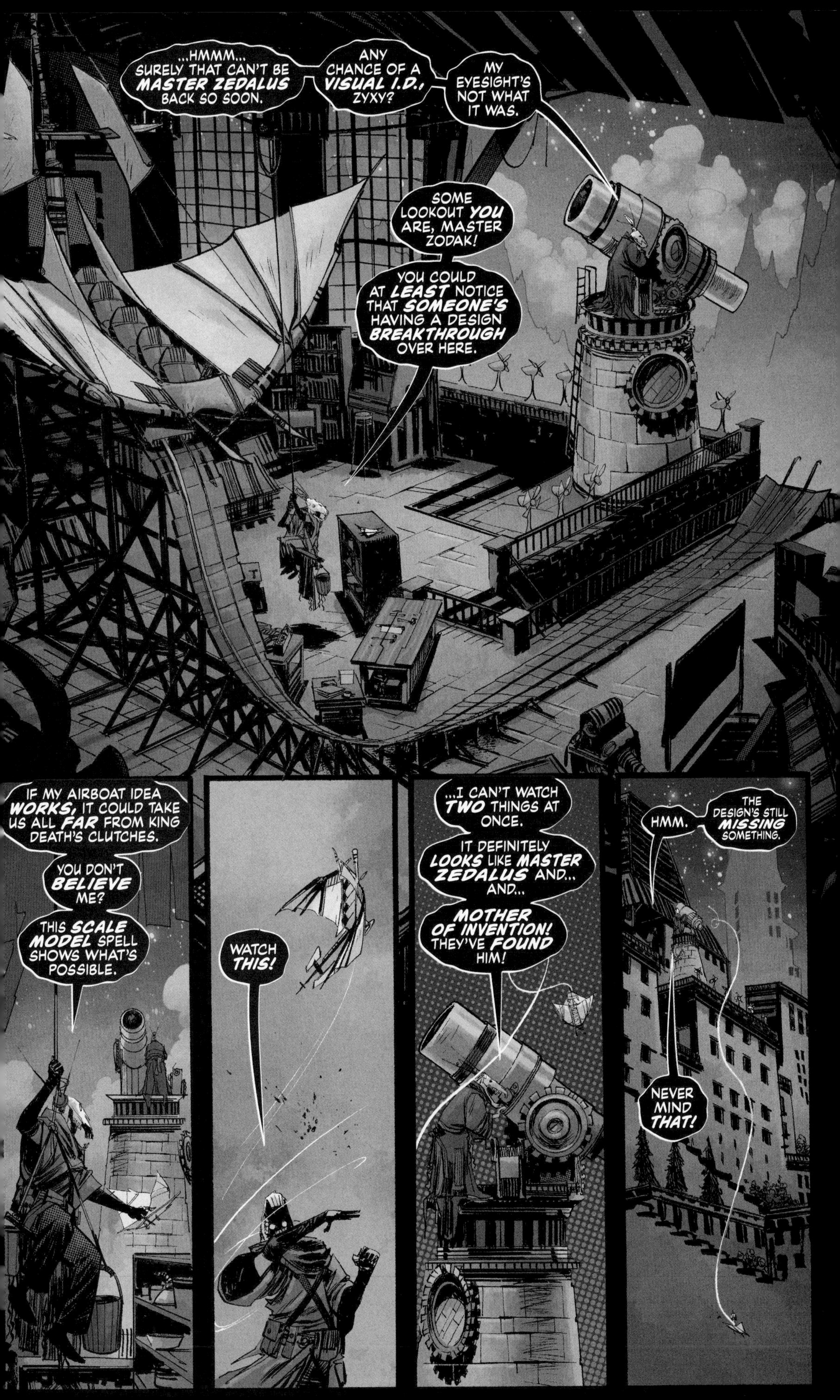
...HMMM... SURELY THAT CAN'T BE **MASTER ZEDALUS** BACK SO SOON.
ANY CHANCE OF A **VISUAL I.D.,** ZYXY?
MY EYESIGHT'S NOT WHAT IT WAS.
SOME LOOKOUT **YOU** ARE, MASTER ZODAK!
YOU COULD AT **LEAST** NOTICE THAT **SOMEONE'S** HAVING A DESIGN **BREAKTHROUGH** OVER HERE.
IF MY AIRBOAT IDEA **WORKS,** IT COULD TAKE US ALL **FAR** FROM KING DEATH'S CLUTCHES.
YOU DON'T **BELIEVE** ME?
THIS **SCALE MODEL** SPELL SHOWS WHAT'S POSSIBLE.
WATCH **THIS!**
...I CAN'T WATCH **TWO** THINGS AT ONCE.
IT DEFINITELY **LOOKS** LIKE **MASTER ZEDALUS** AND... AND...
MOTHER OF INVENTION! THEY'VE **FOUND** HIM!
HMM.
THE DESIGN'S STILL **MISSING** SOMETHING.
NEVER MIND **THAT!**

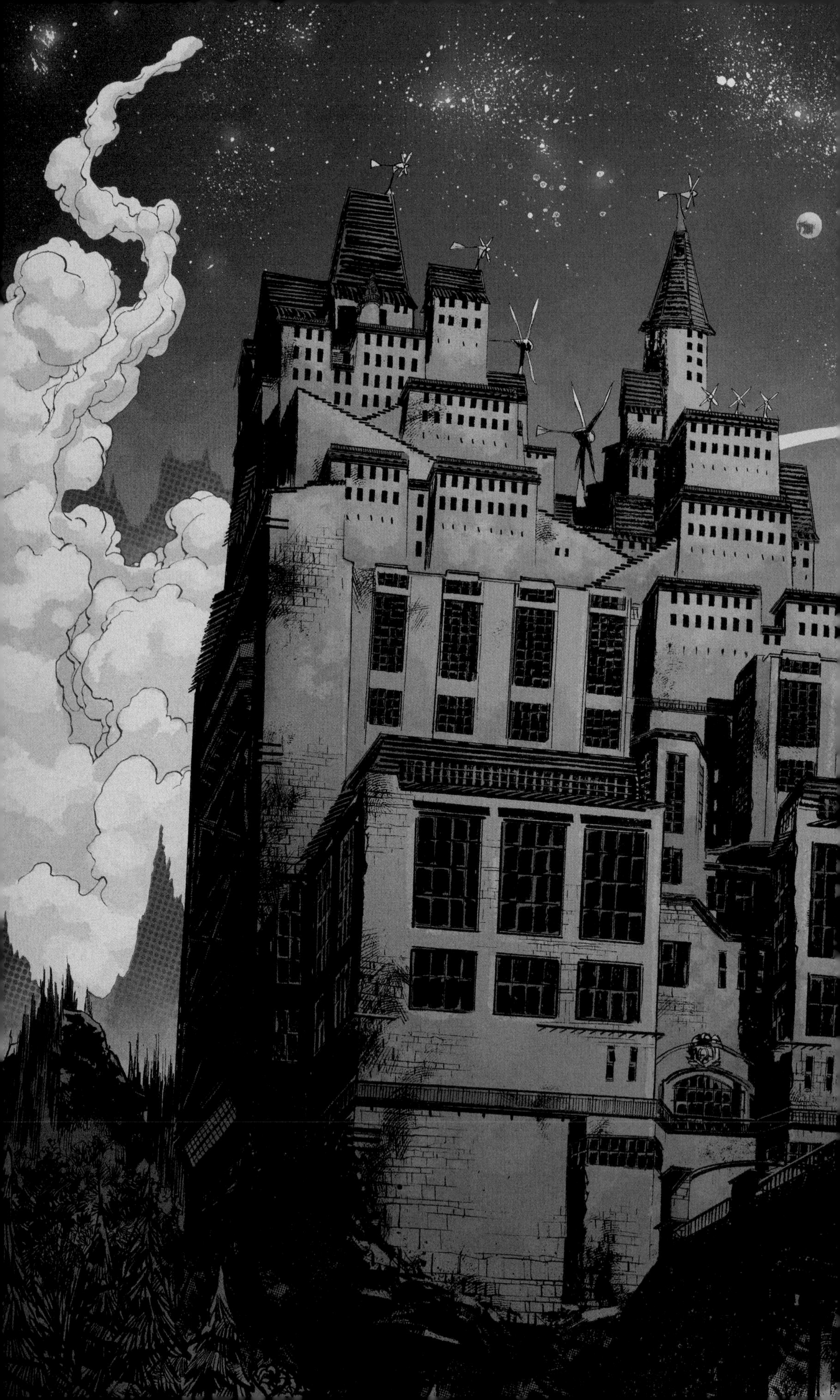

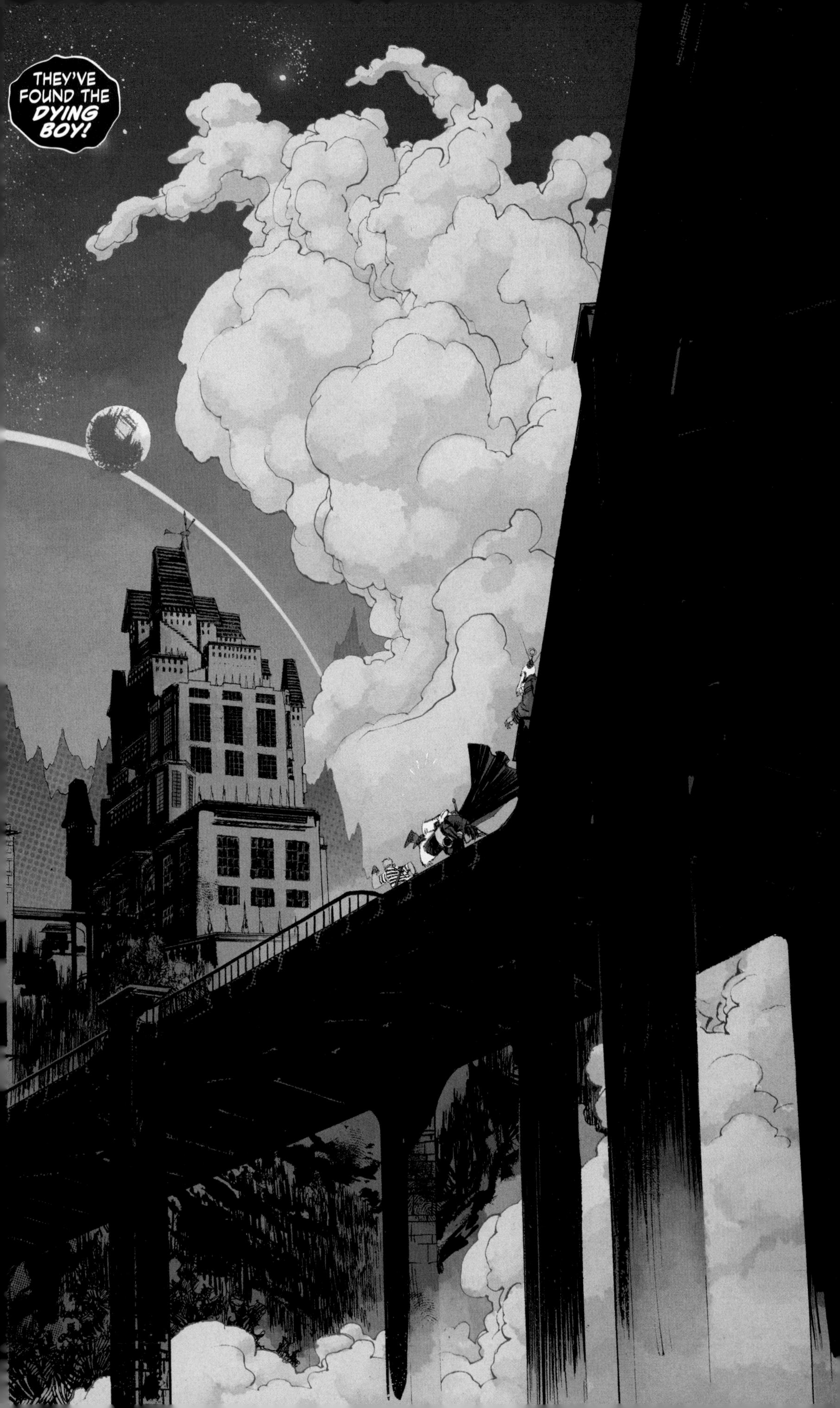
THEY'VE FOUND THE DYING BOY!

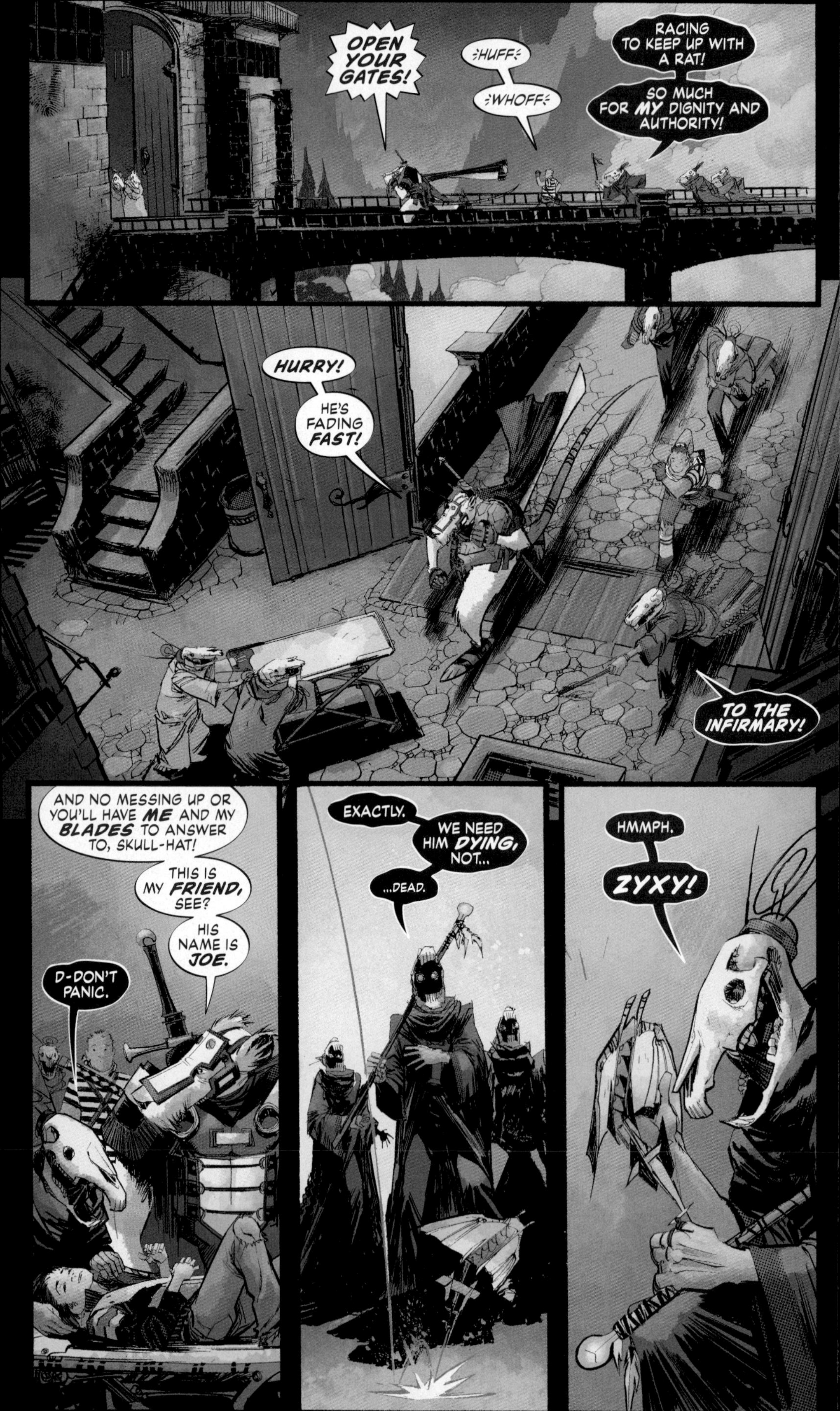
OPEN YOUR GATES!
HUFF
WHOFF
RACING TO KEEP UP WITH A RAT!
SO MUCH FOR MY DIGNITY AND AUTHORITY!
HURRY!
HE'S FADING FAST!
TO THE INFIRMARY!
AND NO MESSING UP OR YOU'LL HAVE ME AND MY BLADES TO ANSWER TO, SKULL-HAT!
THIS IS MY FRIEND, SEE?
HIS NAME IS JOE.
D-DON'T PANIC.
EXACTLY.
WE NEED HIM DYING, NOT...
...DEAD.
HMMPH.
ZYXY!

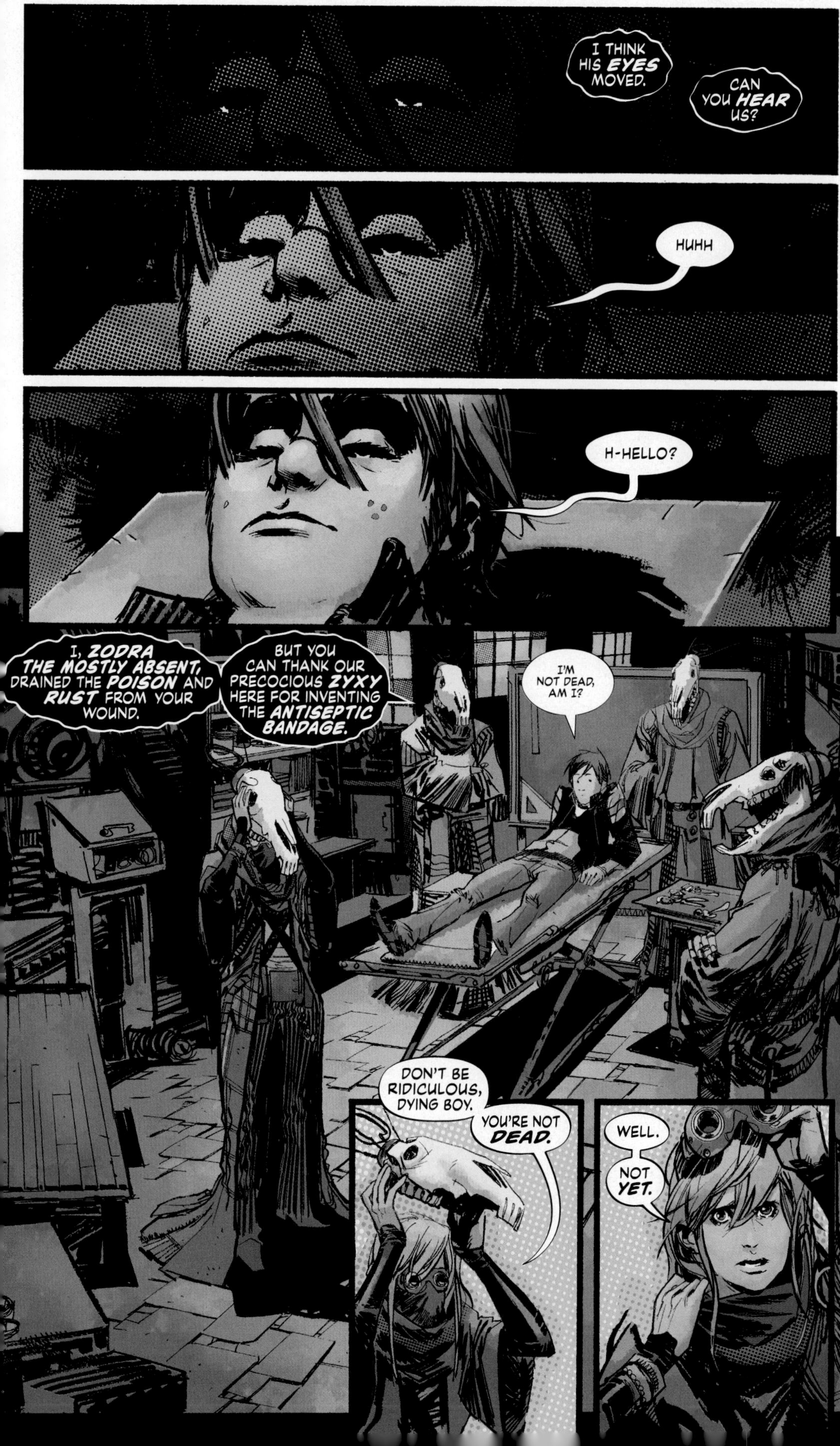

I THINK HIS EYES MOVED.
CAN YOU HEAR US?
HUHH
H-HELLO?
I, ZODRA THE MOSTLY ABSENT, DRAINED THE POISON AND RUST FROM YOUR WOUND.
BUT YOU CAN THANK OUR PRECOCIOUS ZYXY HERE FOR INVENTING THE ANTISEPTIC BANDAGE.
I'M NOT DEAD, AM I?
DON'T BE RIDICULOUS, DYING BOY.
YOU'RE NOT DEAD.
WELL.
NOT YET.

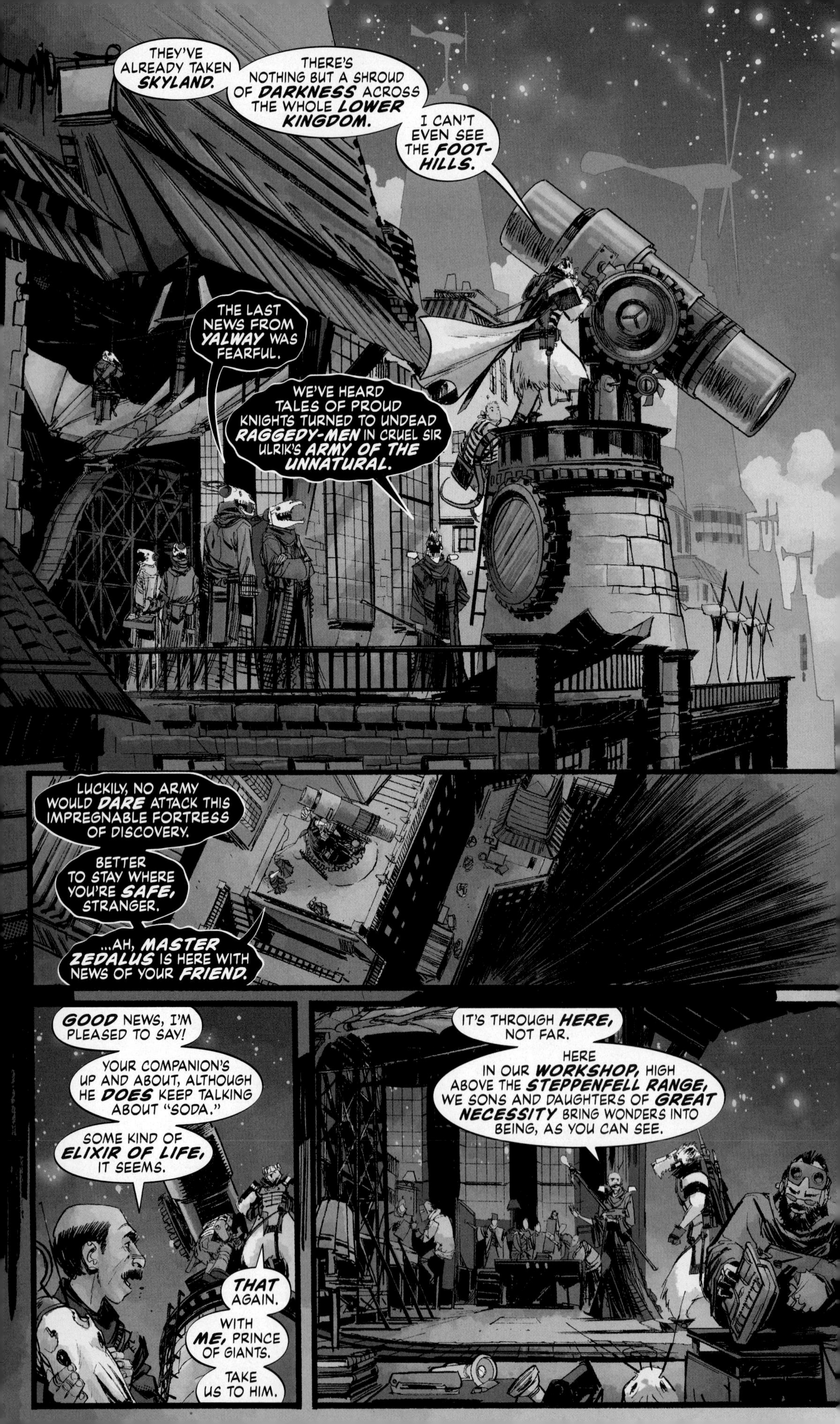
THEY'VE ALREADY TAKEN SKYLAND.
THERE'S NOTHING BUT A SHROUD OF DARKNESS ACROSS THE WHOLE LOWER KINGDOM.
I CAN'T EVEN SEE THE FOOT-HILLS.
THE LAST NEWS FROM YALWAY WAS FEARFUL.
WE'VE HEARD TALES OF PROUD KNIGHTS TURNED TO UNDEAD RAGGEDY-MEN IN CRUEL SIR ULRIK'S ARMY OF THE UNNATURAL.
LUCKILY, NO ARMY WOULD DARE ATTACK THIS IMPREGNABLE FORTRESS OF DISCOVERY.
BETTER TO STAY WHERE YOU'RE SAFE, STRANGER.
...AH, MASTER ZEDALUS IS HERE WITH NEWS OF YOUR FRIEND.
GOOD NEWS, I'M PLEASED TO SAY!
YOUR COMPANION'S UP AND ABOUT, ALTHOUGH HE DOES KEEP TALKING ABOUT "SODA."
SOME KIND OF ELIXIR OF LIFE, IT SEEMS.
THAT AGAIN.
WITH ME, PRINCE OF GIANTS.
TAKE US TO HIM.
IT'S THROUGH HERE, NOT FAR.
HERE IN OUR WORKSHOP, HIGH ABOVE THE STEPPENFELL RANGE, WE SONS AND DAUGHTERS OF GREAT NECESSITY BRING WONDERS INTO BEING, AS YOU CAN SEE.

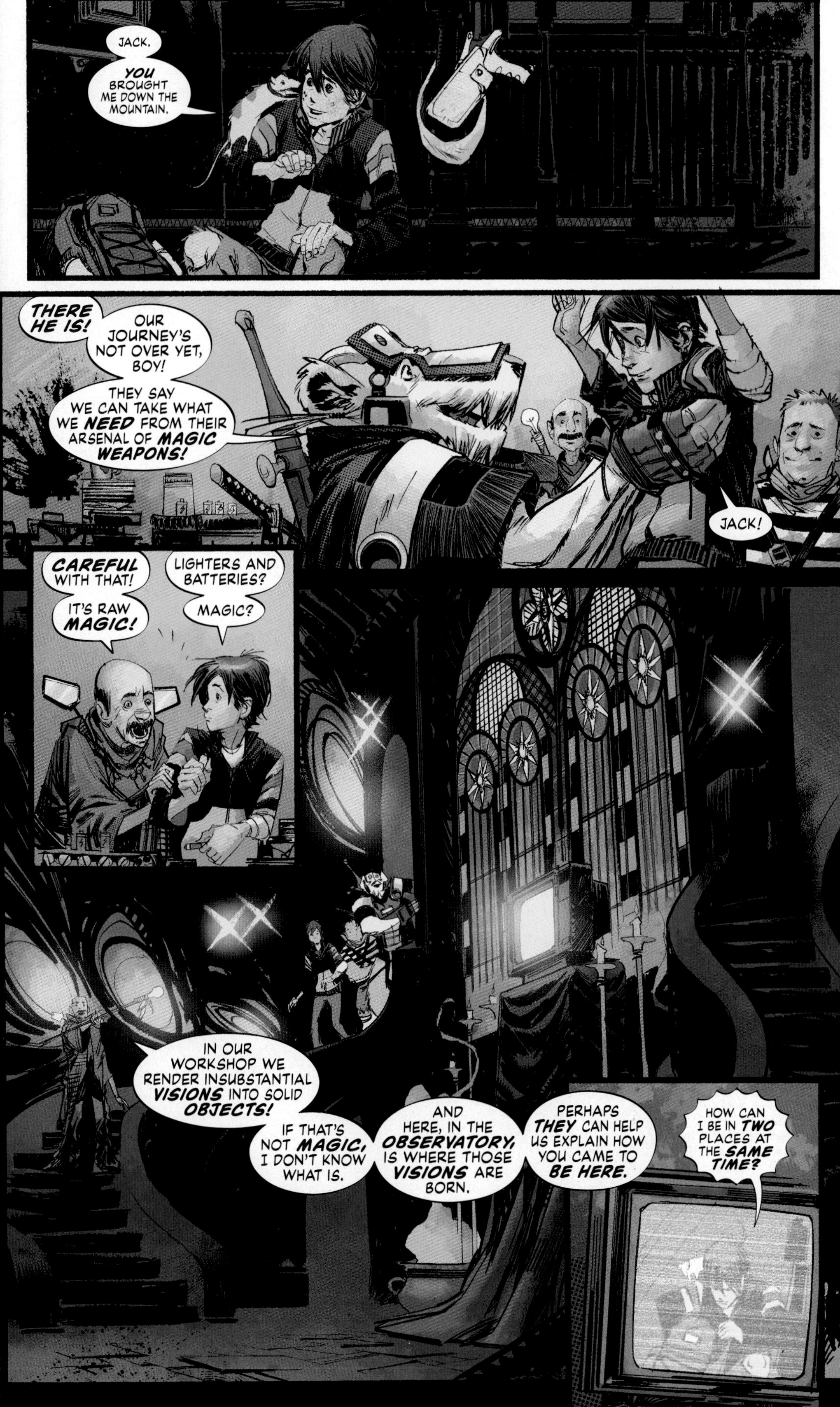
JACK.
YOU BROUGHT ME DOWN THE MOUNTAIN.
THERE HE IS!
OUR JOURNEY'S NOT OVER YET, BOY!
THEY SAY WE CAN TAKE WHAT WE NEED FROM THEIR ARSENAL OF MAGIC WEAPONS!
JACK!
CAREFUL WITH THAT!
IT'S RAW MAGIC!
LIGHTERS AND BATTERIES?
MAGIC?
IN OUR WORKSHOP WE RENDER INSUBSTANTIAL VISIONS INTO SOLID OBJECTS!
IF THAT'S NOT MAGIC, I DON'T KNOW WHAT IS.
AND HERE, IN THE OBSERVATORY, IS WHERE THOSE VISIONS ARE BORN.
PERHAPS THEY CAN HELP US EXPLAIN HOW YOU CAME TO BE HERE.
HOW CAN I BE IN TWO PLACES AT THE SAME TIME?

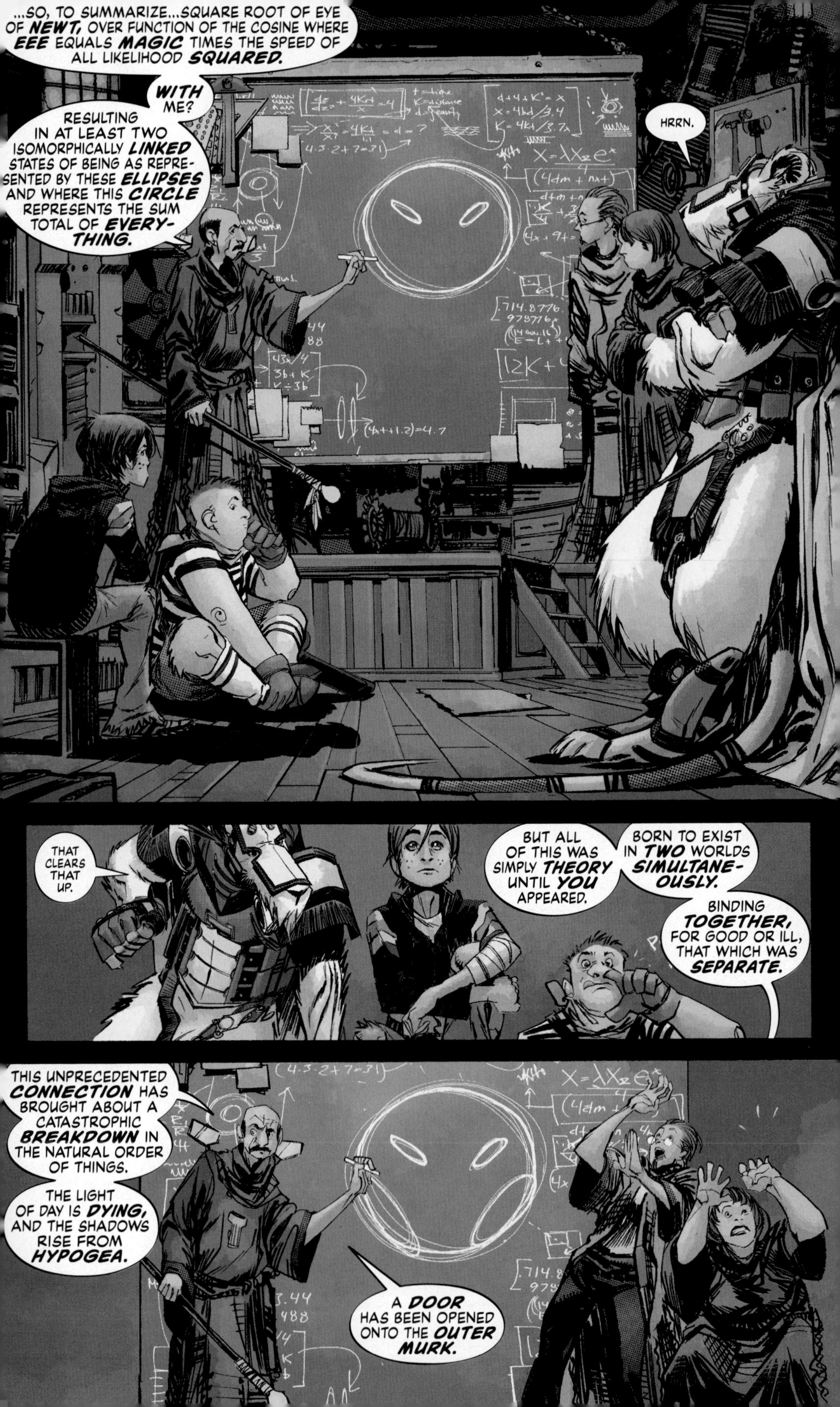

...SO, TO SUMMARIZE...SQUARE ROOT OF EYE OF NEWT, OVER FUNCTION OF THE COSINE WHERE EEE EQUALS MAGIC TIMES THE SPEED OF ALL LIKELIHOOD SQUARED.
WITH ME?
RESULTING IN AT LEAST TWO ISOMORPHICALLY LINKED STATES OF BEING AS REPRESENTED BY THESE ELLIPSES AND WHERE THIS CIRCLE REPRESENTS THE SUM TOTAL OF EVERYTHING.
HRRN.
THAT CLEARS THAT UP.
BUT ALL OF THIS WAS SIMPLY THEORY UNTIL YOU APPEARED.
BORN TO EXIST IN TWO WORLDS SIMULTANEOUSLY.
BINDING TOGETHER, FOR GOOD OR ILL, THAT WHICH WAS SEPARATE.
THIS UNPRECEDENTED CONNECTION HAS BROUGHT ABOUT A CATASTROPHIC BREAKDOWN IN THE NATURAL ORDER OF THINGS.
THE LIGHT OF DAY IS DYING, AND THE SHADOWS RISE FROM HYPOGEA.
A DOOR HAS BEEN OPENED ONTO THE OUTER MURK.

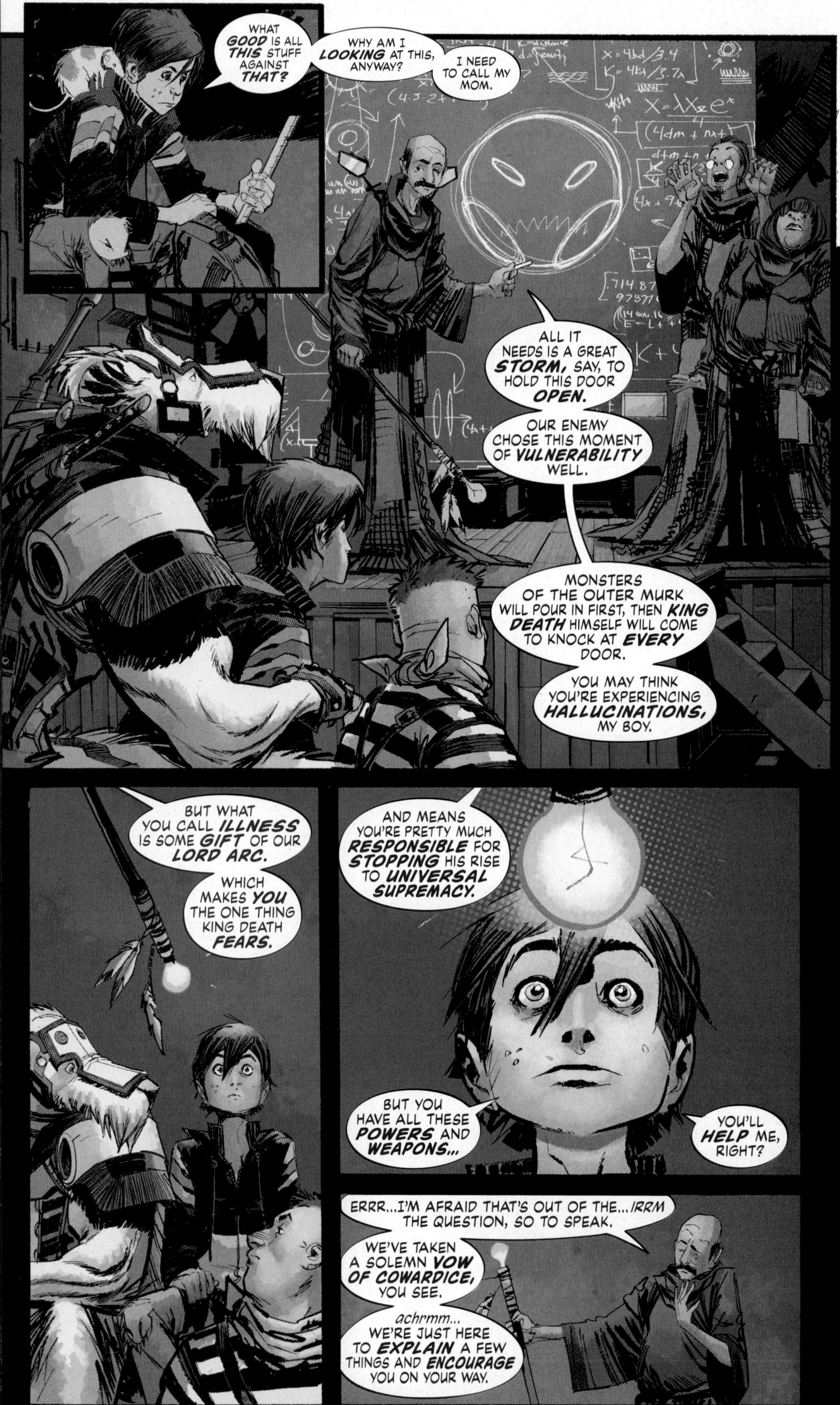
WHAT GOOD IS ALL THIS STUFF AGAINST THAT?
WHY AM I LOOKING AT THIS, ANYWAY?
I NEED TO CALL MY MOM.
ALL IT NEEDS IS A GREAT STORM, SAY, TO HOLD THIS DOOR OPEN.
OUR ENEMY CHOSE THIS MOMENT OF VULNERABILITY WELL.
MONSTERS OF THE OUTER MURK WILL POUR IN FIRST, THEN KING DEATH HIMSELF WILL COME TO KNOCK AT EVERY DOOR.
YOU MAY THINK YOU'RE EXPERIENCING HALLUCINATIONS, MY BOY.
BUT WHAT YOU CALL ILLNESS IS SOME GIFT OF OUR LORD ARC.
WHICH MAKES YOU THE ONE THING KING DEATH FEARS.
AND MEANS YOU'RE PRETTY MUCH RESPONSIBLE FOR STOPPING HIS RISE TO UNIVERSAL SUPREMACY.
BUT YOU HAVE ALL THESE POWERS AND WEAPONS...
YOU'LL HELP ME, RIGHT?
ERRR...I'M AFRAID THAT'S OUT OF THE...IRRM THE QUESTION, SO TO SPEAK.
WE'VE TAKEN A SOLEMN VOW OF COWARDICE, YOU SEE.
achrmm... WE'RE JUST HERE TO EXPLAIN A FEW THINGS AND ENCOURAGE YOU ON YOUR WAY.

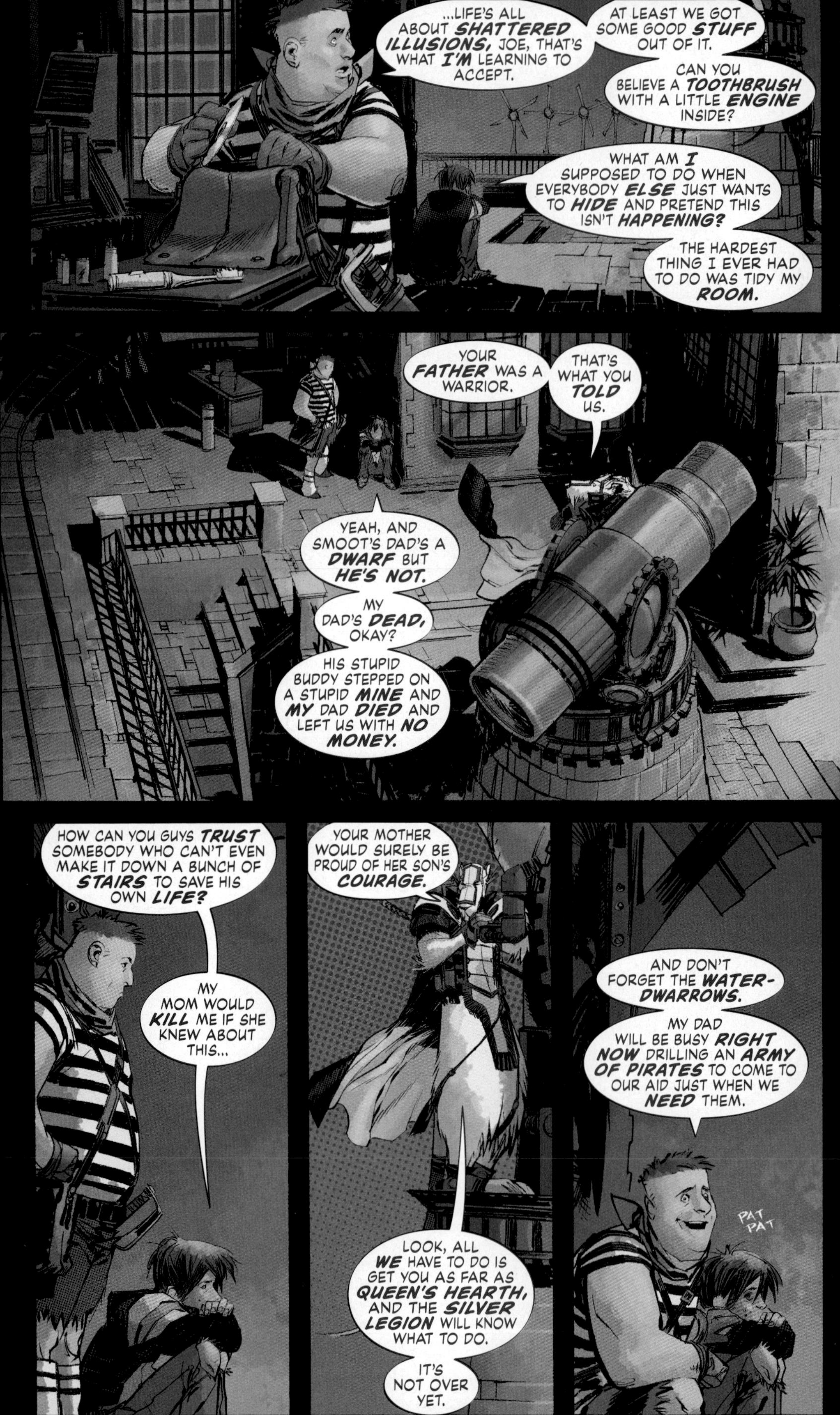
...LIFE'S ALL ABOUT SHATTERED ILLUSIONS, JOE, THAT'S WHAT I'M LEARNING TO ACCEPT.
AT LEAST WE GOT SOME GOOD STUFF OUT OF IT.
CAN YOU BELIEVE A TOOTHBRUSH WITH A LITTLE ENGINE INSIDE?
WHAT AM I SUPPOSED TO DO WHEN EVERYBODY ELSE JUST WANTS TO HIDE AND PRETEND THIS ISN'T HAPPENING?
THE HARDEST THING I EVER HAD TO DO WAS TIDY MY ROOM.
YOUR FATHER WAS A WARRIOR.
THAT'S WHAT YOU TOLD US.
YEAH, AND SMOOT'S DAD'S A DWARF BUT HE'S NOT.
MY DAD'S DEAD, OKAY?
HIS STUPID BUDDY STEPPED ON A STUPID MINE AND MY DAD DIED AND LEFT US WITH NO MONEY.
HOW CAN YOU GUYS TRUST SOMEBODY WHO CAN'T EVEN MAKE IT DOWN A BUNCH OF STAIRS TO SAVE HIS OWN LIFE?
MY MOM WOULD KILL ME IF SHE KNEW ABOUT THIS...
YOUR MOTHER WOULD SURELY BE PROUD OF HER SON'S COURAGE.
LOOK, ALL WE HAVE TO DO IS GET YOU AS FAR AS QUEEN'S HEARTH, AND THE SILVER LEGION WILL KNOW WHAT TO DO.
IT'S NOT OVER YET.
AND DON'T FORGET THE WATER-DWARROWS.
MY DAD WILL BE BUSY RIGHT NOW DRILLING AN ARMY OF PIRATES TO COME TO OUR AID JUST WHEN WE NEED THEM.
PAT PAT

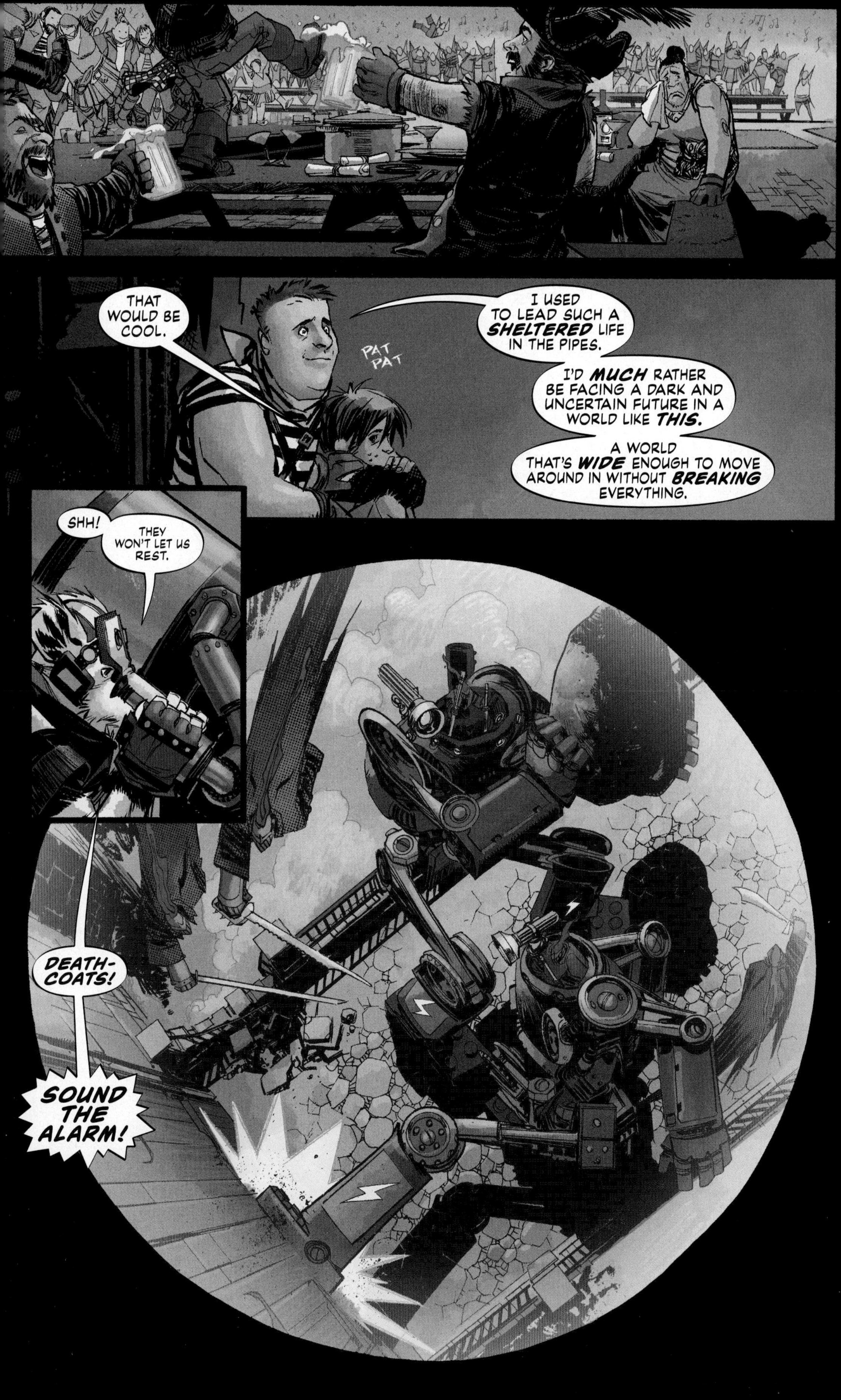
THAT WOULD BE COOL.
I USED TO LEAD SUCH A SHELTERED LIFE IN THE PIPES.
PAT PAT
I'D MUCH RATHER BE FACING A DARK AND UNCERTAIN FUTURE IN A WORLD LIKE THIS.
A WORLD THAT'S WIDE ENOUGH TO MOVE AROUND IN WITHOUT BREAKING EVERYTHING.
SHH!
THEY WON'T LET US REST.
DEATH-COATS!
SOUND THE ALARM!

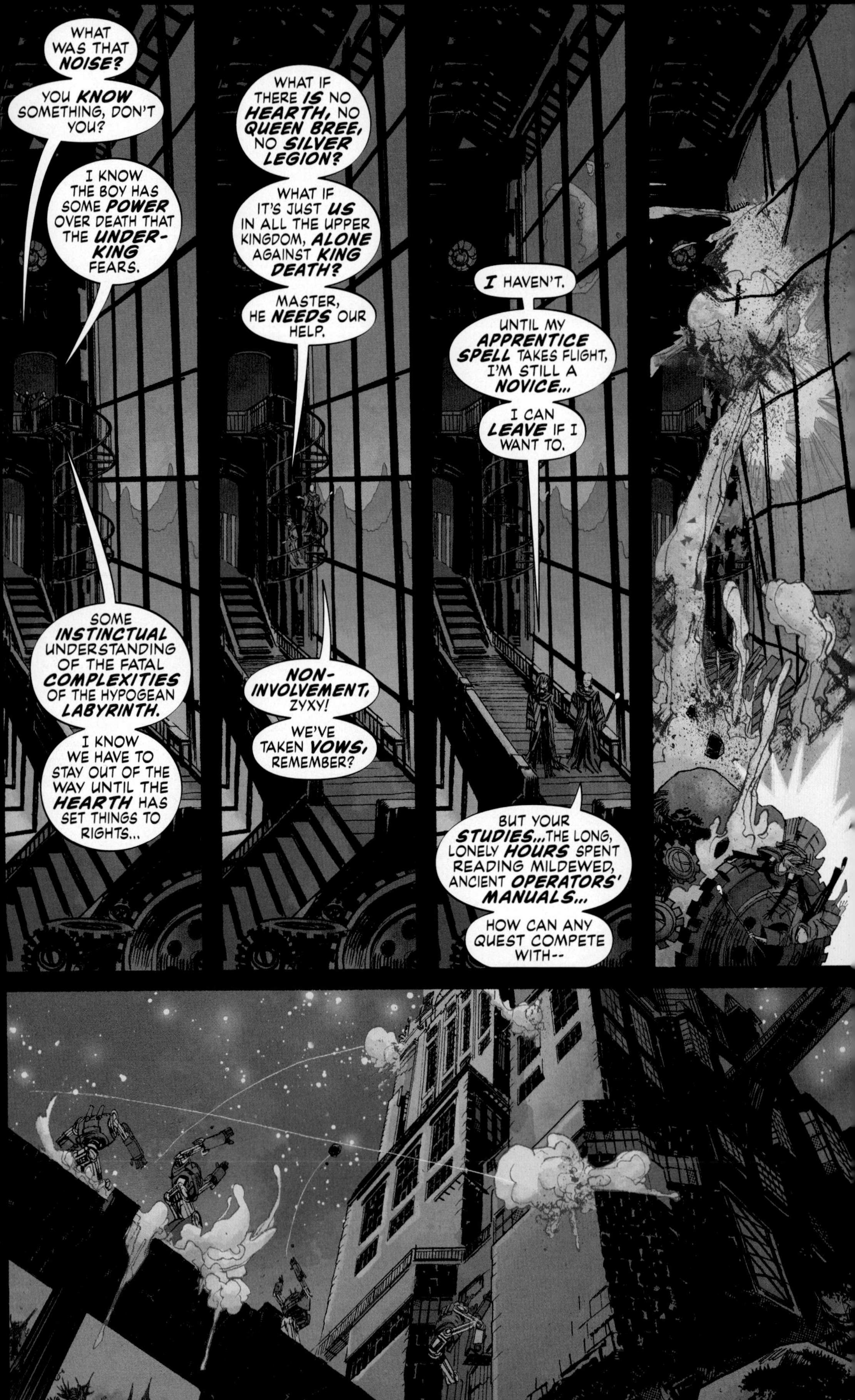

WHAT WAS THAT NOISE?
YOU KNOW SOMETHING, DON'T YOU?
I KNOW THE BOY HAS SOME POWER OVER DEATH THAT THE UNDER-KING FEARS.
SOME INSTINCTUAL UNDERSTANDING OF THE FATAL COMPLEXITIES OF THE HYPOGEAN LABYRINTH.
I KNOW WE HAVE TO STAY OUT OF THE WAY UNTIL THE HEARTH HAS SET THINGS TO RIGHTS...
WHAT IF THERE IS NO HEARTH, NO QUEEN BREE, NO SILVER LEGION?
WHAT IF IT'S JUST US IN ALL THE UPPER KINGDOM, ALONE AGAINST KING DEATH?
MASTER, HE NEEDS OUR HELP.
NON-INVOLVEMENT, ZYXY!
WE'VE TAKEN VOWS, REMEMBER?
I HAVEN'T.
UNTIL MY APPRENTICE SPELL TAKES FLIGHT, I'M STILL A NOVICE...
I CAN LEAVE IF I WANT TO.
BUT YOUR STUDIES...THE LONG, LONELY HOURS SPENT READING MILDEWED, ANCIENT OPERATORS' MANUALS...
HOW CAN ANY QUEST COMPETE WITH--

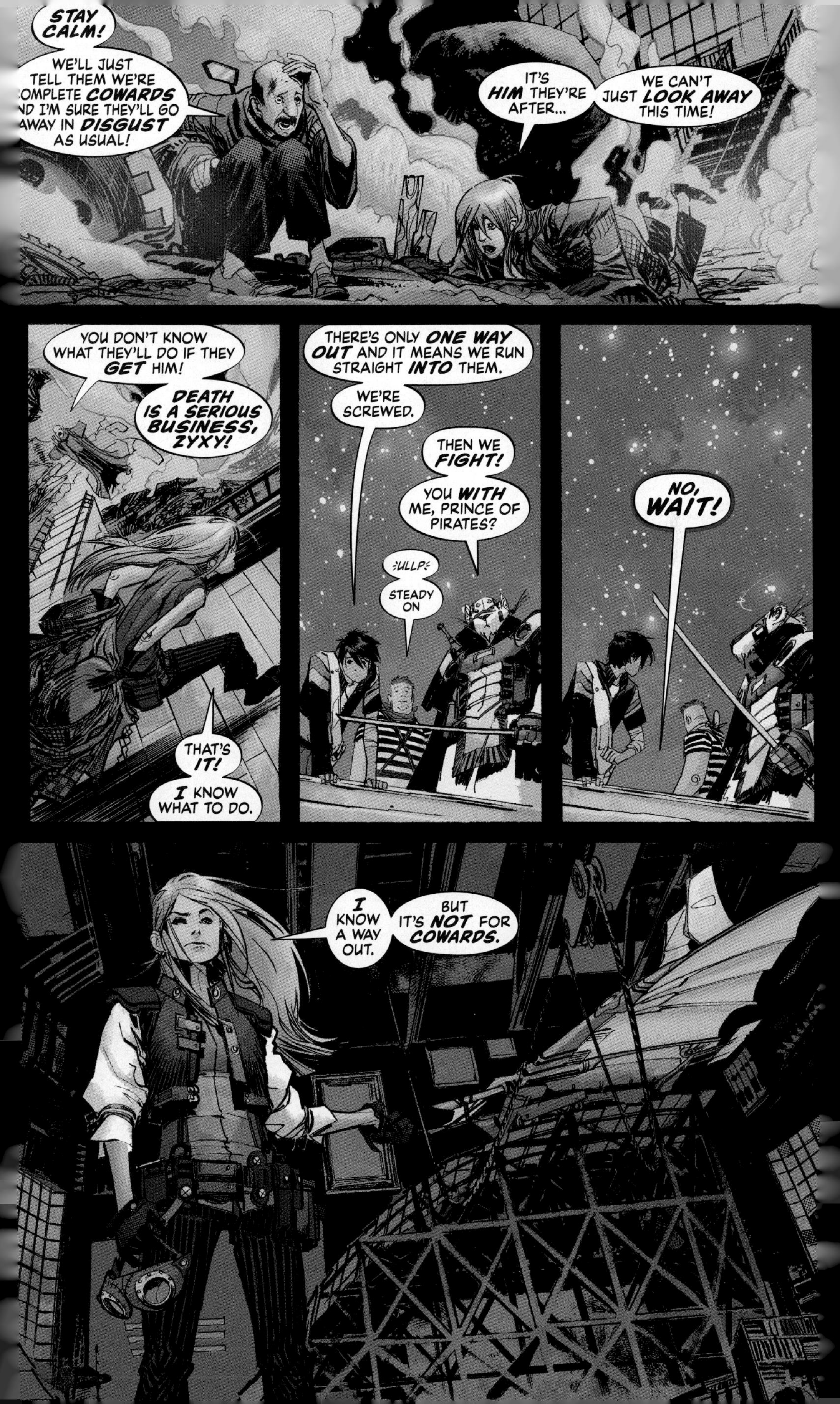
STAY CALM!
WE'LL JUST TELL THEM WE'RE COMPLETE COWARDS AND I'M SURE THEY'LL GO AWAY IN DISGUST AS USUAL!
IT'S HIM THEY'RE AFTER...
WE CAN'T JUST LOOK AWAY THIS TIME!
YOU DON'T KNOW WHAT THEY'LL DO IF THEY GET HIM!
DEATH IS A SERIOUS BUSINESS, ZYXY!
THAT'S IT!
I KNOW WHAT TO DO.
THERE'S ONLY ONE WAY OUT AND IT MEANS WE RUN STRAIGHT INTO THEM.
WE'RE SCREWED.
THEN WE FIGHT!
YOU WITH ME, PRINCE OF PIRATES?
ULLP
STEADY ON
NO, WAIT!
I KNOW A WAY OUT.
BUT IT'S NOT FOR COWARDS.

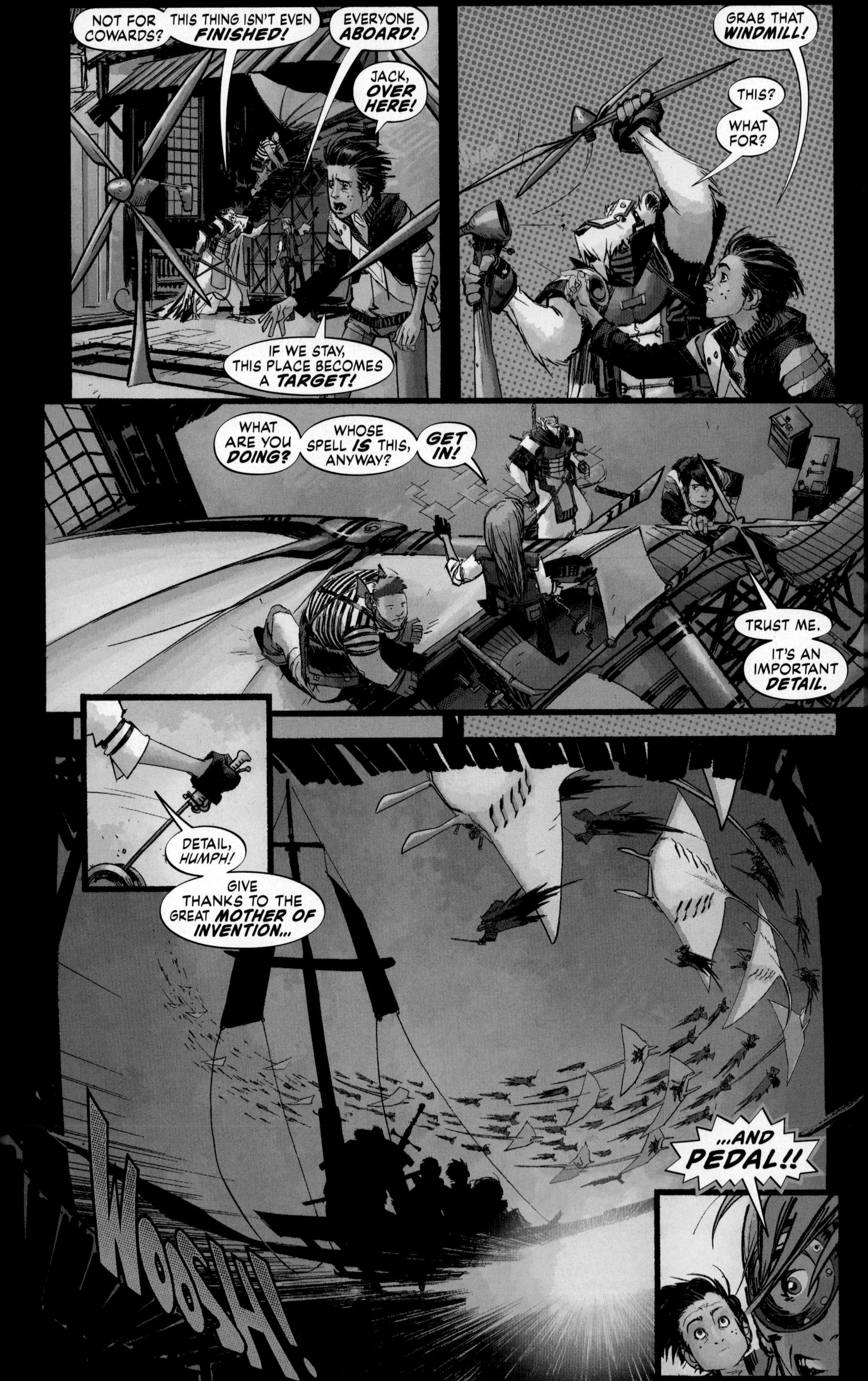
NOT FOR COWARDS?
THIS THING ISN'T EVEN FINISHED!
EVERYONE ABOARD!
JACK, OVER HERE!
IF WE STAY, THIS PLACE BECOMES A TARGET!
GRAB THAT WINDMILL!
THIS?
WHAT FOR?
WHAT ARE YOU DOING?
WHOSE SPELL IS THIS, ANYWAY?
GET IN!
TRUST ME.
IT'S AN IMPORTANT DETAIL.
DETAIL, HUMPH!
GIVE THANKS TO THE GREAT MOTHER OF INVENTION...
...AND PEDAL!!
WOOSH!

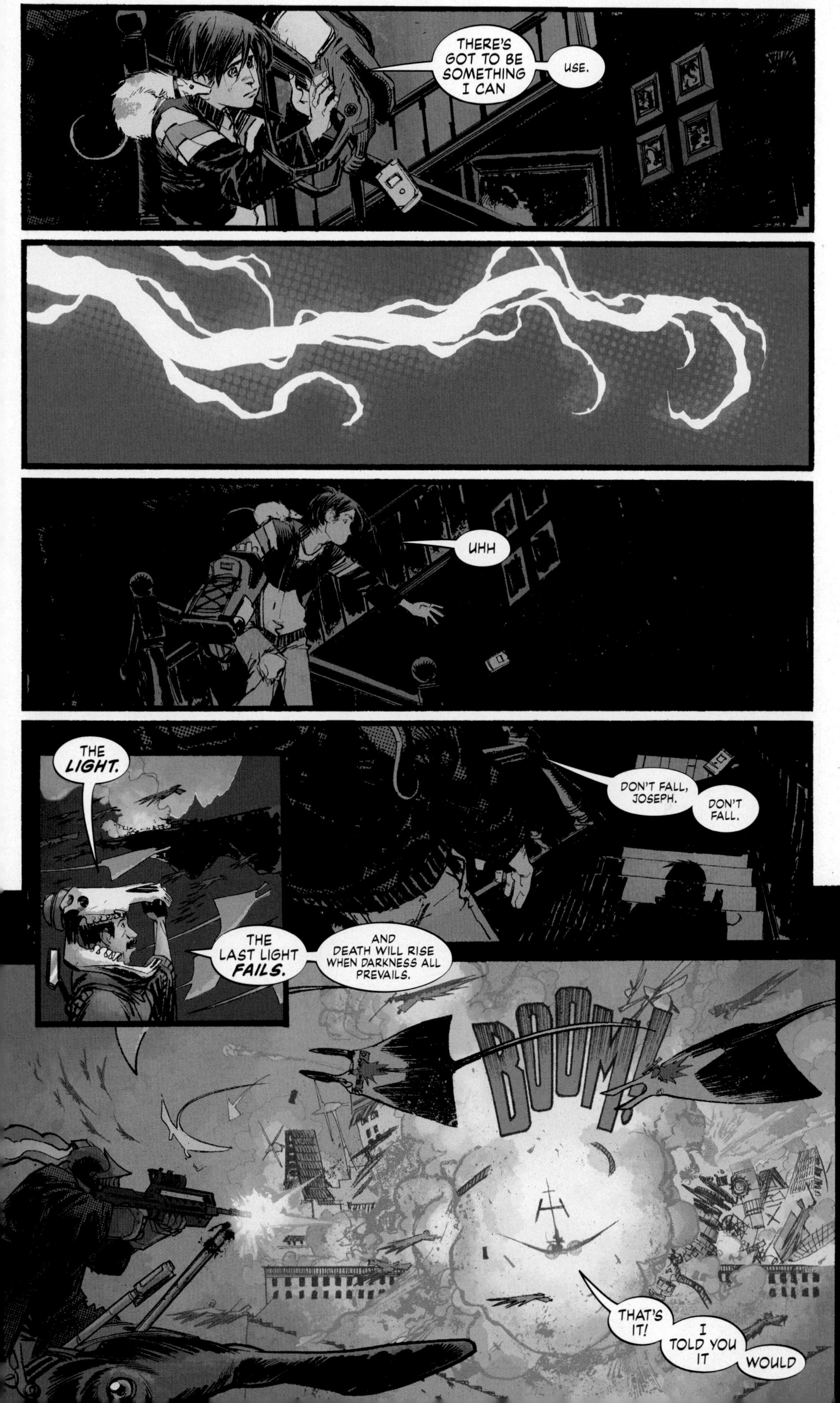
THERE'S GOT TO BE SOMETHING I CAN
USE.
UHH
THE *LIGHT.*
DON'T FALL, JOSEPH.
DON'T FALL.
THE LAST LIGHT *FAILS.*
AND DEATH WILL RISE WHEN DARKNESS ALL PREVAILS.
BOOM!
THAT'S IT!
I TOLD YOU IT
WOULD

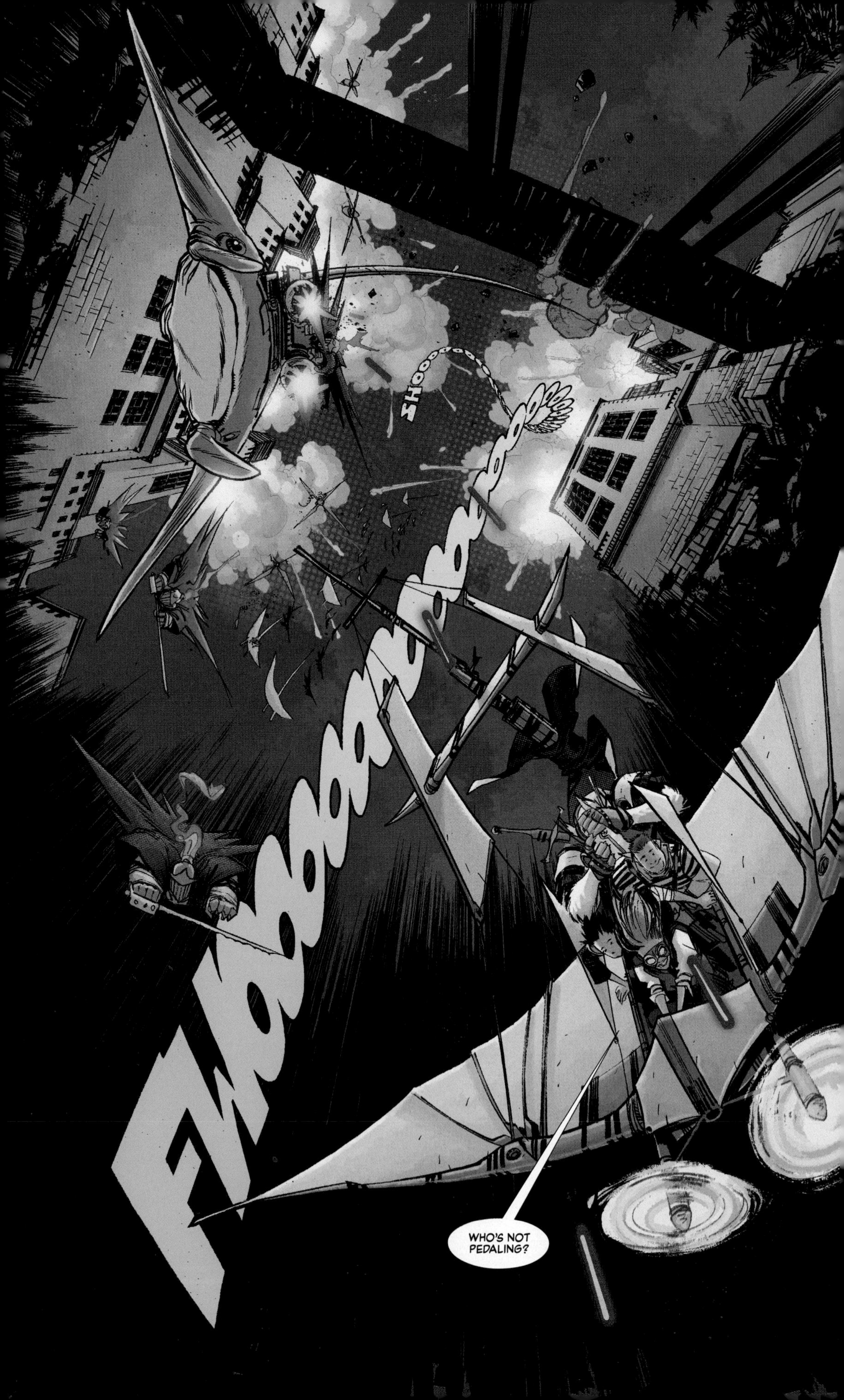

SHOOOOOO
FWOOOOOOOOOOOOOO
WHO'S NOT PEDALING?

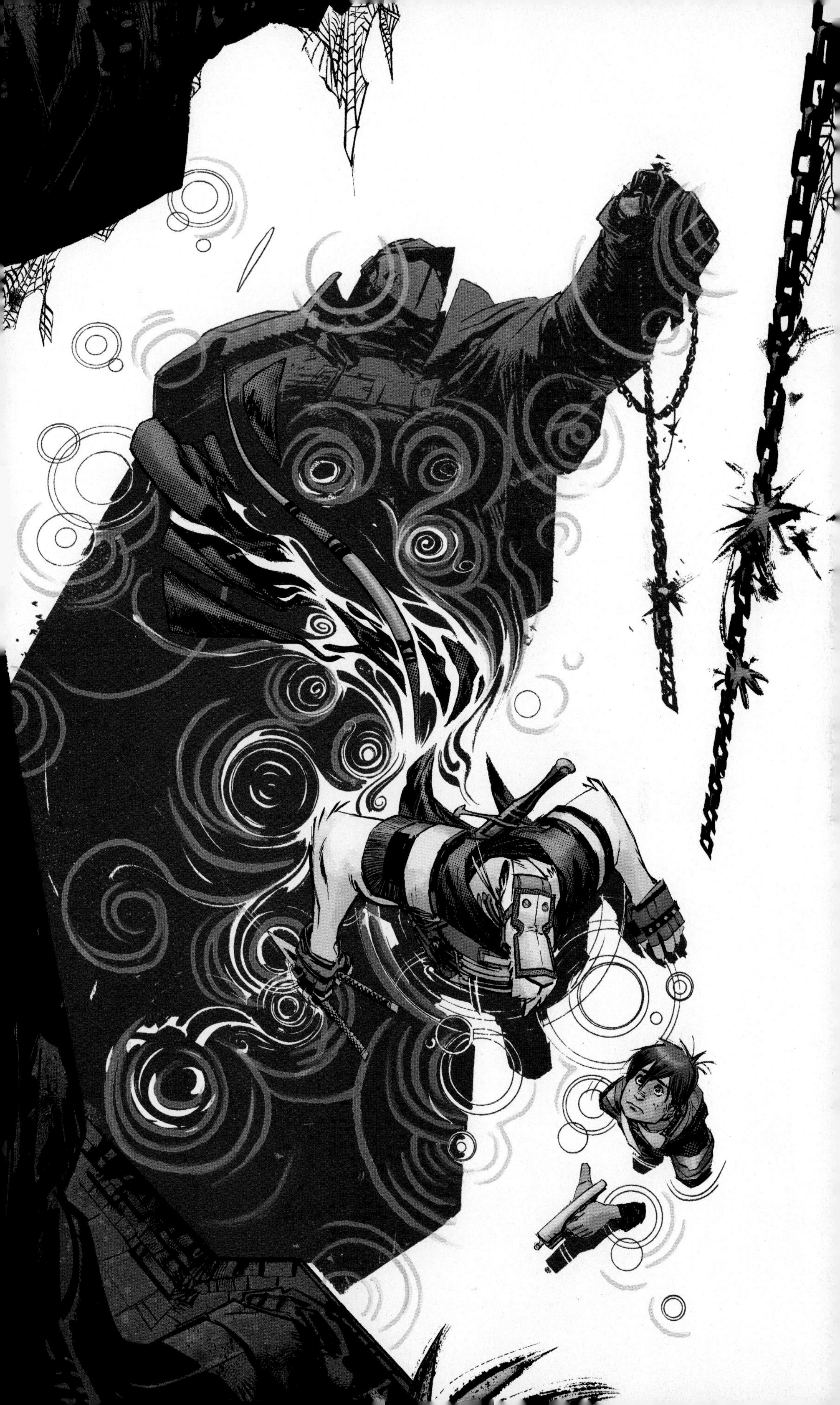

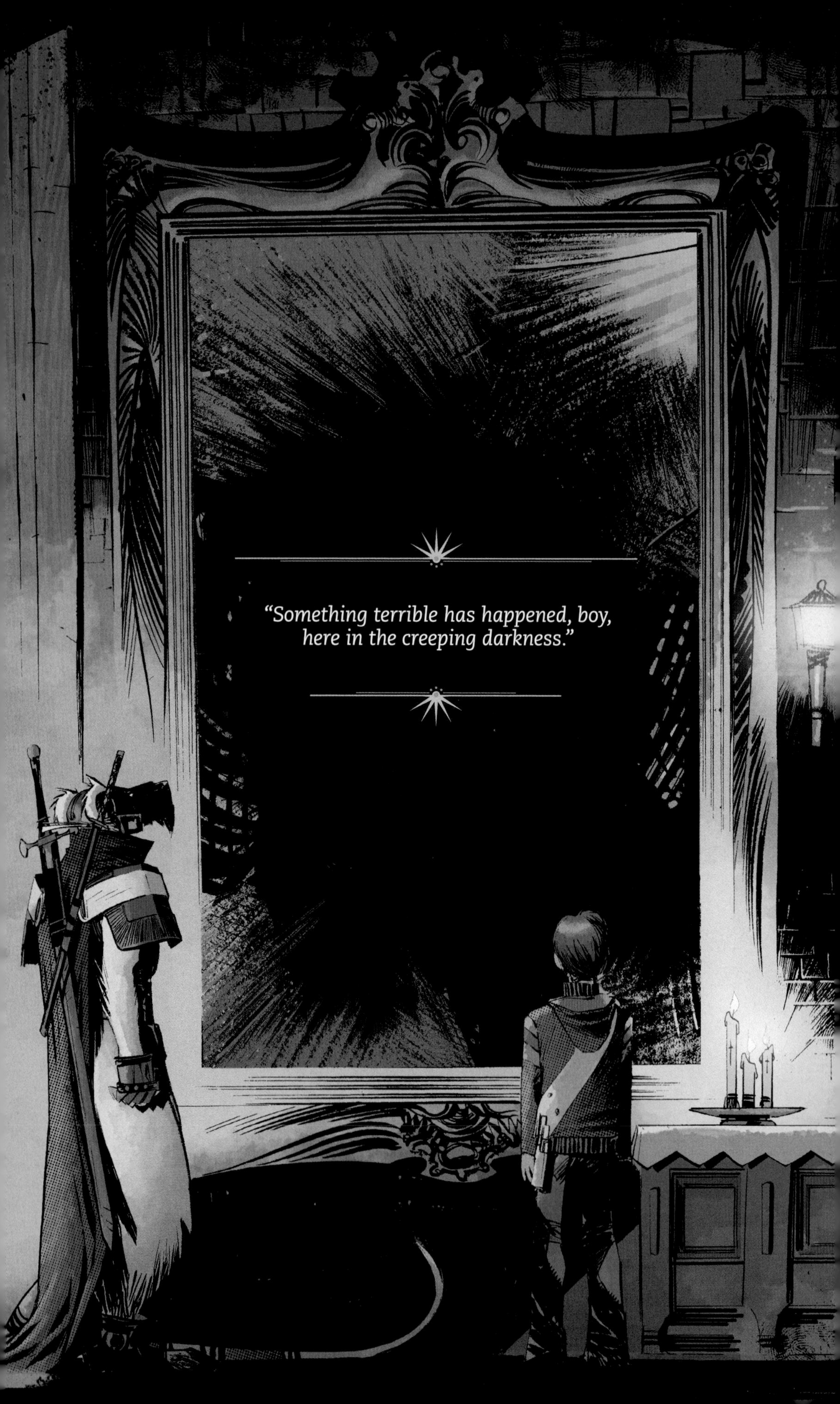
"Something terrible has happened, boy,
here in the creeping darkness."

chapter 5: from never to always

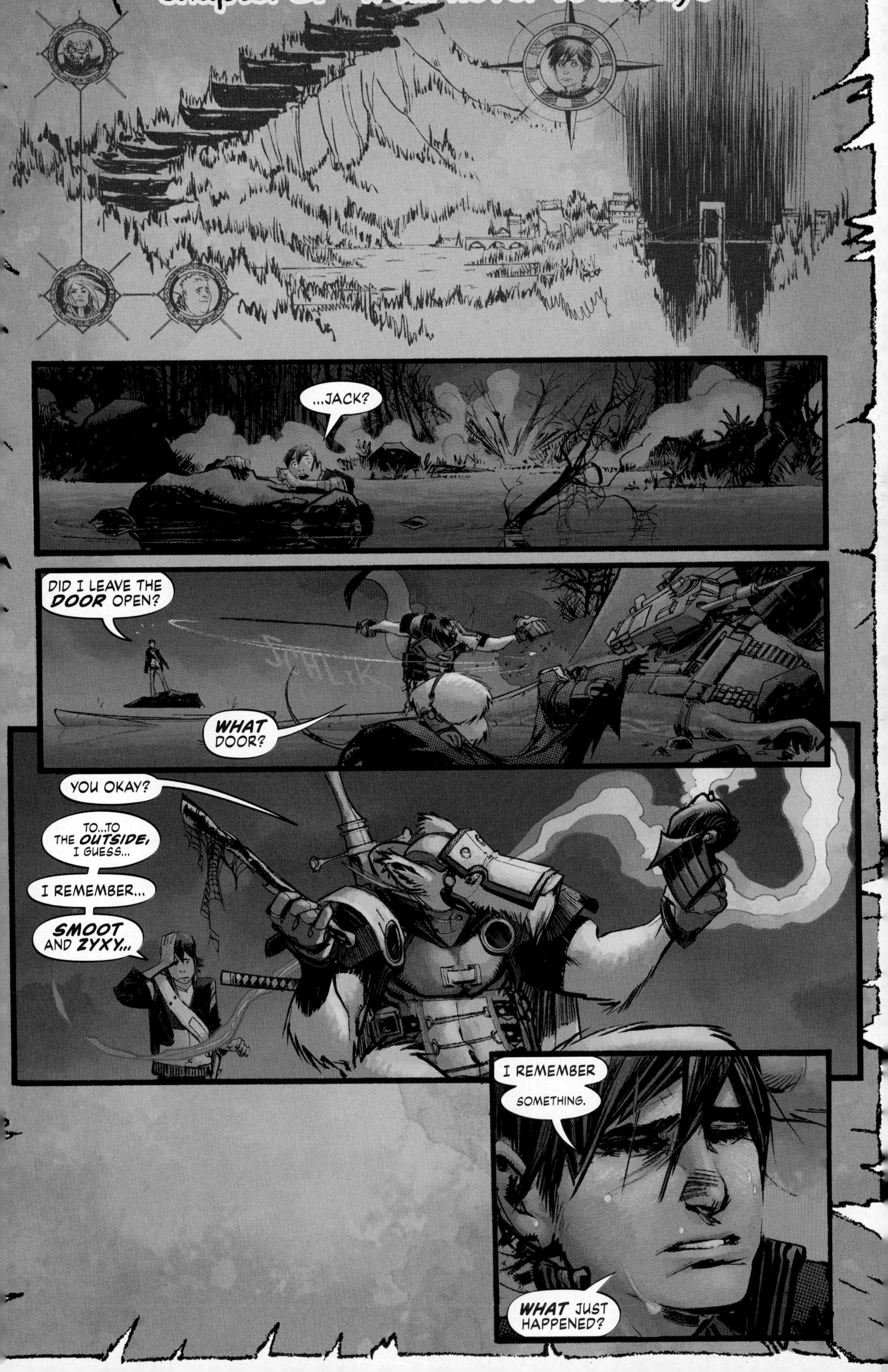
...JACK?
DID I LEAVE THE DOOR OPEN?
SCHLIK
WHAT DOOR?
YOU OKAY?
TO...TO THE OUTSIDE, I GUESS...
I REMEMBER...
SMOOT AND ZYXY...
I REMEMBER SOMETHING.
WHAT JUST HAPPENED?

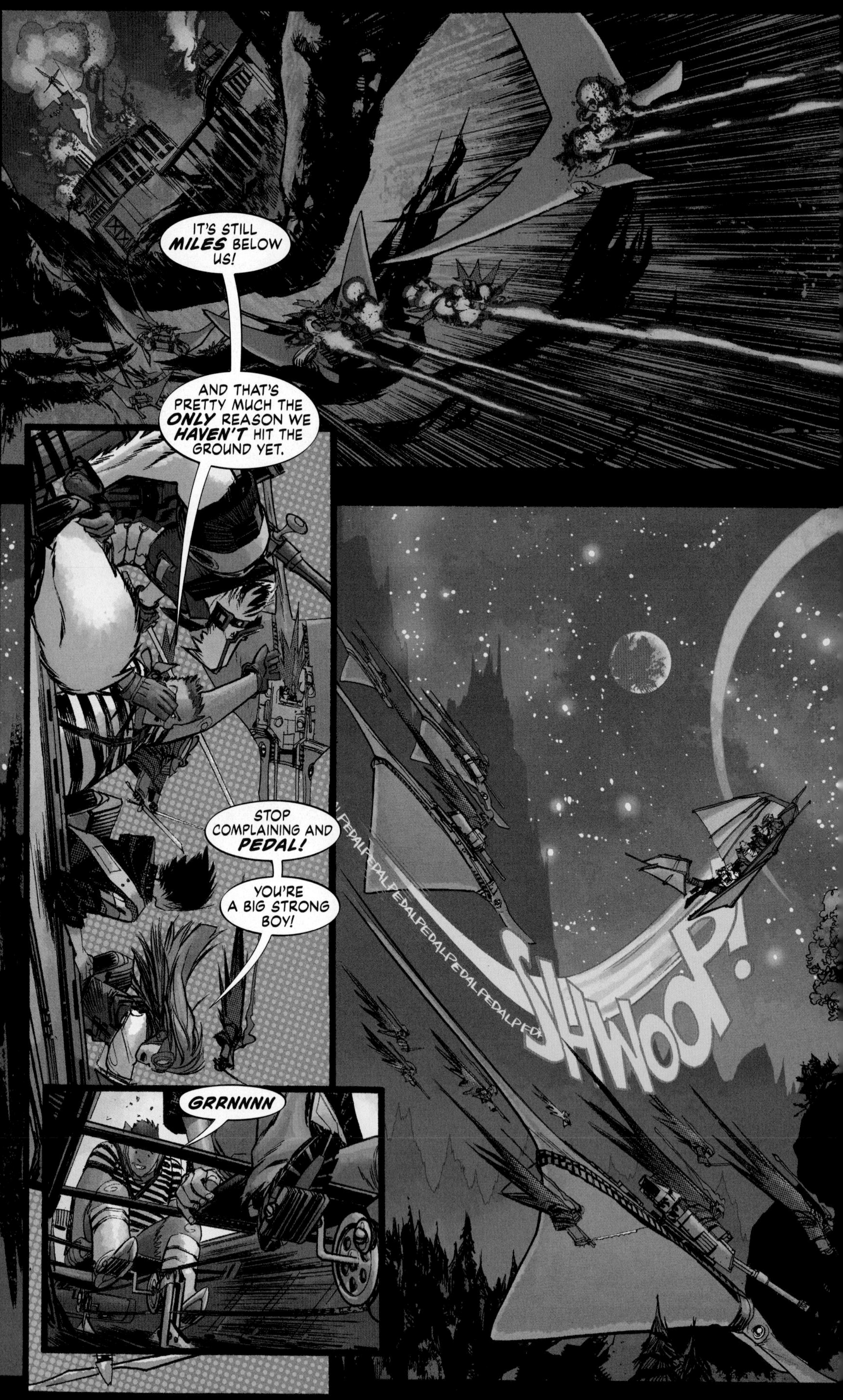
IT'S STILL MILES BELOW US!
AND THAT'S PRETTY MUCH THE ONLY REASON WE HAVEN'T HIT THE GROUND YET.
STOP COMPLAINING AND PEDAL!
YOU'RE A BIG STRONG BOY!
PEDALPEDALPEDALPEDALPEDALPEDALPED
SHWOOP!
GRRNNNN

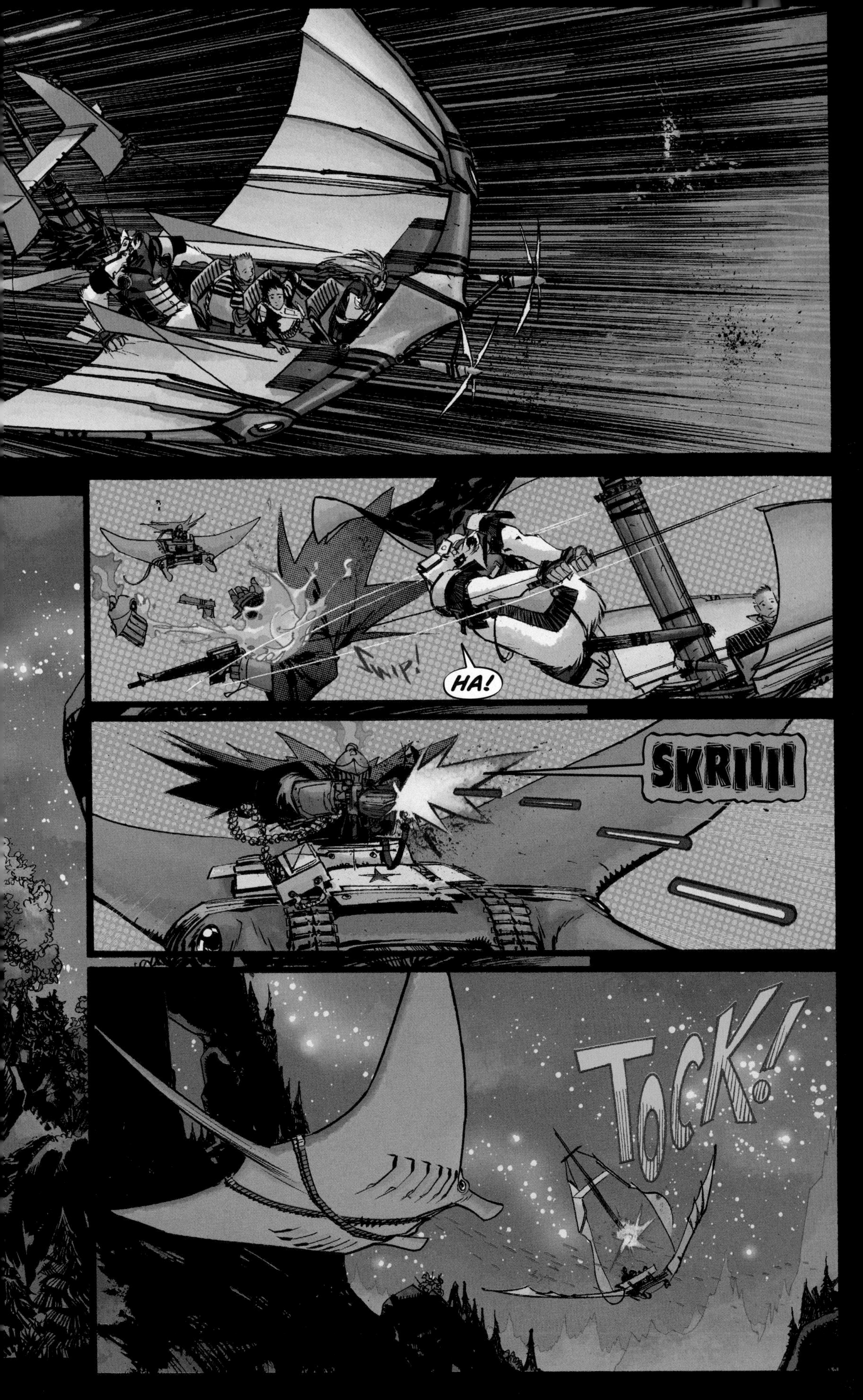
SWIP!
HA!
SKRIIII
TOCK!

THE *FAN* IN FRONT WAS A REALLY GOOD INNOVATION.

PROPELLERS WEREN'T REALLY *MY* IDEA.

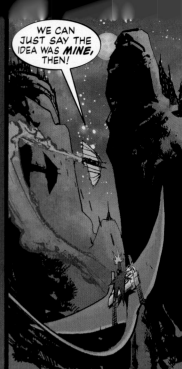

WE CAN JUST SAY THE IDEA WAS *MINE*, THEN!

THIS MANTA RIDER IS A PAIN IN MY ASS!

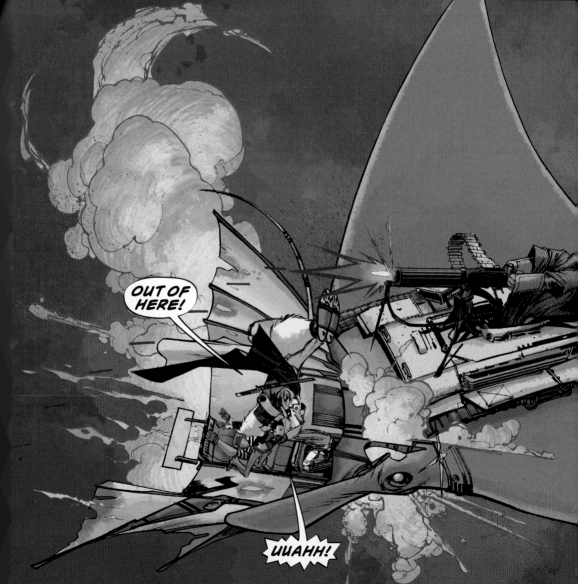

OUT OF HERE!

UUAHH!

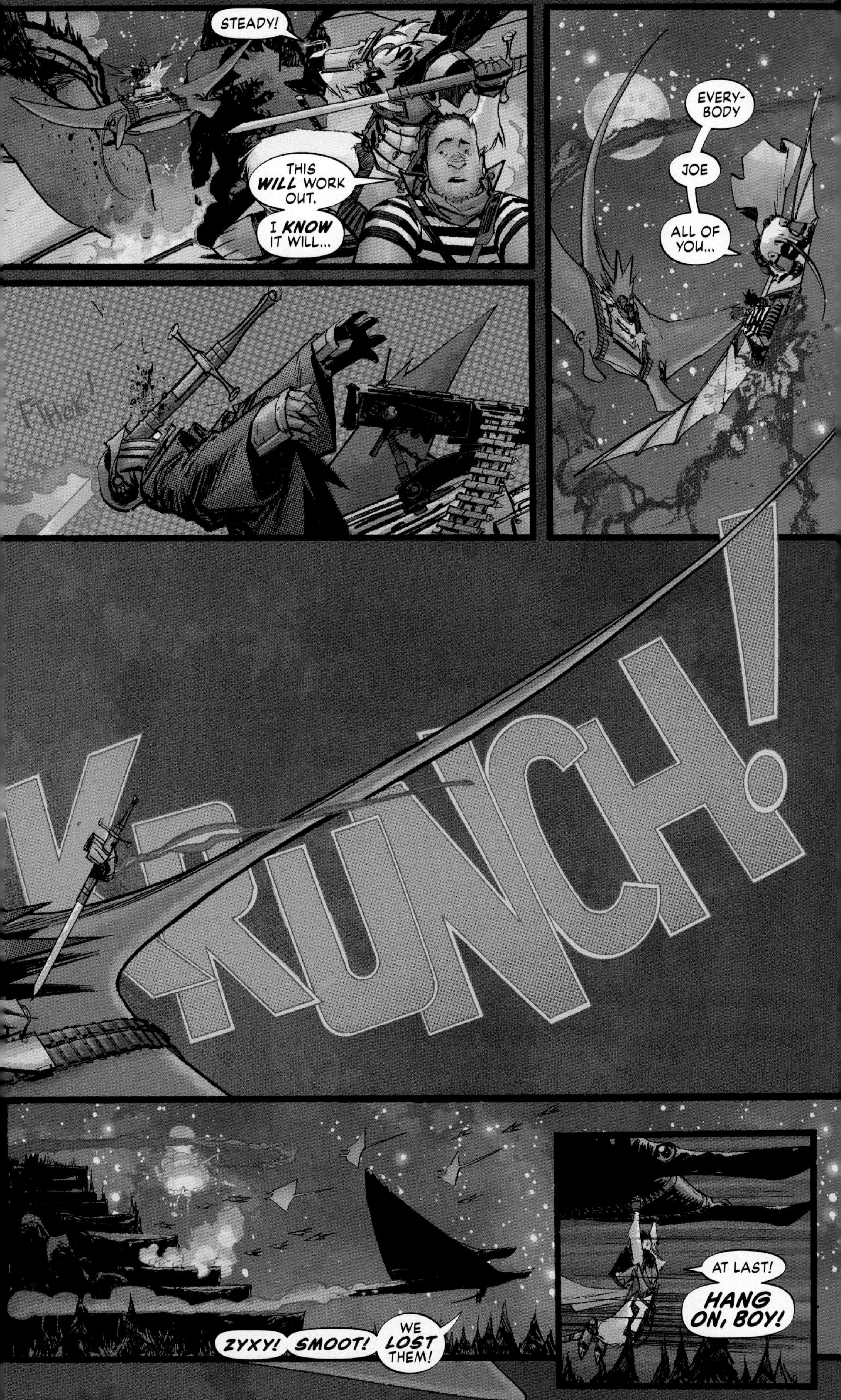
STEADY!
THIS WILL WORK OUT.
I KNOW IT WILL...
EVERY-BODY
JOE
ALL OF YOU...
FTHOK!
KRUNCH!
ZYXY!
SMOOT!
WE LOST THEM!
AT LAST!
HANG ON, BOY!

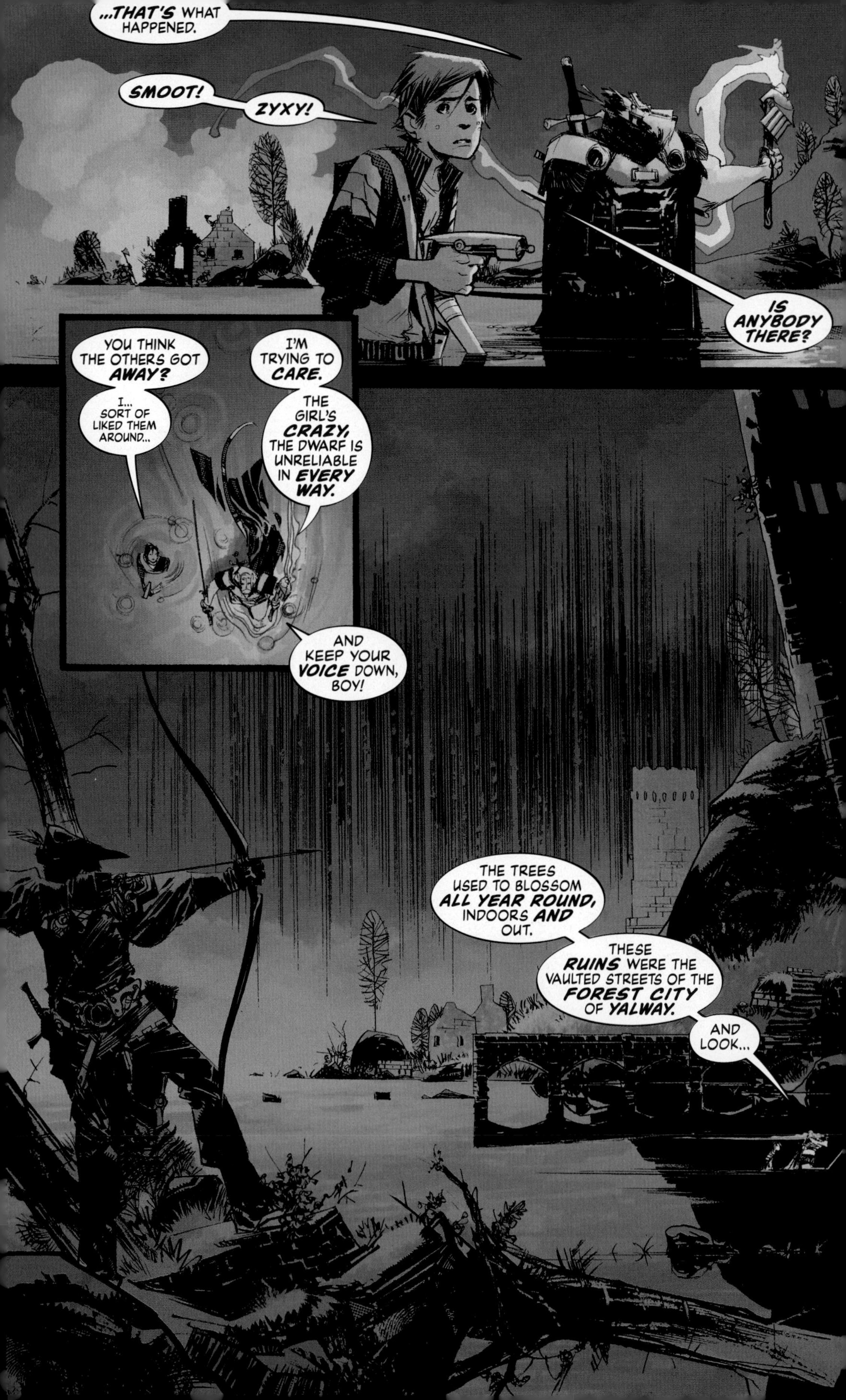
...THAT'S WHAT HAPPENED.
SMOOT!
ZYXY!
IS ANYBODY THERE?
YOU THINK THE OTHERS GOT AWAY?
I... SORT OF LIKED THEM AROUND...
I'M TRYING TO CARE.
THE GIRL'S CRAZY, THE DWARF IS UNRELIABLE IN EVERY WAY.
AND KEEP YOUR VOICE DOWN, BOY!
THE TREES USED TO BLOSSOM ALL YEAR ROUND, INDOORS AND OUT.
THESE RUINS WERE THE VAULTED STREETS OF THE FOREST CITY OF YALWAY.
AND LOOK...

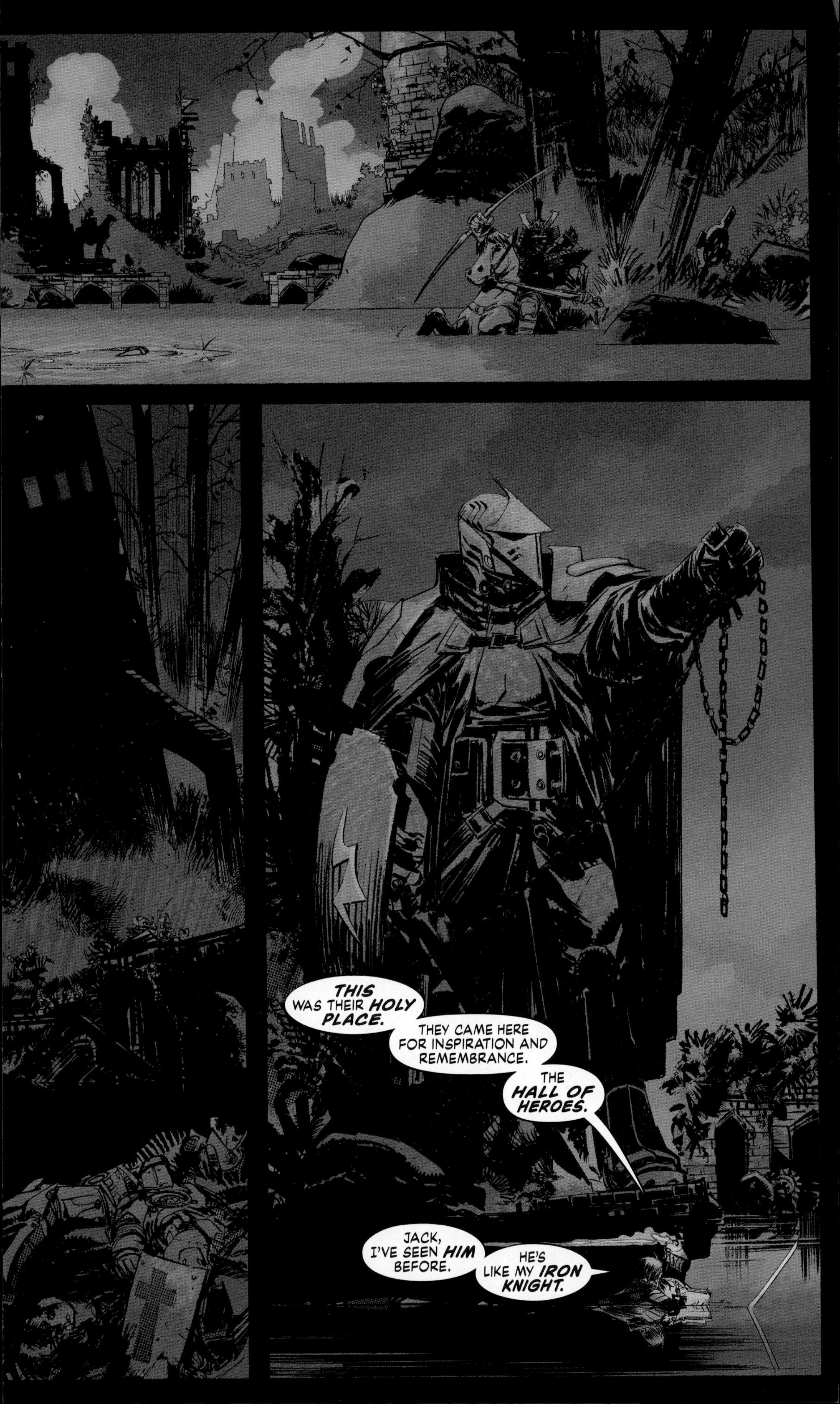
THIS WAS THEIR HOLY PLACE.
THEY CAME HERE FOR INSPIRATION AND REMEMBRANCE.
THE HALL OF HEROES.
JACK, I'VE SEEN HIM BEFORE.
HE'S LIKE MY IRON KNIGHT.

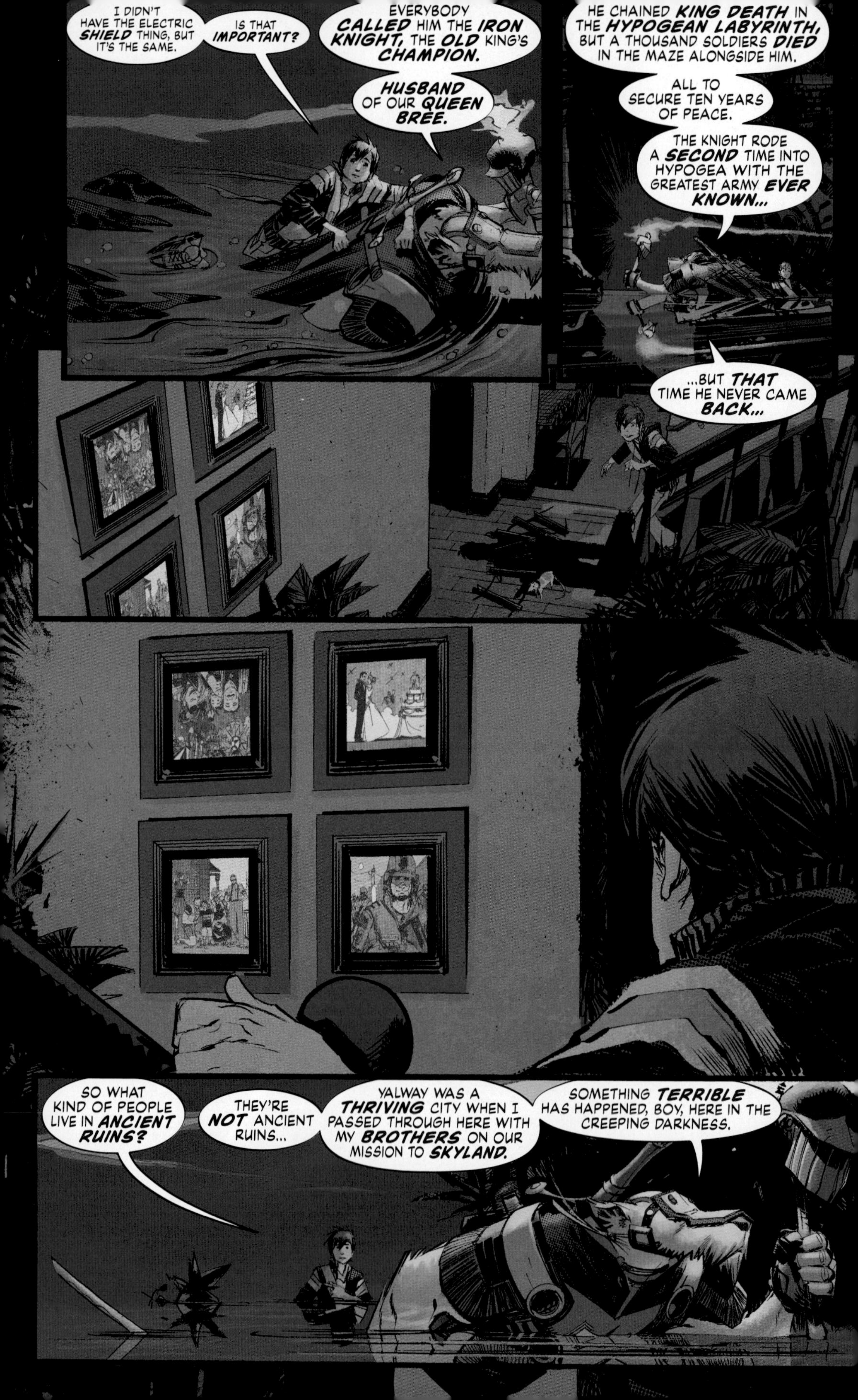
I DIDN'T HAVE THE ELECTRIC SHIELD THING, BUT IT'S THE SAME.
IS THAT IMPORTANT?
EVERYBODY CALLED HIM THE IRON KNIGHT, THE OLD KING'S CHAMPION.
HUSBAND OF OUR QUEEN BREE.
HE CHAINED KING DEATH IN THE HYPOGEAN LABYRINTH, BUT A THOUSAND SOLDIERS DIED IN THE MAZE ALONGSIDE HIM.
ALL TO SECURE TEN YEARS OF PEACE.
THE KNIGHT RODE A SECOND TIME INTO HYPOGEA WITH THE GREATEST ARMY EVER KNOWN...
...BUT THAT TIME HE NEVER CAME BACK...
SO WHAT KIND OF PEOPLE LIVE IN ANCIENT RUINS?
THEY'RE NOT ANCIENT RUINS...
YALWAY WAS A THRIVING CITY WHEN I PASSED THROUGH HERE WITH MY BROTHERS ON OUR MISSION TO SKYLAND.
SOMETHING TERRIBLE HAS HAPPENED, BOY, HERE IN THE CREEPING DARKNESS.

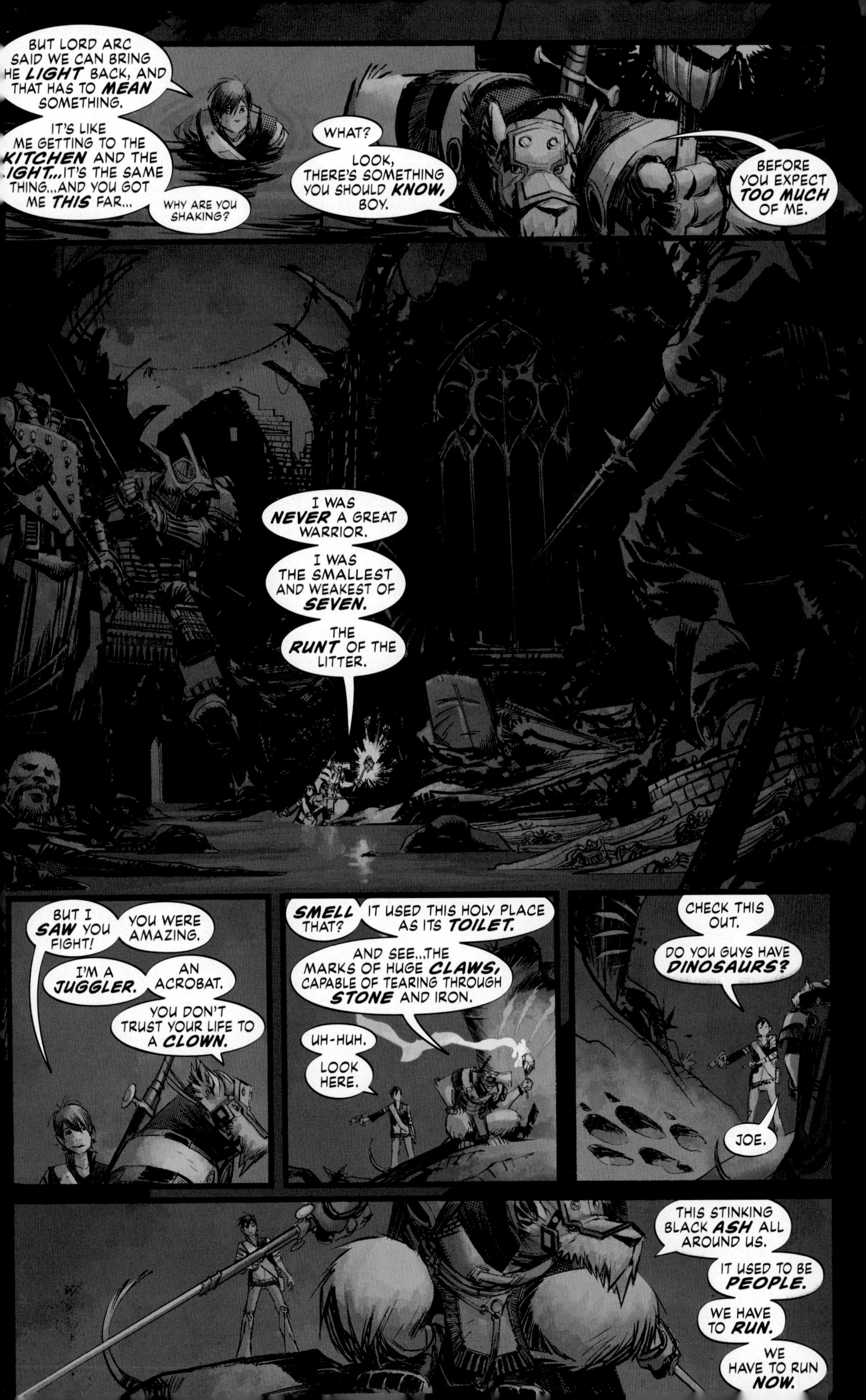
BUT LORD ARC SAID WE CAN BRING HE LIGHT BACK, AND THAT HAS TO MEAN SOMETHING.
IT'S LIKE ME GETTING TO THE KITCHEN AND THE IGHT...IT'S THE SAME THING...AND YOU GOT ME THIS FAR...
WHY ARE YOU SHAKING?
WHAT?
LOOK, THERE'S SOMETHING YOU SHOULD KNOW, BOY.
BEFORE YOU EXPECT TOO MUCH OF ME.
I WAS NEVER A GREAT WARRIOR.
I WAS THE SMALLEST AND WEAKEST OF SEVEN.
THE RUNT OF THE LITTER.
BUT I SAW YOU FIGHT!
YOU WERE AMAZING.
I'M A JUGGLER.
AN ACROBAT.
YOU DON'T TRUST YOUR LIFE TO A CLOWN.
SMELL THAT?
IT USED THIS HOLY PLACE AS ITS TOILET.
AND SEE...THE MARKS OF HUGE CLAWS, CAPABLE OF TEARING THROUGH STONE AND IRON.
UH-HUH.
LOOK HERE.
CHECK THIS OUT.
DO YOU GUYS HAVE DINOSAURS?
JOE.
THIS STINKING BLACK ASH ALL AROUND US.
IT USED TO BE PEOPLE.
WE HAVE TO RUN.
WE HAVE TO RUN NOW.

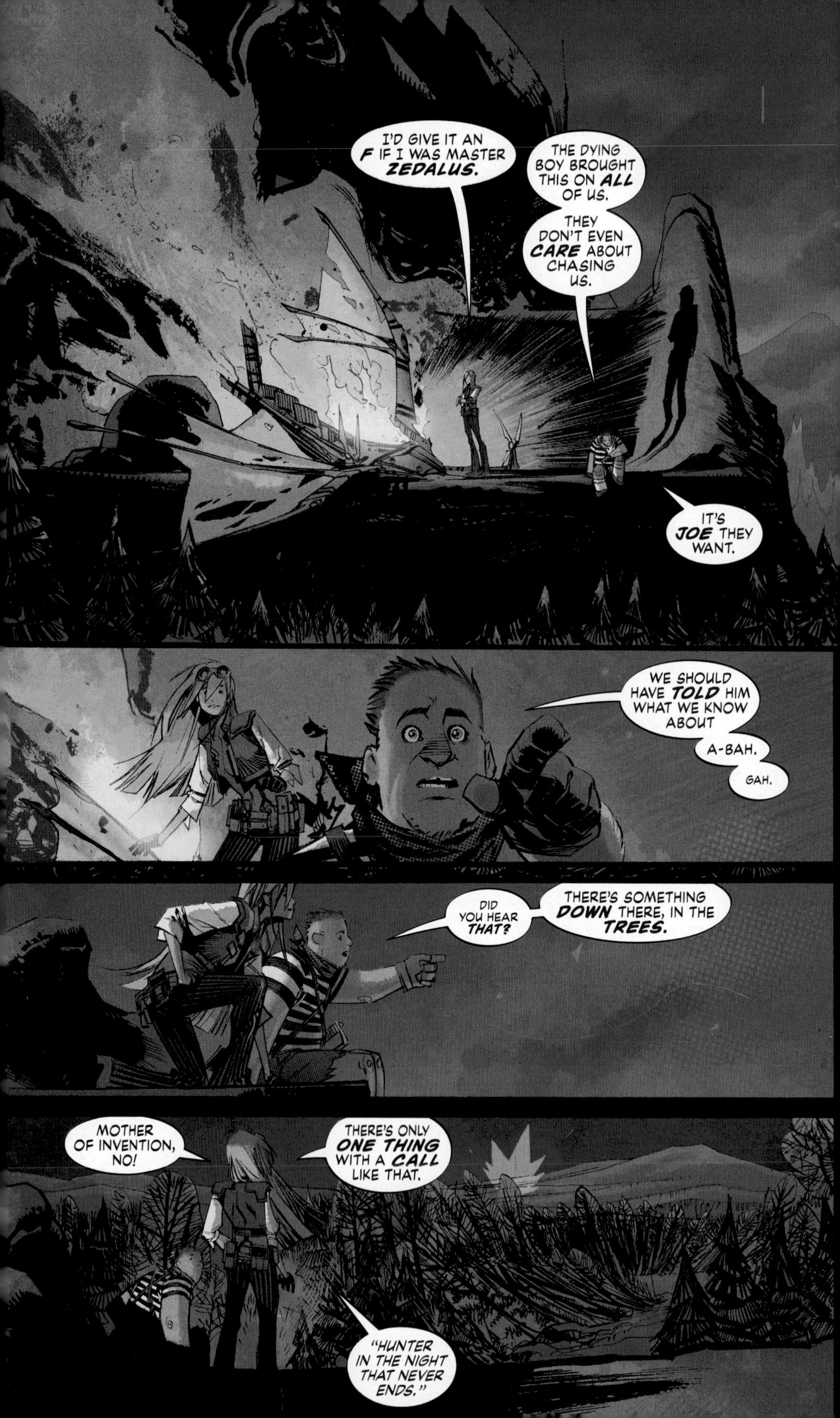
I'D GIVE IT AN *F* IF I WAS MASTER **ZEDALUS.**
THE DYING BOY BROUGHT THIS ON **ALL** OF US.
THEY DON'T EVEN **CARE** ABOUT CHASING US.
IT'S **JOE** THEY WANT.
WE SHOULD HAVE **TOLD** HIM WHAT WE KNOW ABOUT
A-BAH.
GAH.
DID YOU HEAR **THAT?**
THERE'S SOMETHING **DOWN** THERE, IN THE **TREES.**
MOTHER OF INVENTION, NO!
THERE'S ONLY **ONE THING** WITH A **CALL** LIKE THAT.
"HUNTER IN THE NIGHT THAT NEVER ENDS."

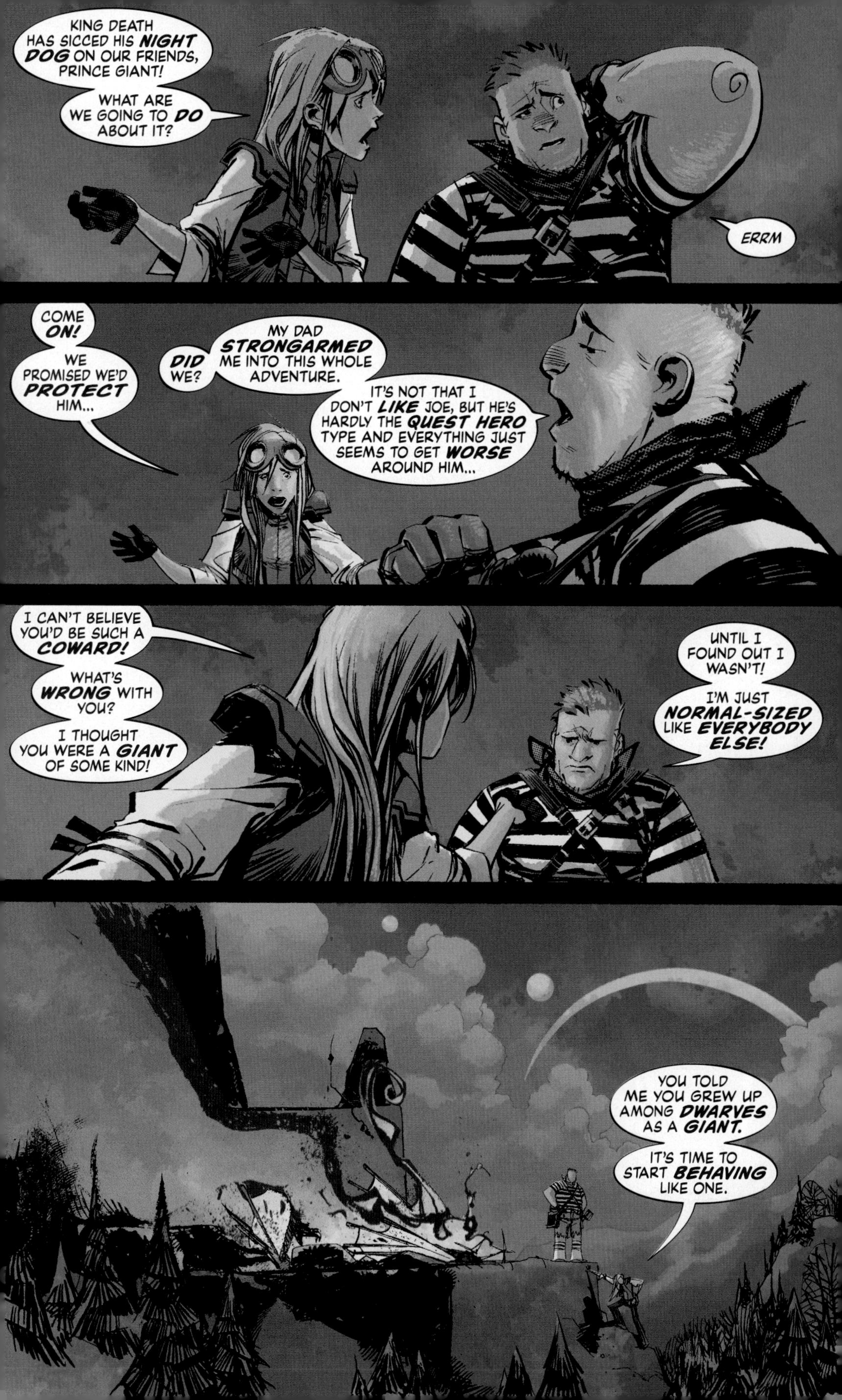

KING DEATH HAS SICCED HIS NIGHT DOG ON OUR FRIENDS, PRINCE GIANT!
WHAT ARE WE GOING TO DO ABOUT IT?
ERRM
COME ON!
WE PROMISED WE'D PROTECT HIM...
DID WE?
MY DAD STRONGARMED ME INTO THIS WHOLE ADVENTURE.
IT'S NOT THAT I DON'T LIKE JOE, BUT HE'S HARDLY THE QUEST HERO TYPE AND EVERYTHING JUST SEEMS TO GET WORSE AROUND HIM...
I CAN'T BELIEVE YOU'D BE SUCH A COWARD!
WHAT'S WRONG WITH YOU?
I THOUGHT YOU WERE A GIANT OF SOME KIND!
UNTIL I FOUND OUT I WASN'T!
I'M JUST NORMAL-SIZED LIKE EVERYBODY ELSE!
YOU TOLD ME YOU GREW UP AMONG DWARVES AS A GIANT.
IT'S TIME TO START BEHAVING LIKE ONE.

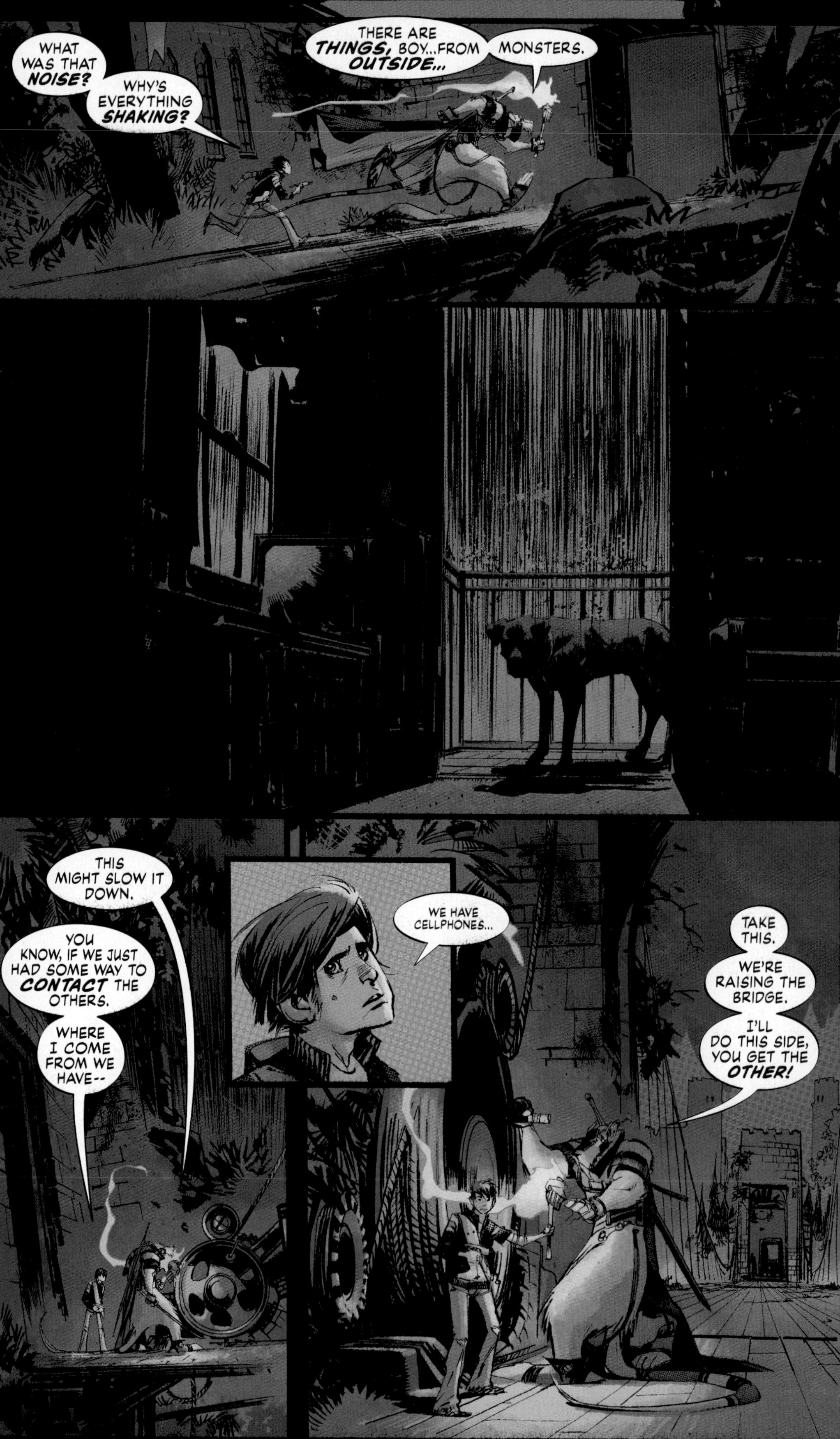

WHAT WAS THAT **NOISE?**
WHY'S EVERYTHING **SHAKING?**
THERE ARE **THINGS,** BOY...FROM **OUTSIDE...**
MONSTERS.
THIS MIGHT SLOW IT DOWN.
YOU KNOW, IF WE JUST HAD SOME WAY TO **CONTACT** THE OTHERS.
WHERE I COME FROM WE HAVE--
WE HAVE CELLPHONES...
TAKE THIS.
WE'RE RAISING THE BRIDGE.
I'LL DO THIS SIDE, YOU GET THE **OTHER!**

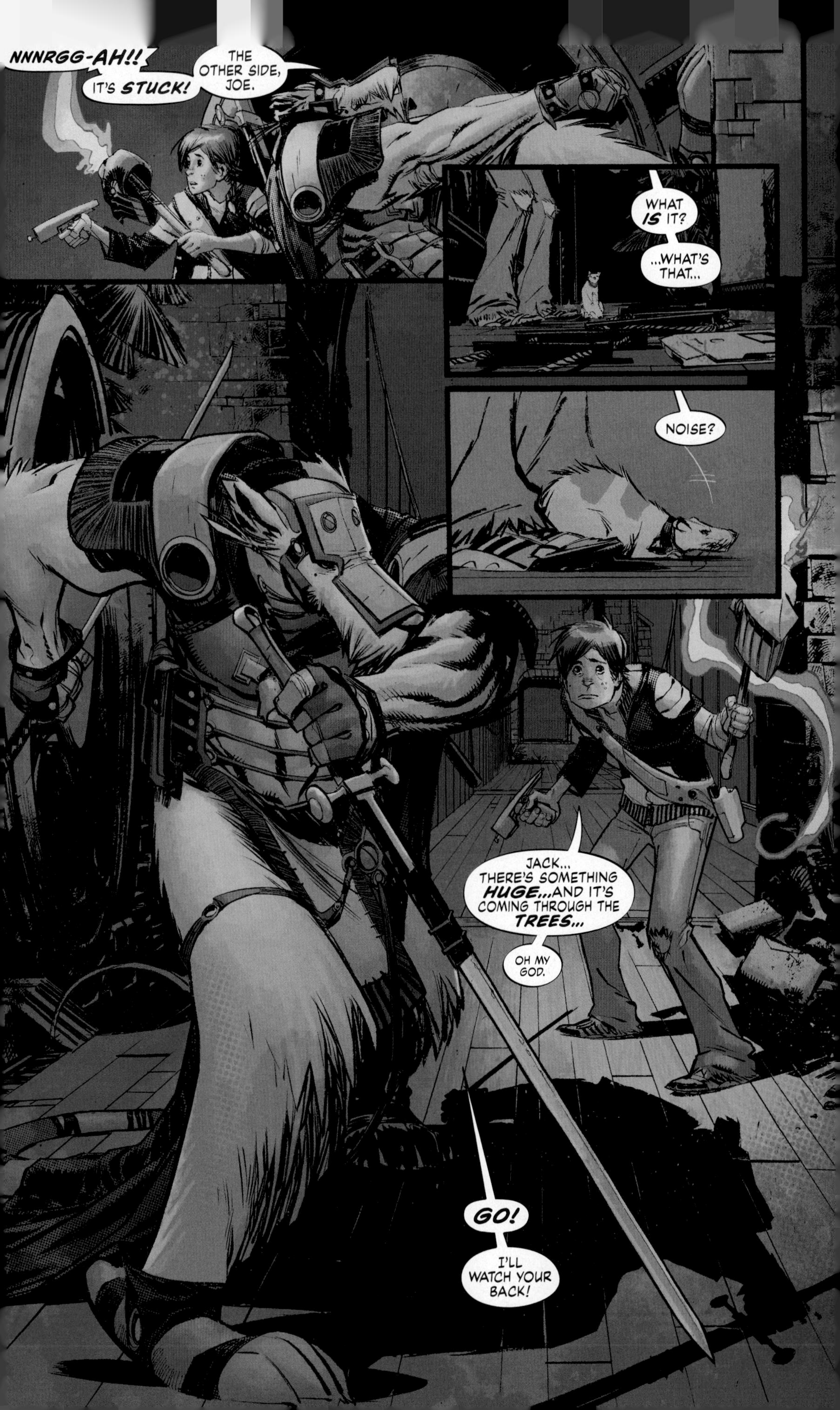
NNNRGG-AH!!
IT'S STUCK!
THE OTHER SIDE, JOE.
WHAT IS IT?
...WHAT'S THAT...
NOISE?
JACK... THERE'S SOMETHING HUGE...AND IT'S COMING THROUGH THE TREES...
OH MY GOD.
GO!
I'LL WATCH YOUR BACK!

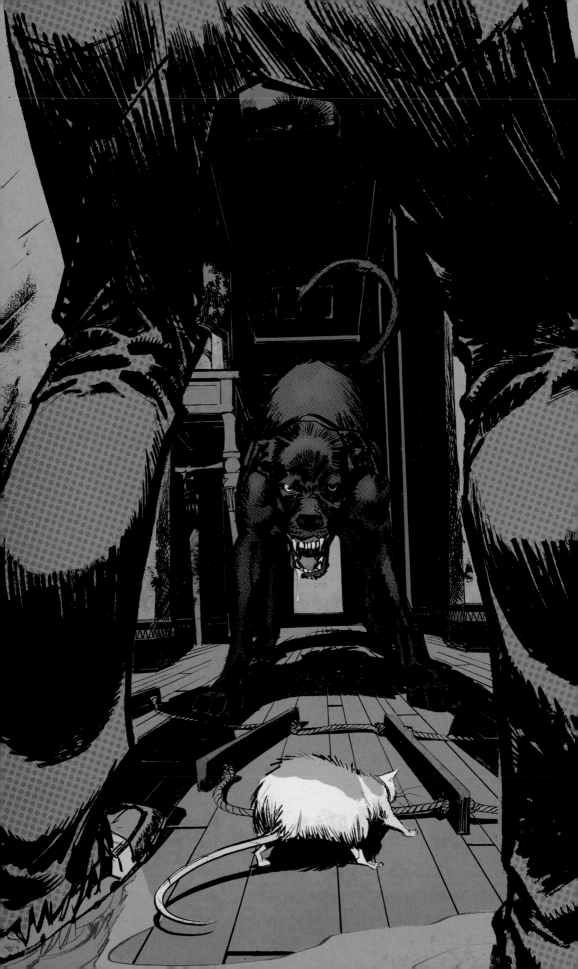

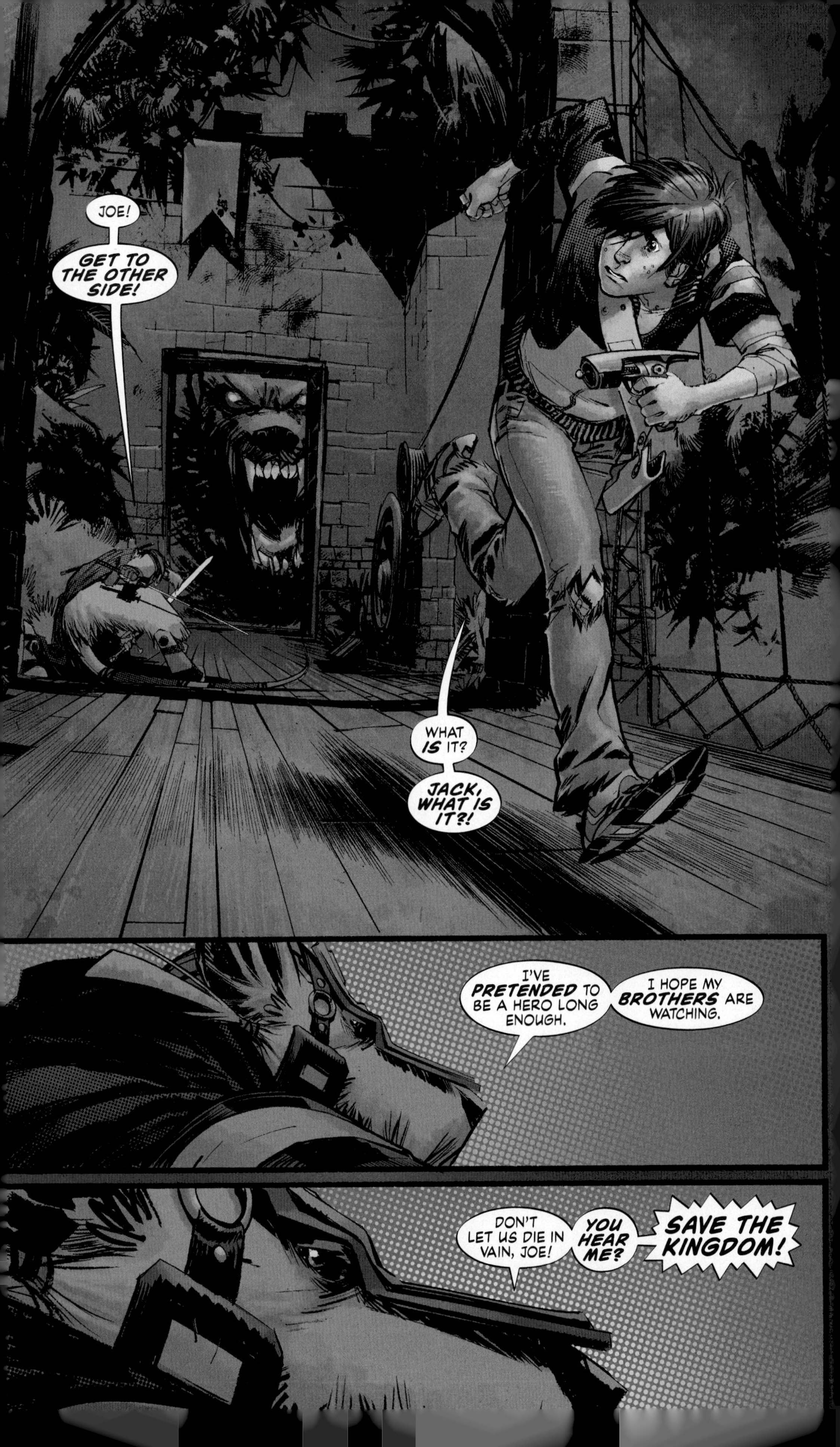
JOE!
GET TO THE OTHER SIDE!
WHAT *IS* IT?
JACK, WHAT IS IT?!
I'VE *PRETENDED* TO BE A HERO LONG ENOUGH.
I HOPE MY *BROTHERS* ARE WATCHING.
DON'T LET US DIE IN VAIN, JOE!
YOU HEAR ME?
SAVE THE KINGDOM!

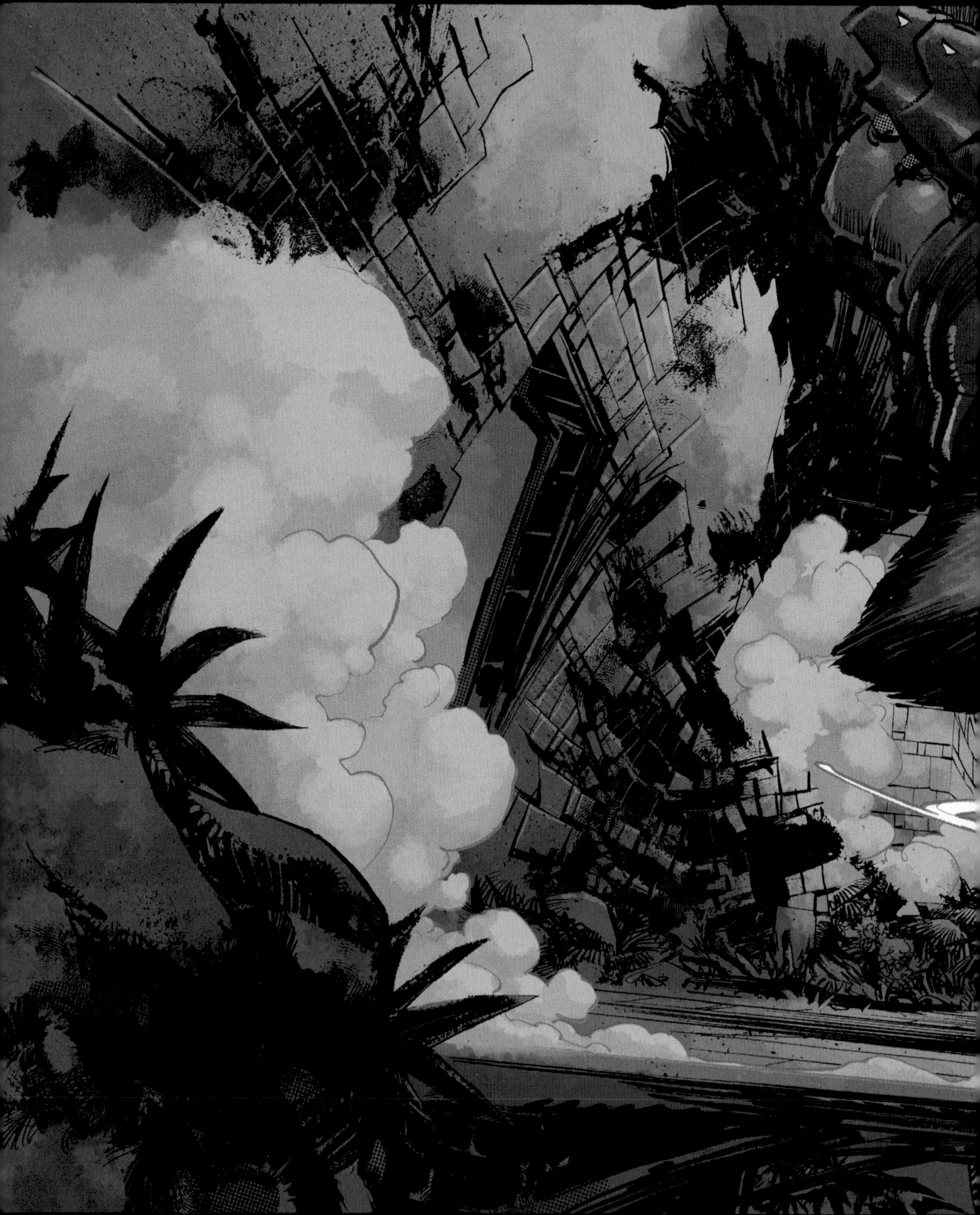

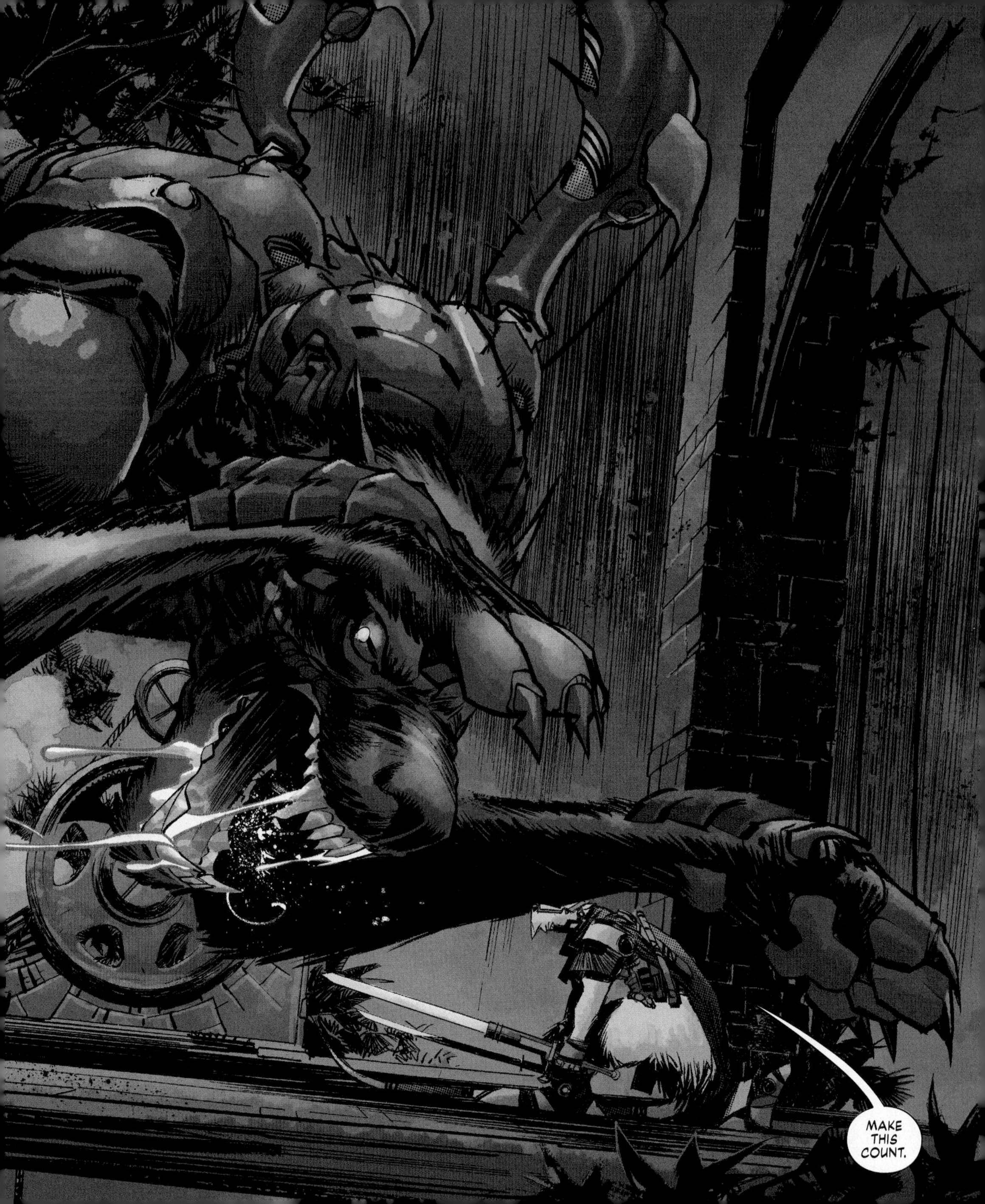
MAKE THIS COUNT.

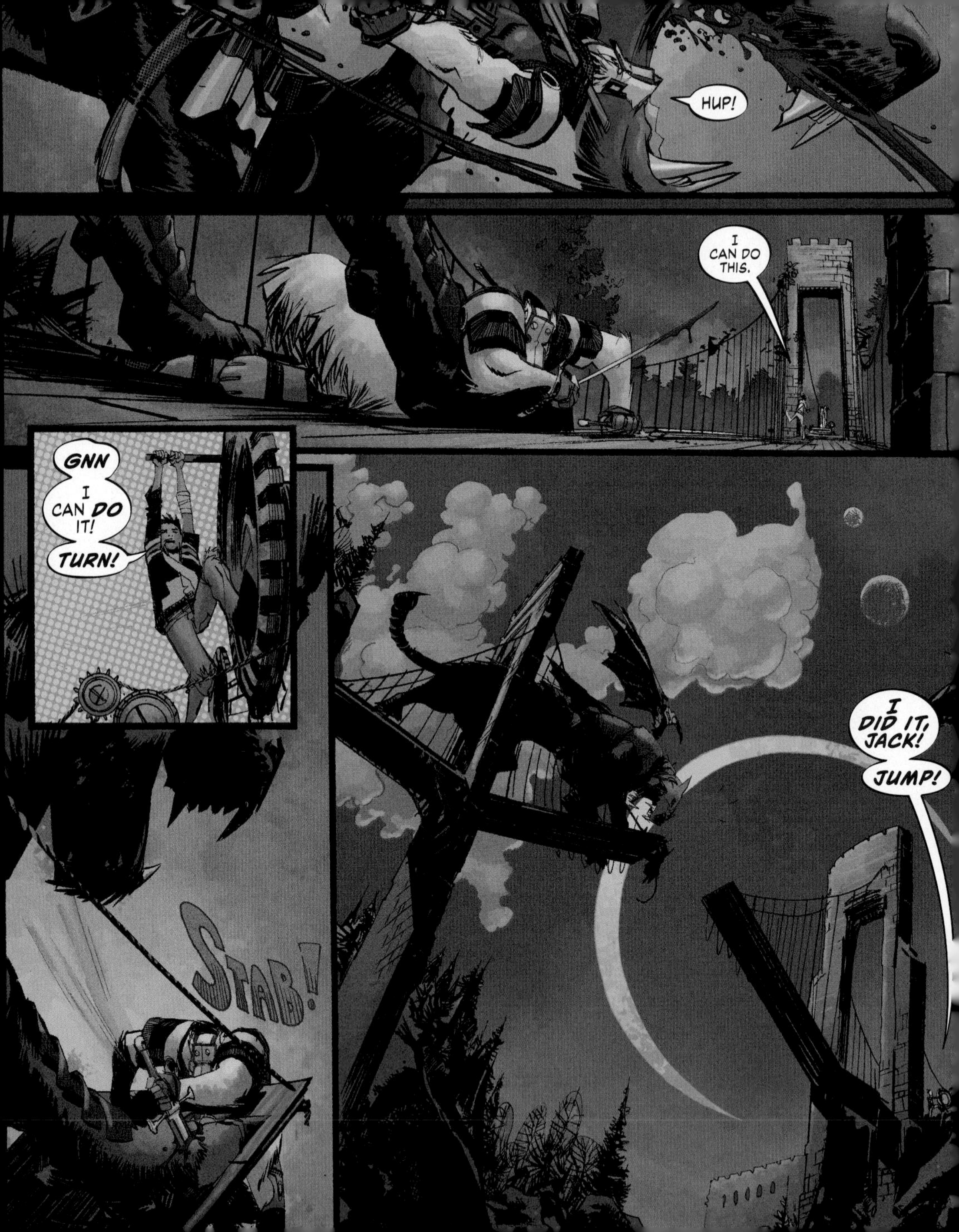
HUP!
I CAN DO THIS.
GNN
I CAN DO IT!
TURN!
STAB!
I DID IT, JACK!
JUMP!

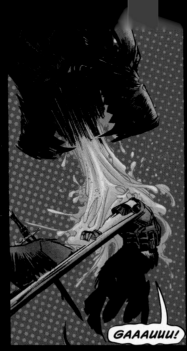

JUMP!

GAAAUUU!

YOU WON'T HAVE HIM.

YOU'LL NEVER TAKE US ALL.

SHLUK!

HA!

JACK! NOW!!

LEAP!

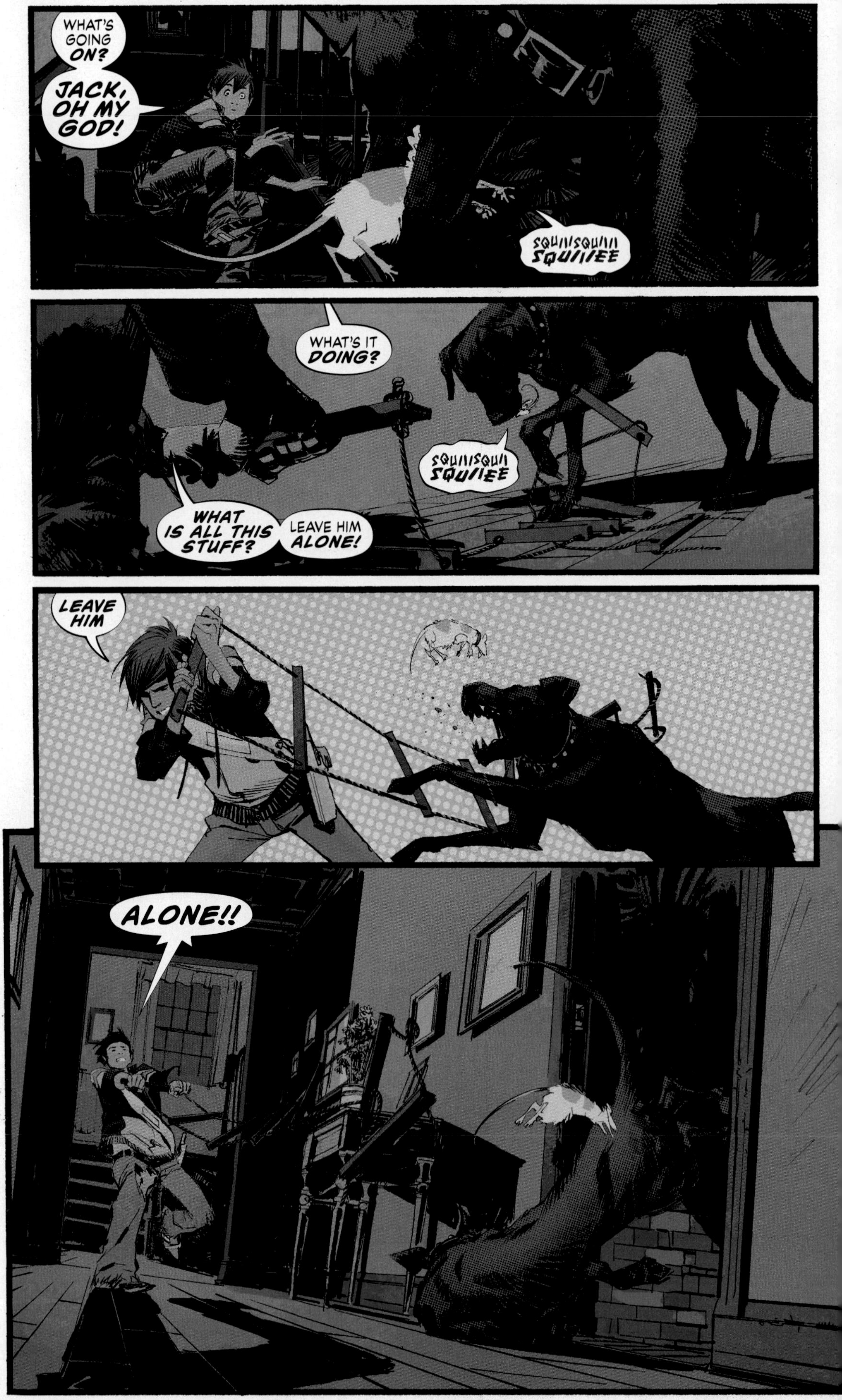
WHAT'S GOING ON?
JACK, OH MY GOD!
SQUIISQUII SQUIIEE
WHAT'S IT DOING?
SQUIISQUII SQUIIEE
WHAT IS ALL THIS STUFF?
LEAVE HIM ALONE!
LEAVE HIM
ALONE!!

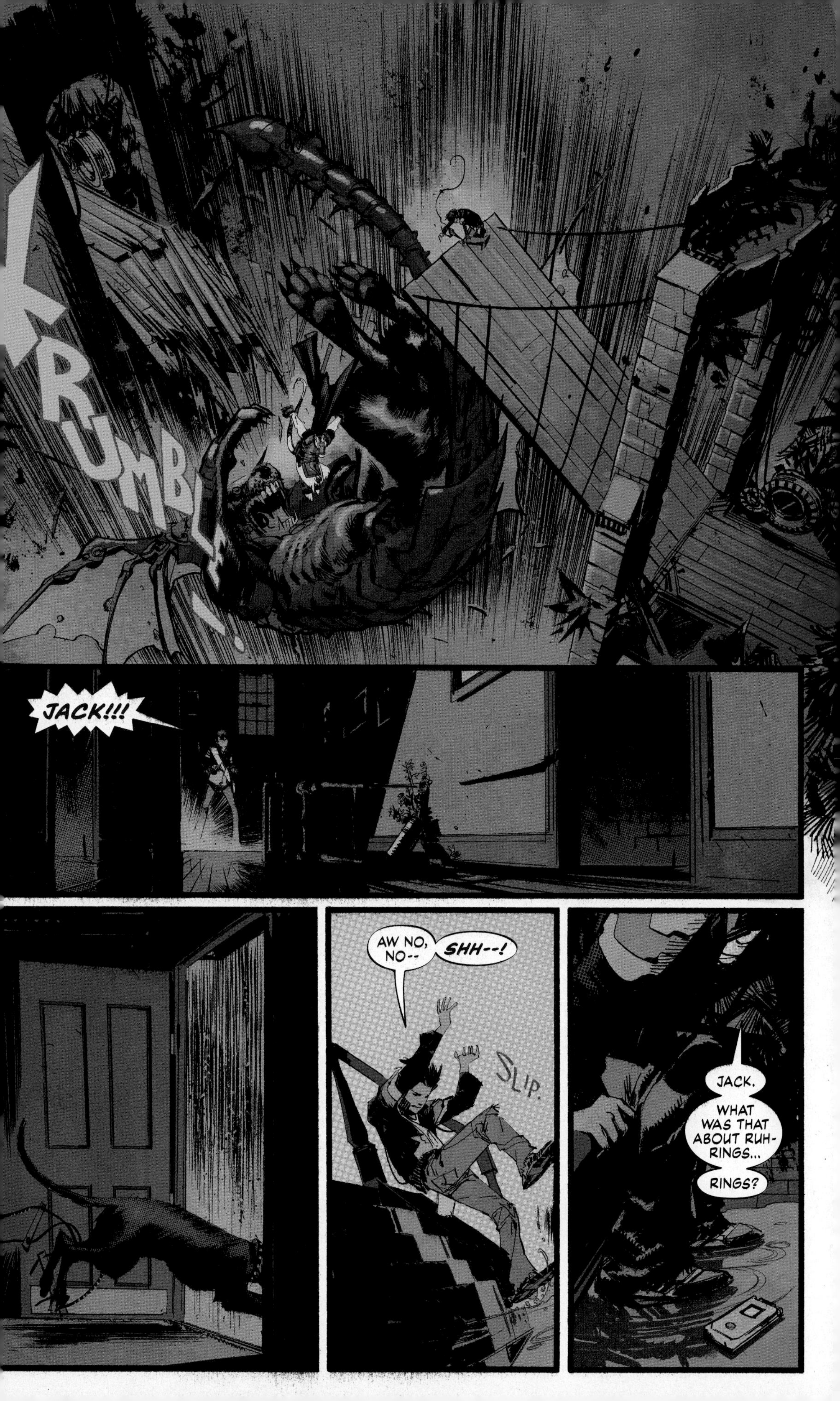
KRUMBLE!
JACK!!!
AW NO, NO--
SHH--!
SLIP.
JACK.
WHAT WAS THAT ABOUT RUH-RINGS...
RINGS?

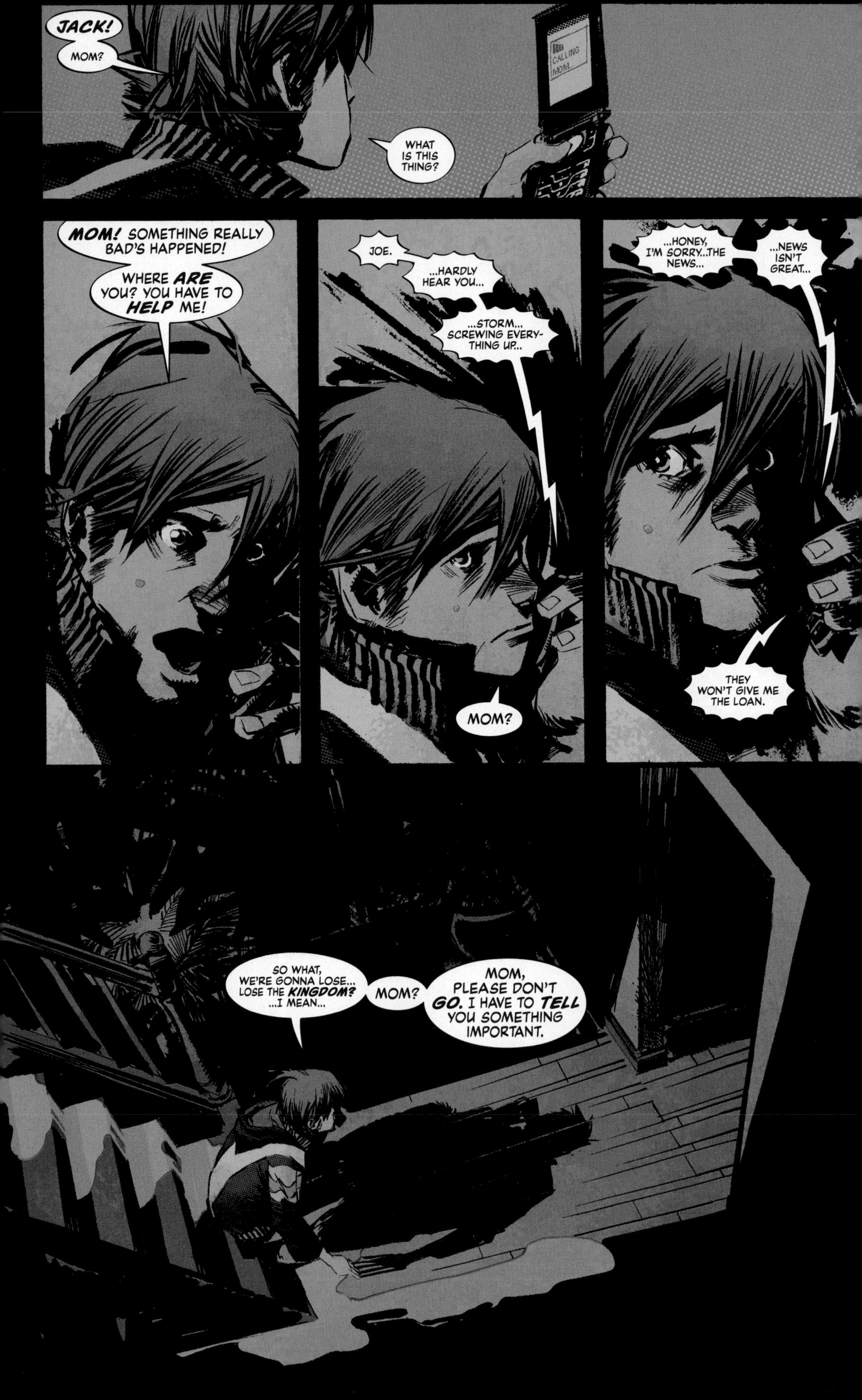

JACK!
MOM?
CALLING MOM...
WHAT IS THIS THING?
MOM! SOMETHING REALLY BAD'S HAPPENED!
WHERE ARE YOU? YOU HAVE TO HELP ME!
JOE.
...HARDLY HEAR YOU...
...STORM... SCREWING EVERY-THING UP...
MOM?
...HONEY, I'M SORRY...THE NEWS...
...NEWS ISN'T GREAT...
THEY WON'T GIVE ME THE LOAN.
SO WHAT, WE'RE GONNA LOSE... LOSE THE KINGDOM? ...I MEAN...
MOM?
MOM, PLEASE DON'T GO. I HAVE TO TELL YOU SOMETHING IMPORTANT.

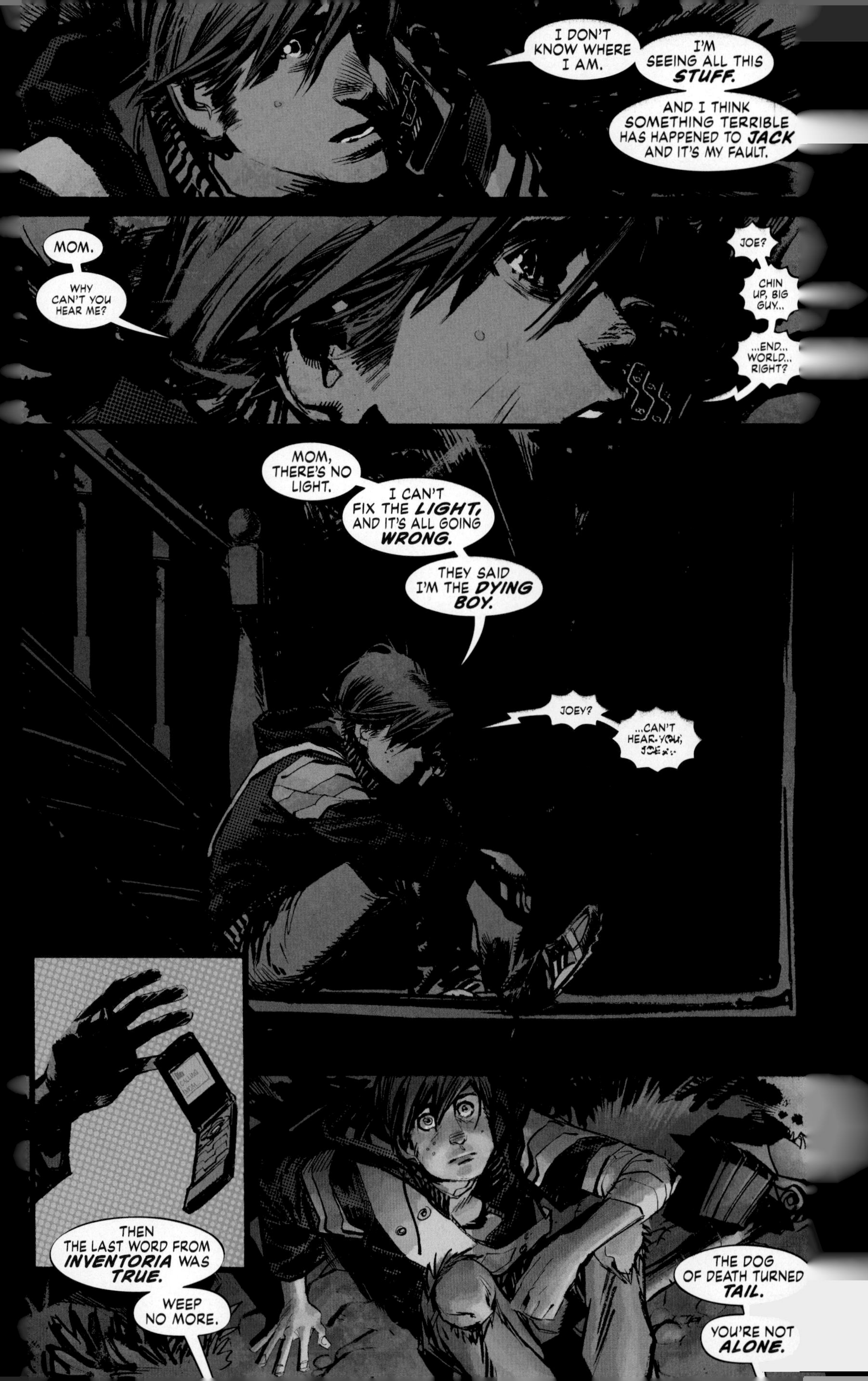
I DON'T KNOW WHERE I AM.
I'M SEEING ALL THIS STUFF.
AND I THINK SOMETHING TERRIBLE HAS HAPPENED TO JACK AND IT'S MY FAULT.
MOM.
WHY CAN'T YOU HEAR ME?
JOE?
CHIN UP, BIG GUY...
...END... WORLD... RIGHT?
MOM, THERE'S NO LIGHT.
I CAN'T FIX THE LIGHT, AND IT'S ALL GOING WRONG.
THEY SAID I'M THE DYING BOY.
JOEY?
...CAN'T HEAR YOU,
THEN THE LAST WORD FROM INVENTORIA WAS TRUE.
WEEP NO MORE.
THE DOG OF DEATH TURNED TAIL.
YOU'RE NOT ALONE.

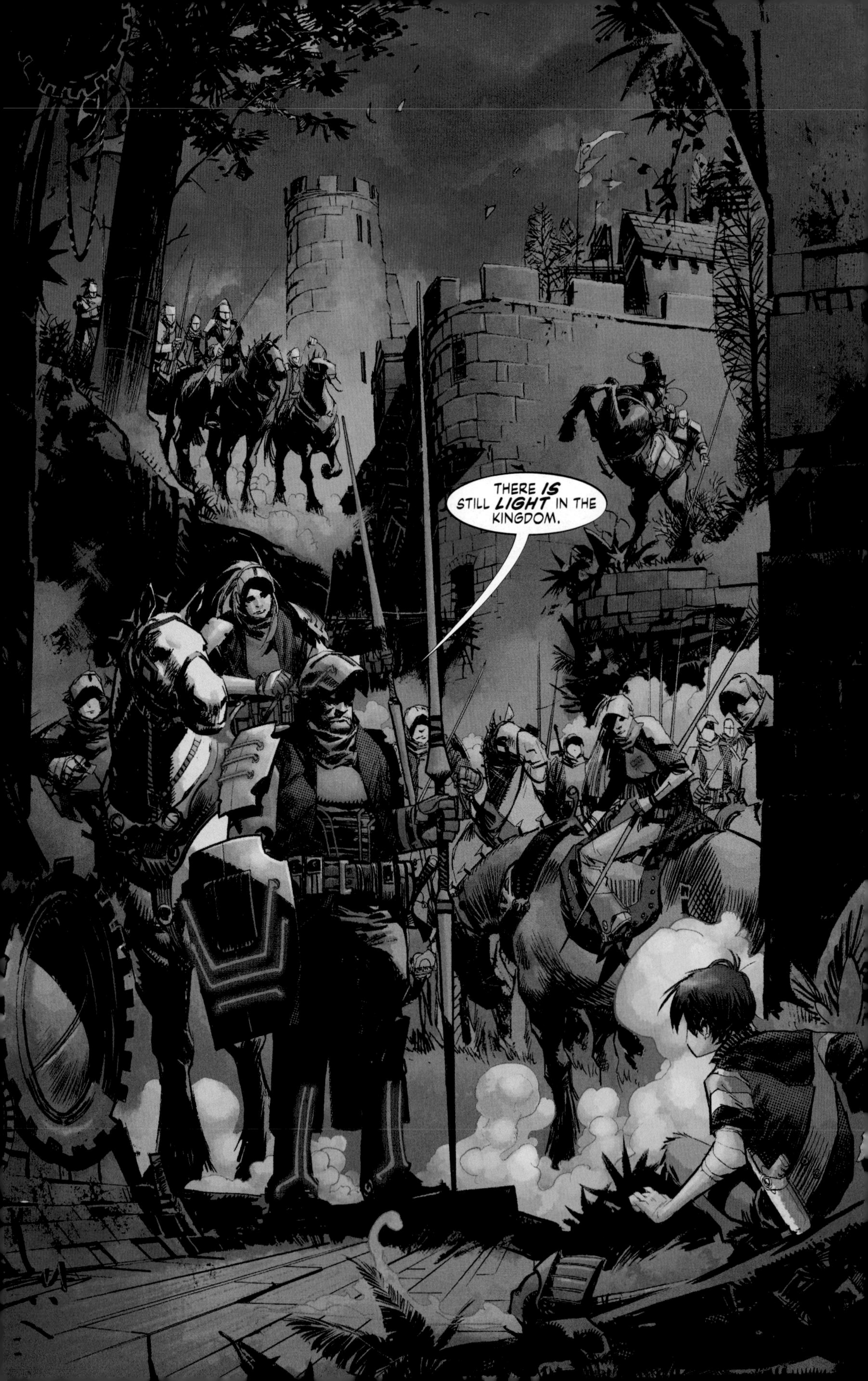
THERE IS STILL LIGHT IN THE KINGDOM.

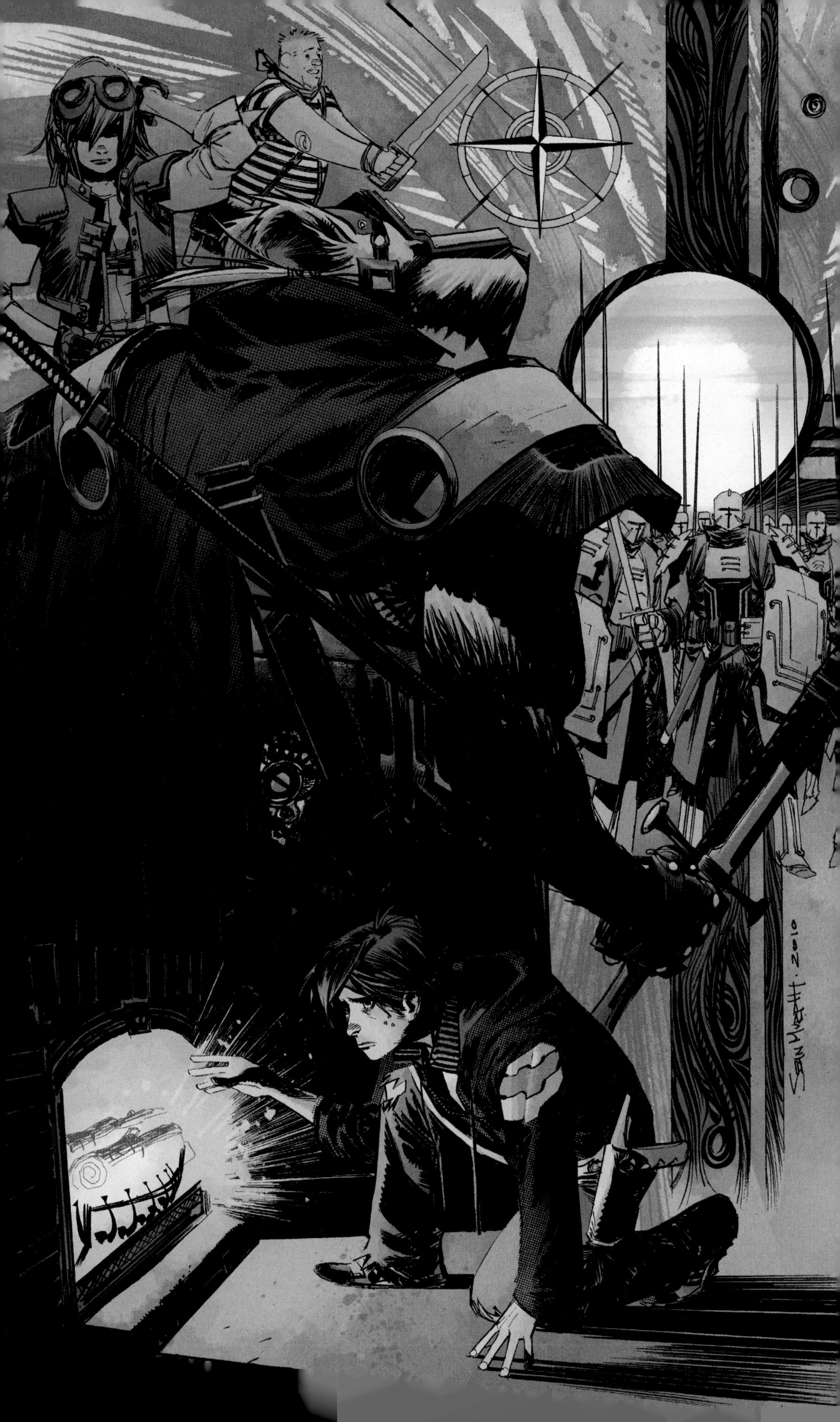

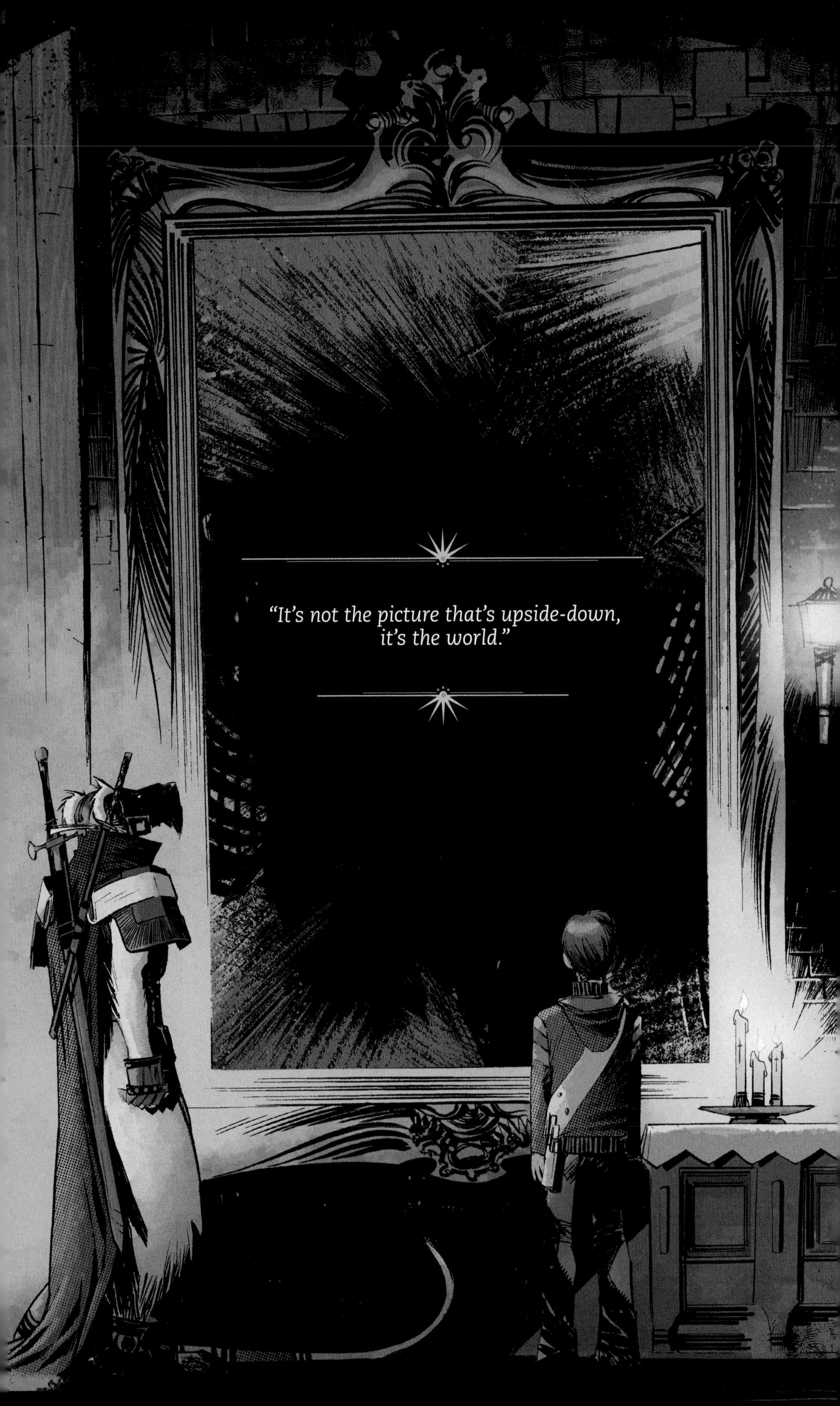
"It's not the picture that's upside-down,
it's the world."

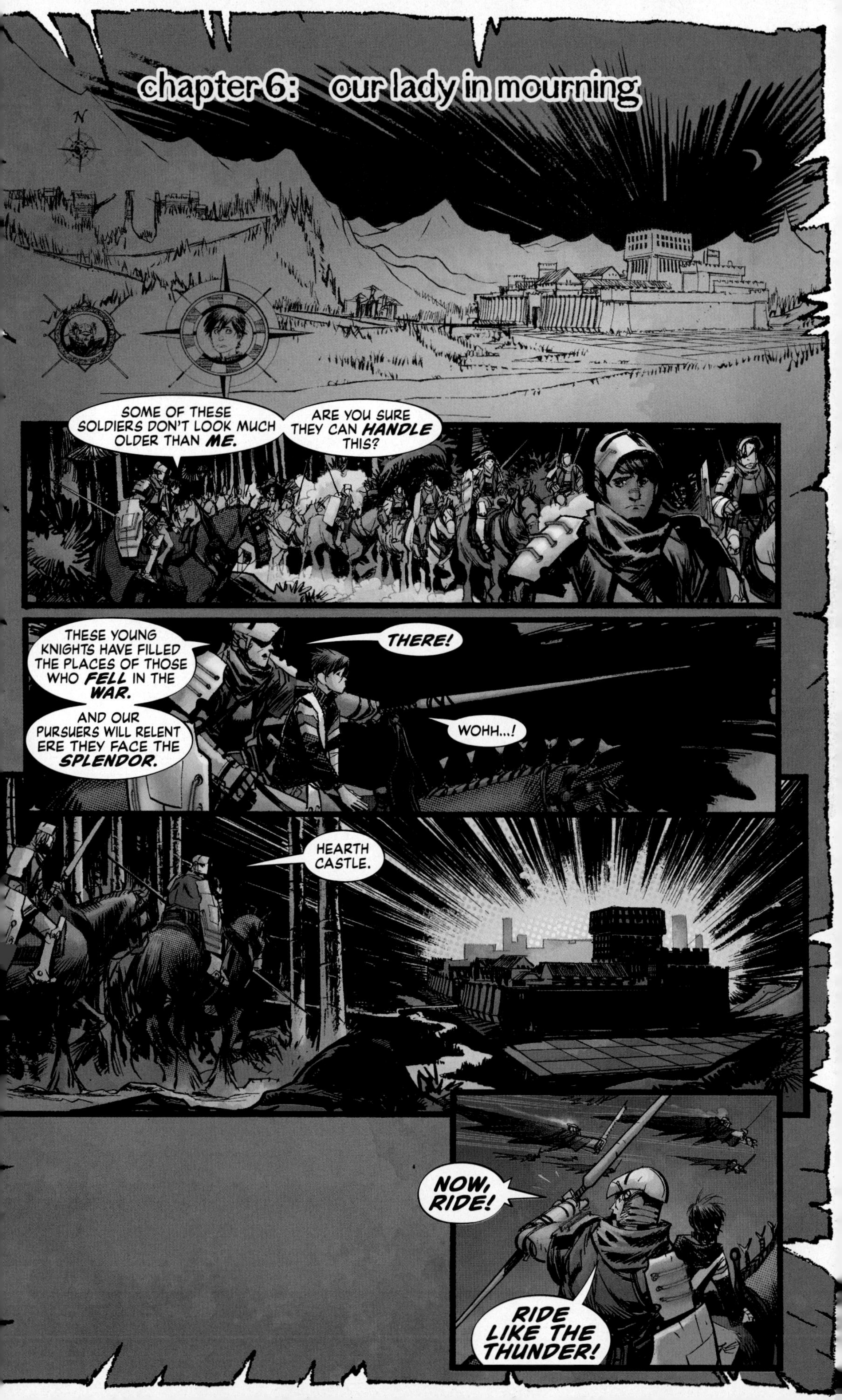
chapter 6: our lady in mourning
N
SOME OF THESE SOLDIERS DON'T LOOK MUCH OLDER THAN ME.
ARE YOU SURE THEY CAN HANDLE THIS?
THESE YOUNG KNIGHTS HAVE FILLED THE PLACES OF THOSE WHO FELL IN THE WAR.
AND OUR PURSUERS WILL RELENT ERE THEY FACE THE SPLENDOR.
THERE!
WOHH...!
HEARTH CASTLE.
NOW, RIDE!
RIDE LIKE THE THUNDER!

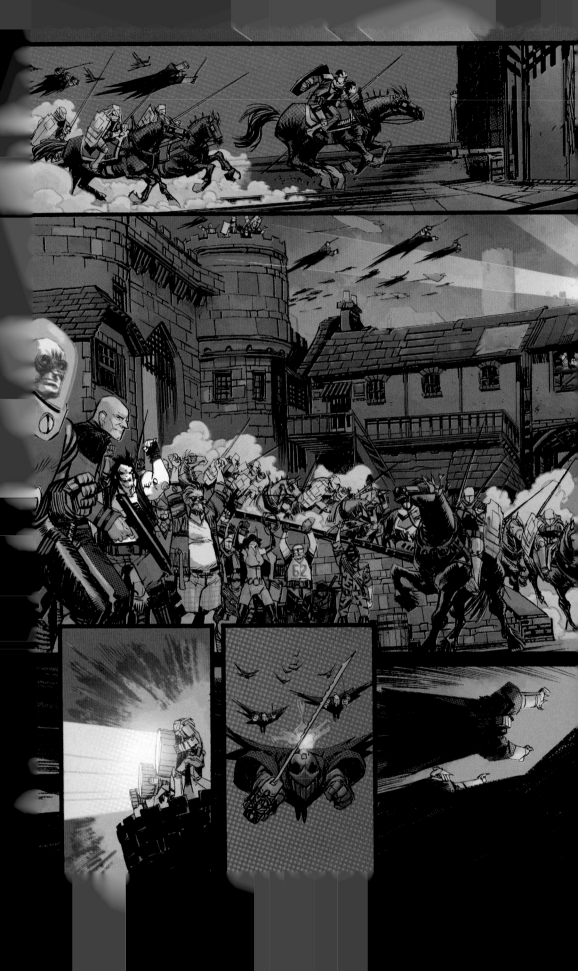

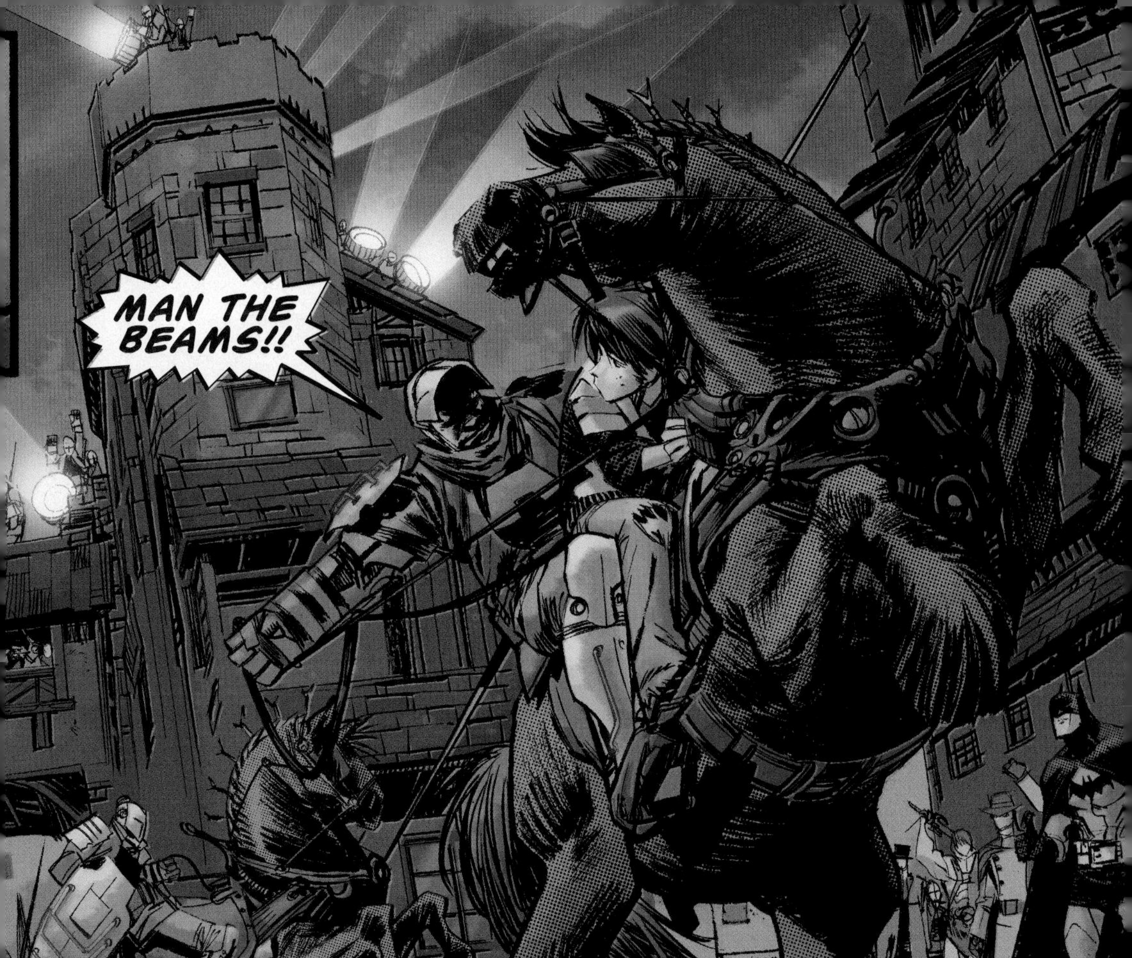
MAN THE BEAMS!!
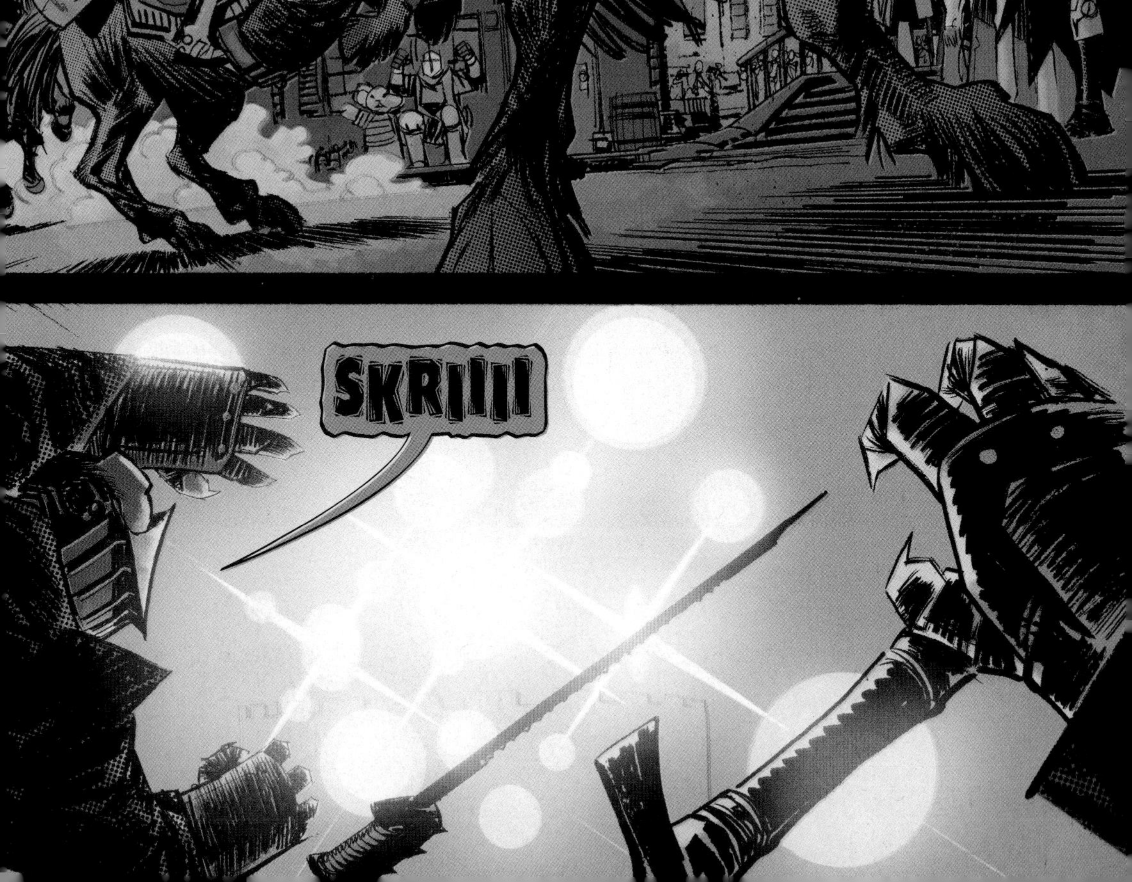
SKRIIII

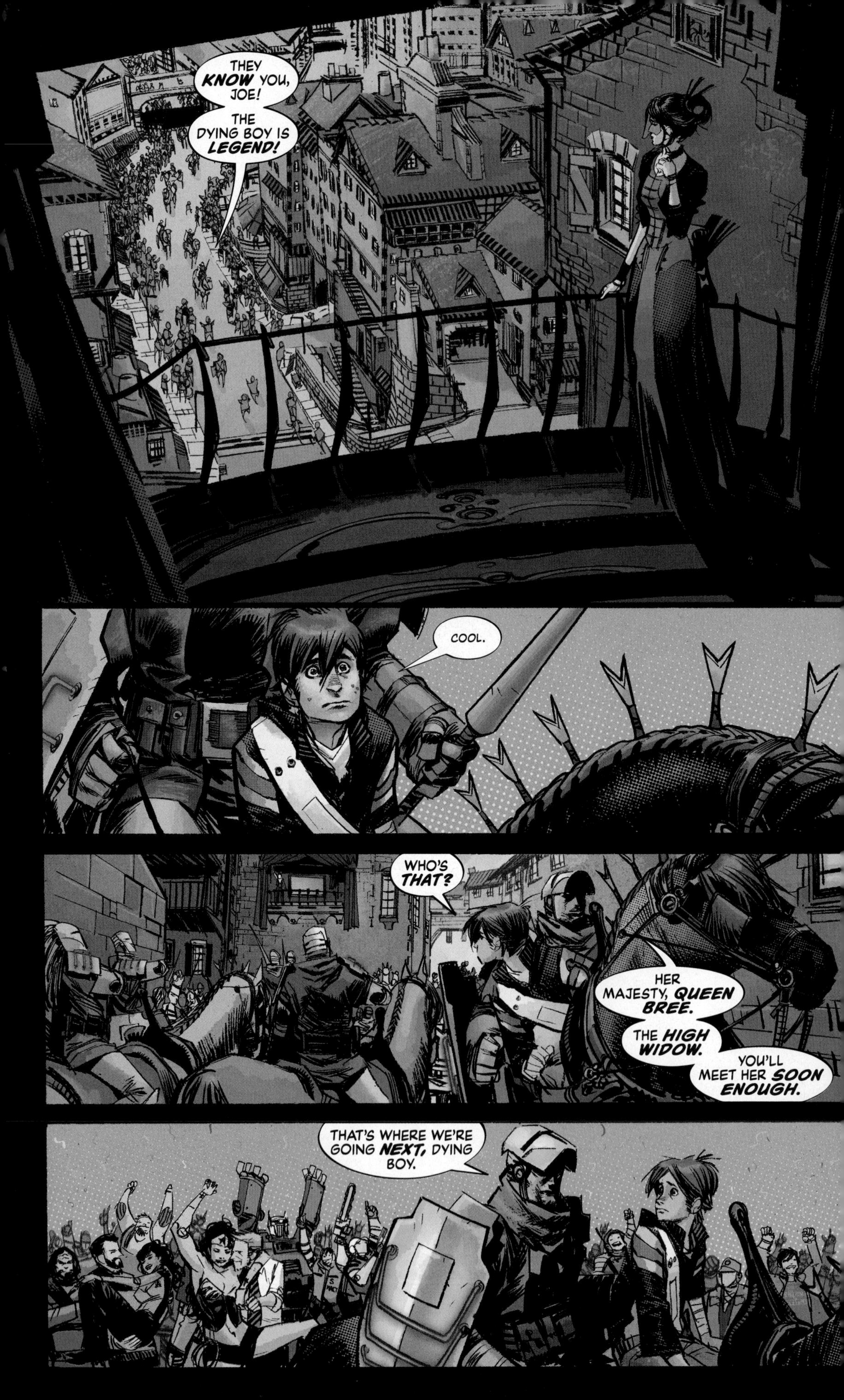
THEY KNOW YOU, JOE!
THE DYING BOY IS LEGEND!
COOL.
WHO'S THAT?
HER MAJESTY, QUEEN BREE.
THE HIGH WIDOW.
YOU'LL MEET HER SOON ENOUGH.
THAT'S WHERE WE'RE GOING NEXT, DYING BOY.

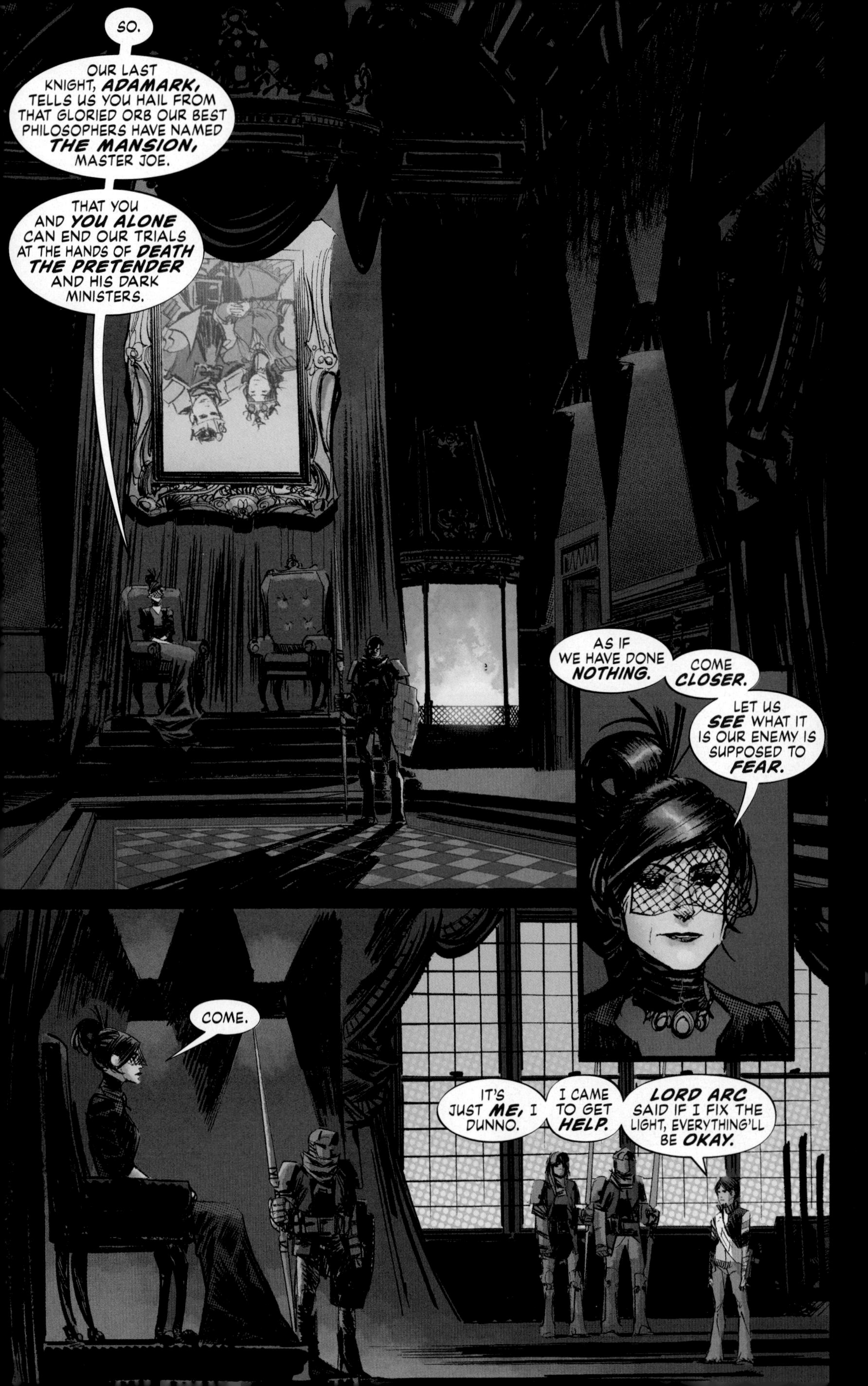
SO.
OUR LAST KNIGHT, ADAMARK, TELLS US YOU HAIL FROM THAT GLORIED ORB OUR BEST PHILOSOPHERS HAVE NAMED THE MANSION, MASTER JOE.
THAT YOU AND YOU ALONE CAN END OUR TRIALS AT THE HANDS OF DEATH THE PRETENDER AND HIS DARK MINISTERS.
AS IF WE HAVE DONE NOTHING.
COME CLOSER.
LET US SEE WHAT IT IS OUR ENEMY IS SUPPOSED TO FEAR.
COME.
IT'S JUST ME, I DUNNO.
I CAME TO GET HELP.
LORD ARC SAID IF I FIX THE LIGHT, EVERYTHING'LL BE OKAY.

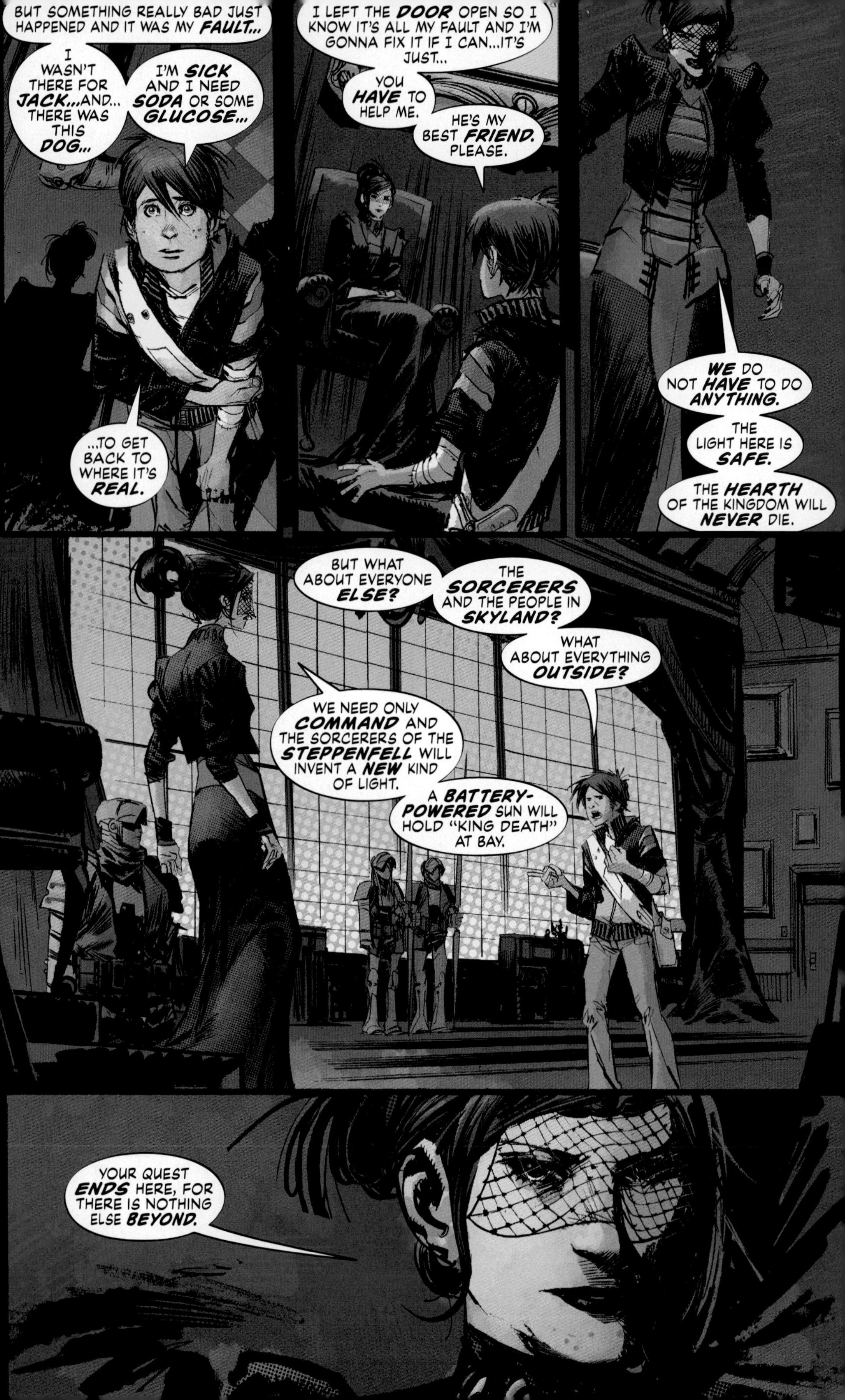
BUT SOMETHING REALLY BAD JUST HAPPENED AND IT WAS MY FAULT...
I WASN'T THERE FOR JACK...AND... THERE WAS THIS DOG...
I'M SICK AND I NEED SODA OR SOME GLUCOSE...
...TO GET BACK TO WHERE IT'S REAL.
I LEFT THE DOOR OPEN SO I KNOW IT'S ALL MY FAULT AND I'M GONNA FIX IT IF I CAN...IT'S JUST...
YOU HAVE TO HELP ME.
HE'S MY BEST FRIEND. PLEASE.
WE DO NOT HAVE TO DO ANYTHING.
THE LIGHT HERE IS SAFE.
THE HEARTH OF THE KINGDOM WILL NEVER DIE.
BUT WHAT ABOUT EVERYONE ELSE?
THE SORCERERS AND THE PEOPLE IN SKYLAND?
WHAT ABOUT EVERYTHING OUTSIDE?
WE NEED ONLY COMMAND AND THE SORCERERS OF THE STEPPENFELL WILL INVENT A NEW KIND OF LIGHT.
A BATTERY-POWERED SUN WILL HOLD "KING DEATH" AT BAY.
YOUR QUEST ENDS HERE, FOR THERE IS NOTHING ELSE BEYOND.

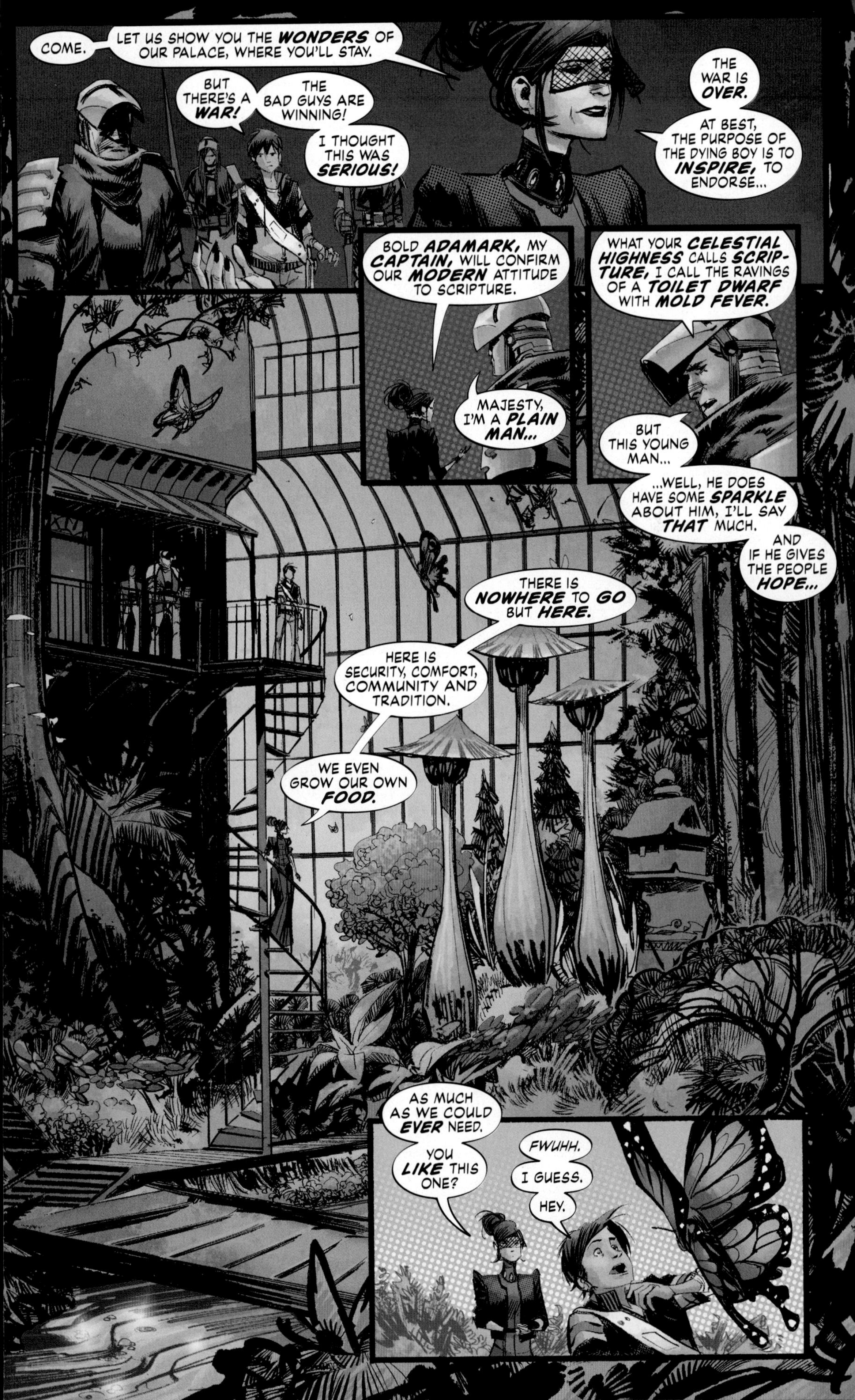
COME.
LET US SHOW YOU THE WONDERS OF OUR PALACE, WHERE YOU'LL STAY.
BUT THERE'S A WAR!
THE BAD GUYS ARE WINNING!
I THOUGHT THIS WAS SERIOUS!
THE WAR IS OVER.
AT BEST, THE PURPOSE OF THE DYING BOY IS TO INSPIRE, TO ENDORSE...
BOLD ADAMARK, MY CAPTAIN, WILL CONFIRM OUR MODERN ATTITUDE TO SCRIPTURE.
MAJESTY, I'M A PLAIN MAN...
WHAT YOUR CELESTIAL HIGHNESS CALLS SCRIPTURE, I CALL THE RAVINGS OF A TOILET DWARF WITH MOLD FEVER.
BUT THIS YOUNG MAN...
...WELL, HE DOES HAVE SOME SPARKLE ABOUT HIM, I'LL SAY THAT MUCH.
AND IF HE GIVES THE PEOPLE HOPE...
THERE IS NOWHERE TO GO BUT HERE.
HERE IS SECURITY, COMFORT, COMMUNITY AND TRADITION.
WE EVEN GROW OUR OWN FOOD.
AS MUCH AS WE COULD EVER NEED.
YOU LIKE THIS ONE?
FWUHH.
I GUESS.
HEY.

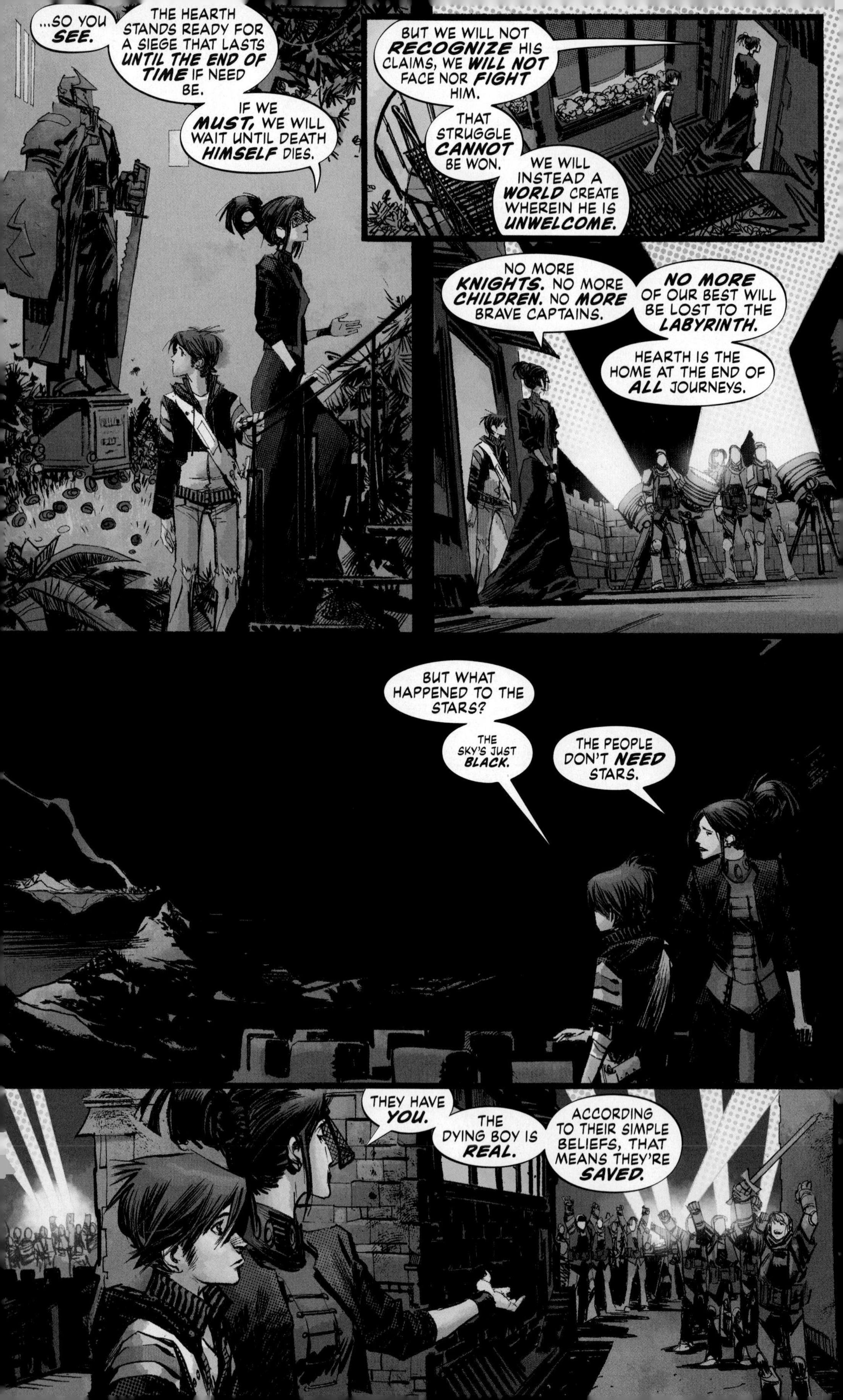

...SO YOU SEE.
THE HEARTH STANDS READY FOR A SIEGE THAT LASTS UNTIL THE END OF TIME IF NEED BE.
IF WE MUST, WE WILL WAIT UNTIL DEATH HIMSELF DIES.
BUT WE WILL NOT RECOGNIZE HIS CLAIMS, WE WILL NOT FACE NOR FIGHT HIM.
THAT STRUGGLE CANNOT BE WON.
WE WILL INSTEAD A WORLD CREATE WHEREIN HE IS UNWELCOME.
NO MORE KNIGHTS. NO MORE CHILDREN. NO MORE BRAVE CAPTAINS.
NO MORE OF OUR BEST WILL BE LOST TO THE LABYRINTH.
HEARTH IS THE HOME AT THE END OF ALL JOURNEYS.
BUT WHAT HAPPENED TO THE STARS?
THE SKY'S JUST BLACK.
THE PEOPLE DON'T NEED STARS.
THEY HAVE YOU.
THE DYING BOY IS REAL.
ACCORDING TO THEIR SIMPLE BELIEFS, THAT MEANS THEY'RE SAVED.

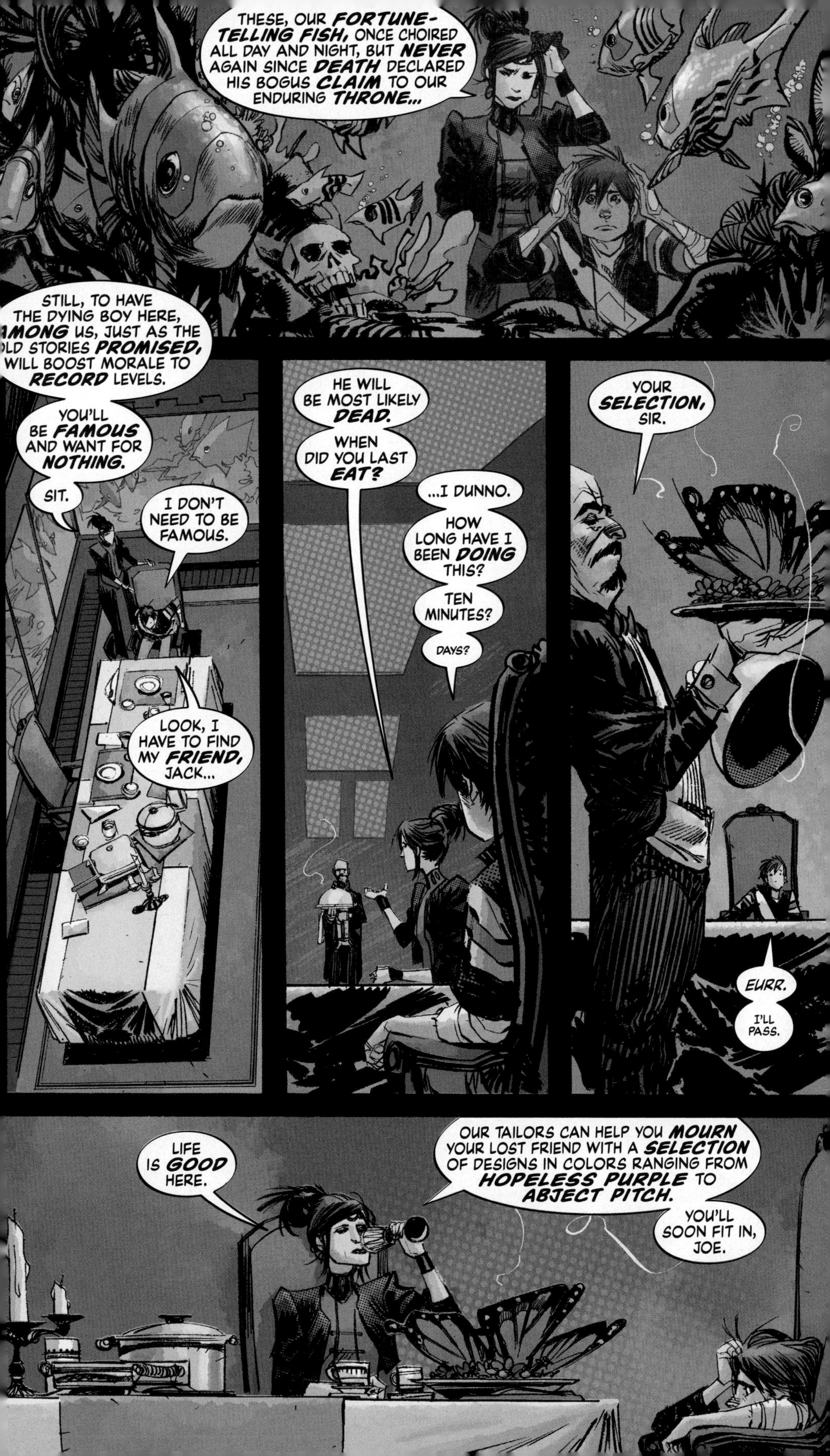
THESE, OUR FORTUNE-TELLING FISH, ONCE CHOIRED ALL DAY AND NIGHT, BUT NEVER AGAIN SINCE DEATH DECLARED HIS BOGUS CLAIM TO OUR ENDURING THRONE...
STILL, TO HAVE THE DYING BOY HERE, AMONG US, JUST AS THE OLD STORIES PROMISED, WILL BOOST MORALE TO RECORD LEVELS.
YOU'LL BE FAMOUS AND WANT FOR NOTHING.
SIT.
I DON'T NEED TO BE FAMOUS.
LOOK, I HAVE TO FIND MY FRIEND, JACK...
HE WILL BE MOST LIKELY DEAD.
WHEN DID YOU LAST EAT?
...I DUNNO.
HOW LONG HAVE I BEEN DOING THIS?
TEN MINUTES?
DAYS?
YOUR SELECTION, SIR.
EURR.
I'LL PASS.
LIFE IS GOOD HERE.
OUR TAILORS CAN HELP YOU MOURN YOUR LOST FRIEND WITH A SELECTION OF DESIGNS IN COLORS RANGING FROM HOPELESS PURPLE TO ABJECT PITCH.
YOU'LL SOON FIT IN, JOE.

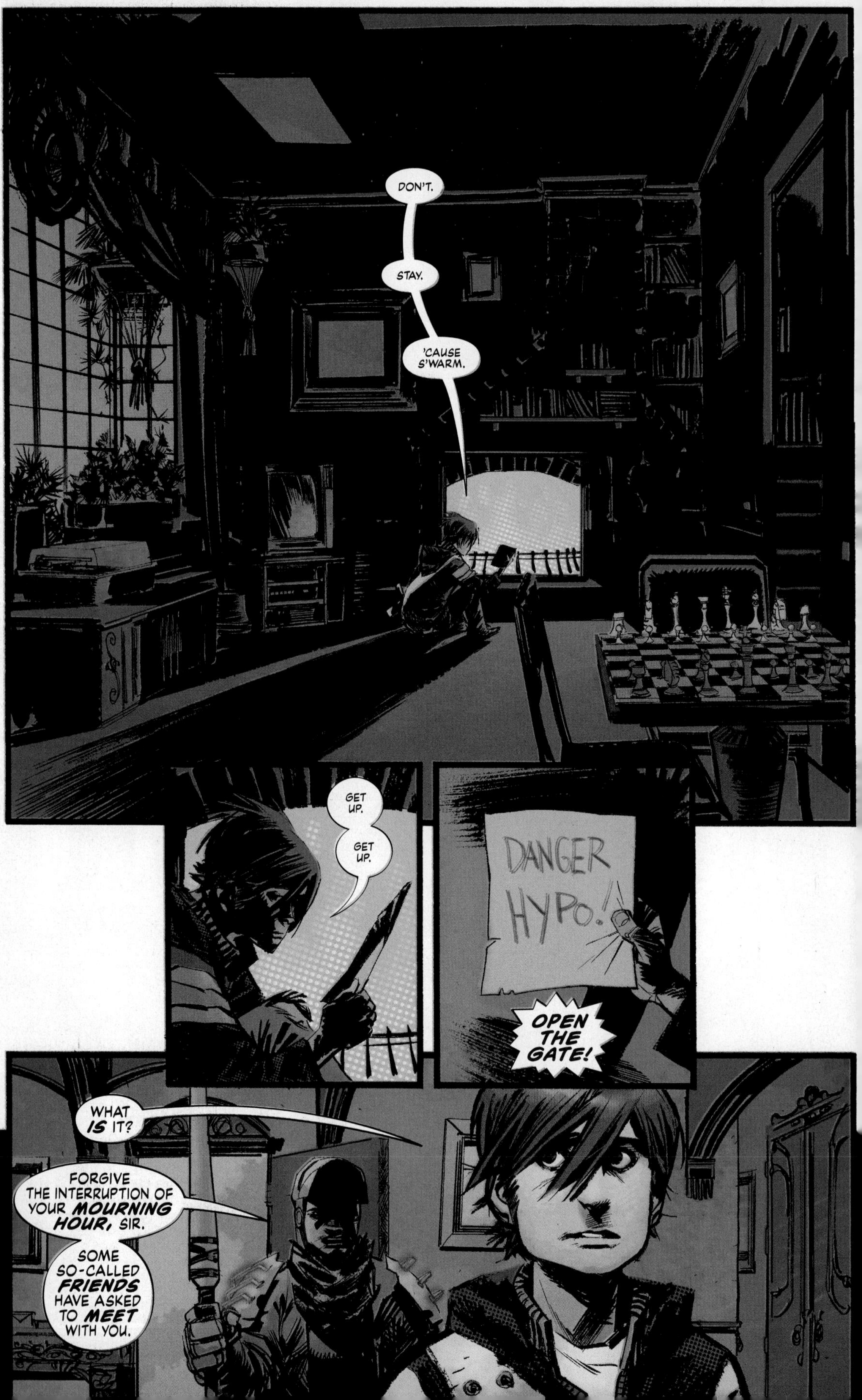
DON'T.
STAY.
'CAUSE S'WARM.
GET UP.
GET UP.
DANGER HYPO.!
OPEN THE GATE!
WHAT *IS* IT?
FORGIVE THE INTERRUPTION OF YOUR *MOURNING HOUR,* SIR.
SOME SO-CALLED *FRIENDS* HAVE ASKED TO *MEET* WITH YOU.

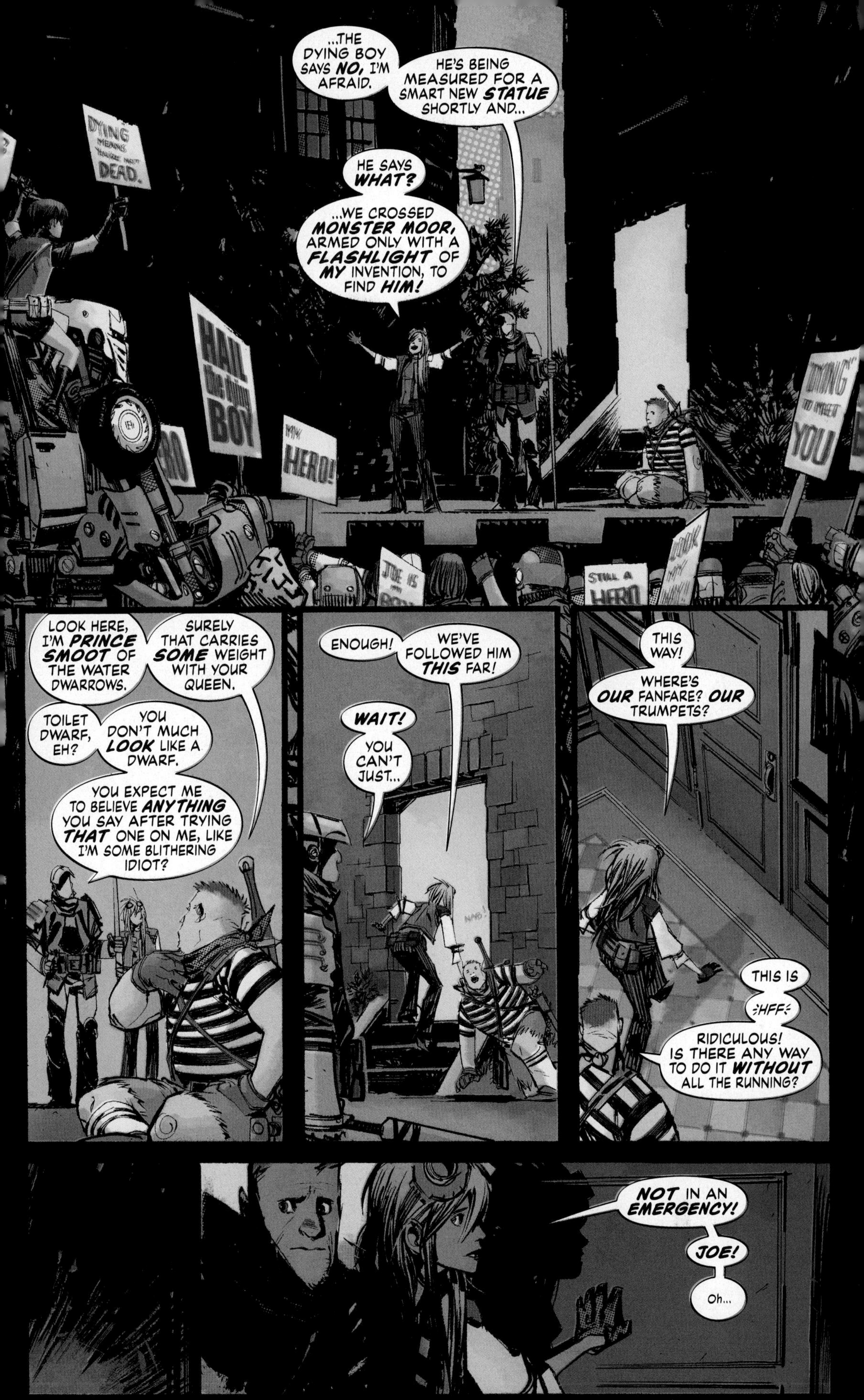

...THE DYING BOY SAYS NO, I'M AFRAID.
HE'S BEING MEASURED FOR A SMART NEW STATUE SHORTLY AND...
HE SAYS WHAT?
...WE CROSSED MONSTER MOOR, ARMED ONLY WITH A FLASHLIGHT OF MY INVENTION, TO FIND HIM!
HERO!
STILL A HERO
LOOK HERE, I'M PRINCE SMOOT OF THE WATER DWARROWS.
SURELY THAT CARRIES SOME WEIGHT WITH YOUR QUEEN.
TOILET DWARF, EH?
YOU DON'T MUCH LOOK LIKE A DWARF.
YOU EXPECT ME TO BELIEVE ANYTHING YOU SAY AFTER TRYING THAT ONE ON ME, LIKE I'M SOME BLITHERING IDIOT?
ENOUGH!
WE'VE FOLLOWED HIM THIS FAR!
WAIT!
YOU CAN'T JUST...
THIS WAY!
WHERE'S OUR FANFARE? OUR TRUMPETS?
THIS IS
HFF
RIDICULOUS! IS THERE ANY WAY TO DO IT WITHOUT ALL THE RUNNING?
NOT IN AN EMERGENCY!
JOE!
Oh...

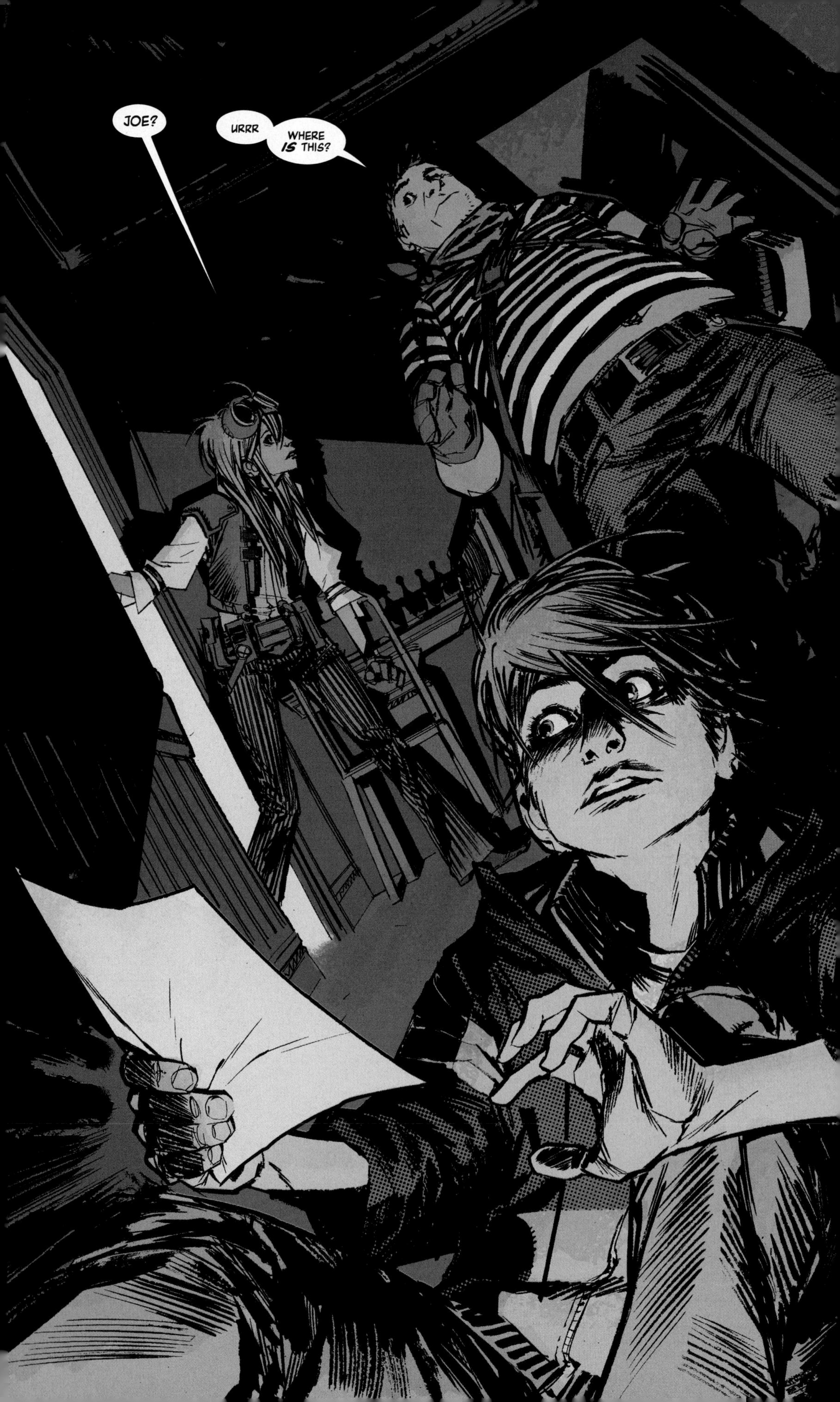
JOE?
URRR
WHERE IS THIS?

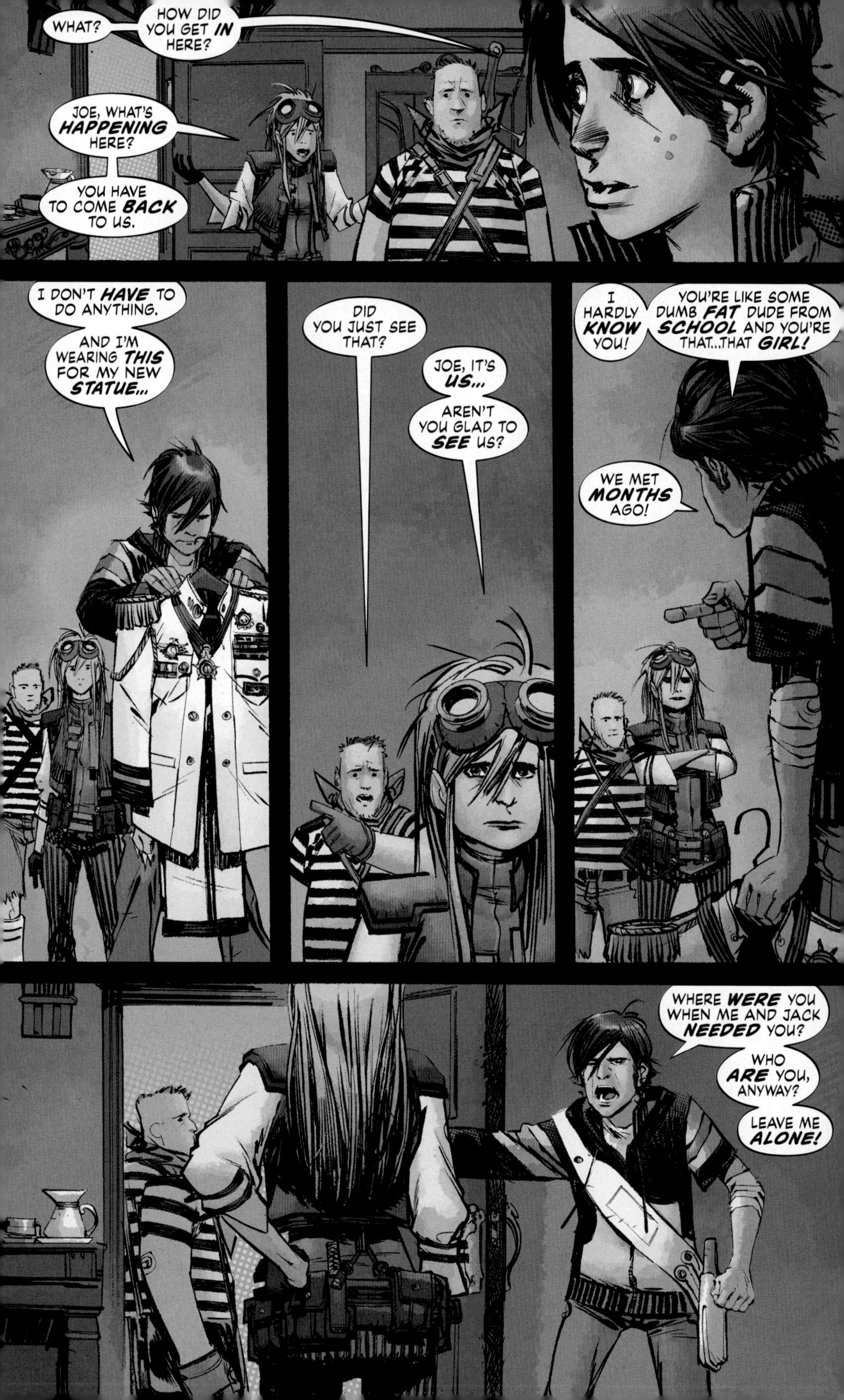
WHAT?
HOW DID YOU GET IN HERE?
JOE, WHAT'S HAPPENING HERE?
YOU HAVE TO COME BACK TO US.
I DON'T HAVE TO DO ANYTHING.
AND I'M WEARING THIS FOR MY NEW STATUE...
DID YOU JUST SEE THAT?
JOE, IT'S US...
AREN'T YOU GLAD TO SEE US?
I HARDLY KNOW YOU!
YOU'RE LIKE SOME DUMB FAT DUDE FROM SCHOOL AND YOU'RE THAT...THAT GIRL!
WE MET MONTHS AGO!
WHERE WERE YOU WHEN ME AND JACK NEEDED YOU?
WHO ARE YOU, ANYWAY?
LEAVE ME ALONE!

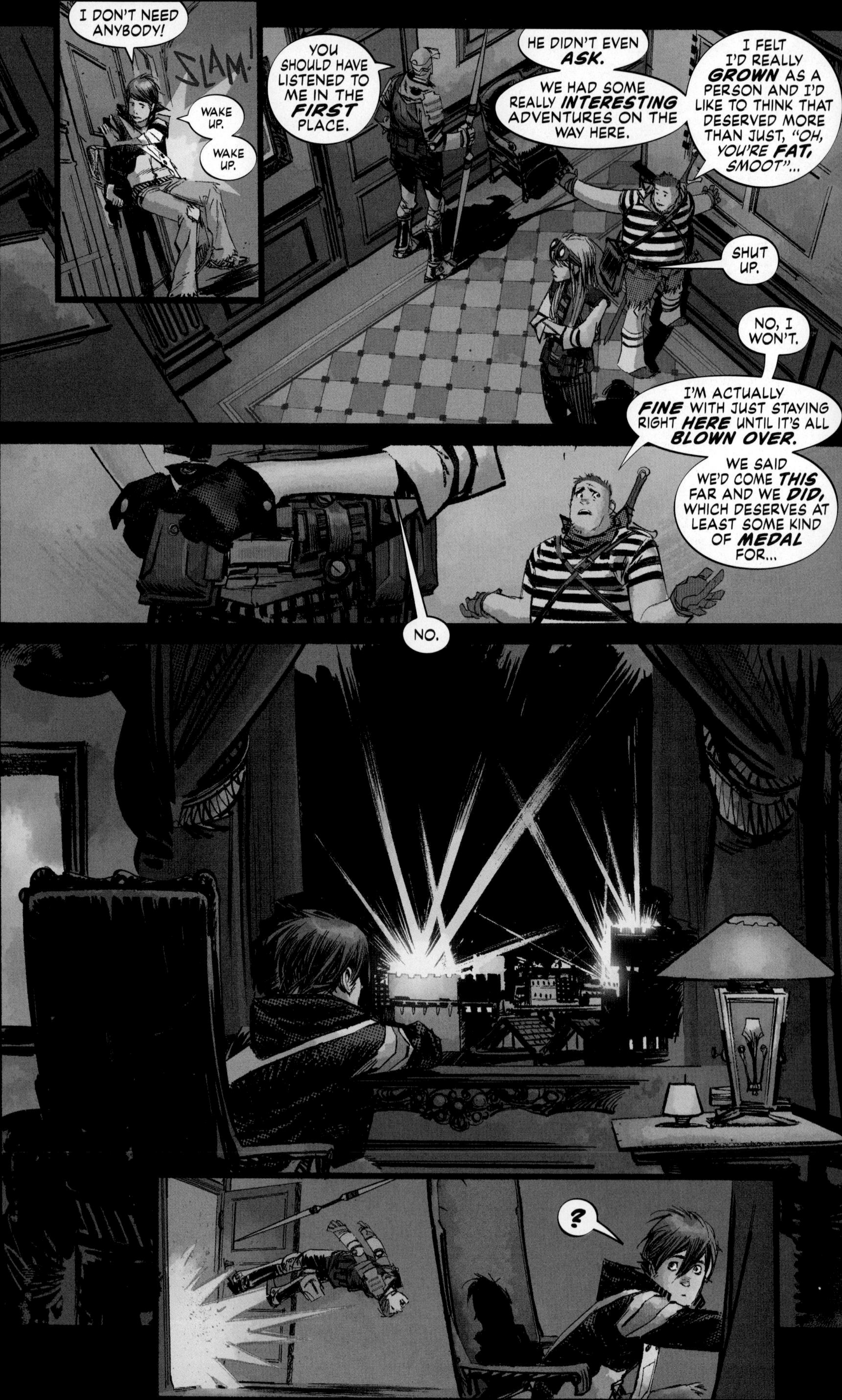
I DON'T NEED ANYBODY!
SLAM!
WAKE UP.
WAKE UP.
YOU SHOULD HAVE LISTENED TO ME IN THE FIRST PLACE.
HE DIDN'T EVEN ASK.
WE HAD SOME REALLY INTERESTING ADVENTURES ON THE WAY HERE.
I FELT I'D REALLY GROWN AS A PERSON AND I'D LIKE TO THINK THAT DESERVED MORE THAN JUST, "OH, YOU'RE FAT, SMOOT"...
SHUT UP.
NO, I WON'T.
I'M ACTUALLY FINE WITH JUST STAYING RIGHT HERE UNTIL IT'S ALL BLOWN OVER.
WE SAID WE'D COME THIS FAR AND WE DID, WHICH DESERVES AT LEAST SOME KIND OF MEDAL FOR...
NO.
?

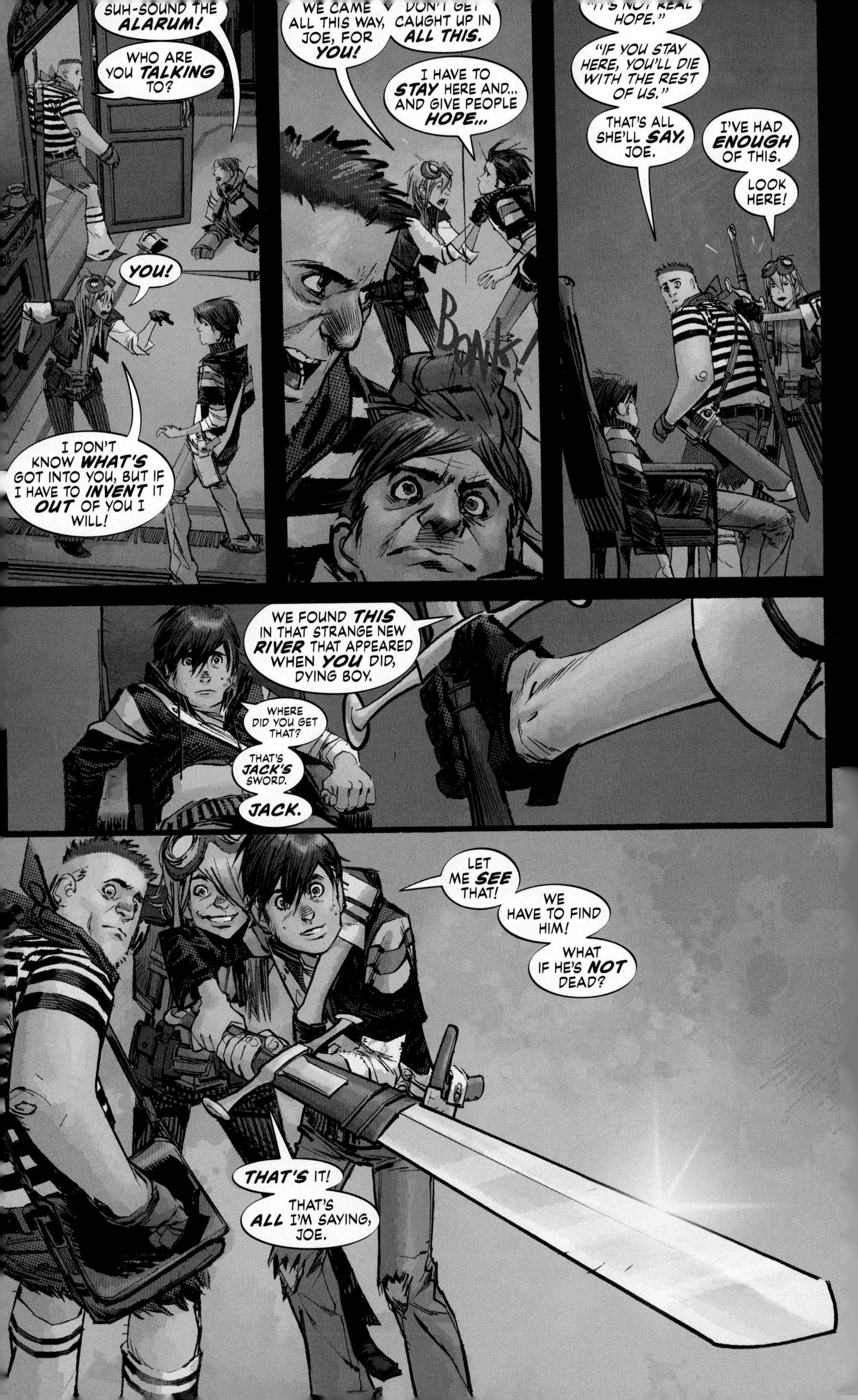
SUH-SOUND THE ALARUM!
WHO ARE YOU TALKING TO?
YOU!
I DON'T KNOW WHAT'S GOT INTO YOU, BUT IF I HAVE TO INVENT IT OUT OF YOU I WILL!
WE CAME ALL THIS WAY, JOE, FOR YOU!
DON'T GET CAUGHT UP IN ALL THIS.
I HAVE TO STAY HERE AND... AND GIVE PEOPLE HOPE...
BONK!
HOPE."
"IF YOU STAY HERE, YOU'LL DIE WITH THE REST OF US."
THAT'S ALL SHE'LL SAY, JOE.
I'VE HAD ENOUGH OF THIS.
LOOK HERE!
WE FOUND THIS IN THAT STRANGE NEW RIVER THAT APPEARED WHEN YOU DID, DYING BOY.
WHERE DID YOU GET THAT?
THAT'S JACK'S SWORD.
JACK.
LET ME SEE THAT!
WE HAVE TO FIND HIM!
WHAT IF HE'S NOT DEAD?
THAT'S IT!
THAT'S ALL I'M SAYING, JOE.

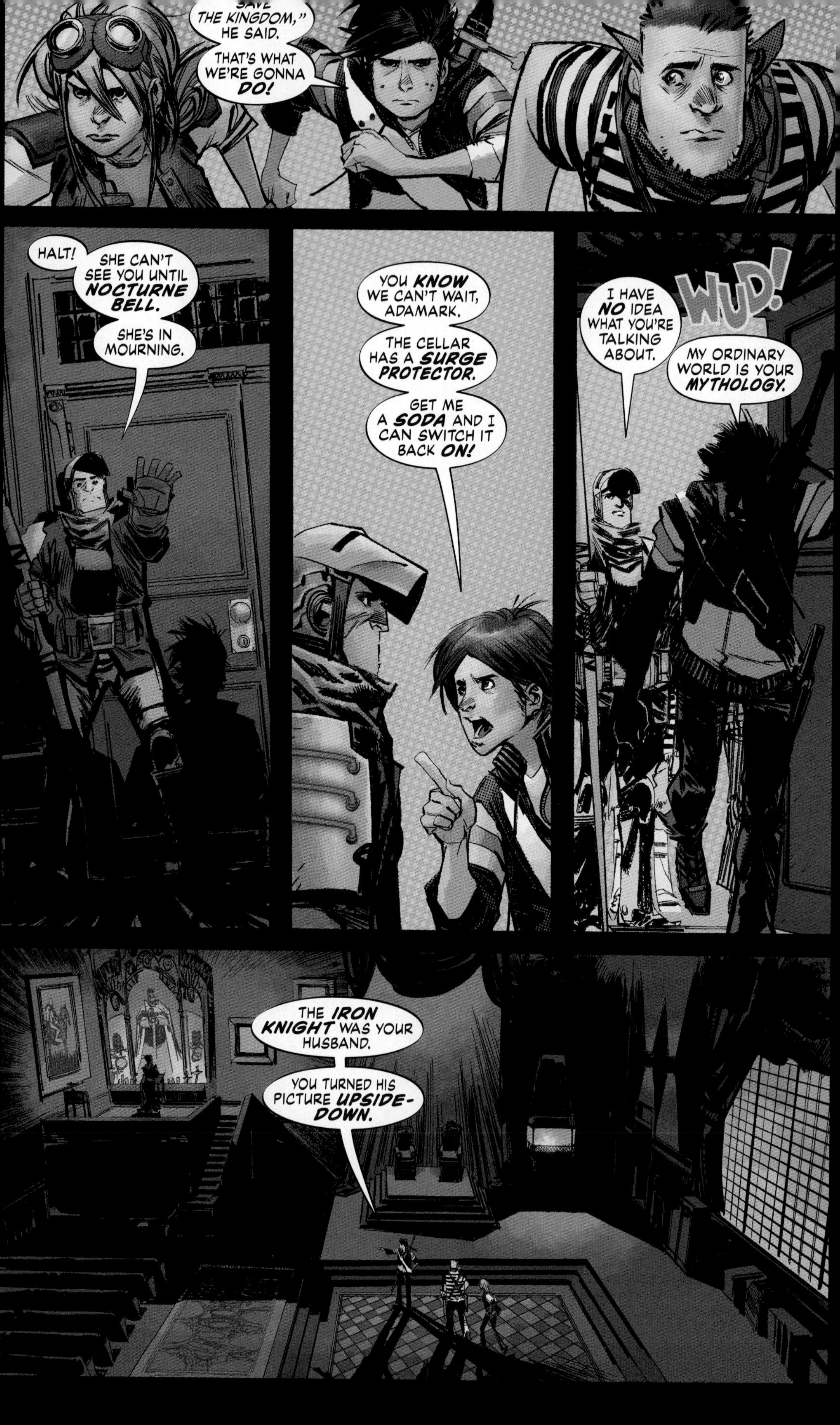
THE KINGDOM," HE SAID.
THAT'S WHAT WE'RE GONNA DO!
HALT!
SHE CAN'T SEE YOU UNTIL NOCTURNE BELL.
SHE'S IN MOURNING.
YOU KNOW WE CAN'T WAIT, ADAMARK.
THE CELLAR HAS A SURGE PROTECTOR.
GET ME A SODA AND I CAN SWITCH IT BACK ON!
WUD!
I HAVE NO IDEA WHAT YOU'RE TALKING ABOUT.
MY ORDINARY WORLD IS YOUR MYTHOLOGY.
THE IRON KNIGHT WAS YOUR HUSBAND.
YOU TURNED HIS PICTURE UPSIDE-DOWN.

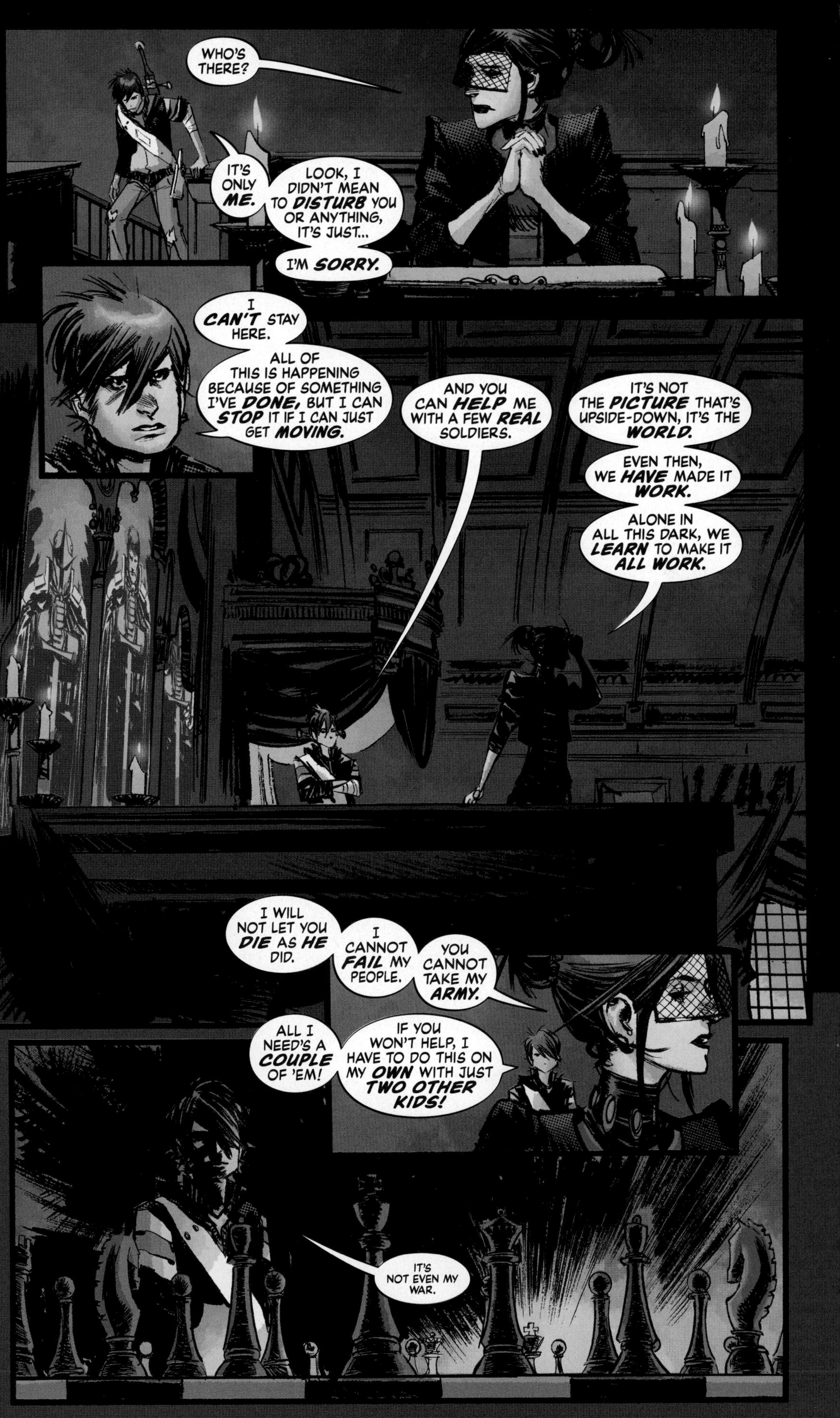
WHO'S THERE?
IT'S ONLY ME.
LOOK, I DIDN'T MEAN TO DISTURB YOU OR ANYTHING, IT'S JUST...
I'M SORRY.
I CAN'T STAY HERE.
ALL OF THIS IS HAPPENING BECAUSE OF SOMETHING I'VE DONE, BUT I CAN STOP IT IF I CAN JUST GET MOVING.
AND YOU CAN HELP ME WITH A FEW REAL SOLDIERS.
IT'S NOT THE PICTURE THAT'S UPSIDE-DOWN, IT'S THE WORLD.
EVEN THEN, WE HAVE MADE IT WORK.
ALONE IN ALL THIS DARK, WE LEARN TO MAKE IT ALL WORK.
I WILL NOT LET YOU DIE AS HE DID.
I CANNOT FAIL MY PEOPLE.
YOU CANNOT TAKE MY ARMY.
ALL I NEED'S A COUPLE OF 'EM!
IF YOU WON'T HELP, I HAVE TO DO THIS ON MY OWN WITH JUST TWO OTHER KIDS!
IT'S NOT EVEN MY WAR.

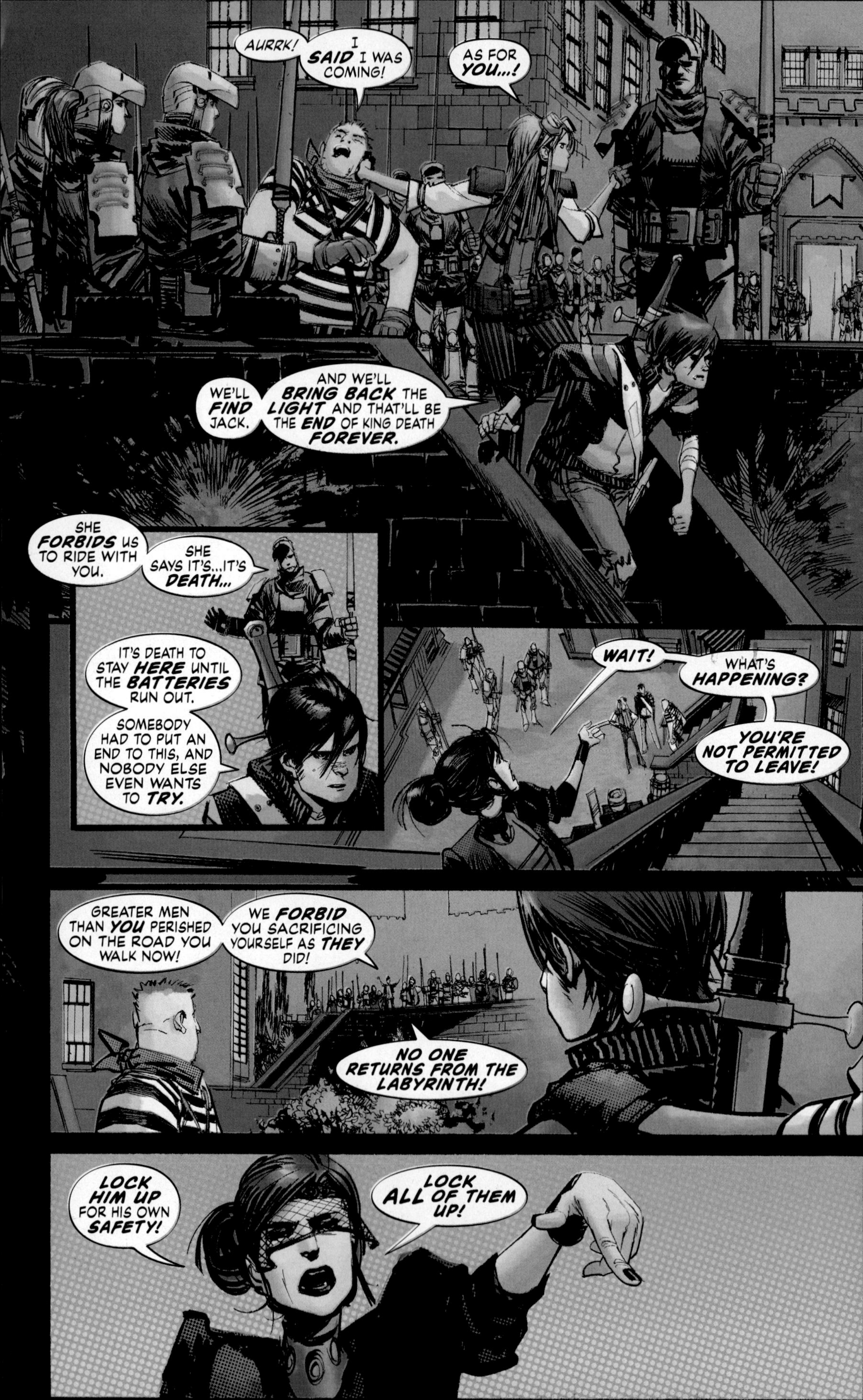

AURRK!
I SAID I WAS COMING!
AS FOR YOU...!
WE'LL FIND JACK.
AND WE'LL BRING BACK THE LIGHT AND THAT'LL BE THE END OF KING DEATH FOREVER.
SHE FORBIDS US TO RIDE WITH YOU.
SHE SAYS IT'S...IT'S DEATH...
IT'S DEATH TO STAY HERE UNTIL THE BATTERIES RUN OUT.
SOMEBODY HAD TO PUT AN END TO THIS, AND NOBODY ELSE EVEN WANTS TO TRY.
WAIT!
WHAT'S HAPPENING?
YOU'RE NOT PERMITTED TO LEAVE!
GREATER MEN THAN YOU PERISHED ON THE ROAD YOU WALK NOW!
WE FORBID YOU SACRIFICING YOURSELF AS THEY DID!
NO ONE RETURNS FROM THE LABYRINTH!
LOCK HIM UP FOR HIS OWN SAFETY!
LOCK ALL OF THEM UP!

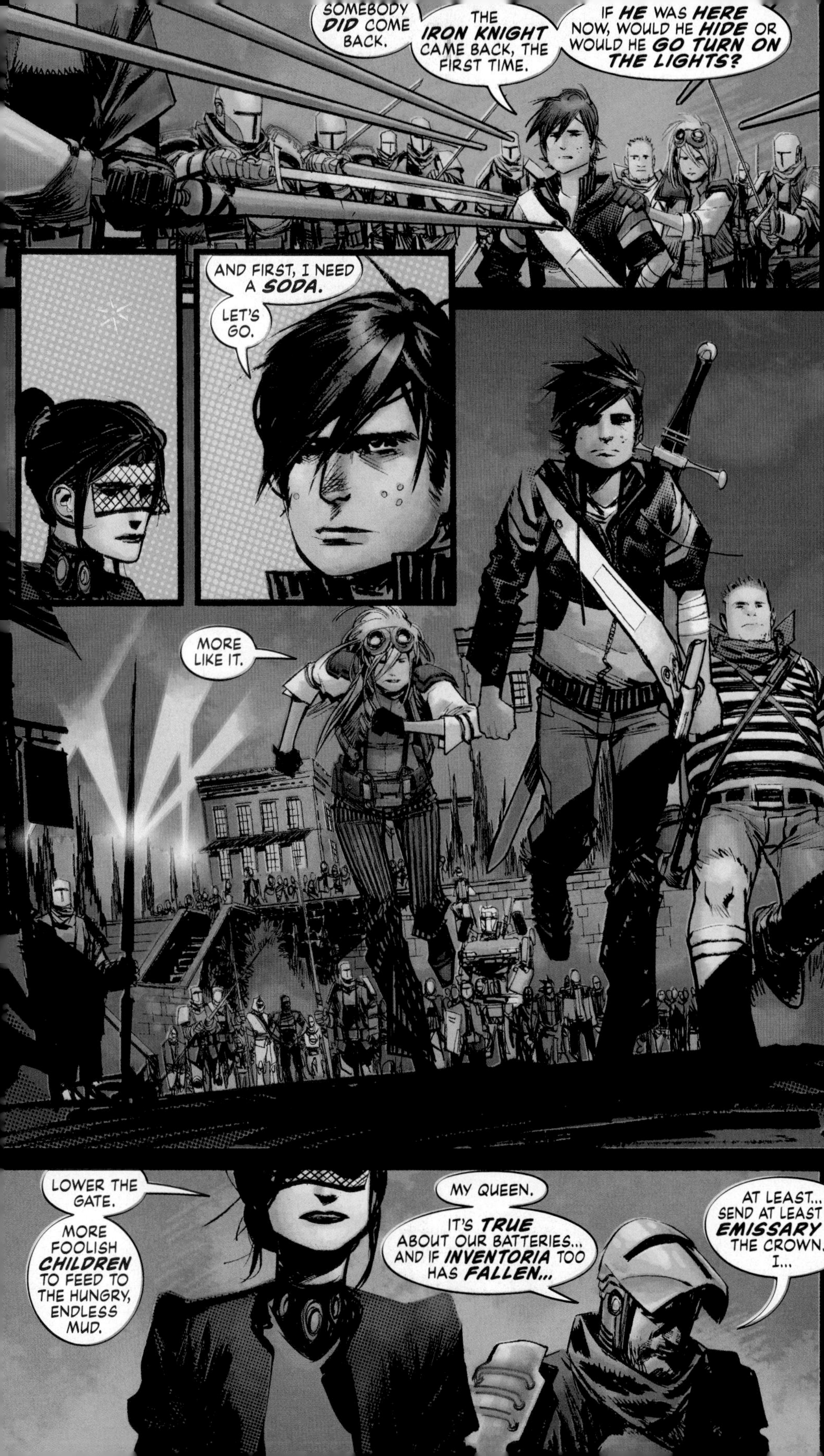
SOMEBODY DID COME BACK.
THE IRON KNIGHT CAME BACK, THE FIRST TIME.
IF HE WAS HERE NOW, WOULD HE HIDE OR WOULD HE GO TURN ON THE LIGHTS?
AND FIRST, I NEED A SODA.
LET'S GO.
MORE LIKE IT.
LOWER THE GATE.
MORE FOOLISH CHILDREN TO FEED TO THE HUNGRY, ENDLESS MUD.
MY QUEEN.
IT'S TRUE ABOUT OUR BATTERIES... AND IF INVENTORIA TOO HAS FALLEN...
AT LEAST... SEND AT LEAST AN EMISSARY OF THE CROWN... I...

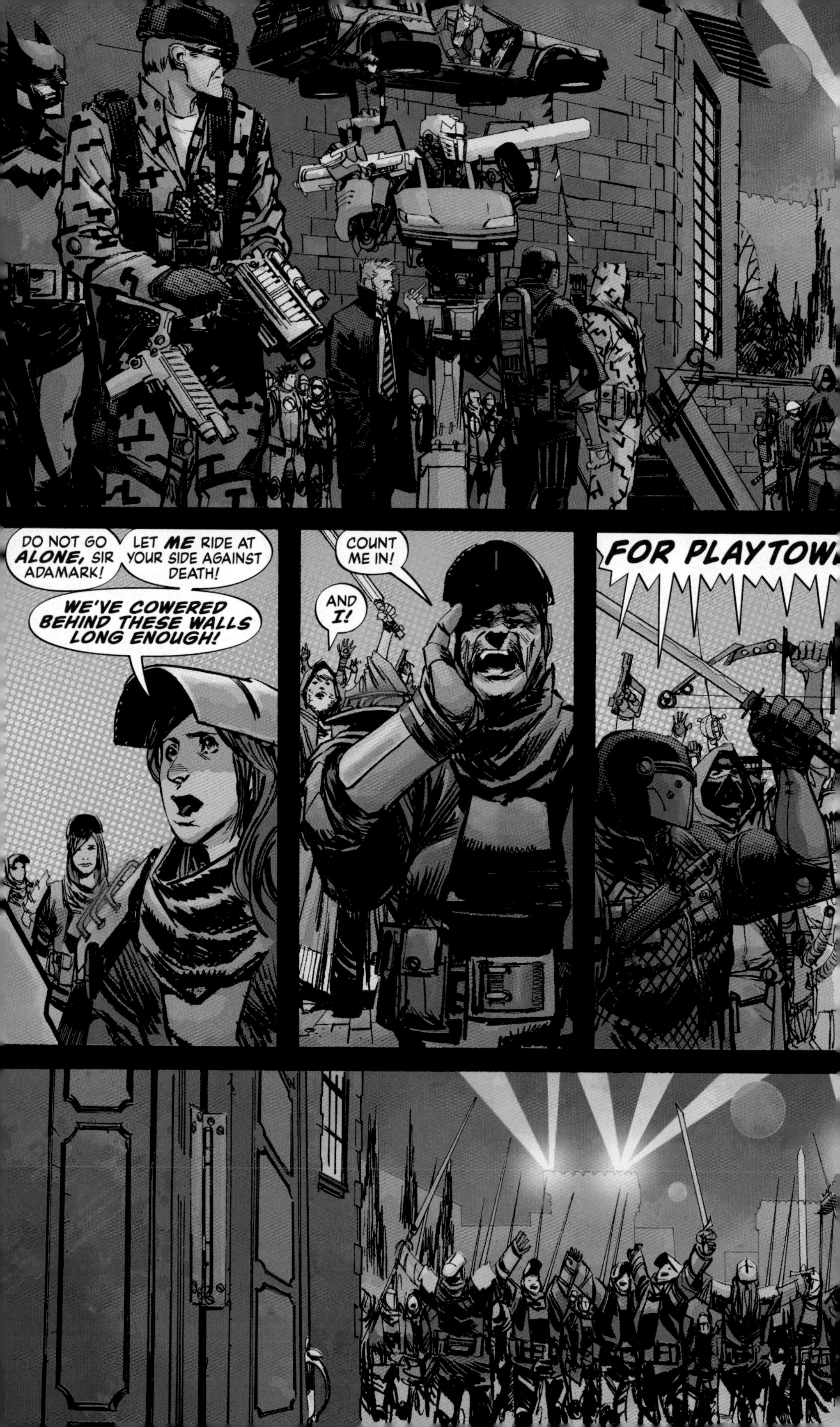

DO NOT GO ALONE, SIR ADAMARK!
LET ME RIDE AT YOUR SIDE AGAINST DEATH!
WE'VE COWERED BEHIND THESE WALLS LONG ENOUGH!
COUNT ME IN!
AND I!
FOR PLAYTOW

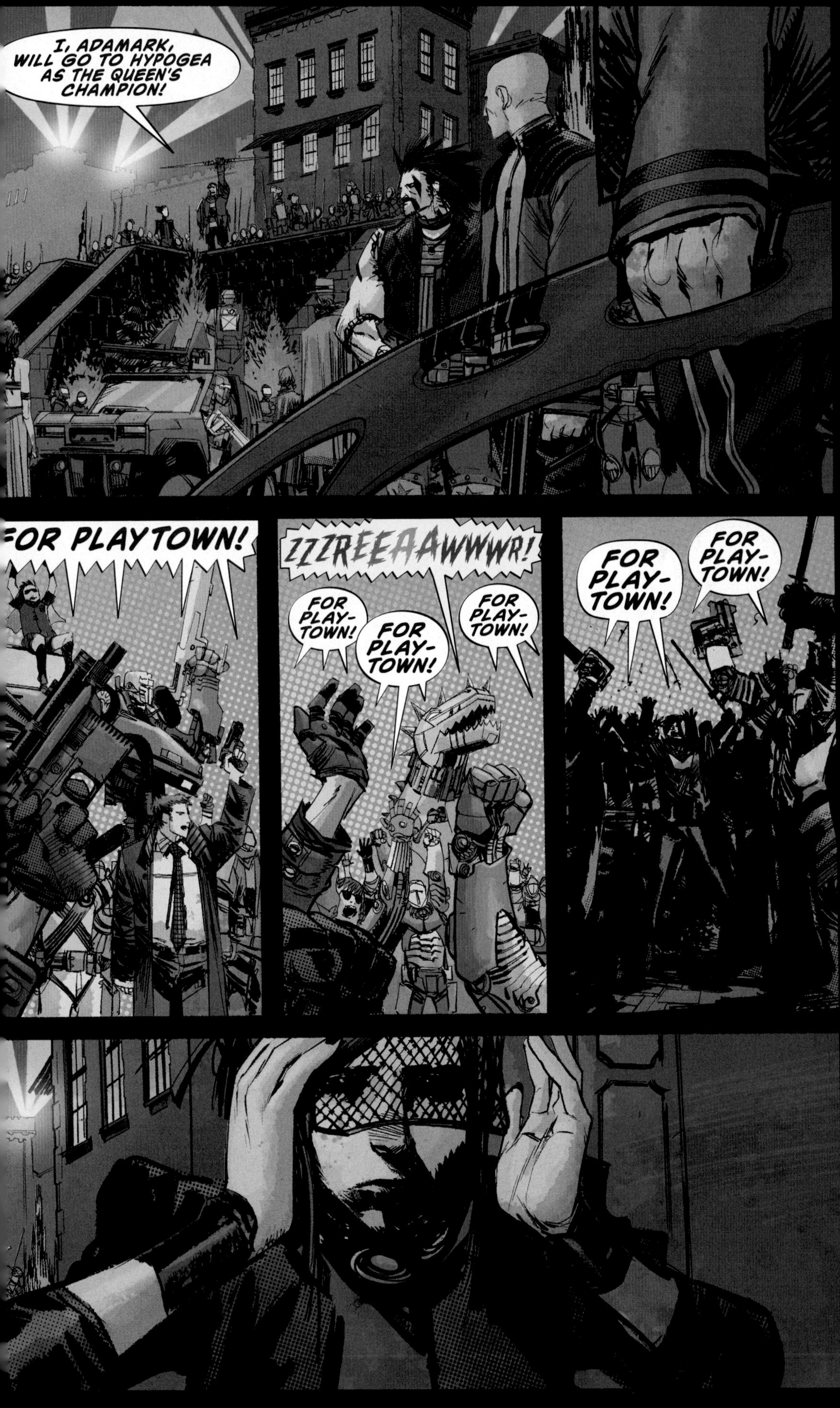
I, ADAMARK, WILL GO TO HYPOGEA AS THE QUEEN'S CHAMPION!
FOR PLAYTOWN!
ZZZREEAAWWWR!
FOR PLAY-TOWN!
FOR PLAY-TOWN!
FOR PLAY-TOWN!
FOR PLAY-TOWN!
FOR PLAY-TOWN!

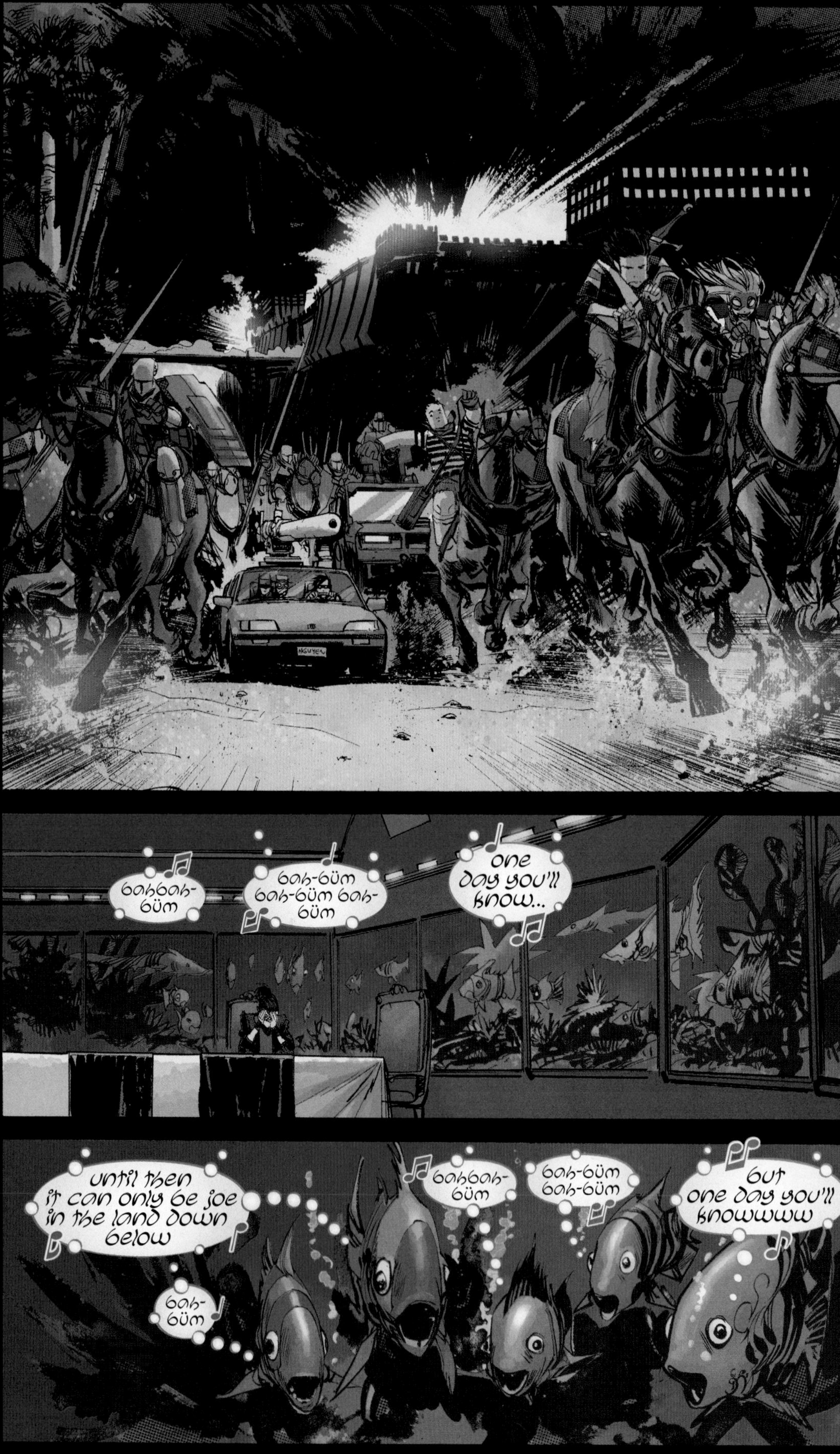
NGUYEN
bahbah-büm
bah-büm bah-büm bah-büm
one day you'll know...
until then it can only be joe in the land down below
bahbah-büm
bah-büm bah-büm
but one day you'll knowwww
bah-büm

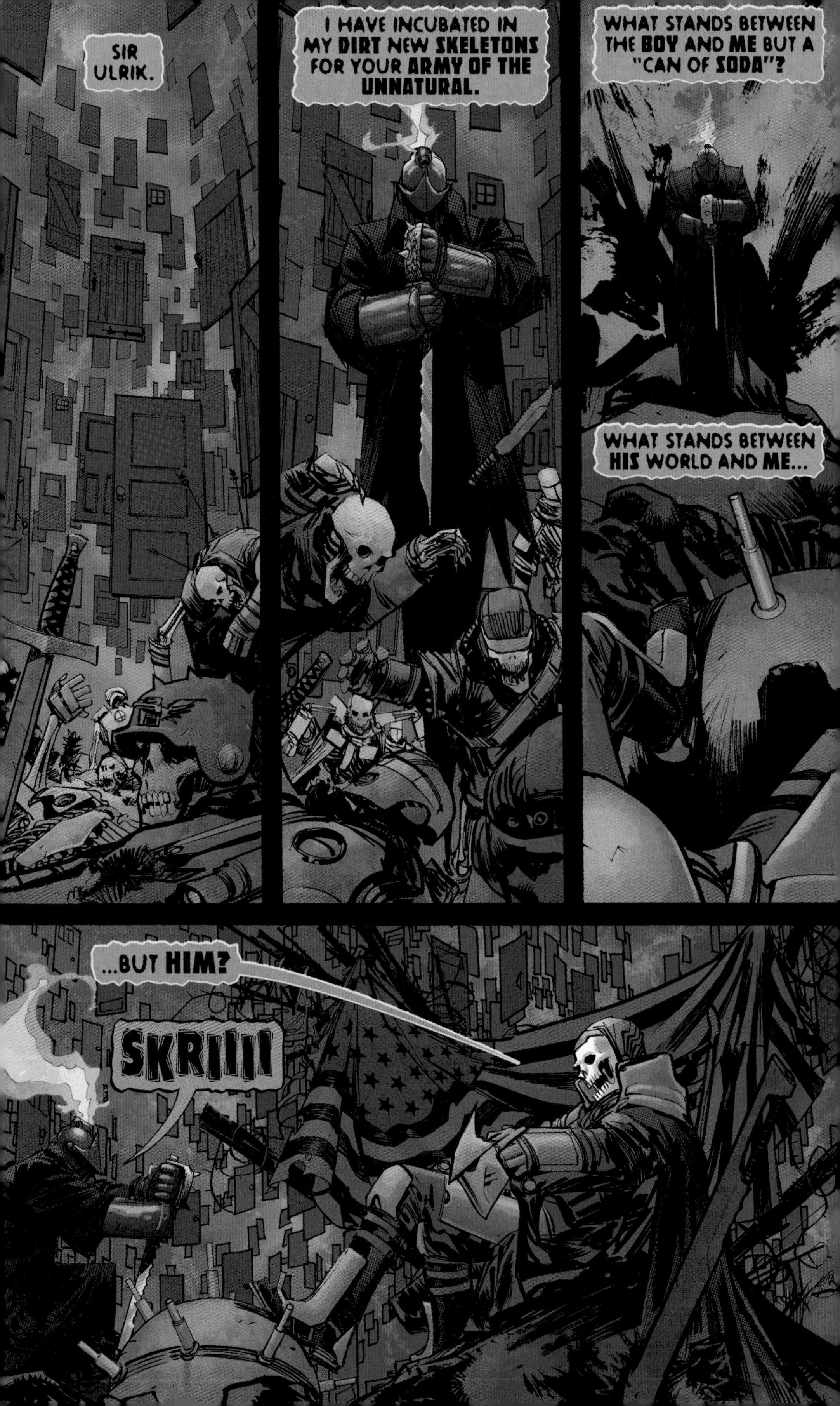
SIR ULRIK.
I HAVE INCUBATED IN MY DIRT NEW SKELETONS FOR YOUR ARMY OF THE UNNATURAL.
WHAT STANDS BETWEEN THE BOY AND ME BUT A "CAN OF SODA"?
WHAT STANDS BETWEEN HIS WORLD AND ME...
...BUT HIM?
SKRIIII

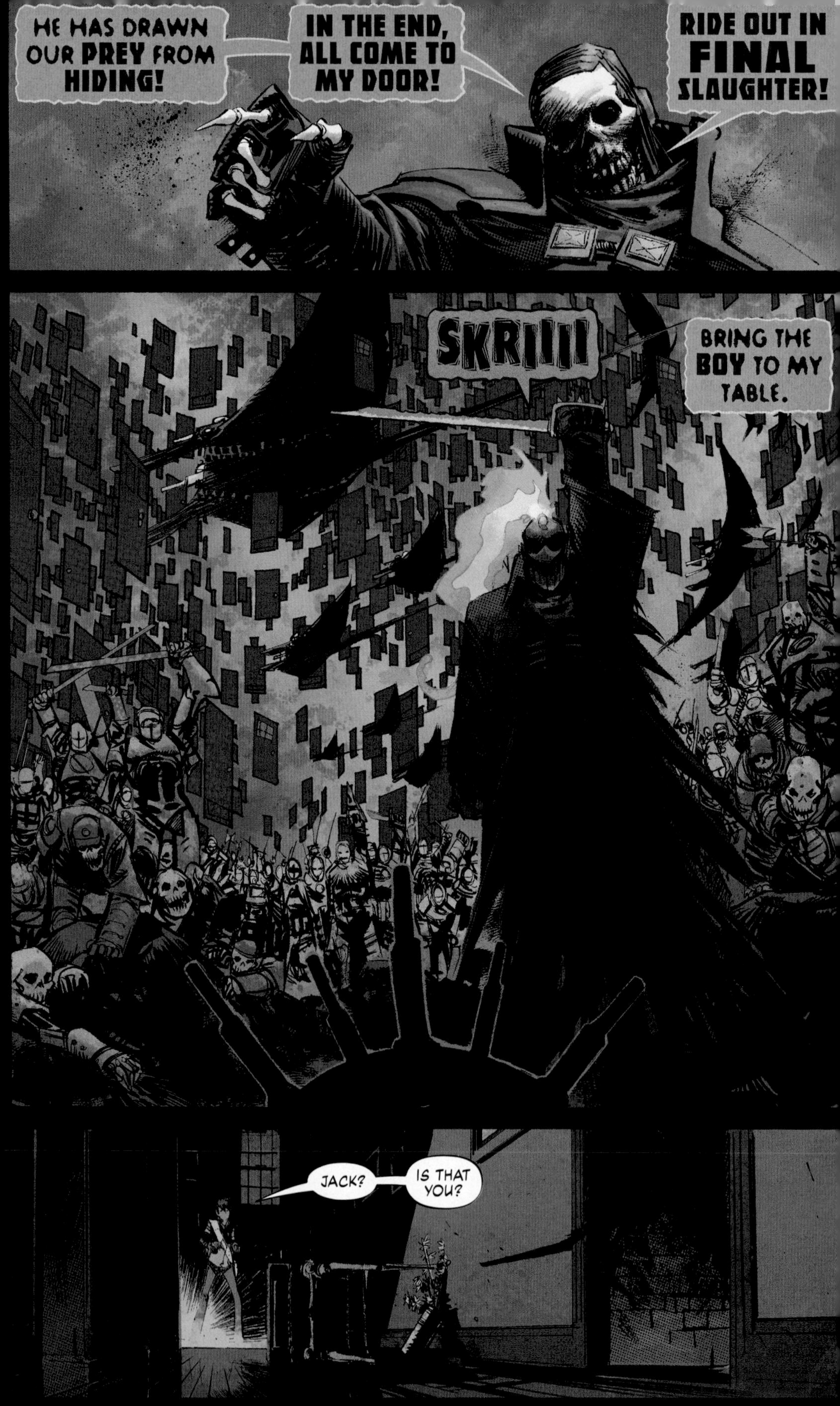
HE HAS DRAWN OUR PREY FROM HIDING!
IN THE END, ALL COME TO MY DOOR!
RIDE OUT IN FINAL SLAUGHTER!
SKRIIII
BRING THE BOY TO MY TABLE.
JACK?
IS THAT YOU?

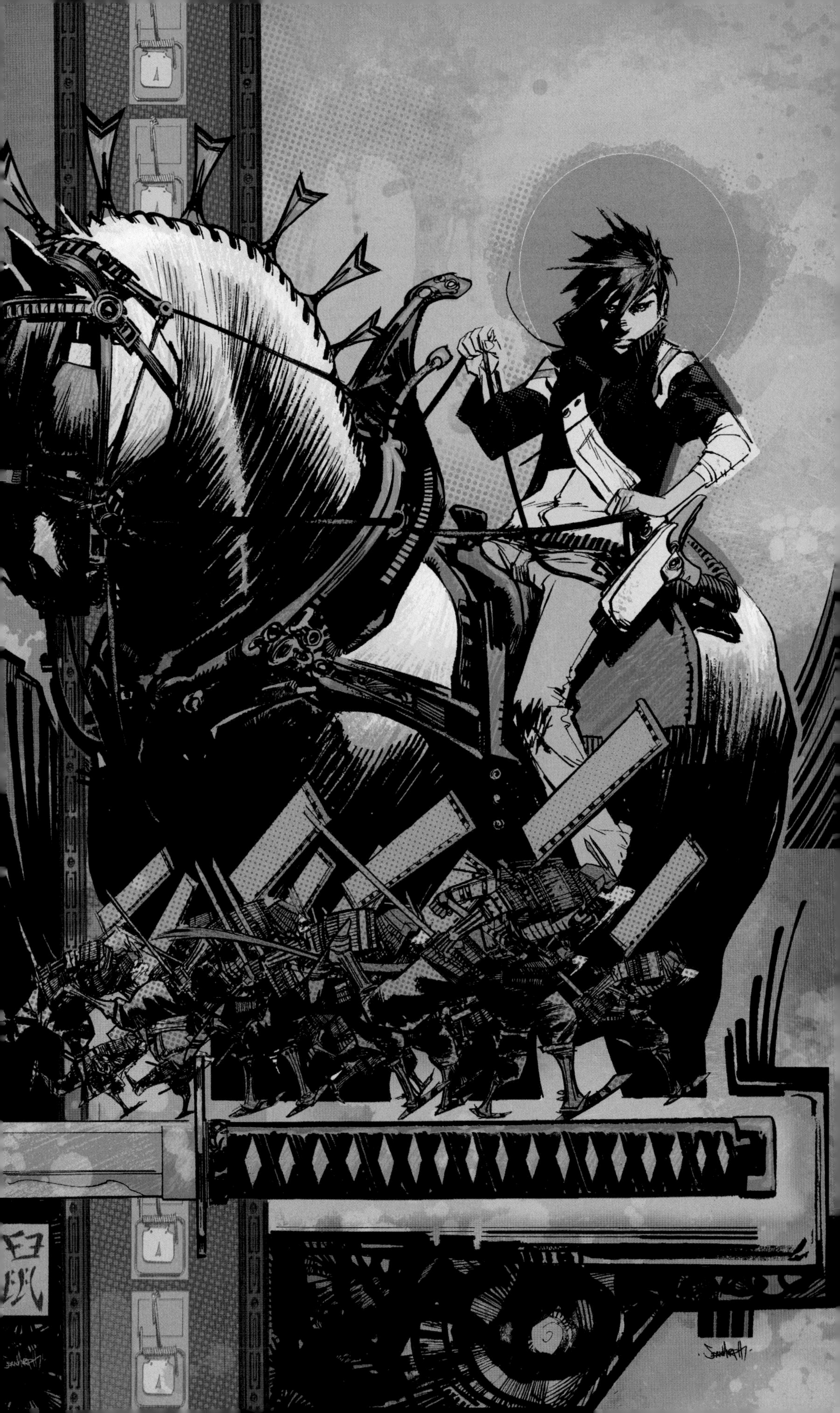

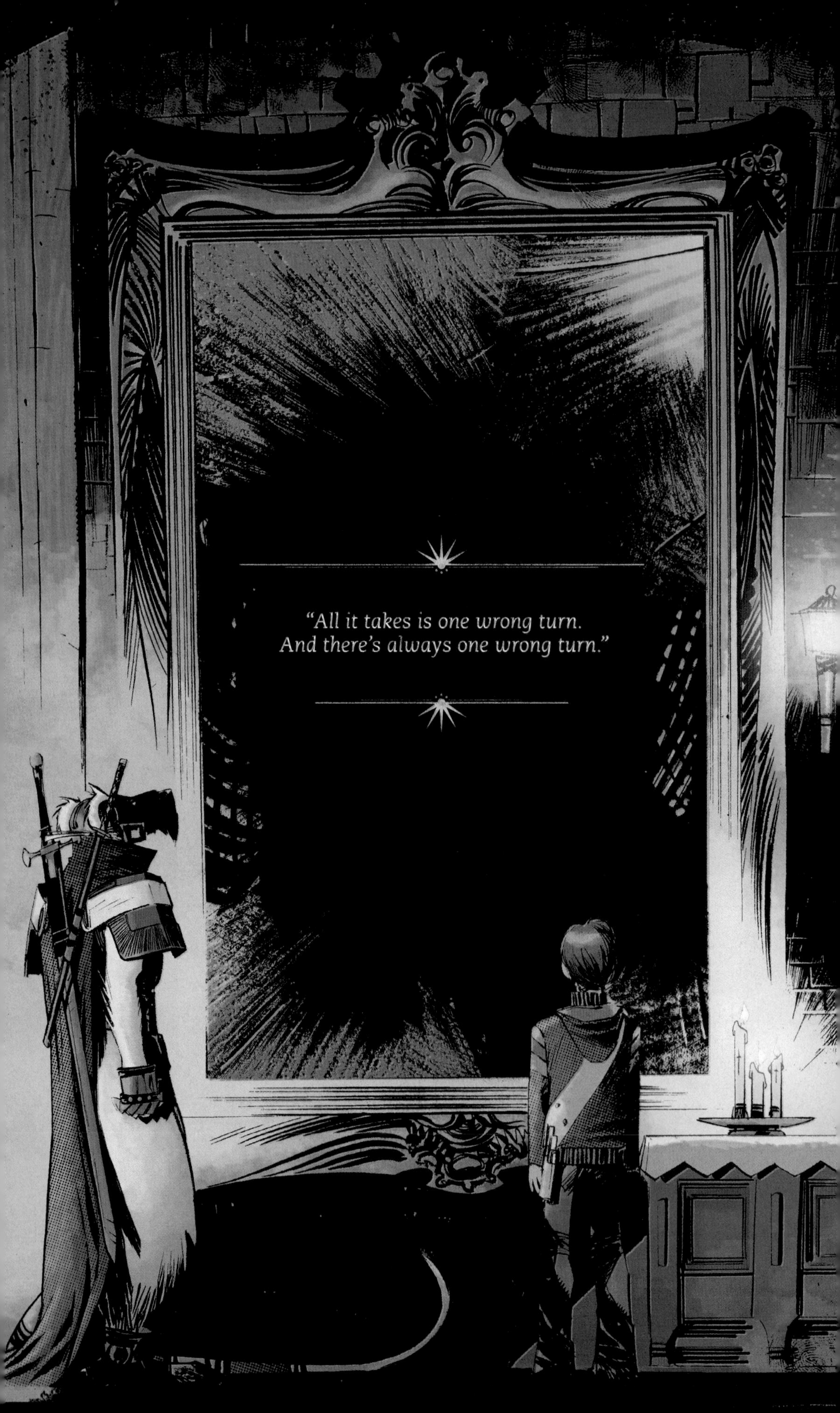
"All it takes is one wrong turn.
And there's always one wrong turn."

chapter 7: labyrinth of the lost

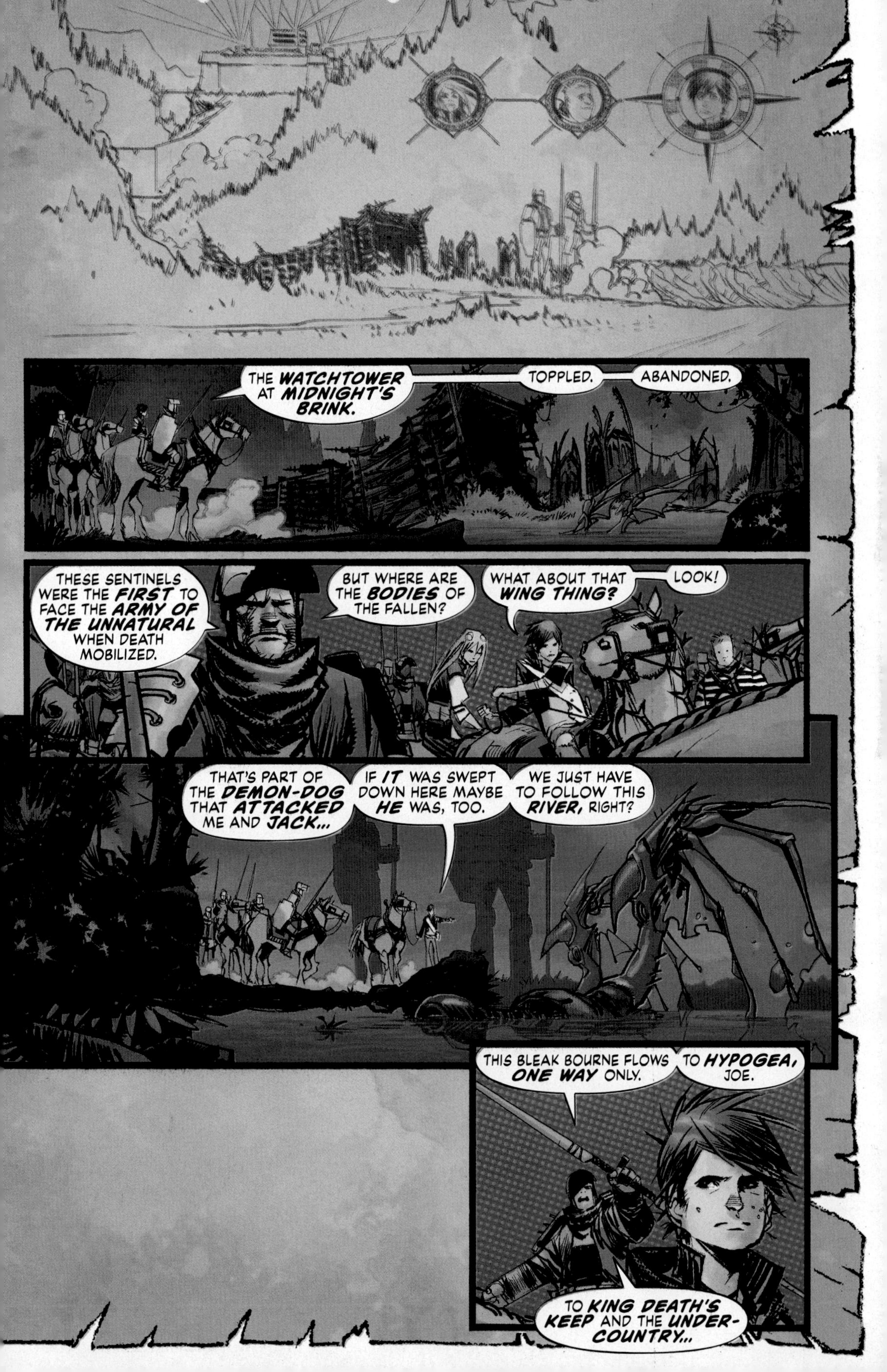
THE WATCHTOWER AT MIDNIGHT'S BRINK.
TOPPLED.
ABANDONED.
THESE SENTINELS WERE THE FIRST TO FACE THE ARMY OF THE UNNATURAL WHEN DEATH MOBILIZED.
BUT WHERE ARE THE BODIES OF THE FALLEN?
WHAT ABOUT THAT WING THING?
LOOK!
THAT'S PART OF THE DEMON-DOG THAT ATTACKED ME AND JACK...
IF IT WAS SWEPT DOWN HERE MAYBE HE WAS, TOO.
WE JUST HAVE TO FOLLOW THIS RIVER, RIGHT?
THIS BLEAK BOURNE FLOWS ONE WAY ONLY.
TO HYPOGEA, JOE.
TO KING DEATH'S KEEP AND THE UNDER-COUNTRY...

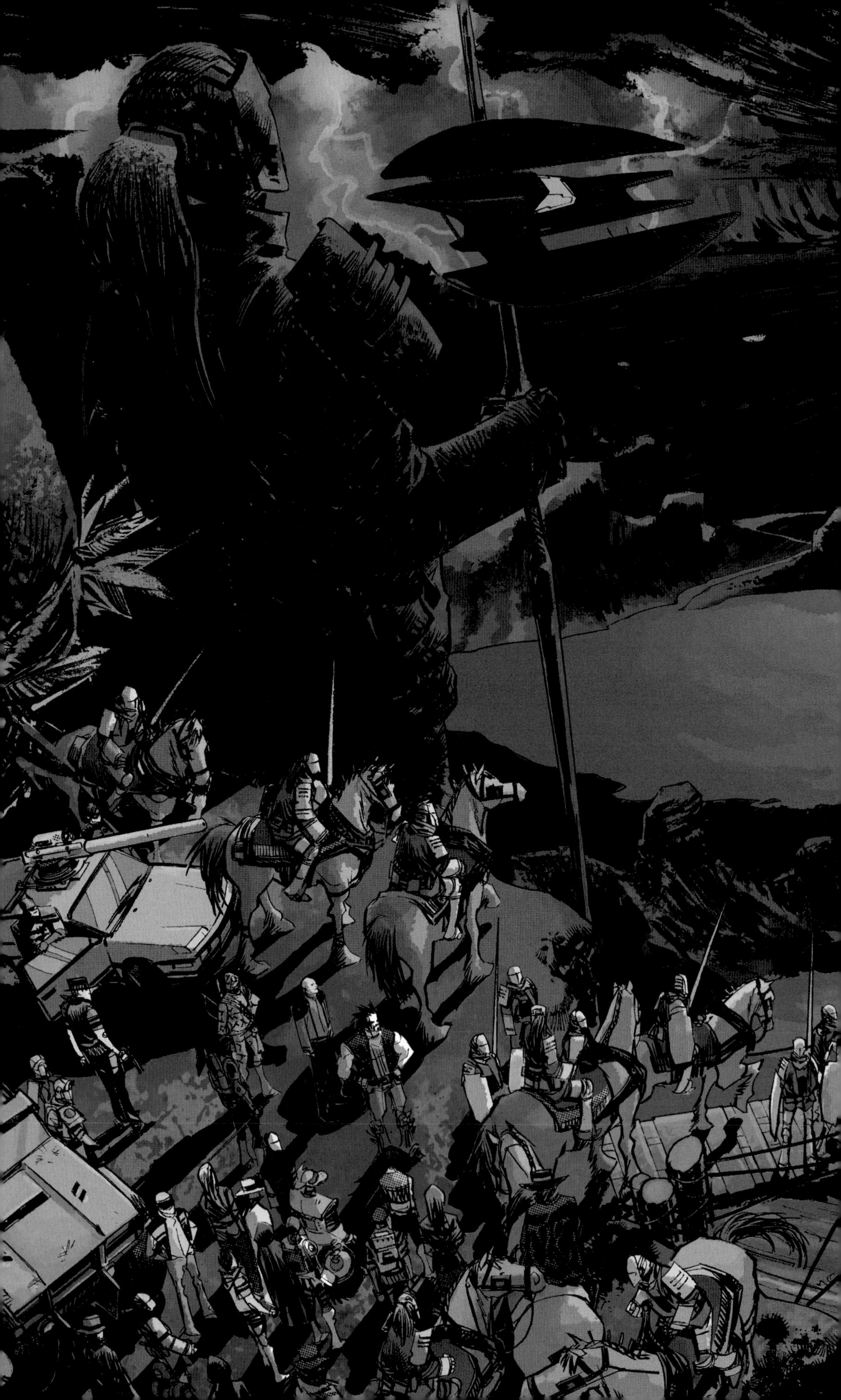

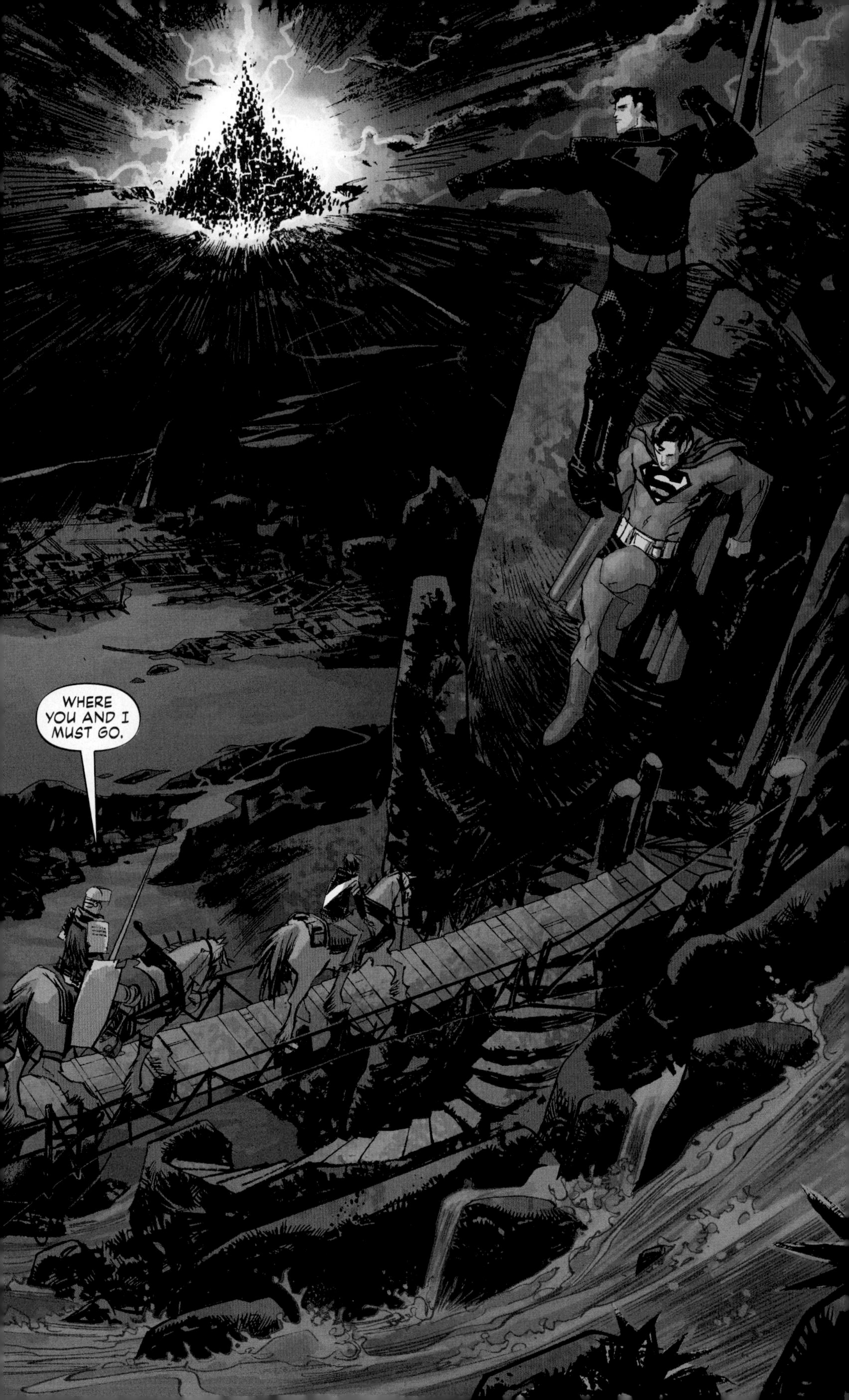
WHERE YOU AND I MUST GO.

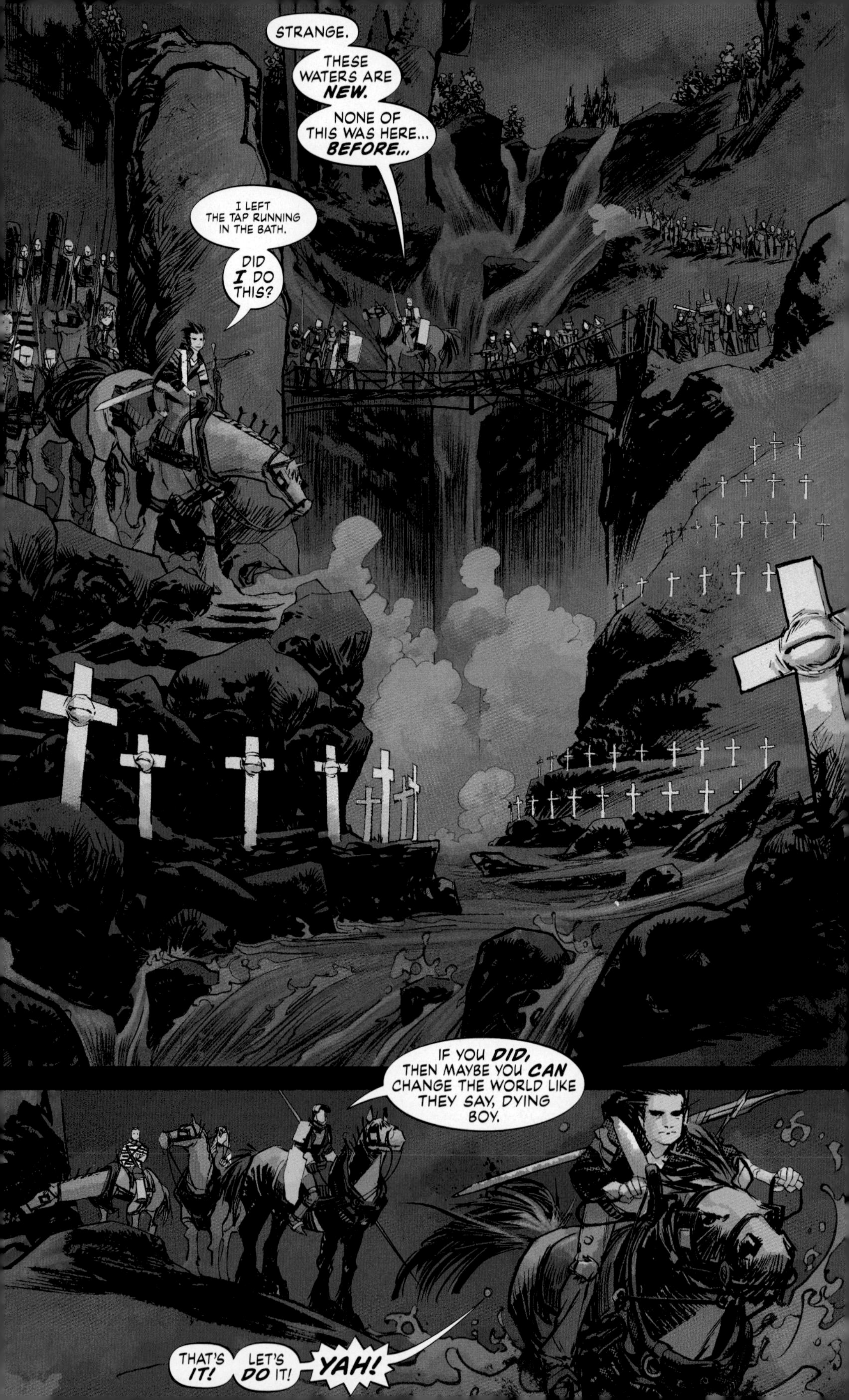
STRANGE.
THESE WATERS ARE NEW.
NONE OF THIS WAS HERE... BEFORE...
I LEFT THE TAP RUNNING IN THE BATH.
DID I DO THIS?
IF YOU DID, THEN MAYBE YOU CAN CHANGE THE WORLD LIKE THEY SAY, DYING BOY.
THAT'S IT!
LET'S DO IT!
YAH!

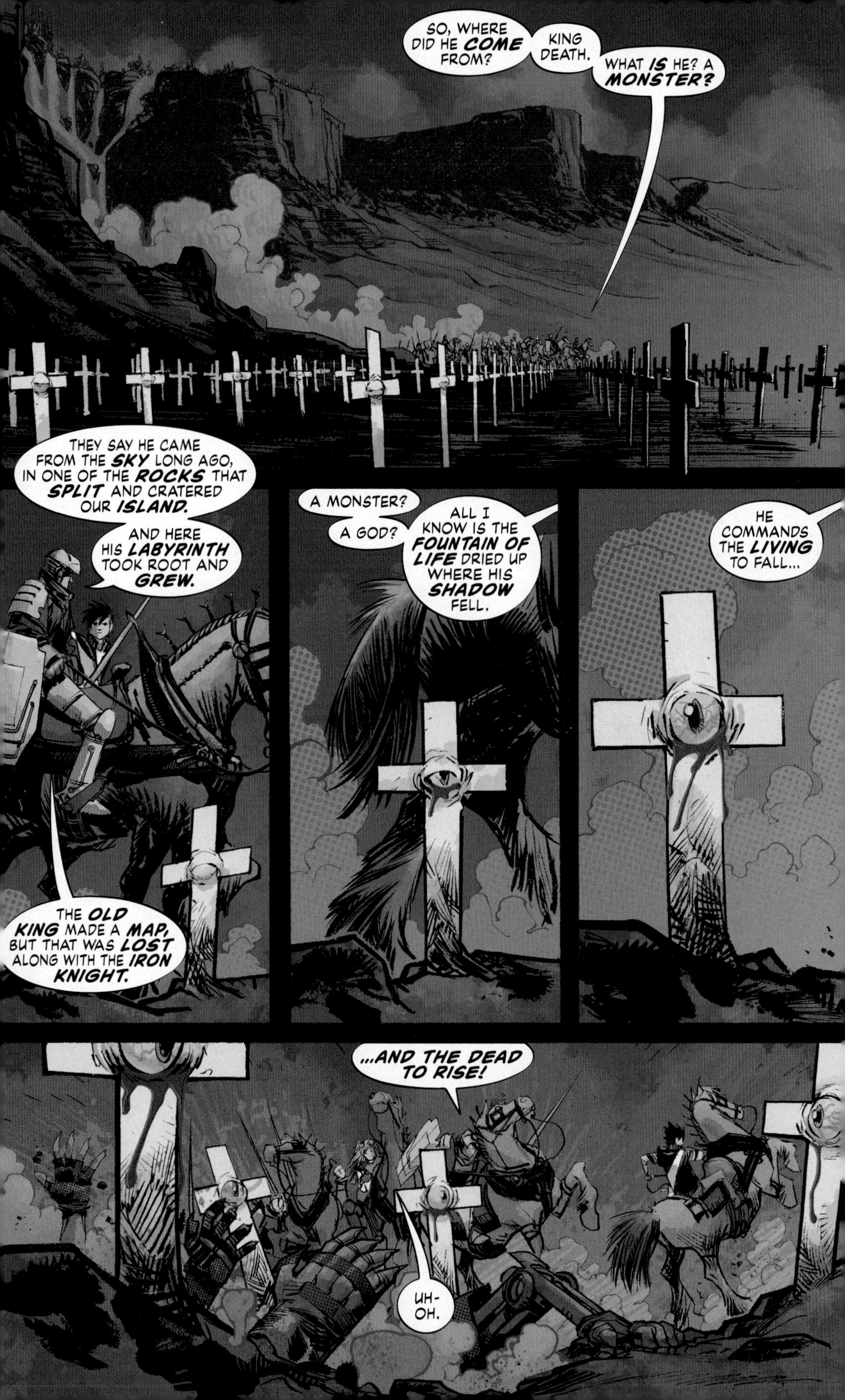
SO, WHERE DID HE COME FROM?
KING DEATH.
WHAT IS HE? A MONSTER?
THEY SAY HE CAME FROM THE SKY LONG AGO, IN ONE OF THE ROCKS THAT SPLIT AND CRATERED OUR ISLAND.
AND HERE HIS LABYRINTH TOOK ROOT AND GREW.
THE OLD KING MADE A MAP, BUT THAT WAS LOST ALONG WITH THE IRON KNIGHT.
A MONSTER?
A GOD?
ALL I KNOW IS THE FOUNTAIN OF LIFE DRIED UP WHERE HIS SHADOW FELL.
HE COMMANDS THE LIVING TO FALL...
...AND THE DEAD TO RISE!
UH-OH.

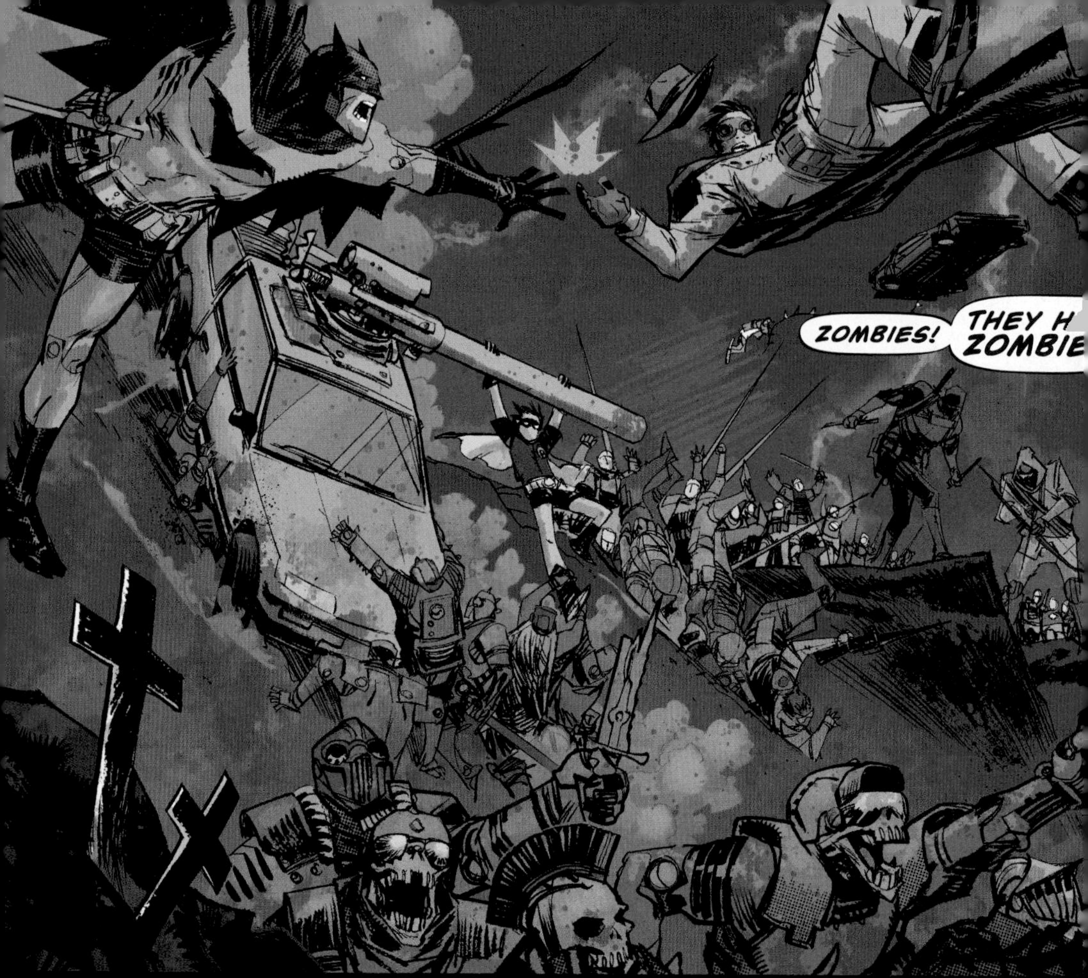
ZOMBIES!
THEY H ZOMBIE

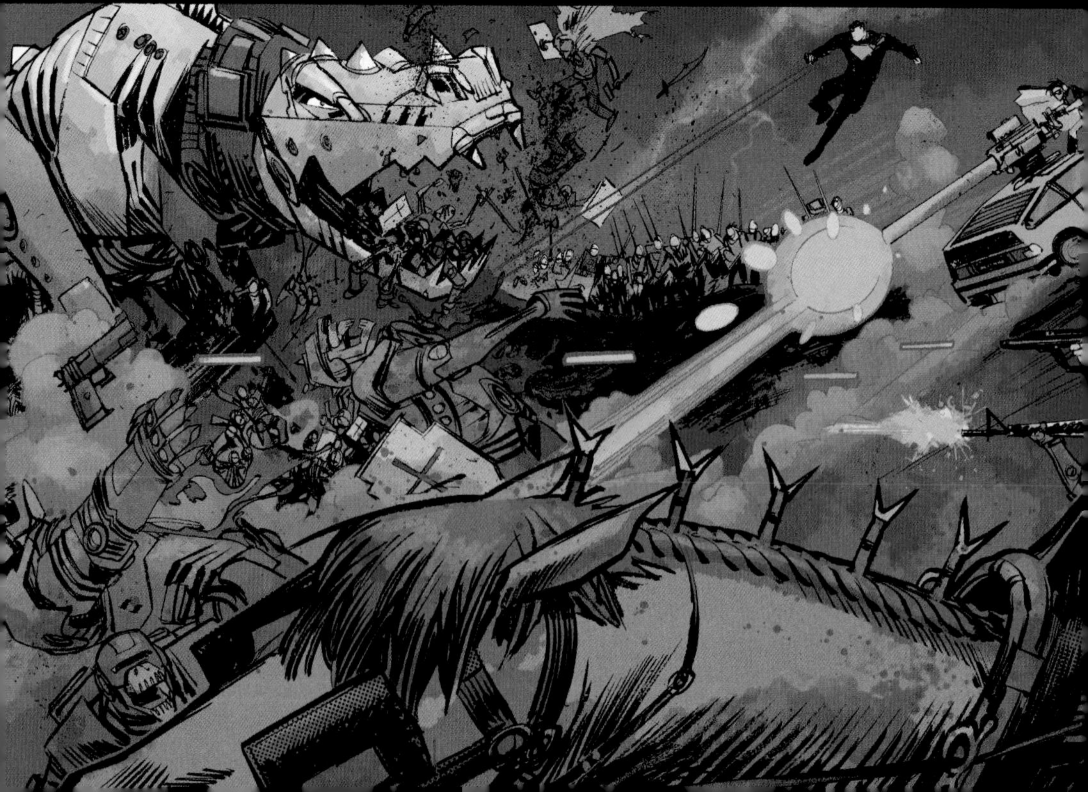

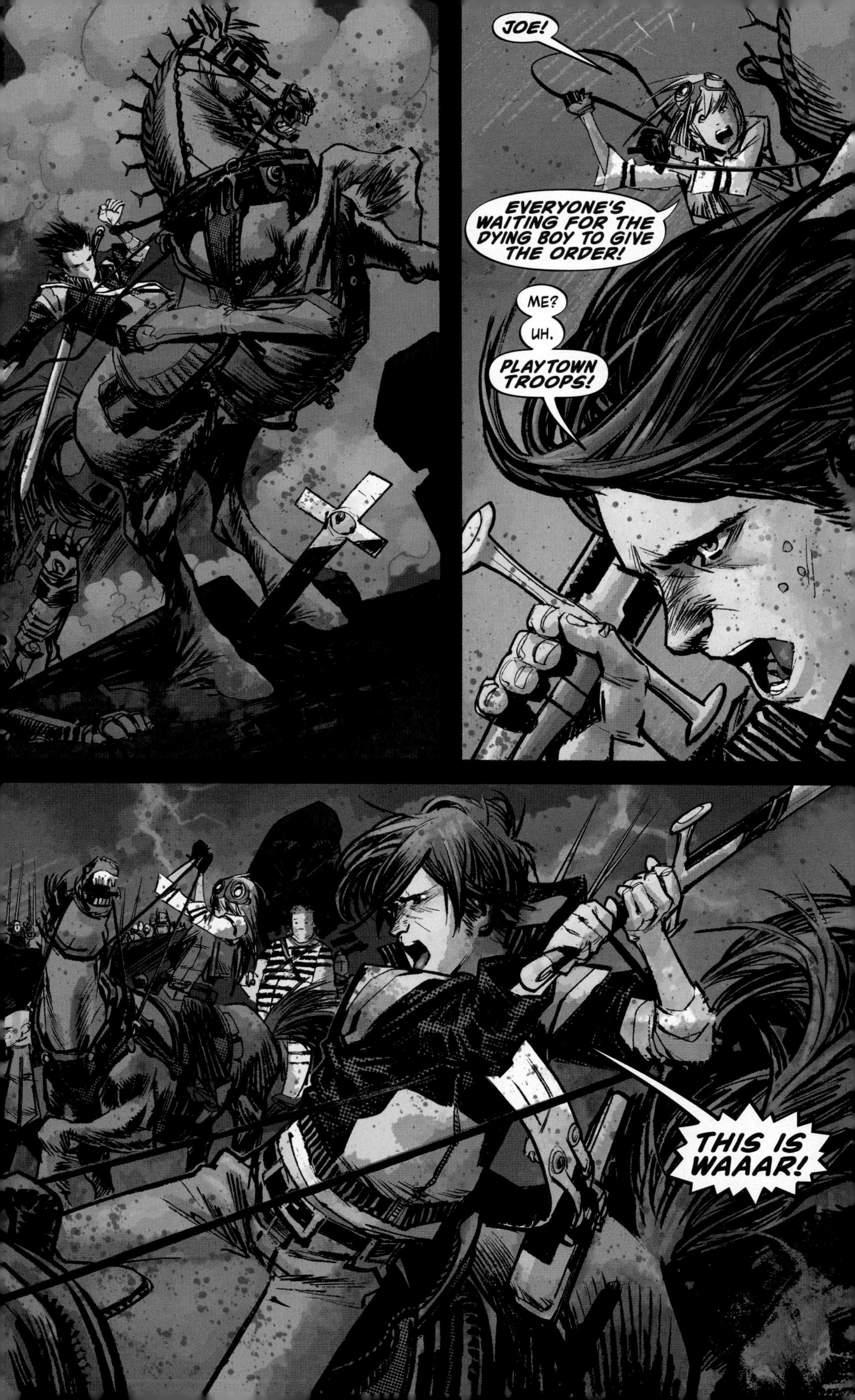
JOE!
EVERYONE'S WAITING FOR THE DYING BOY TO GIVE THE ORDER!
ME?
UH.
PLAYTOWN TROOPS!
THIS IS WAAAR!

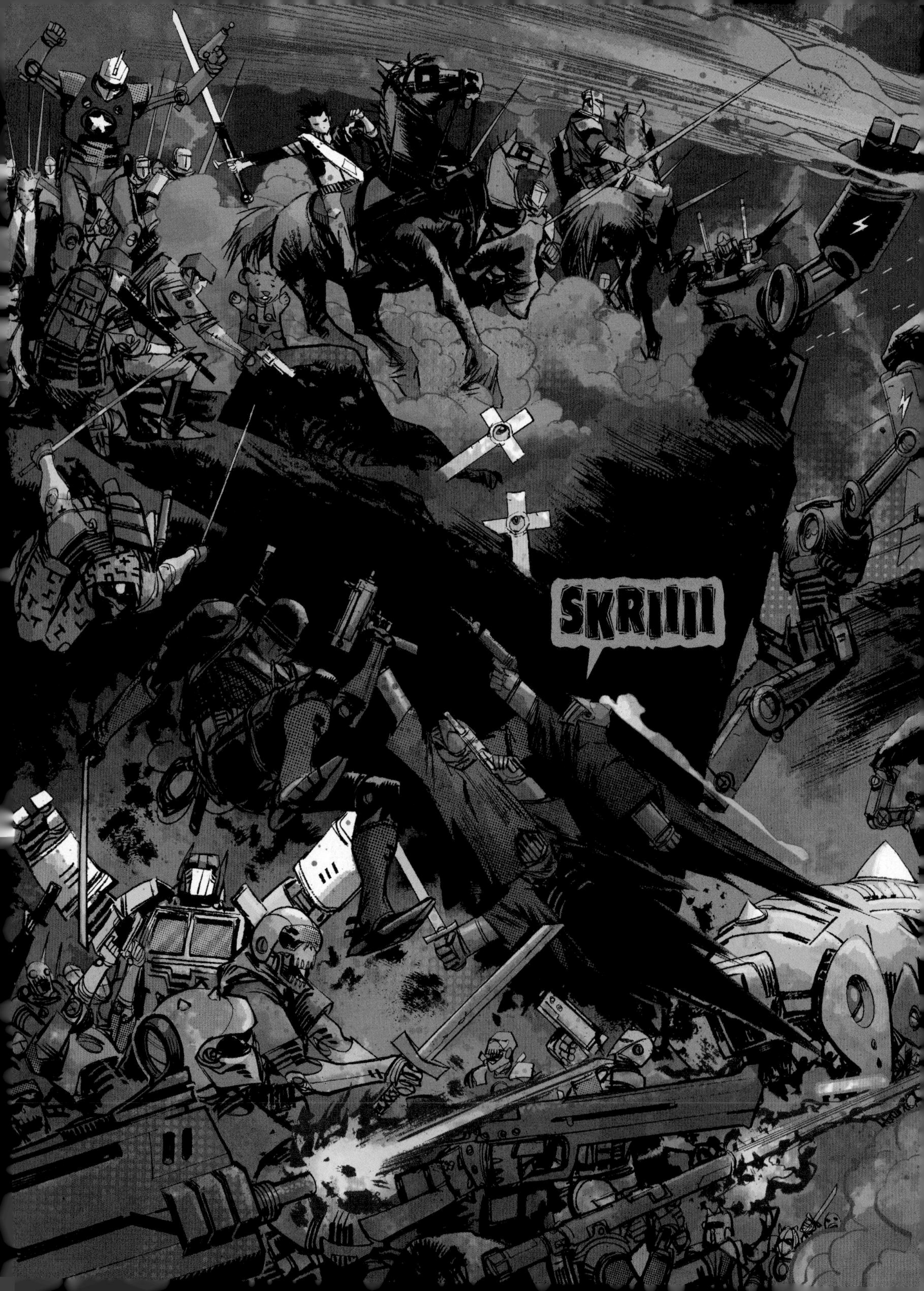
SKRIIII

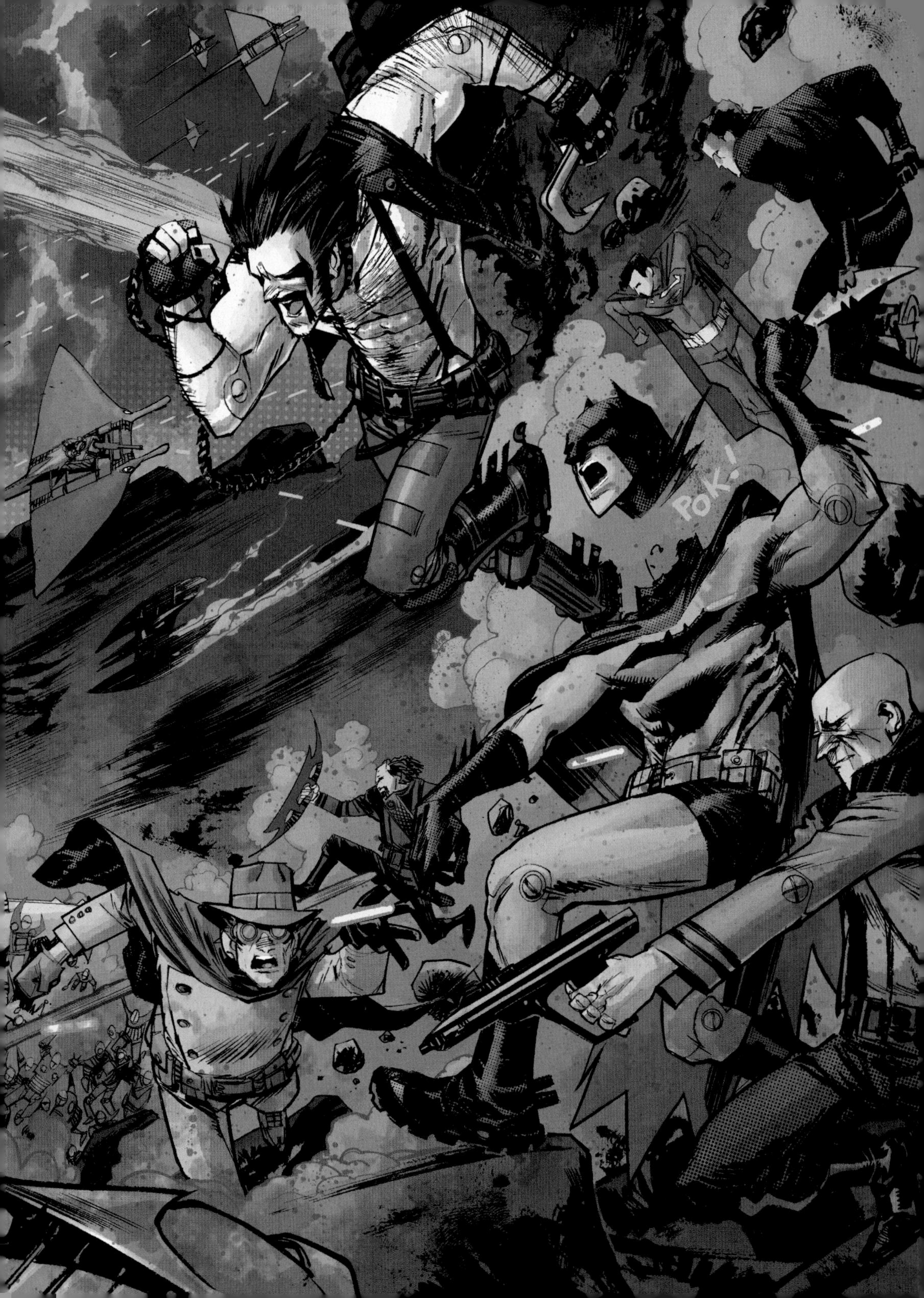
POK!

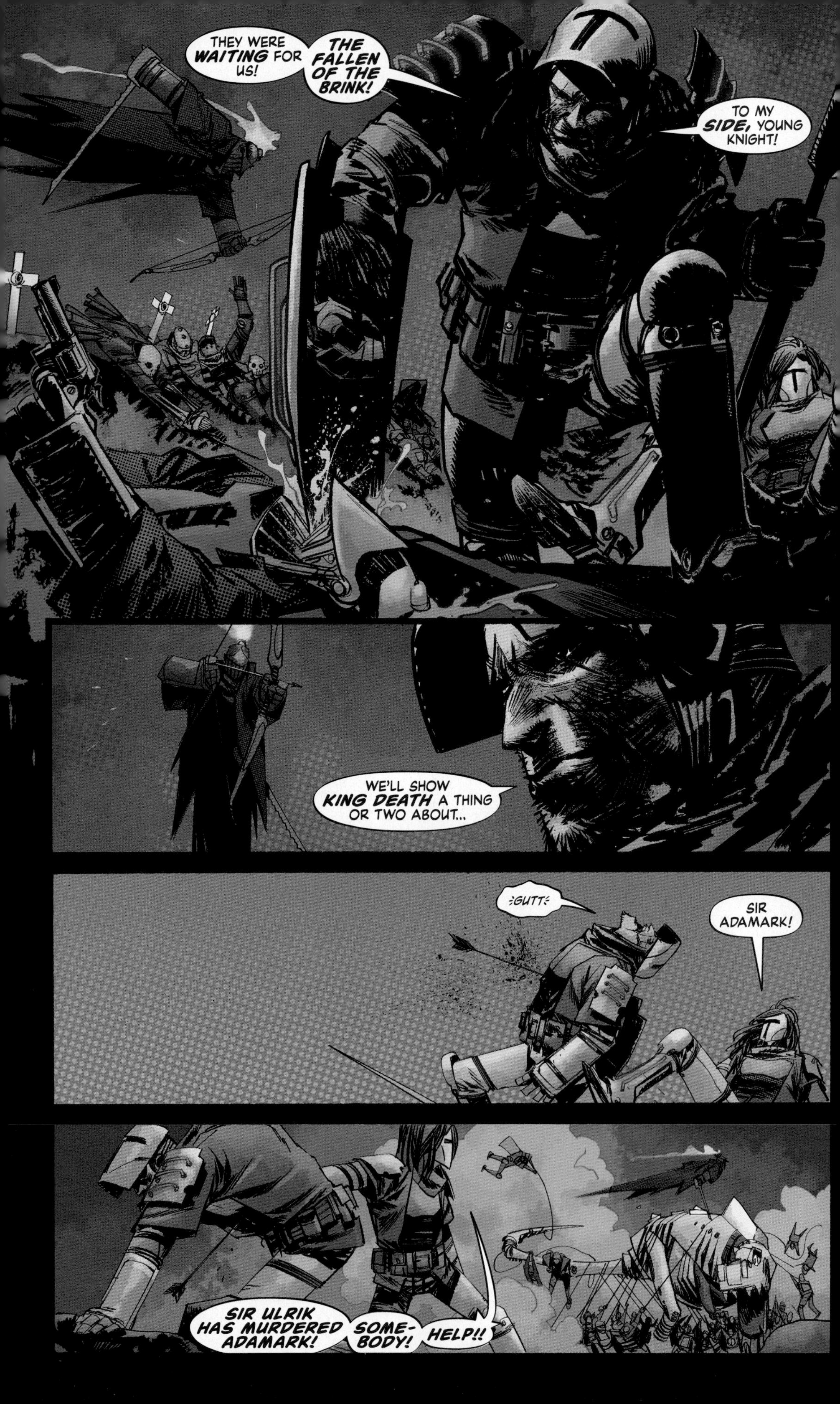
THEY WERE WAITING FOR US!
THE FALLEN OF THE BRINK!
TO MY SIDE, YOUNG KNIGHT!
WE'LL SHOW KING DEATH A THING OR TWO ABOUT...
GUTT
SIR ADAMARK!
SIR ULRIK HAS MURDERED ADAMARK!
SOME-BODY!
HELP!!

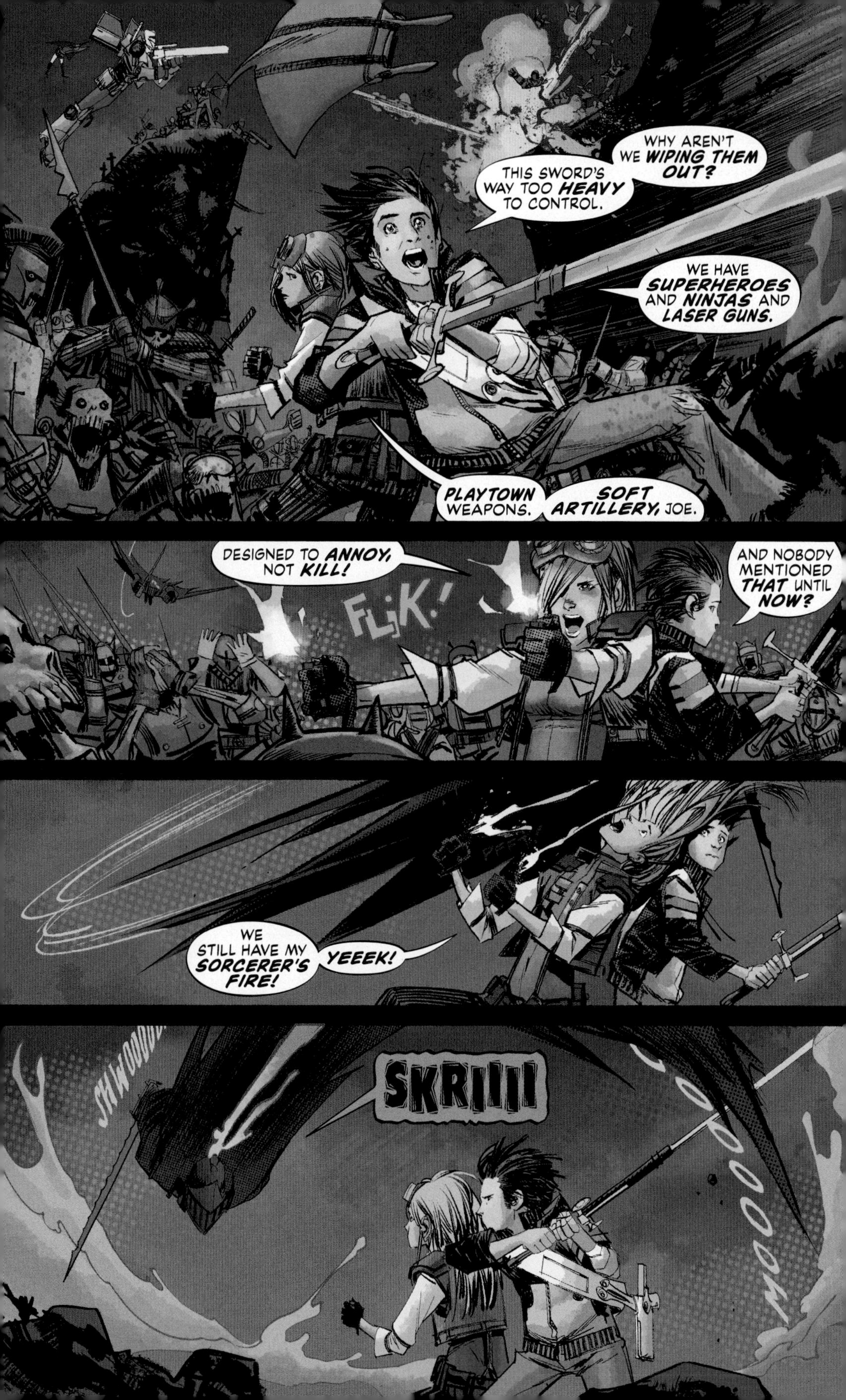
THIS SWORD'S WAY TOO HEAVY TO CONTROL.
WHY AREN'T WE WIPING THEM OUT?
WE HAVE SUPERHEROES AND NINJAS AND LASER GUNS.
PLAYTOWN WEAPONS.
SOFT ARTILLERY, JOE.
DESIGNED TO ANNOY, NOT KILL!
FLIK!
AND NOBODY MENTIONED THAT UNTIL NOW?
WE STILL HAVE MY SORCERER'S FIRE!
YEEEK!
SKRIIII

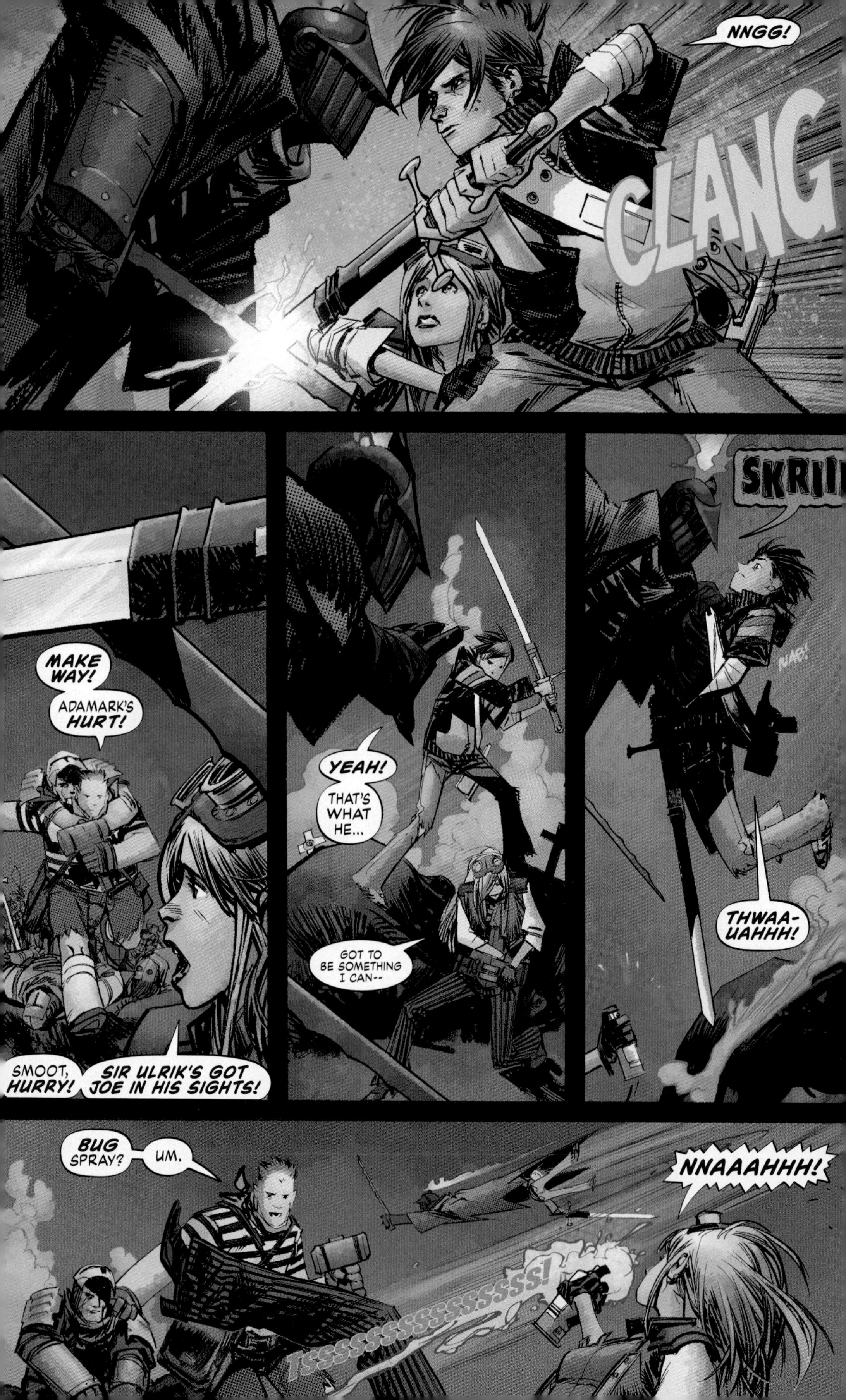
NNGG!
CLANG
MAKE WAY!
ADAMARK'S HURT!
SMOOT, HURRY!
SIR ULRIK'S GOT JOE IN HIS SIGHTS!
YEAH!
THAT'S WHAT HE...
GOT TO BE SOMETHING I CAN--
SKRIII
NAB!
THWAA-UAHHH!
BUG SPRAY?
UM.
NNAAAHHH!
TSSSSSSSSSSSSSSSSSS!

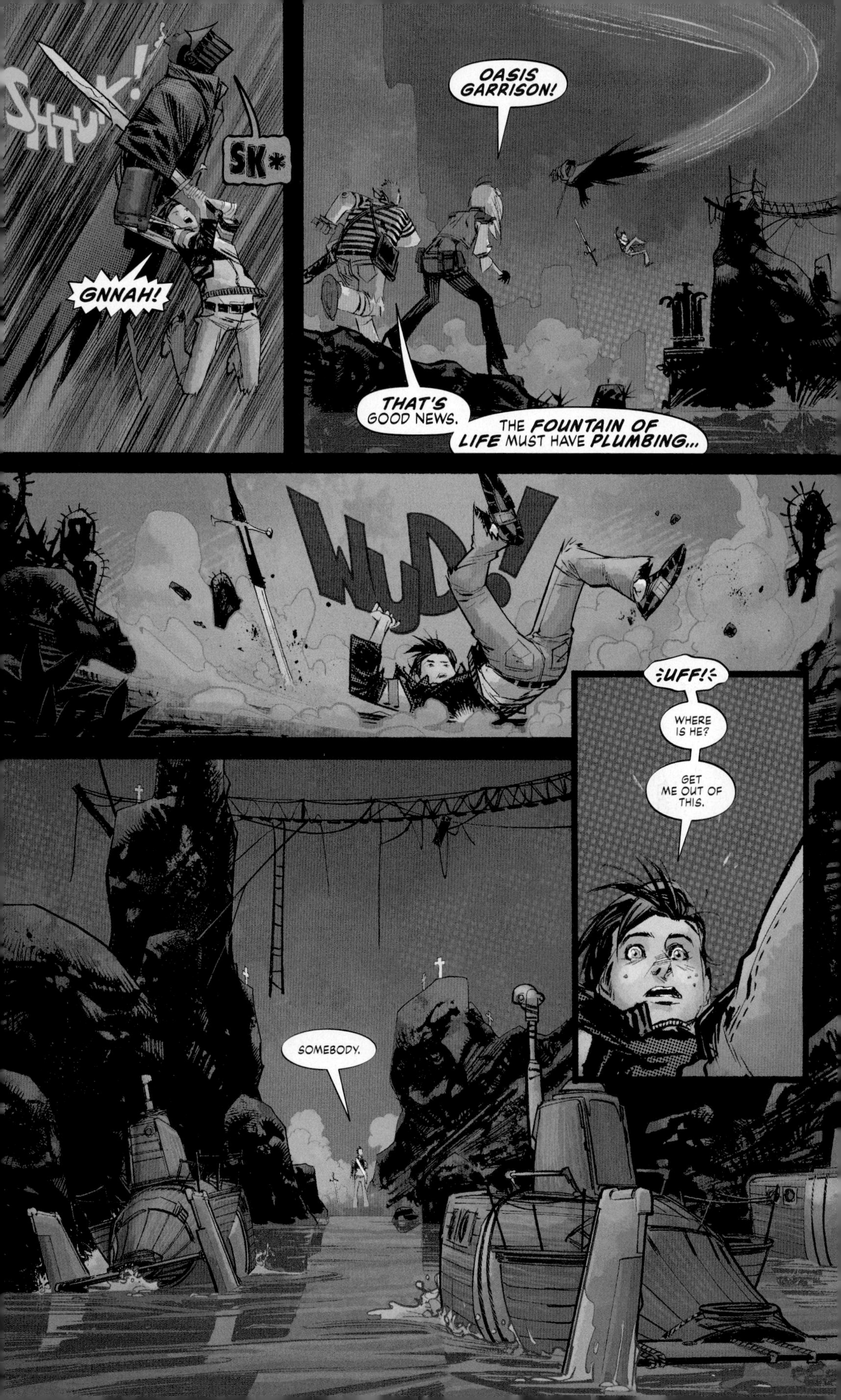
SHTUK!
SK*
GNNAH!
OASIS GARRISON!
THAT'S GOOD NEWS.
THE FOUNTAIN OF LIFE MUST HAVE PLUMBING...
WUD!
UFF!
WHERE IS HE?
GET ME OUT OF THIS.
SOMEBODY.

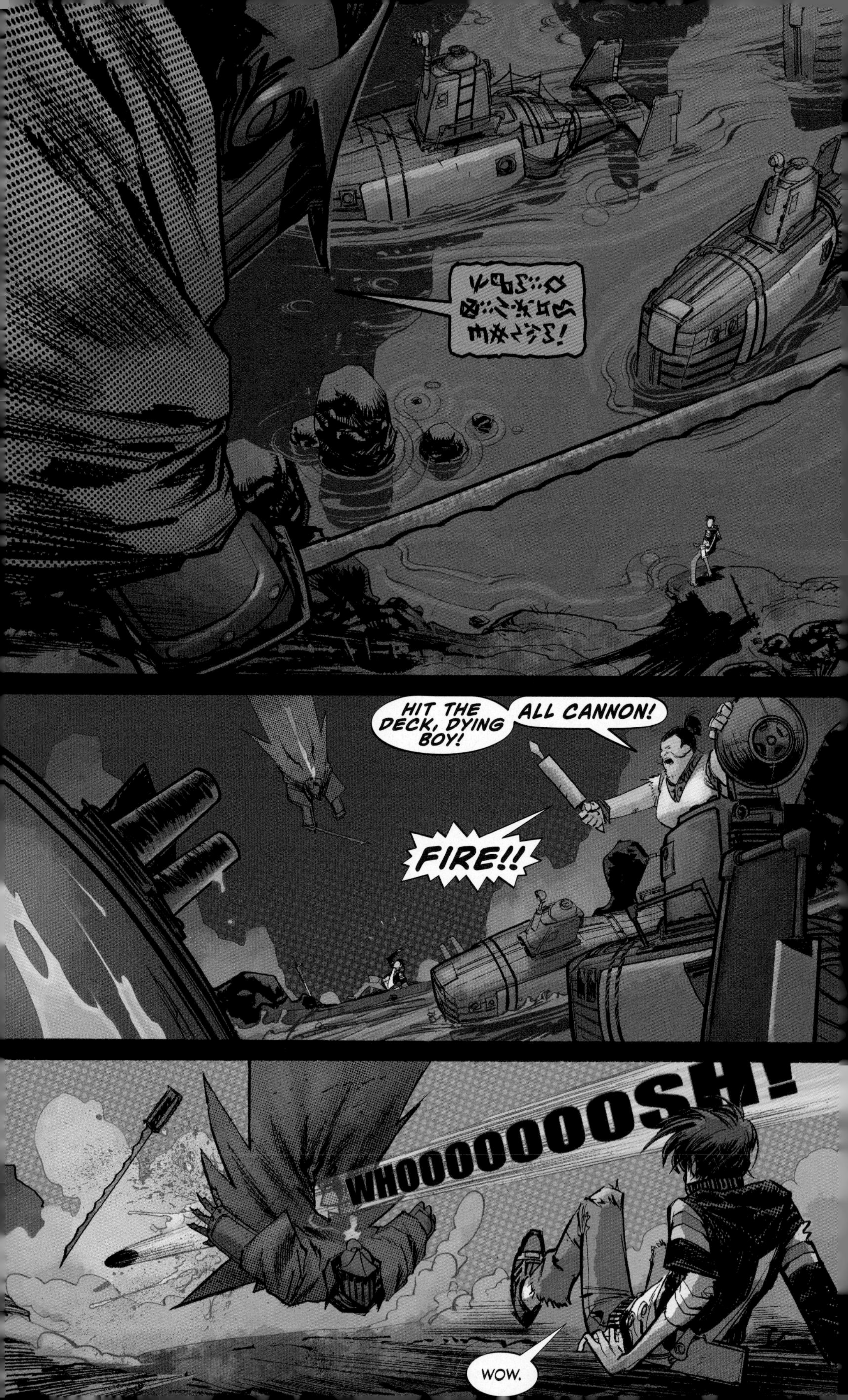
HIT THE DECK, DYING BOY!
ALL CANNON!
FIRE!!
WHOOOOOOOSH!
WOW.

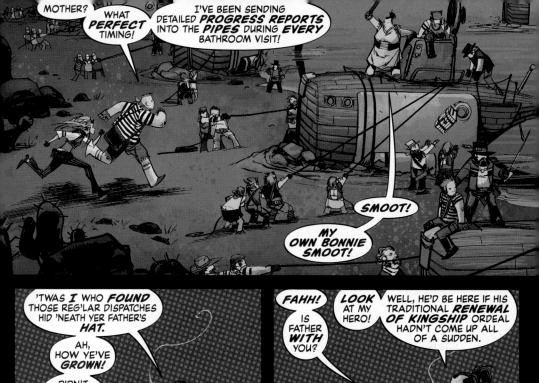

MOTHER? WHAT **PERFECT** TIMING!

I'VE BEEN SENDING DETAILED **PROGRESS REPORTS** INTO THE **PIPES** DURING **EVERY** BATHROOM VISIT!

SMOOT!

MY OWN BONNIE SMOOT!

'TWAS **I** WHO **FOUND** THOSE REG'LAR DISPATCHES HID 'NEATH YER FATHER'S **HAT.**

AH, HOW YE'VE **GROWN!**

DIDN'T I ALWAYS **SAY** THERE WAS **GIANT** IN YE?!

MMRRMMFF

FMMBBL

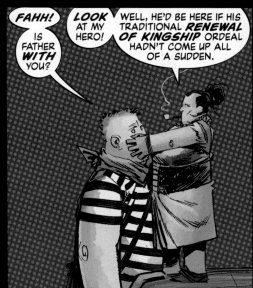

FAHH! IS FATHER **WITH** YOU?

LOOK AT MY **HERO!** WELL, HE'D BE HERE IF HIS TRADITIONAL **RENEWAL OF KINGSHIP** ORDEAL HADN'T COME UP ALL OF A SUDDEN.

SO I'M **QUEEN** OF THE PIRATES 'TIL THE **BLUE CRAB MIGRATION SEASON'S** DONE.

WHAT **I** SAY GOES.

AN' I WON'T SEE MY **BOY** FIGHT A WHOLE **WAR** ON HIS **OWN!**

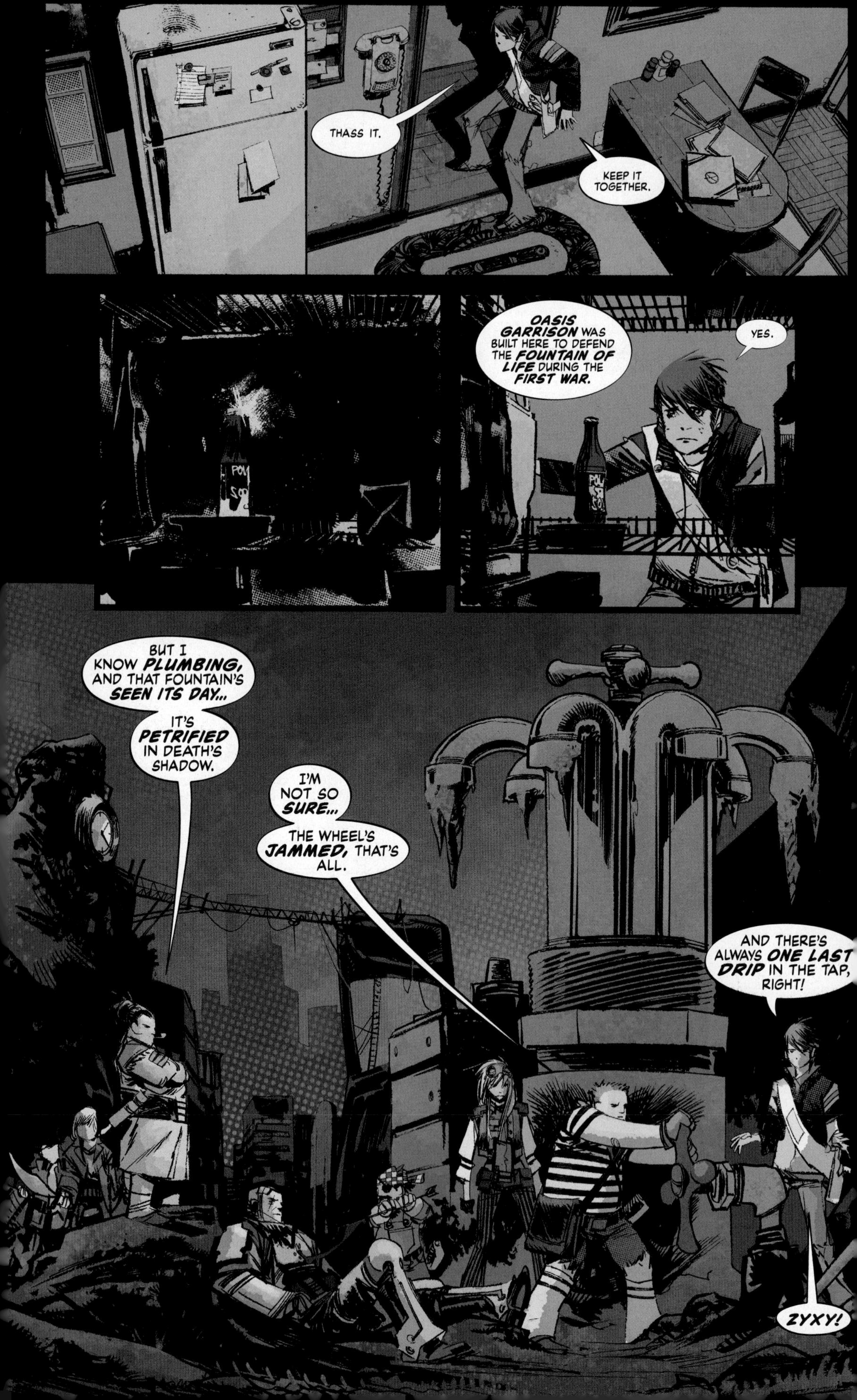
THASS IT.
KEEP IT TOGETHER.
OASIS GARRISON WAS BUILT HERE TO DEFEND THE FOUNTAIN OF LIFE DURING THE FIRST WAR.
YES.
BUT I KNOW PLUMBING, AND THAT FOUNTAIN'S SEEN ITS DAY...
IT'S PETRIFIED IN DEATH'S SHADOW.
I'M NOT SO SURE...
THE WHEEL'S JAMMED, THAT'S ALL.
AND THERE'S ALWAYS ONE LAST DRIP IN THE TAP, RIGHT!
ZYXY!

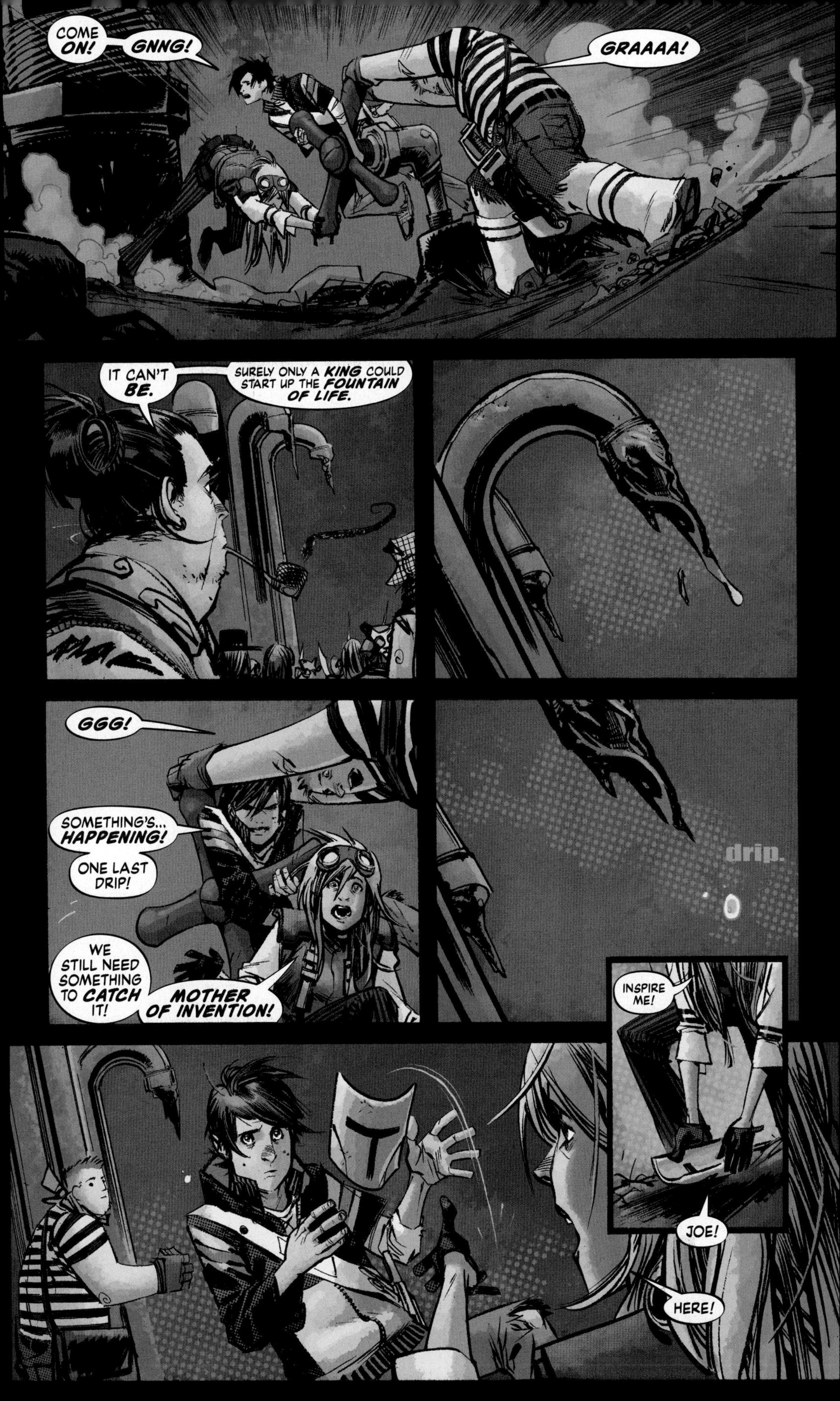
COME ON!
GNNG!
GRAAAA!
IT CAN'T BE.
SURELY ONLY A KING COULD START UP THE FOUNTAIN OF LIFE.
GGG!
SOMETHING'S... HAPPENING!
ONE LAST DRIP!
WE STILL NEED SOMETHING TO CATCH IT!
MOTHER OF INVENTION!
drip.
INSPIRE ME!
JOE!
HERE!

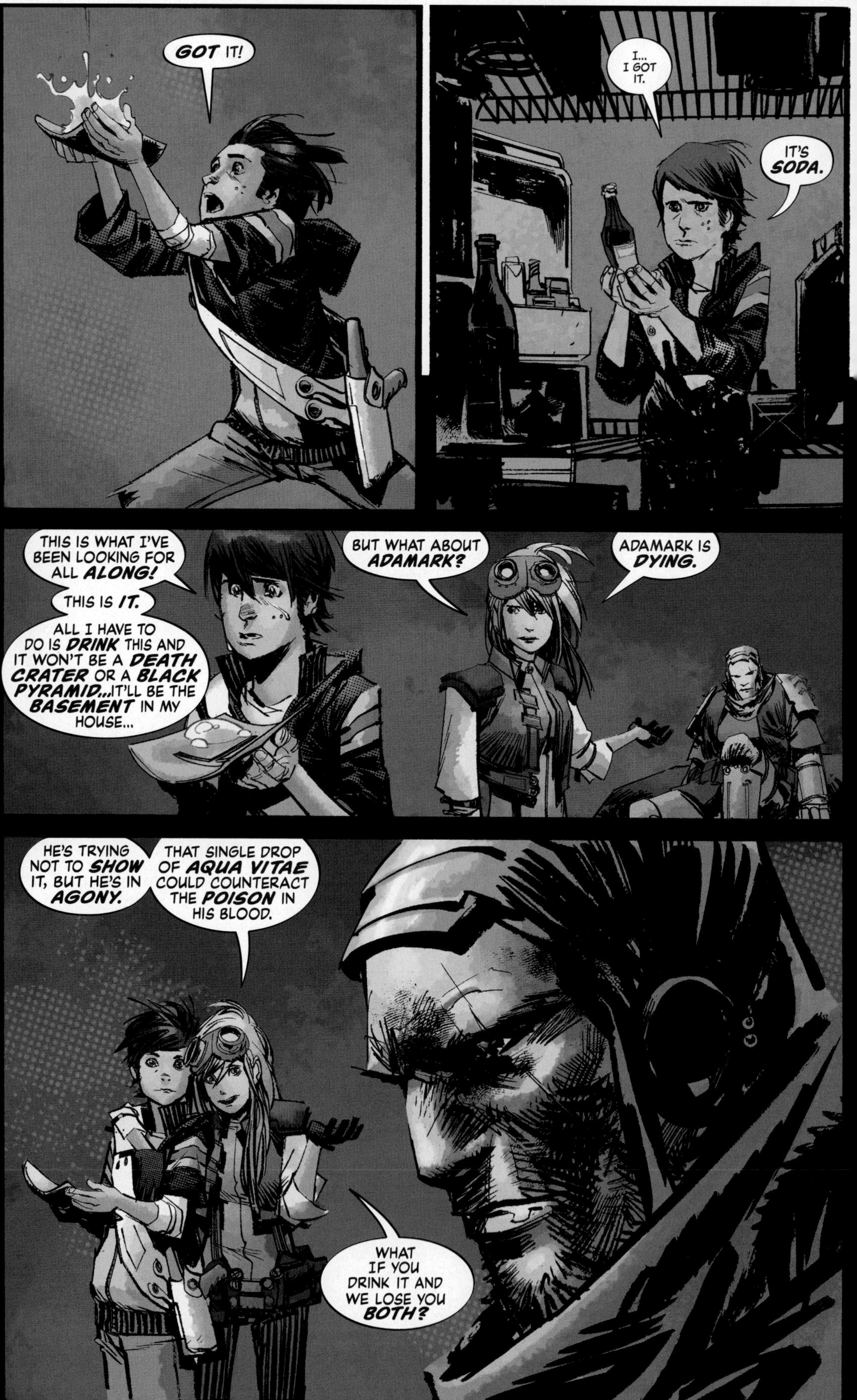
GOT IT!
I... I GOT IT.
IT'S SODA.
THIS IS WHAT I'VE BEEN LOOKING FOR ALL ALONG!
THIS IS IT.
ALL I HAVE TO DO IS DRINK THIS AND IT WON'T BE A DEATH CRATER OR A BLACK PYRAMID...IT'LL BE THE BASEMENT IN MY HOUSE...
BUT WHAT ABOUT ADAMARK?
ADAMARK IS DYING.
HE'S TRYING NOT TO SHOW IT, BUT HE'S IN AGONY.
THAT SINGLE DROP OF AQUA VITAE COULD COUNTERACT THE POISON IN HIS BLOOD.
WHAT IF YOU DRINK IT AND WE LOSE YOU BOTH?

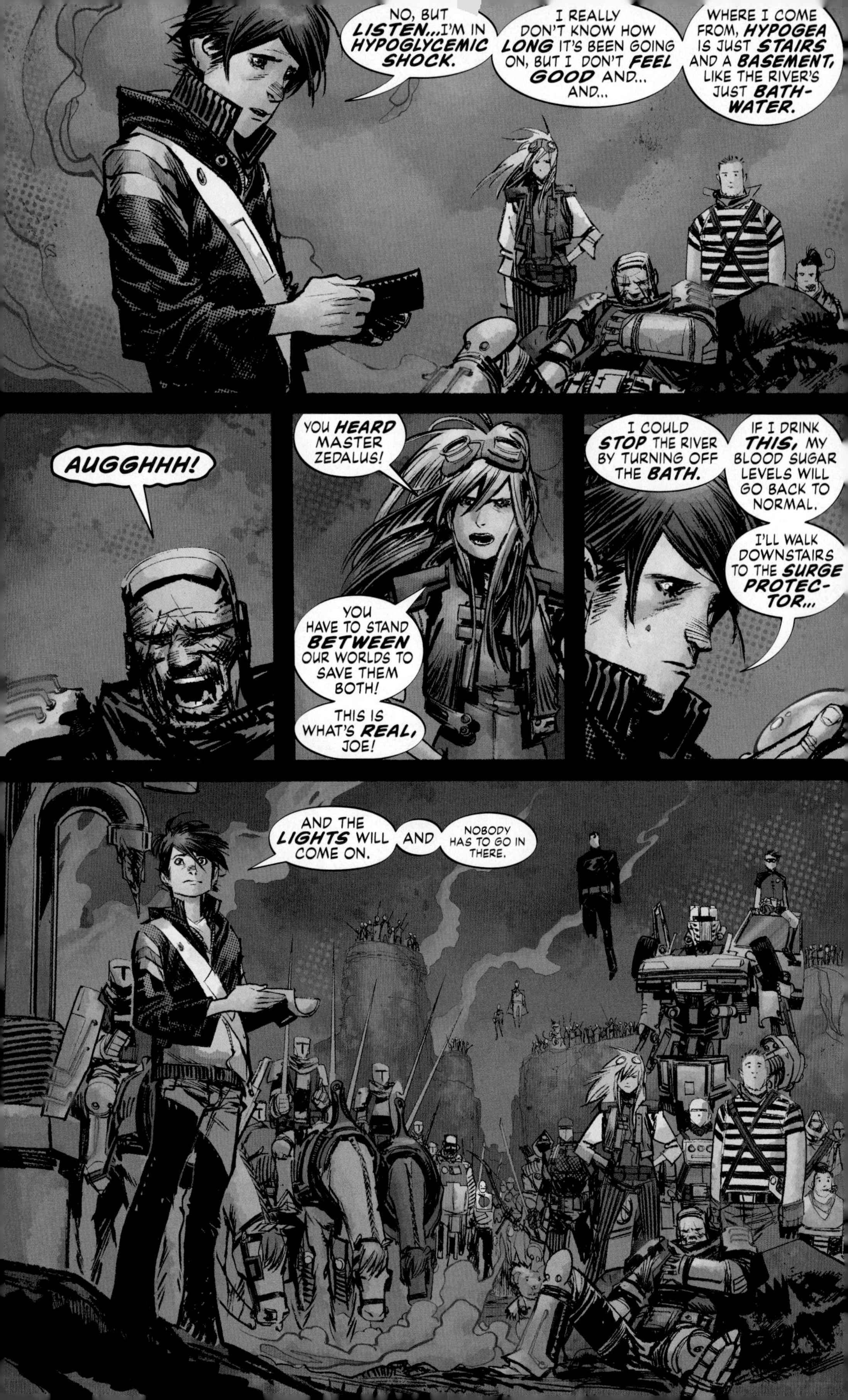
NO, BUT LISTEN...I'M IN HYPOGLYCEMIC SHOCK.
I REALLY DON'T KNOW HOW LONG IT'S BEEN GOING ON, BUT I DON'T FEEL GOOD AND... AND...
WHERE I COME FROM, HYPOGEA IS JUST STAIRS AND A BASEMENT, LIKE THE RIVER'S JUST BATH-WATER.
AUGGHHH!
YOU HEARD MASTER ZEDALUS!
YOU HAVE TO STAND BETWEEN OUR WORLDS TO SAVE THEM BOTH!
THIS IS WHAT'S REAL, JOE!
I COULD STOP THE RIVER BY TURNING OFF THE BATH.
IF I DRINK THIS, MY BLOOD SUGAR LEVELS WILL GO BACK TO NORMAL.
I'LL WALK DOWNSTAIRS TO THE SURGE PROTEC-TOR...
AND THE LIGHTS WILL COME ON.
AND
NOBODY HAS TO GO IN THERE.

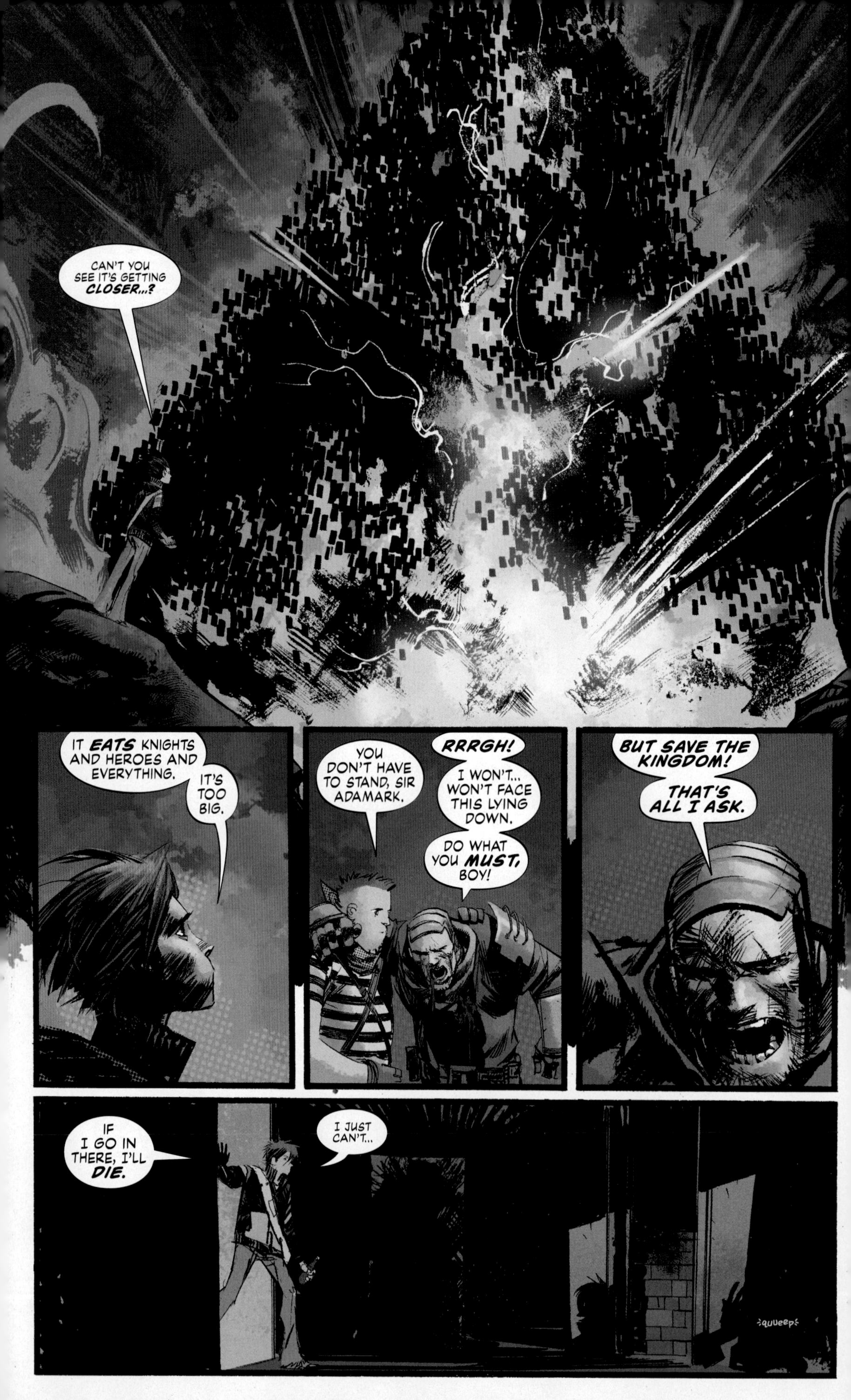
CAN'T YOU SEE IT'S GETTING CLOSER...?
IT EATS KNIGHTS AND HEROES AND EVERYTHING.
IT'S TOO BIG.
YOU DON'T HAVE TO STAND, SIR ADAMARK.
RRRGH!
I WON'T... WON'T FACE THIS LYING DOWN.
DO WHAT YOU MUST, BOY!
BUT SAVE THE KINGDOM!
THAT'S ALL I ASK.
IF I GO IN THERE, I'LL DIE.
I JUST CAN'T...
quueep

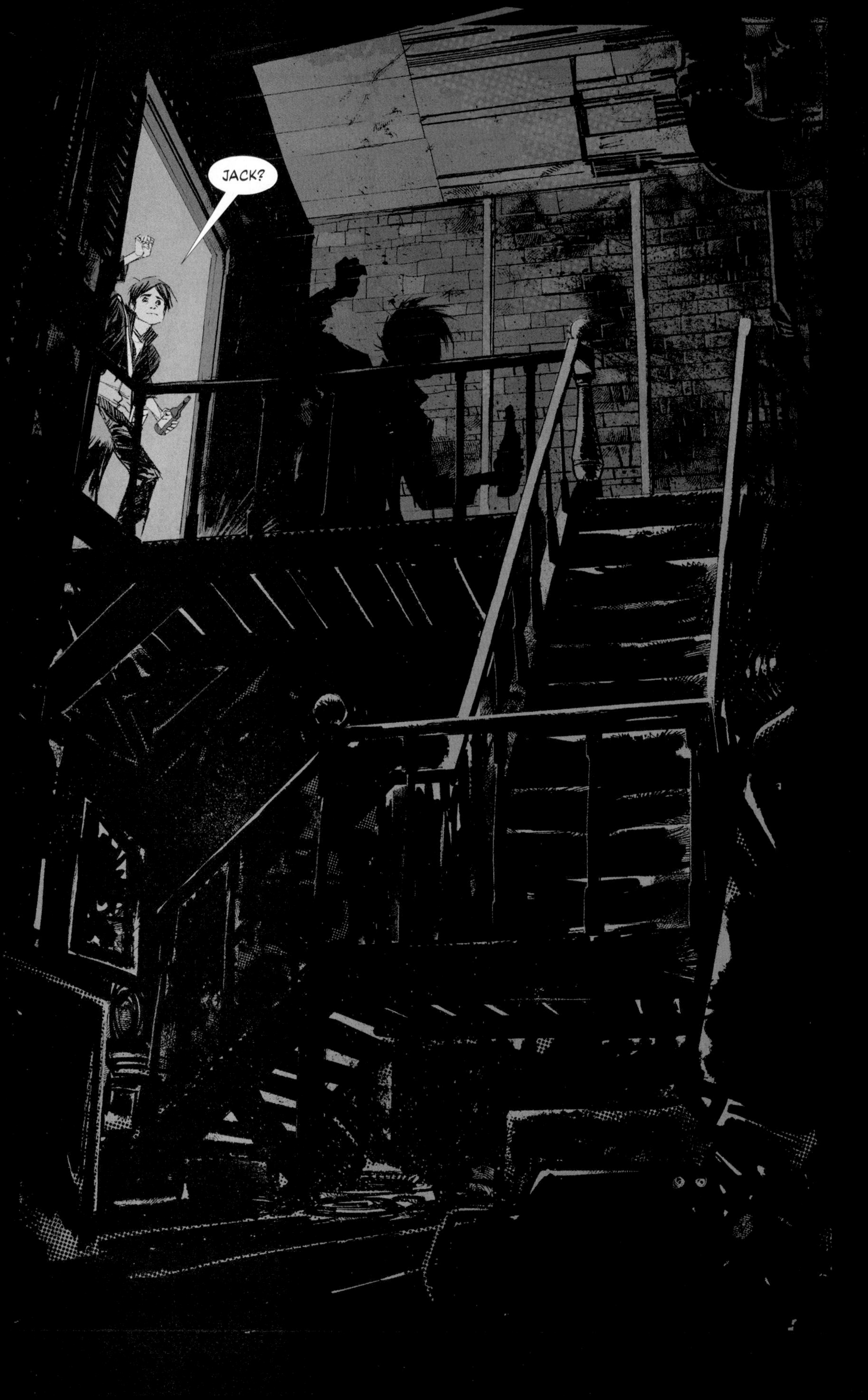
JACK?

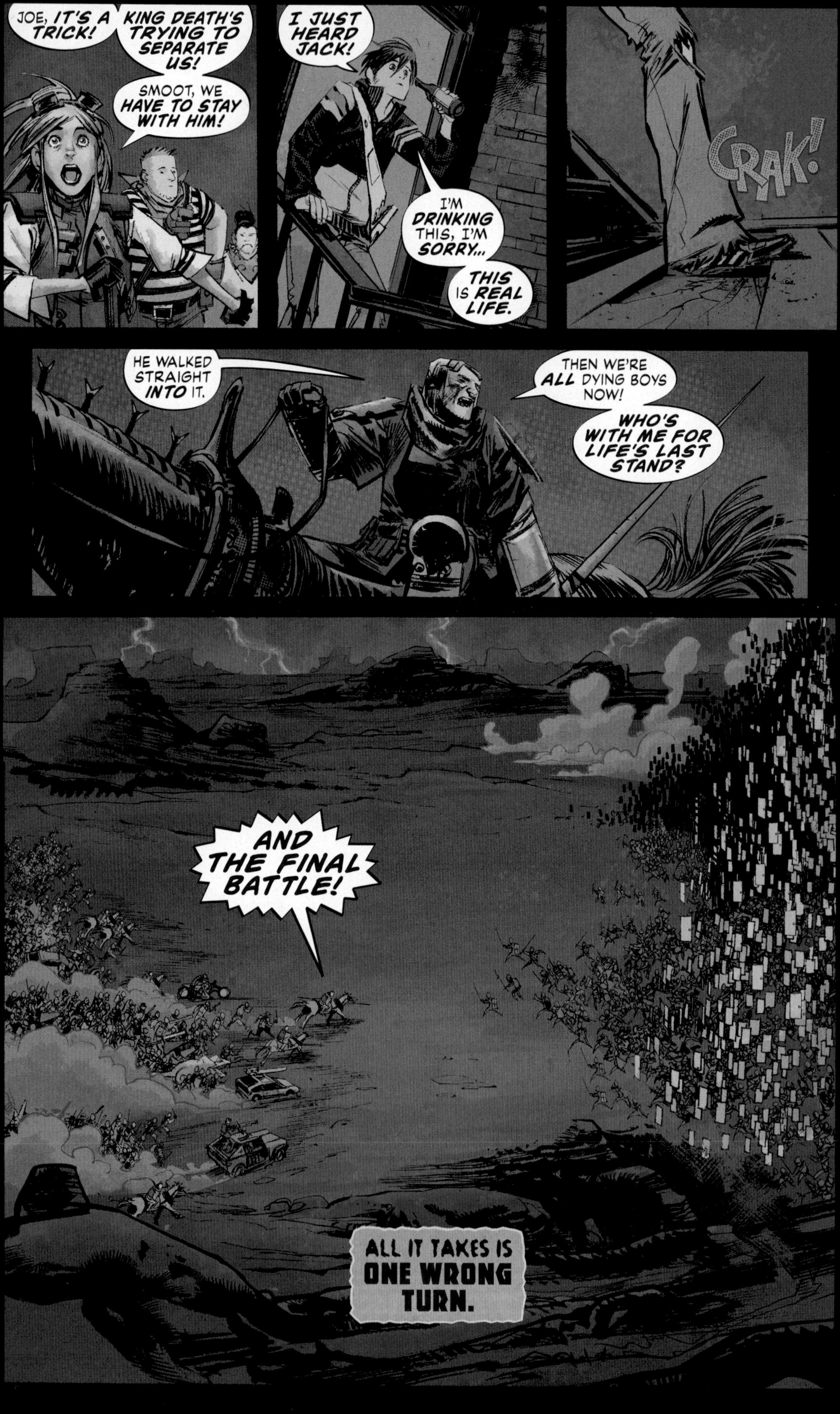

JOE, IT'S A TRICK!
KING DEATH'S TRYING TO SEPARATE US!
SMOOT, WE HAVE TO STAY WITH HIM!
I JUST HEARD JACK!
I'M DRINKING THIS, I'M SORRY...
THIS IS REAL LIFE.
CRAK!
HE WALKED STRAIGHT INTO IT.
THEN WE'RE ALL DYING BOYS NOW!
WHO'S WITH ME FOR LIFE'S LAST STAND?
AND THE FINAL BATTLE!
ALL IT TAKES IS ONE WRONG TURN.

AND THERE'S **ALWAYS** **ONE** **WRONG** **TURN.**

THROUGH A **DOOR**, INTO A **ROOM** YOU'LL **NEVER** LEAVE.

A DOOR THAT LEADS YOU TO **ME.**

THE DOOR YOU LEFT **UNLOCKED.**

THE DOOR YOU LEFT OPEN FOR **DEATH.**

DRIP.

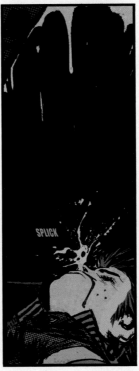

SPLICK

WELCOME, JOSEPH.

UPSIDE DOWN

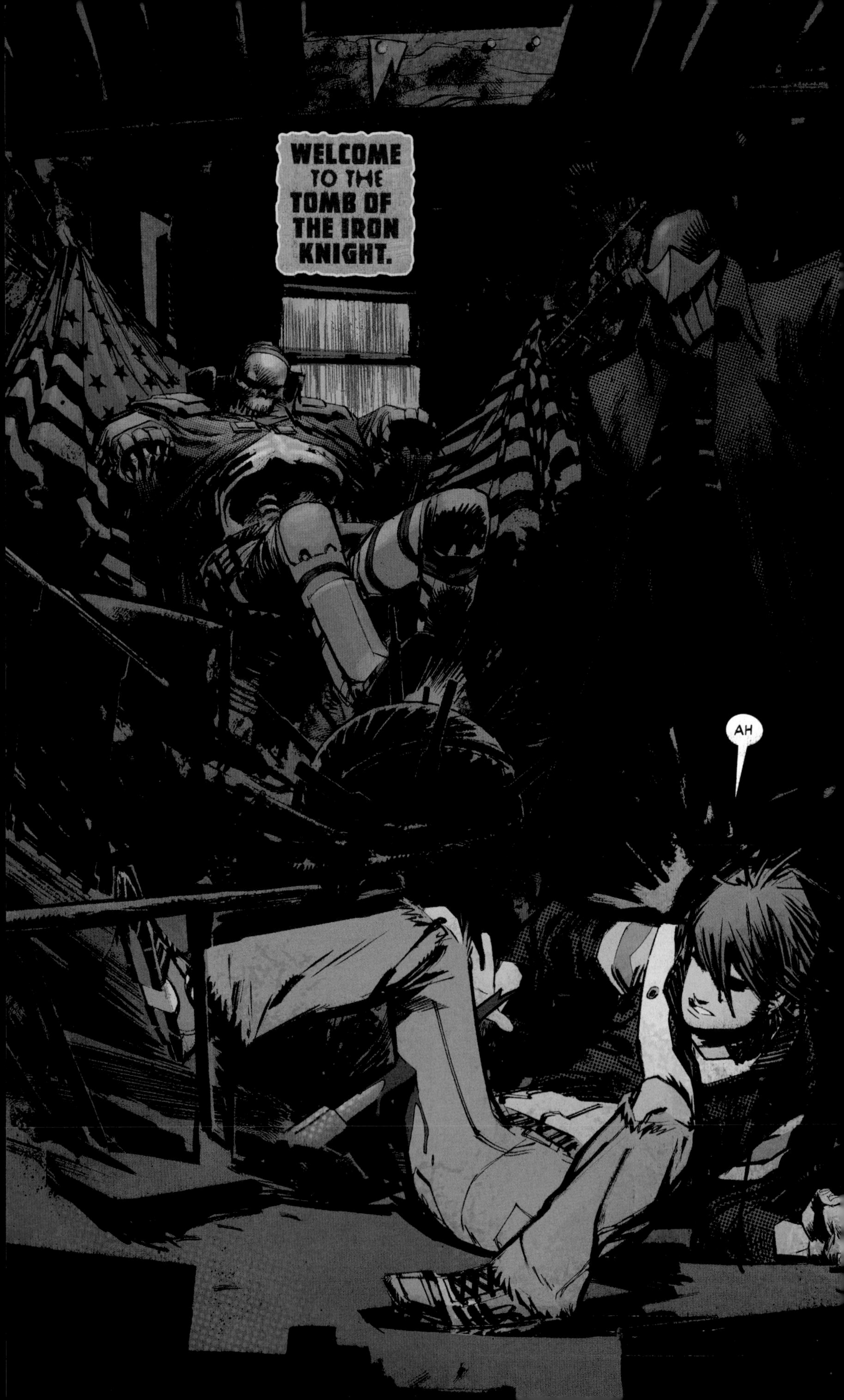
WELCOME TO THE TOMB OF THE IRON KNIGHT.
AH

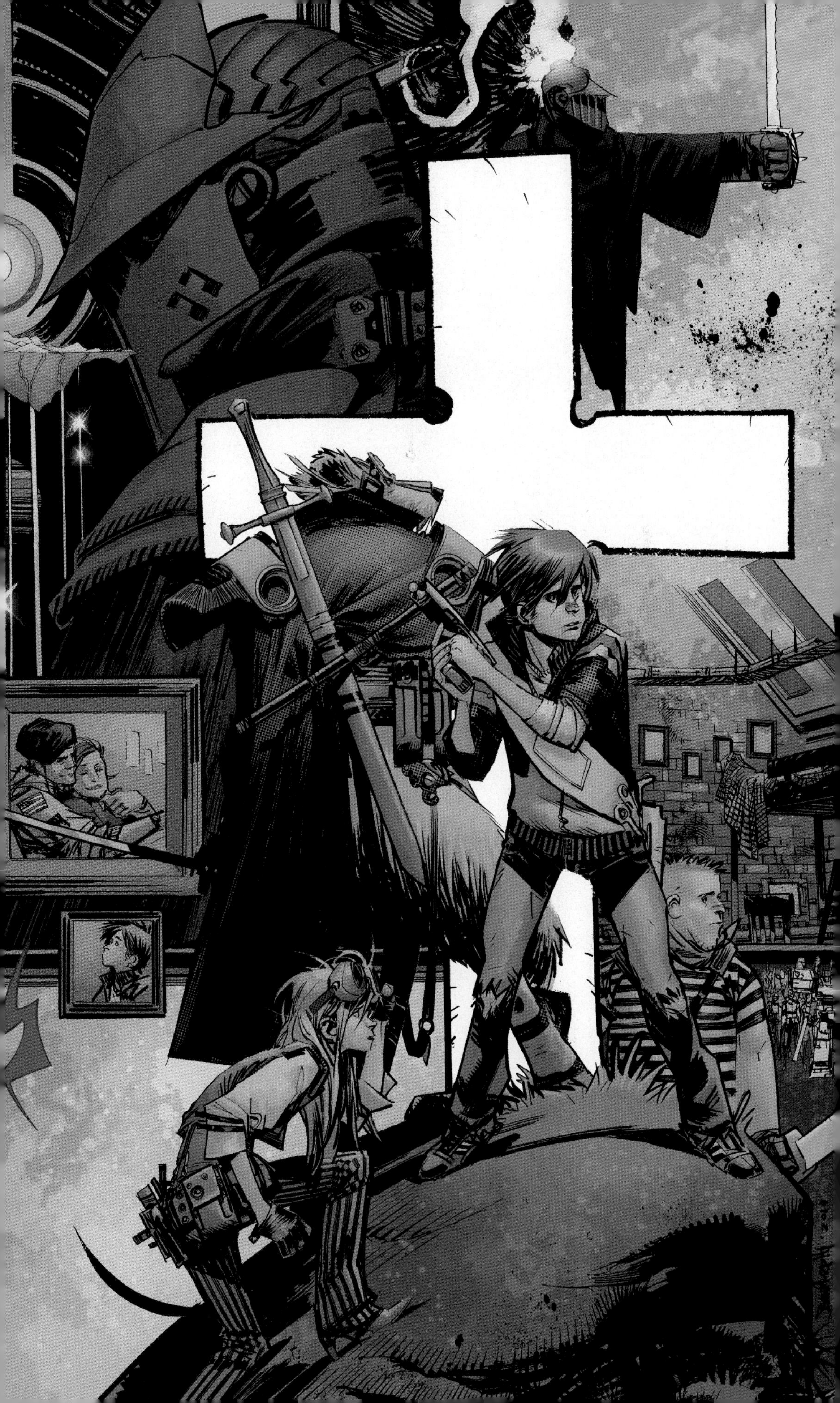

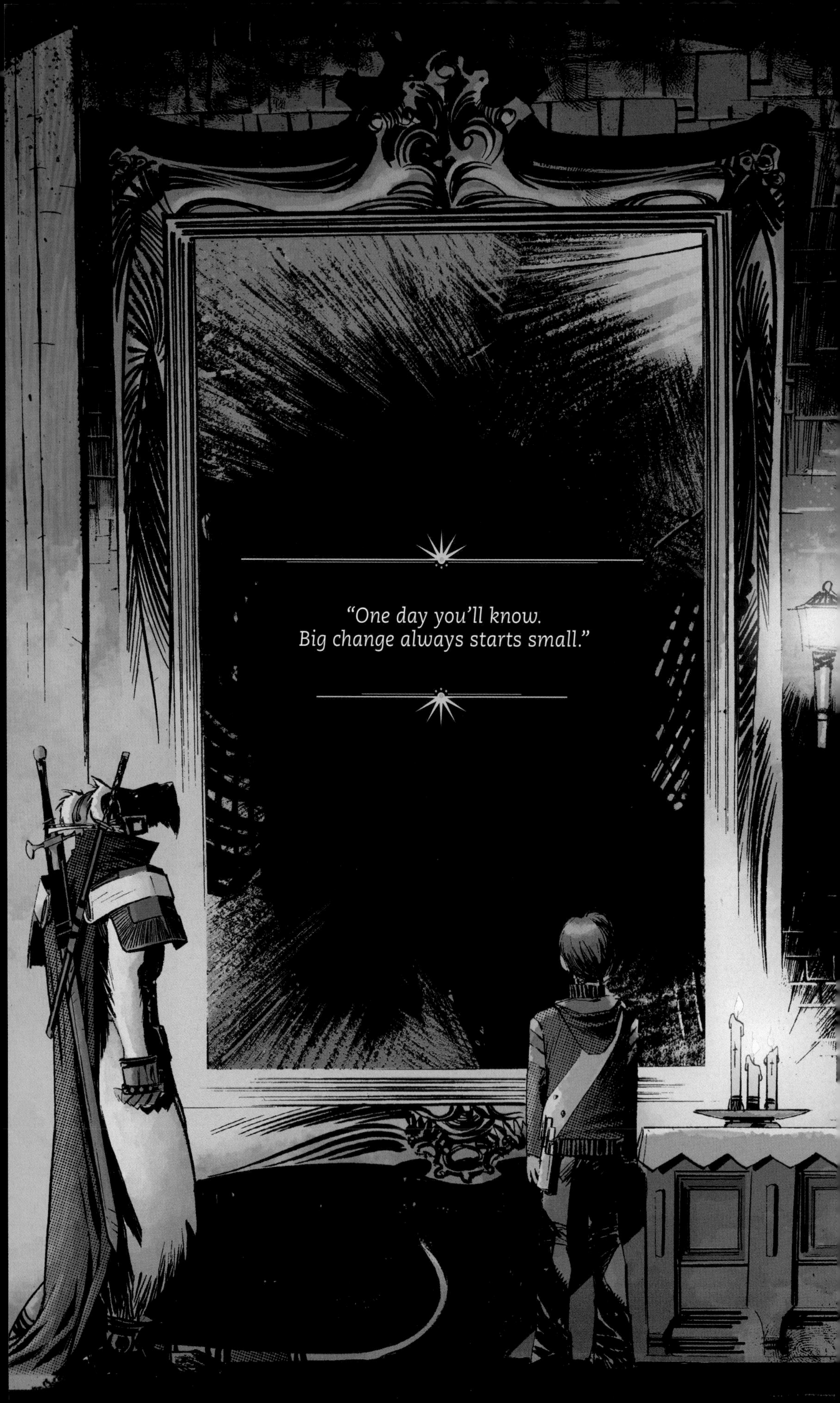
"One day you'll know.
Big change always starts small."

chapter 8: tomb of the iron knight

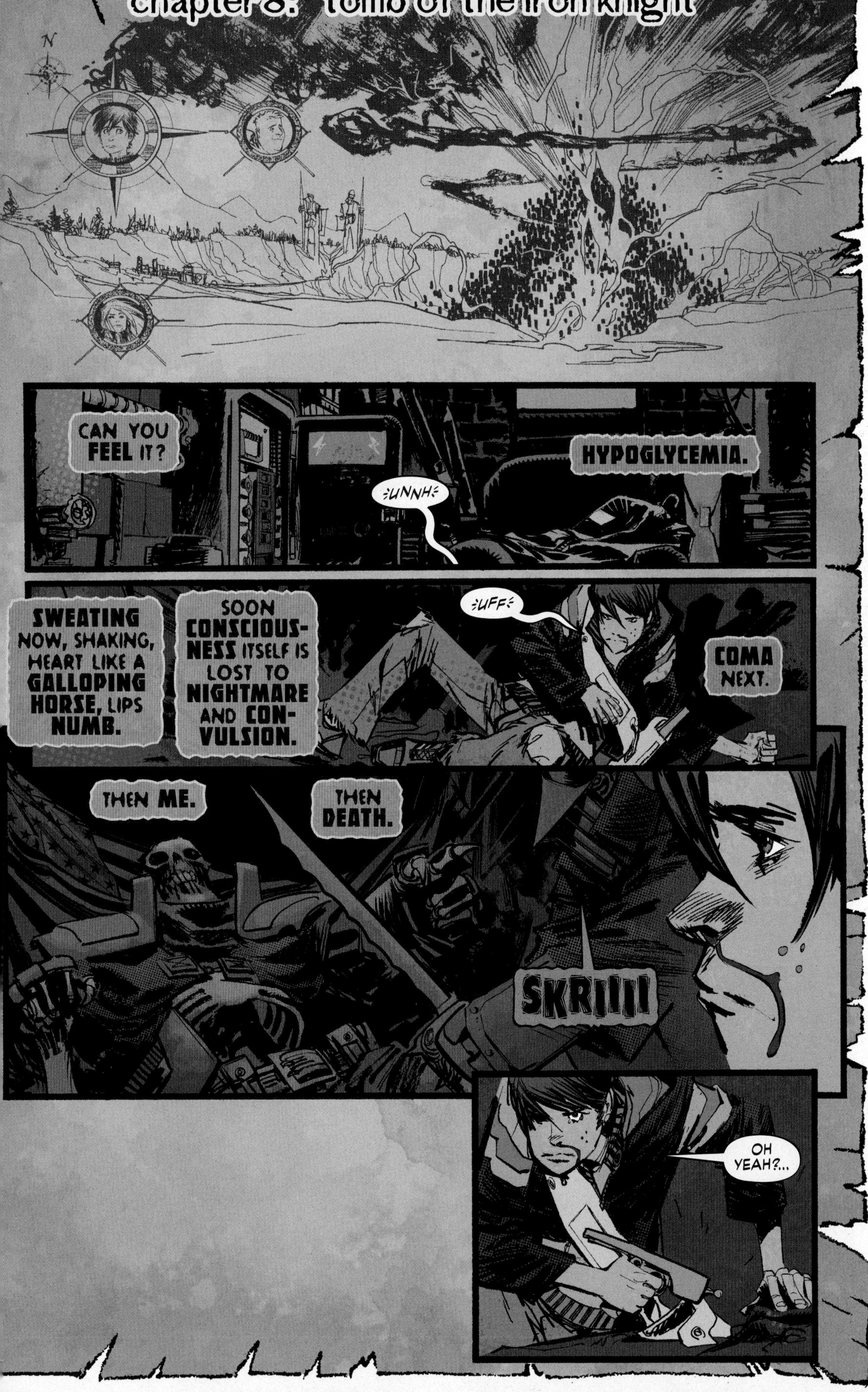

N
CAN YOU FEEL IT?
UNNH
HYPOGLYCEMIA.
SWEATING NOW, SHAKING, HEART LIKE A GALLOPING HORSE, LIPS NUMB.
SOON CONSCIOUSNESS ITSELF IS LOST TO NIGHTMARE AND CONVULSION.
UFF
COMA NEXT.
THEN ME.
THEN DEATH.
SKRIIII
OH YEAH?...

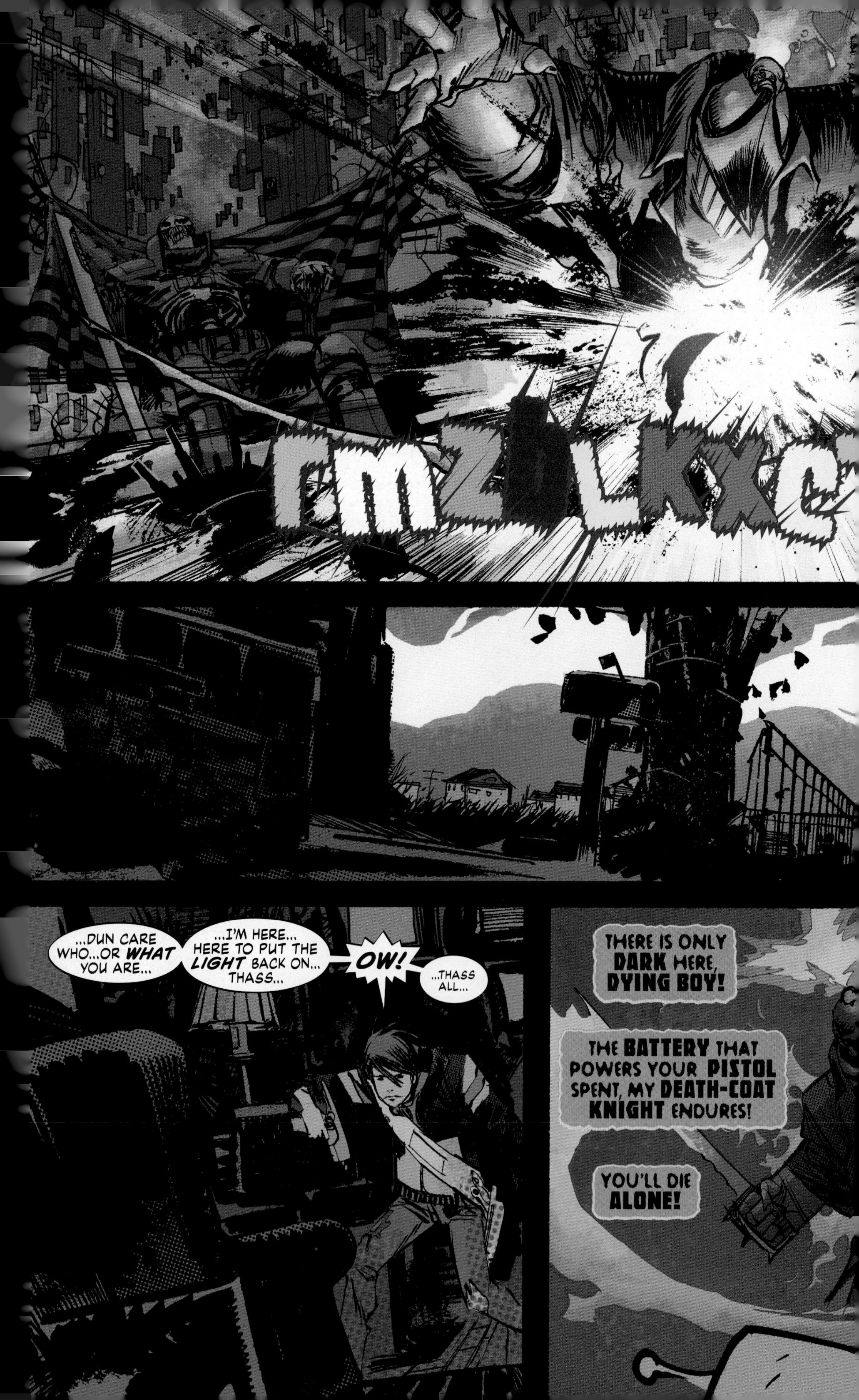
CMZLKXC
...DUN CARE WHO...OR WHAT YOU ARE...
...I'M HERE... HERE TO PUT THE LIGHT BACK ON... THASS...
OW!
...THASS ALL...
THERE IS ONLY DARK HERE, DYING BOY!
THE BATTERY THAT POWERS YOUR PISTOL SPENT, MY DEATH-COAT KNIGHT ENDURES!
YOU'LL DIE ALONE!

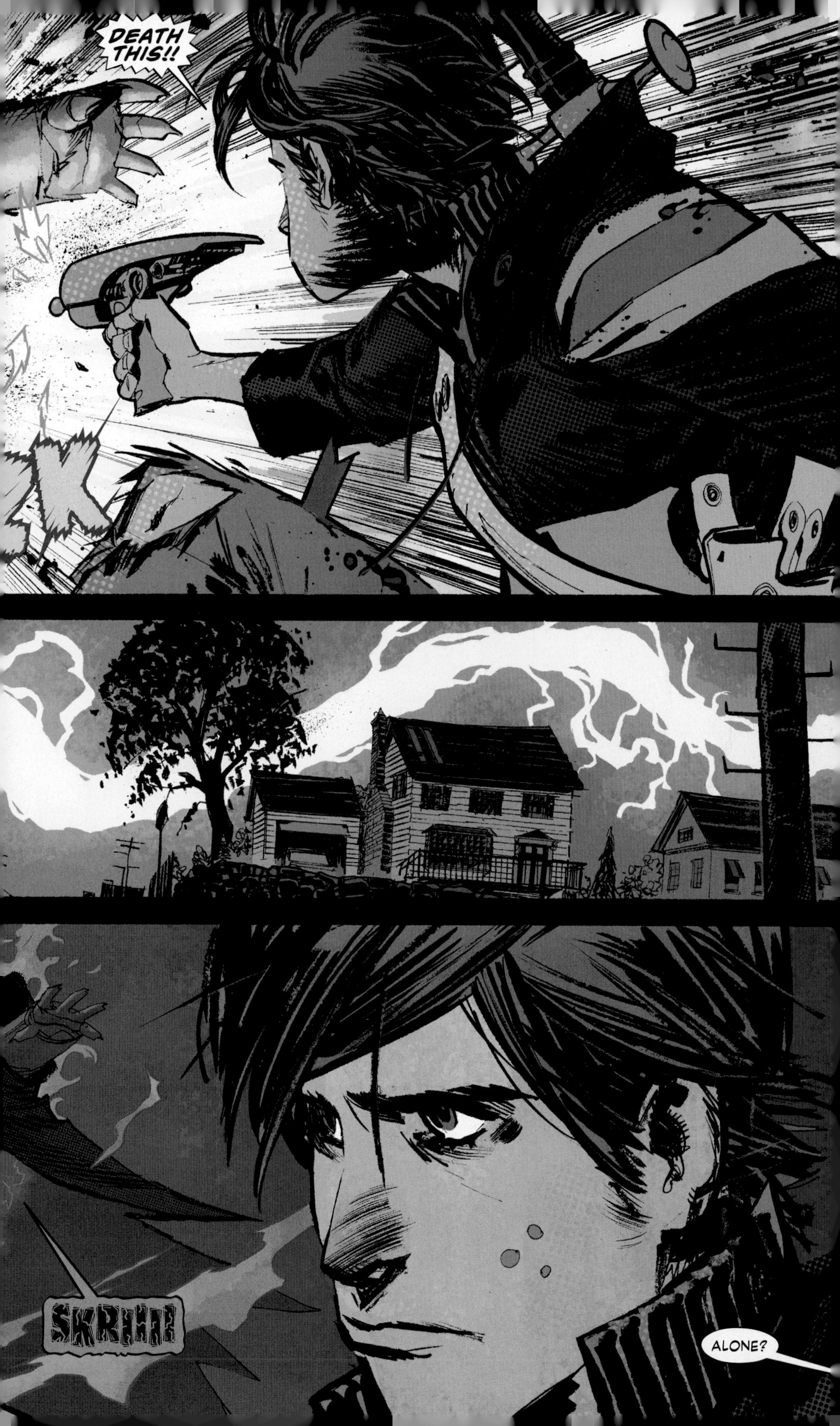
DEATH THIS!!
SKRIII!
ALONE?

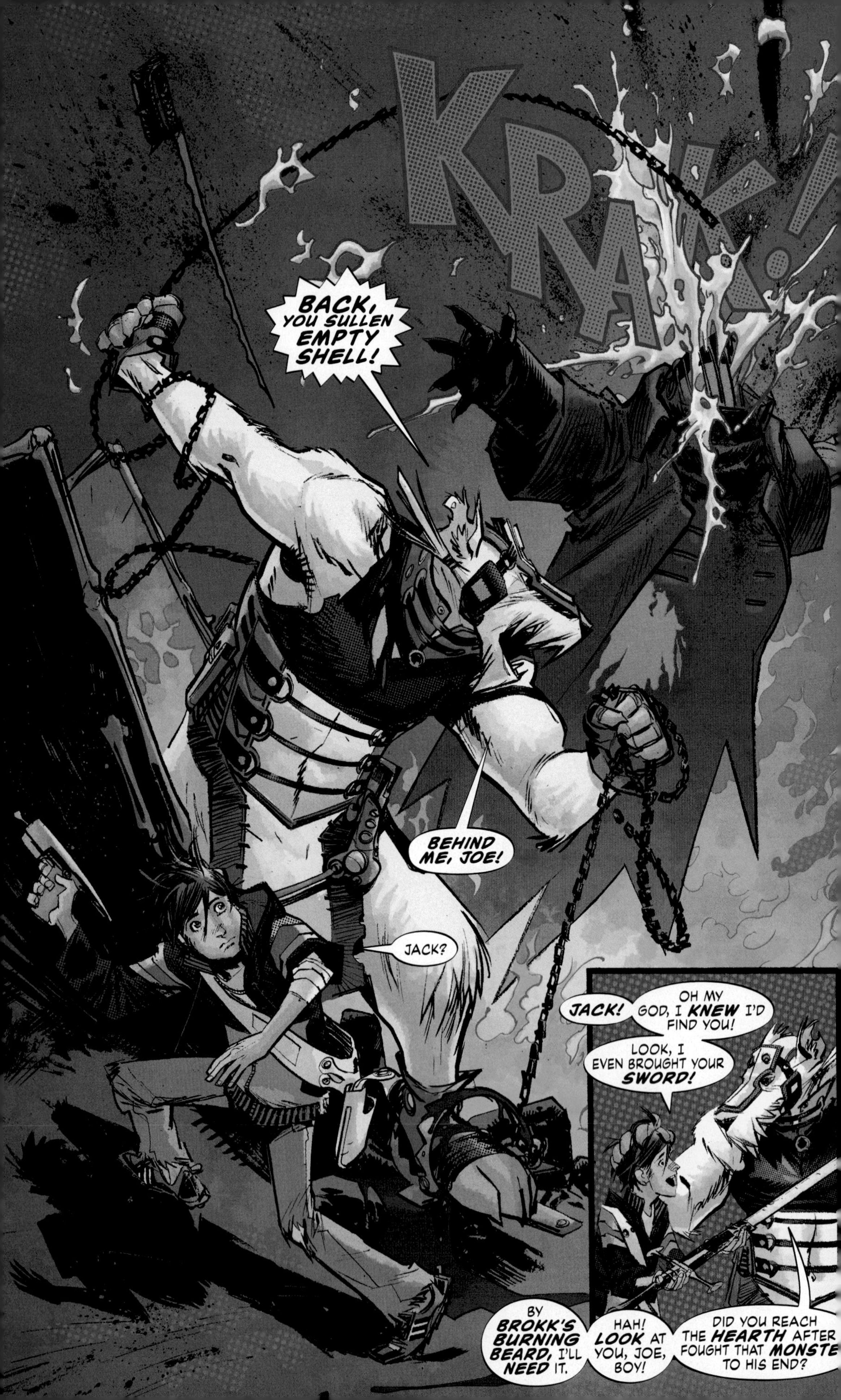
KRAK!!
BACK, YOU SULLEN EMPTY SHELL!
BEHIND ME, JOE!
JACK?
JACK!
OH MY GOD, I KNEW I'D FIND YOU!
LOOK, I EVEN BROUGHT YOUR SWORD!
BY BROKK'S BURNING BEARD, I'LL NEED IT.
HAH! LOOK AT YOU, JOE, BOY!
DID YOU REACH THE HEARTH AFTER FOUGHT THAT MONSTE TO HIS END?

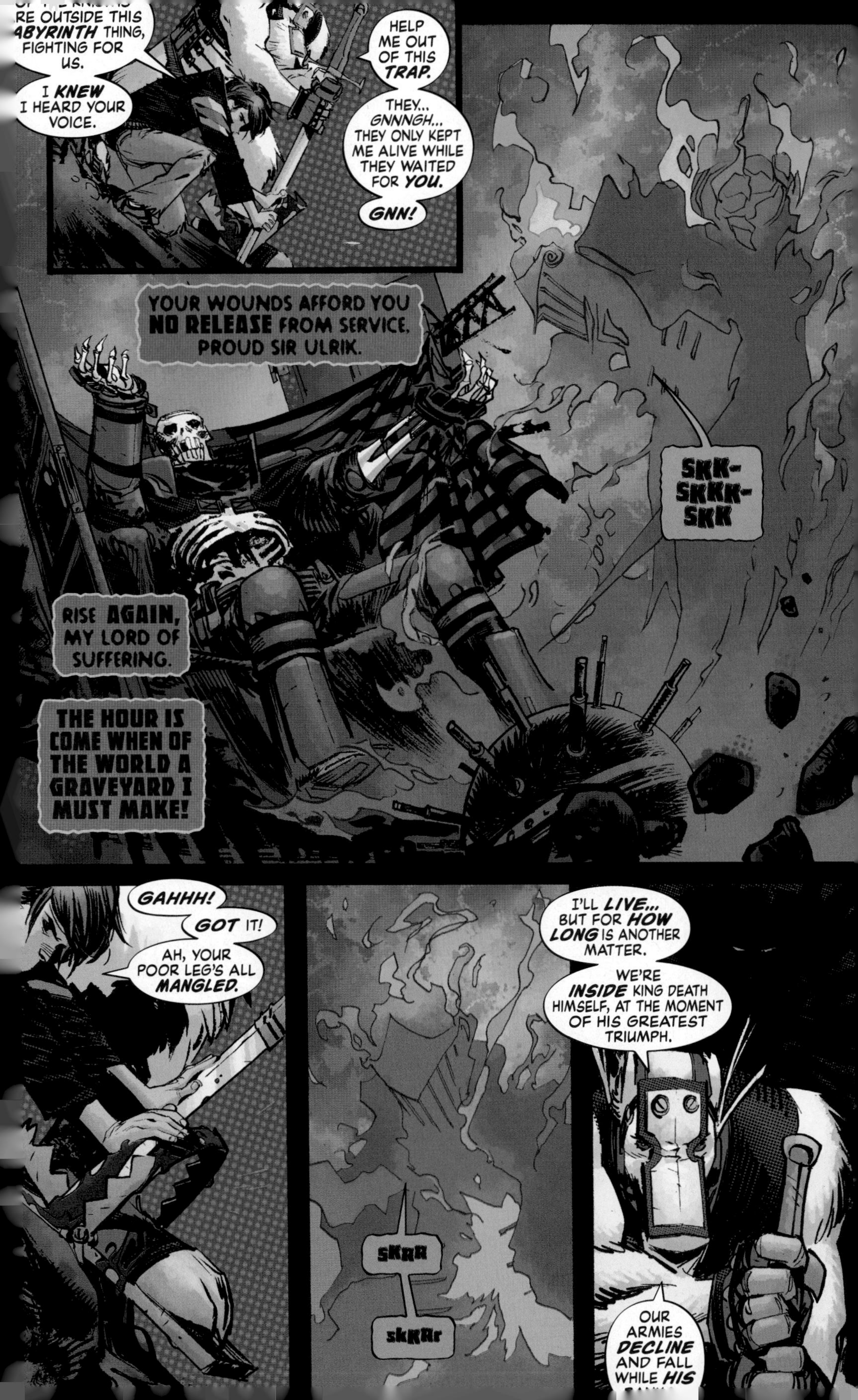
RE OUTSIDE THIS ABYRINTH THING, FIGHTING FOR US.
I KNEW I HEARD YOUR VOICE.
HELP ME OUT OF THIS TRAP.
THEY... GNNNGH... THEY ONLY KEPT ME ALIVE WHILE THEY WAITED FOR YOU.
GNN!
YOUR WOUNDS AFFORD YOU NO RELEASE FROM SERVICE, PROUD SIR ULRIK.
SKK-SKKK-SKK
RISE AGAIN, MY LORD OF SUFFERING.
THE HOUR IS COME WHEN OF THE WORLD A GRAVEYARD I MUST MAKE!
GAHHH!
GOT IT!
AH, YOUR POOR LEG'S ALL MANGLED.
SKRR
SKRRr
I'LL LIVE... BUT FOR HOW LONG IS ANOTHER MATTER.
WE'RE INSIDE KING DEATH HIMSELF, AT THE MOMENT OF HIS GREATEST TRIUMPH.
OUR ARMIES DECLINE AND FALL WHILE HIS

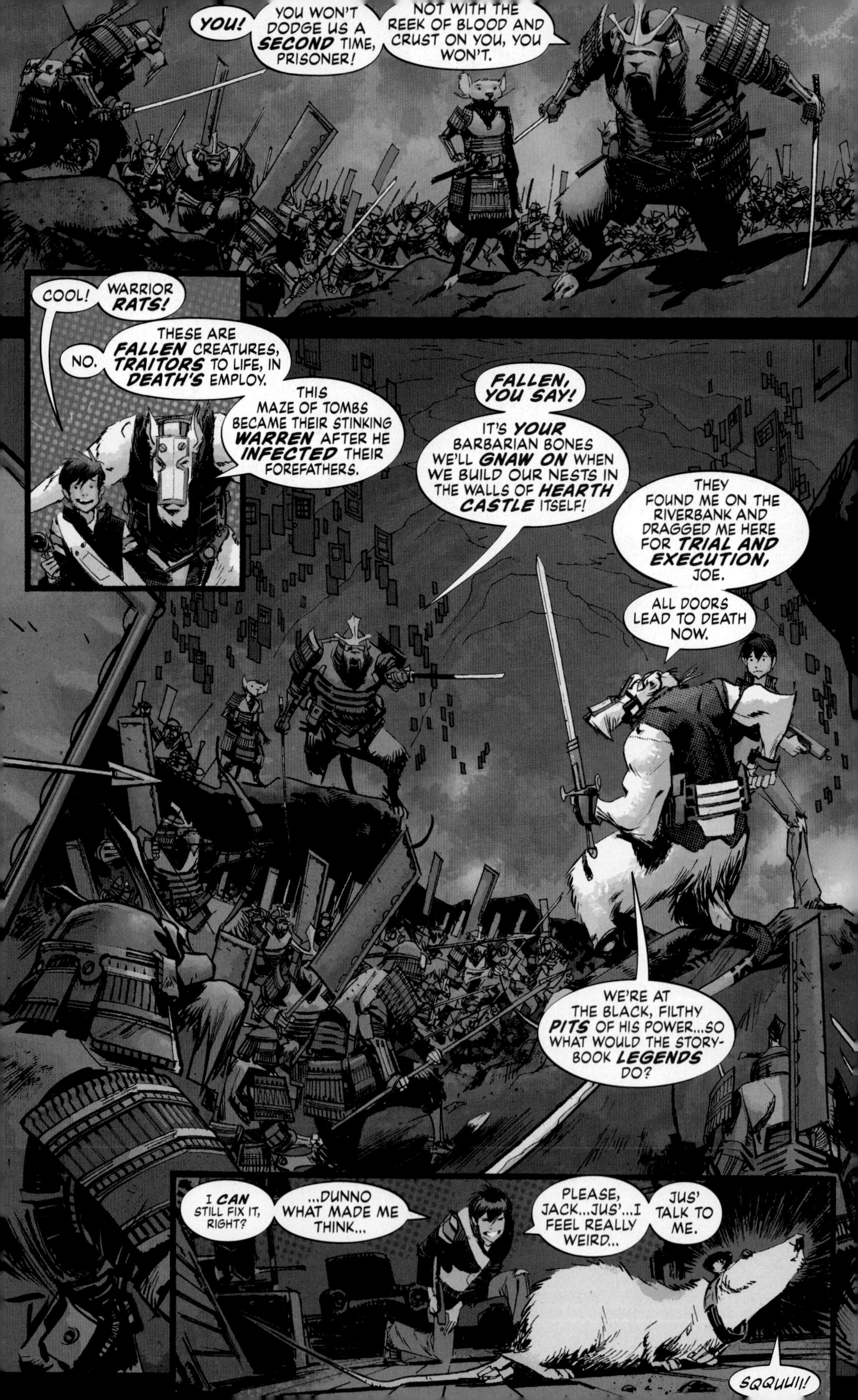
YOU!
YOU WON'T DODGE US A SECOND TIME, PRISONER!
NOT WITH THE REEK OF BLOOD AND CRUST ON YOU, YOU WON'T.
COOL!
WARRIOR RATS!
NO.
THESE ARE FALLEN CREATURES, TRAITORS TO LIFE, IN DEATH'S EMPLOY.
THIS MAZE OF TOMBS BECAME THEIR STINKING WARREN AFTER HE INFECTED THEIR FOREFATHERS.
FALLEN, YOU SAY!
IT'S YOUR BARBARIAN BONES WE'LL GNAW ON WHEN WE BUILD OUR NESTS IN THE WALLS OF HEARTH CASTLE ITSELF!
THEY FOUND ME ON THE RIVERBANK AND DRAGGED ME HERE FOR TRIAL AND EXECUTION, JOE.
ALL DOORS LEAD TO DEATH NOW.
WE'RE AT THE BLACK, FILTHY PITS OF HIS POWER...SO WHAT WOULD THE STORY-BOOK LEGENDS DO?
I CAN STILL FIX IT, RIGHT?
...DUNNO WHAT MADE ME THINK...
PLEASE, JACK...JUS'...I FEEL REALLY WEIRD...
JUS' TALK TO ME.
SQQUUII!

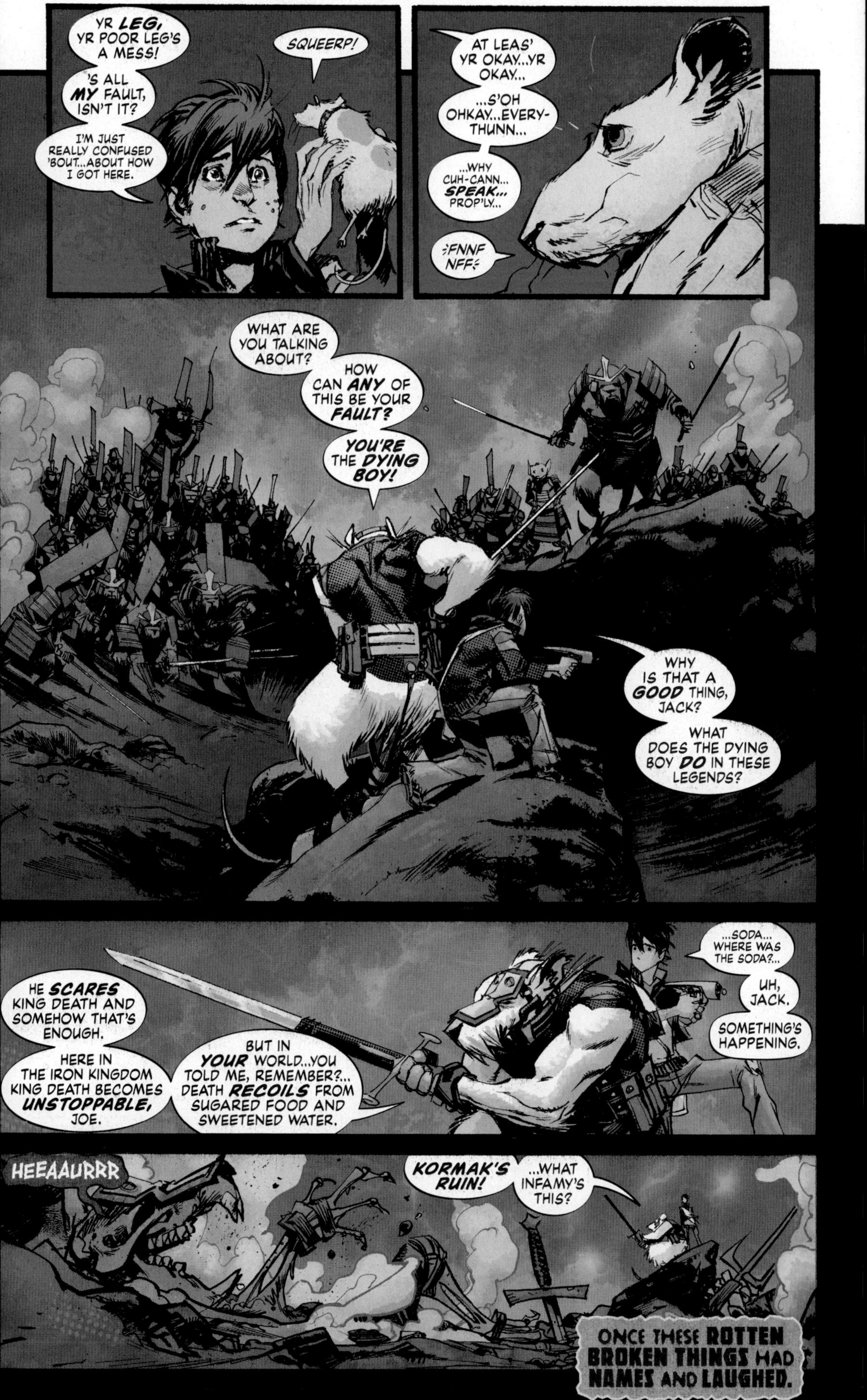

YR LEG, YR POOR LEG'S A MESS!
'S ALL MY FAULT, ISN'T IT?
I'M JUST REALLY CONFUSED 'BOUT...ABOUT HOW I GOT HERE.
SQUEERP!
AT LEAS' YR OKAY...YR OKAY...
...S'OH OHKAY...EVERY-THUNN...
...WHY CUH-CANN... SPEAK... PROP'LY...
FNNF NFF
WHAT ARE YOU TALKING ABOUT?
HOW CAN ANY OF THIS BE YOUR FAULT?
YOU'RE THE DYING BOY!
WHY IS THAT A GOOD THING, JACK?
WHAT DOES THE DYING BOY DO IN THESE LEGENDS?
HE SCARES KING DEATH AND SOMEHOW THAT'S ENOUGH.
HERE IN THE IRON KINGDOM KING DEATH BECOMES UNSTOPPABLE, JOE.
BUT IN YOUR WORLD...YOU TOLD ME, REMEMBER?... DEATH RECOILS FROM SUGARED FOOD AND SWEETENED WATER.
...SODA... WHERE WAS THE SODA?...
UH, JACK.
SOMETHING'S HAPPENING.
HEEAAURRR
KORMAK'S RUIN!
...WHAT INFAMY'S THIS?
ONCE THESE ROTTEN BROKEN THINGS HAD NAMES AND LAUGHED.

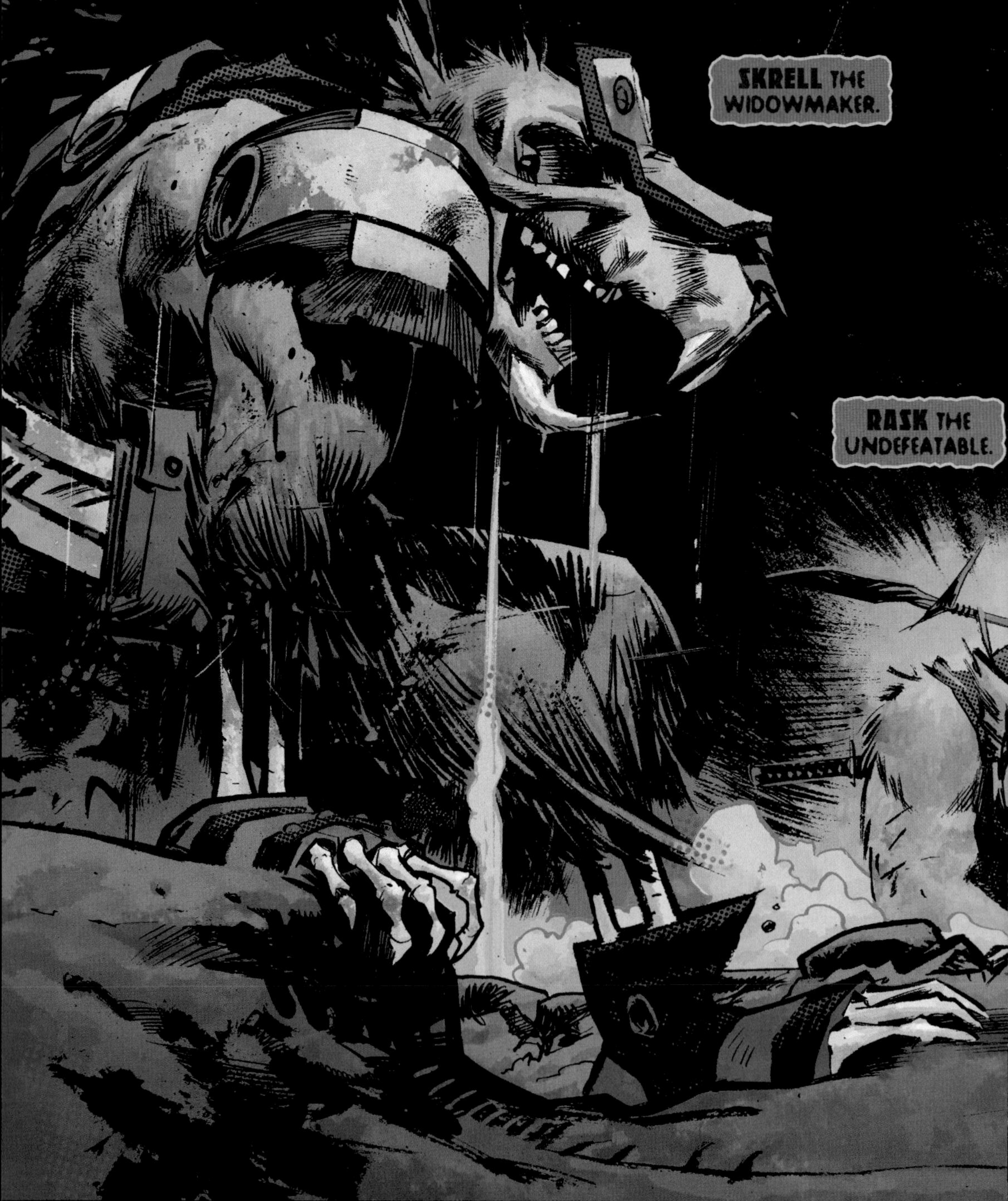
SKRELL THE WIDOWMAKER.
RASK THE UNDEFEATABLE.

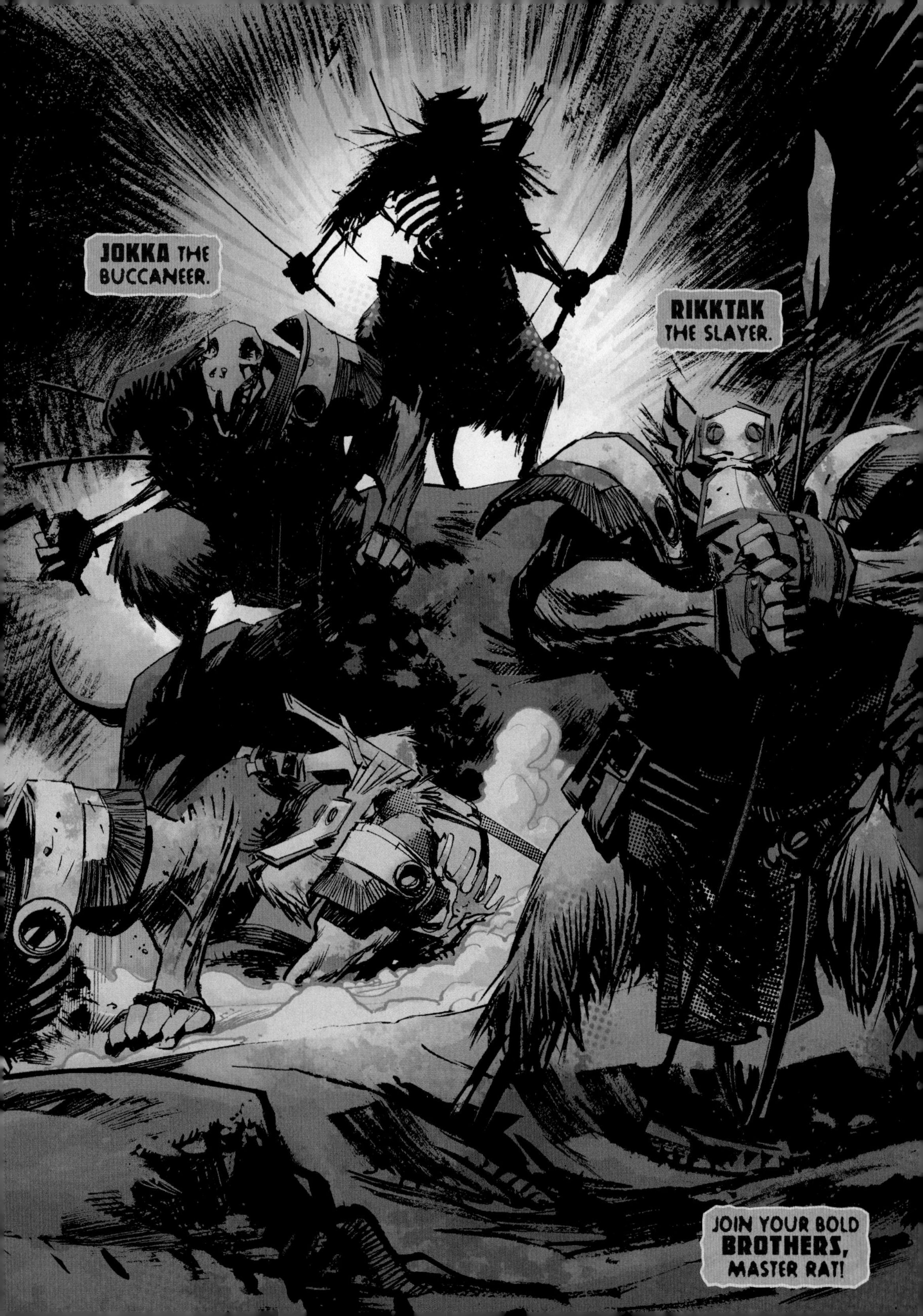
JOKKA THE BUCCANEER.
RIKKTAK THE SLAYER.
JOIN YOUR BOLD BROTHERS, MASTER RAT!

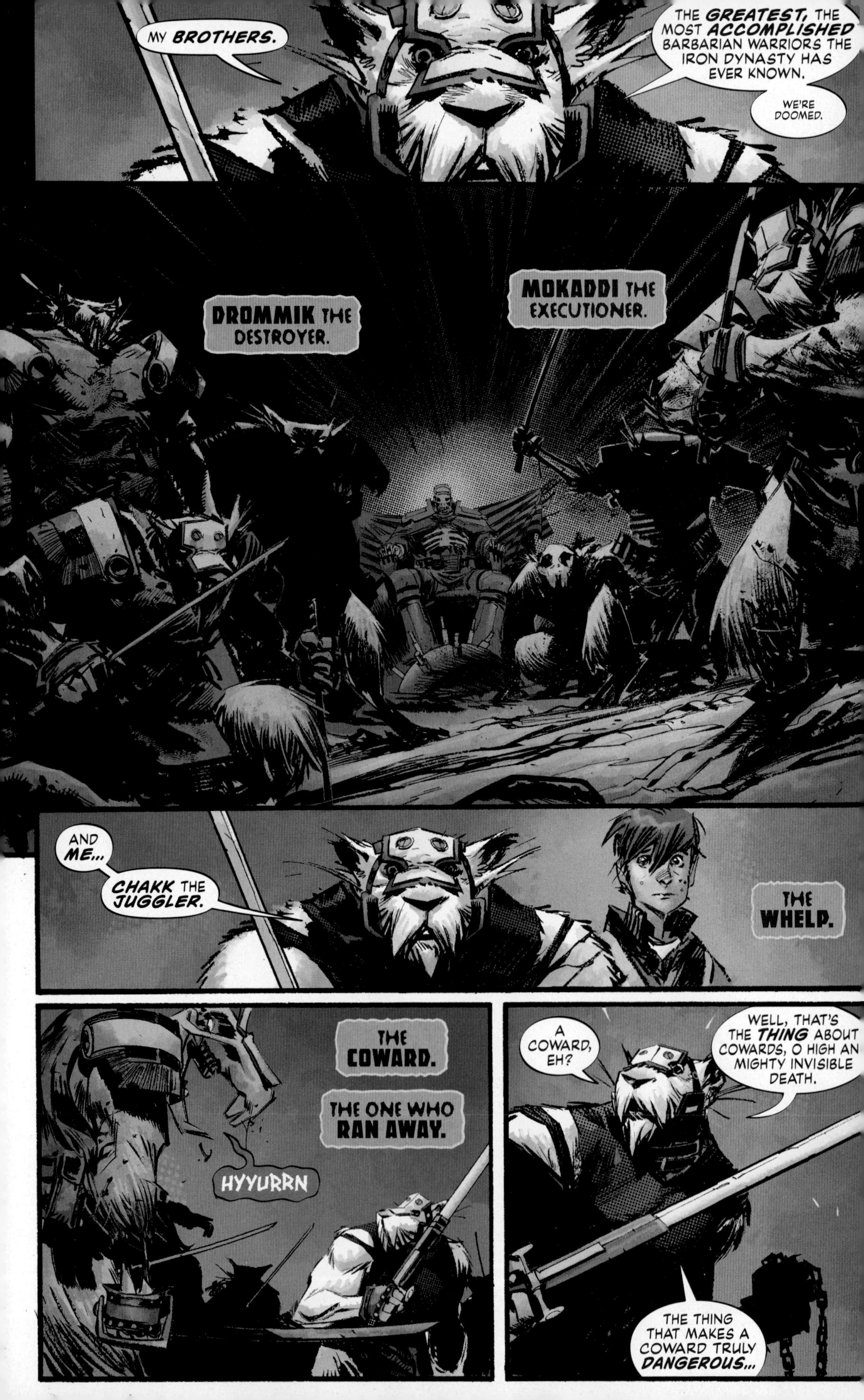
MY BROTHERS.
THE GREATEST, THE MOST ACCOMPLISHED BARBARIAN WARRIORS THE IRON DYNASTY HAS EVER KNOWN.
WE'RE DOOMED.
DROMMIK THE DESTROYER.
MOKADDI THE EXECUTIONER.
AND ME...
CHAKK THE JUGGLER.
THE WHELP.
THE COWARD.
THE ONE WHO RAN AWAY.
HYYURRN
A COWARD, EH?
WELL, THAT'S THE THING ABOUT COWARDS, O HIGH AN MIGHTY INVISIBLE DEATH.
THE THING THAT MAKES A COWARD TRULY DANGEROUS...

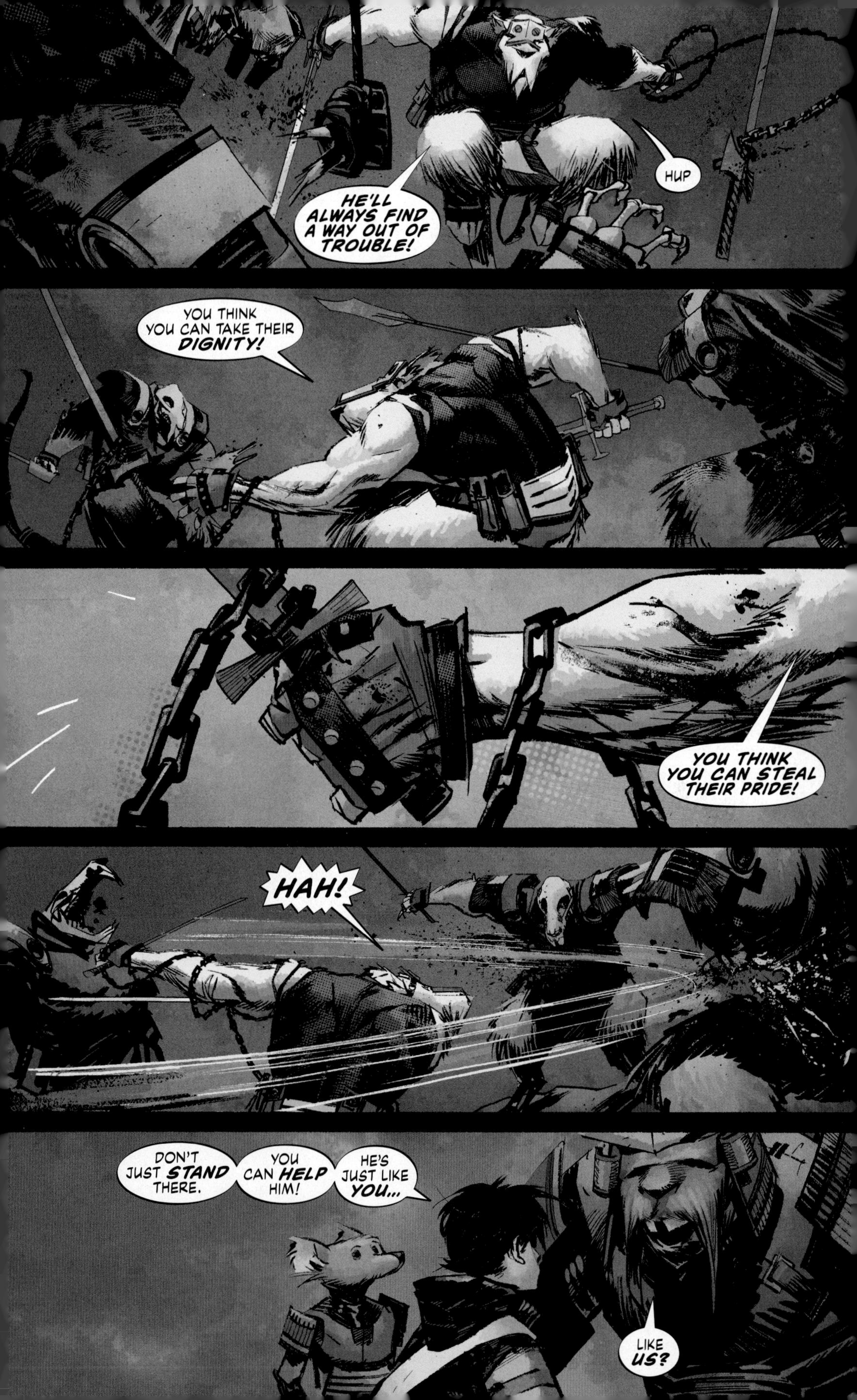
HE'LL ALWAYS FIND A WAY OUT OF TROUBLE!
HUP
YOU THINK YOU CAN TAKE THEIR DIGNITY!
YOU THINK YOU CAN STEAL THEIR PRIDE!
HAH!
DON'T JUST STAND THERE.
YOU CAN HELP HIM!
HE'S JUST LIKE YOU...
LIKE US?

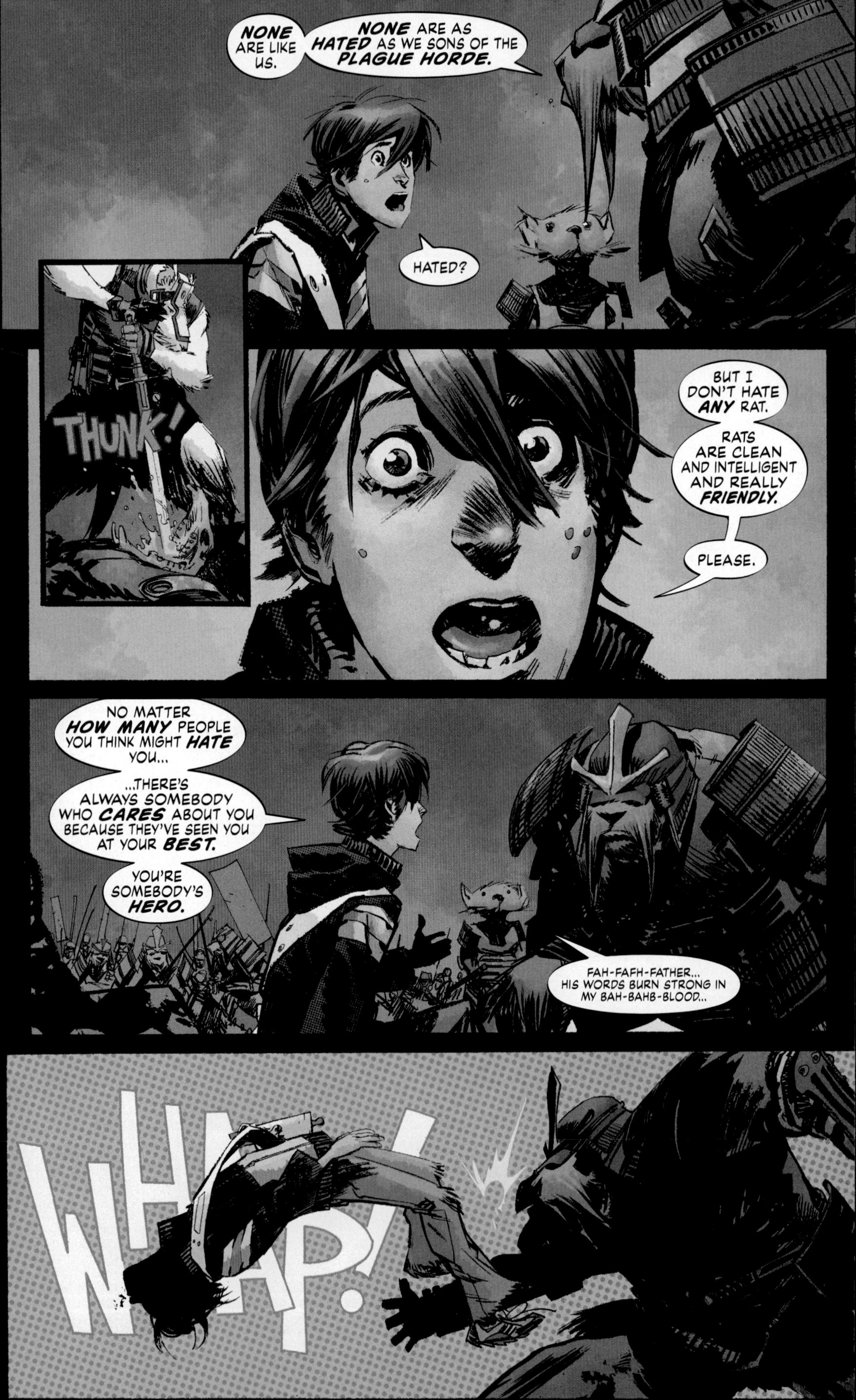
NONE ARE LIKE US.
NONE ARE AS HATED AS WE SONS OF THE PLAGUE HORDE.
HATED?
THUNK!
BUT I DON'T HATE ANY RAT.
RATS ARE CLEAN AND INTELLIGENT AND REALLY FRIENDLY.
PLEASE.
NO MATTER HOW MANY PEOPLE YOU THINK MIGHT HATE YOU...
...THERE'S ALWAYS SOMEBODY WHO CARES ABOUT YOU BECAUSE THEY'VE SEEN YOU AT YOUR BEST.
YOU'RE SOMEBODY'S HERO.
FAH-FAFH-FATHER... HIS WORDS BURN STRONG IN MY BAH-BAHB-BLOOD...
WHAP!

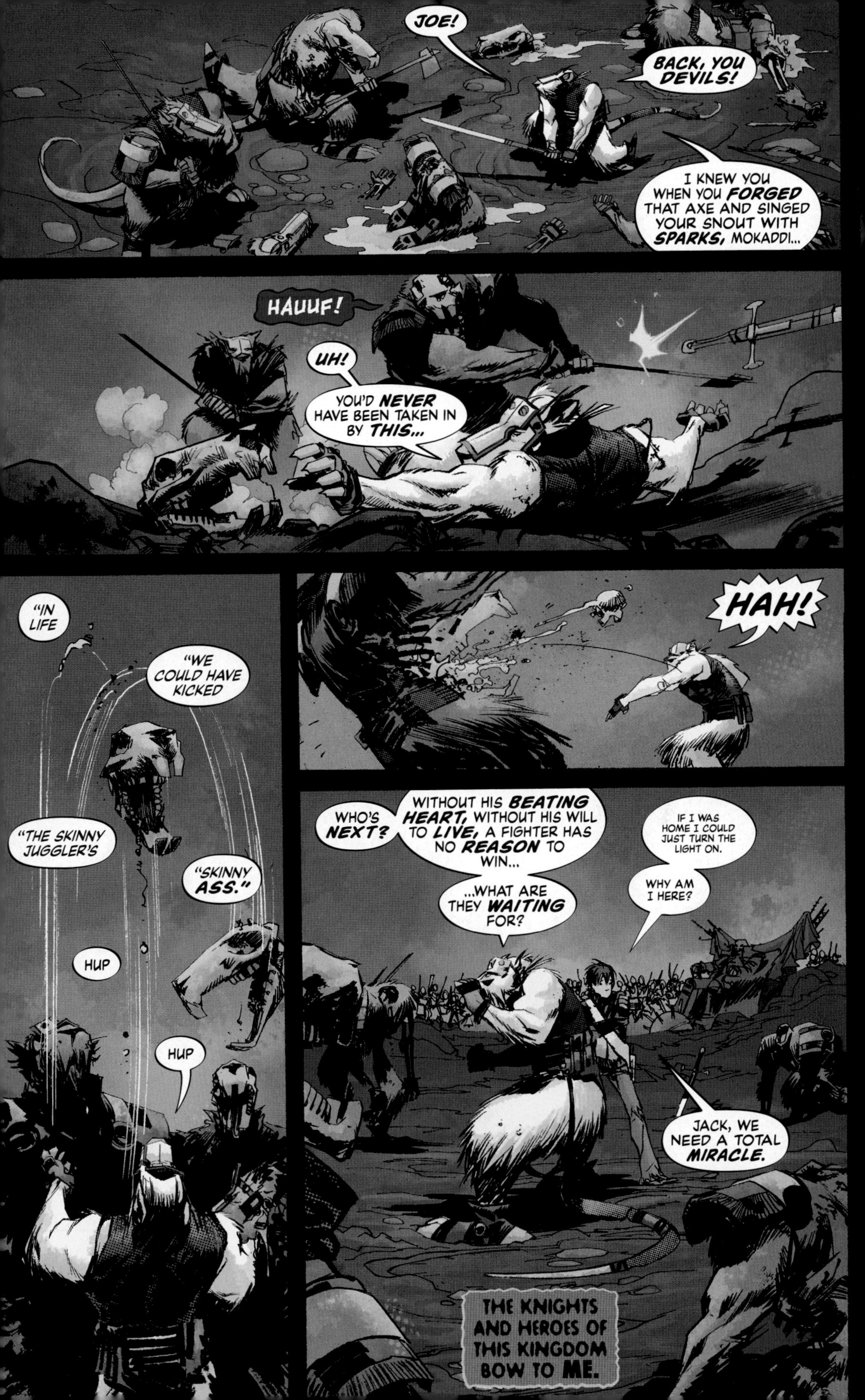
JOE!
BACK, YOU DEVILS!
I KNEW YOU WHEN YOU FORGED THAT AXE AND SINGED YOUR SNOUT WITH SPARKS, MOKADDI...
HAUUF!
UH!
YOU'D NEVER HAVE BEEN TAKEN IN BY THIS...
"IN LIFE
"WE COULD HAVE KICKED
"THE SKINNY JUGGLER'S
"SKINNY ASS."
HUP
HUP
HAH!
WHO'S NEXT?
WITHOUT HIS BEATING HEART, WITHOUT HIS WILL TO LIVE, A FIGHTER HAS NO REASON TO WIN...
...WHAT ARE THEY WAITING FOR?
IF I WAS HOME I COULD JUST TURN THE LIGHT ON.
WHY AM I HERE?
JACK, WE NEED A TOTAL MIRACLE.
THE KNIGHTS AND HEROES OF THIS KINGDOM BOW TO ME.

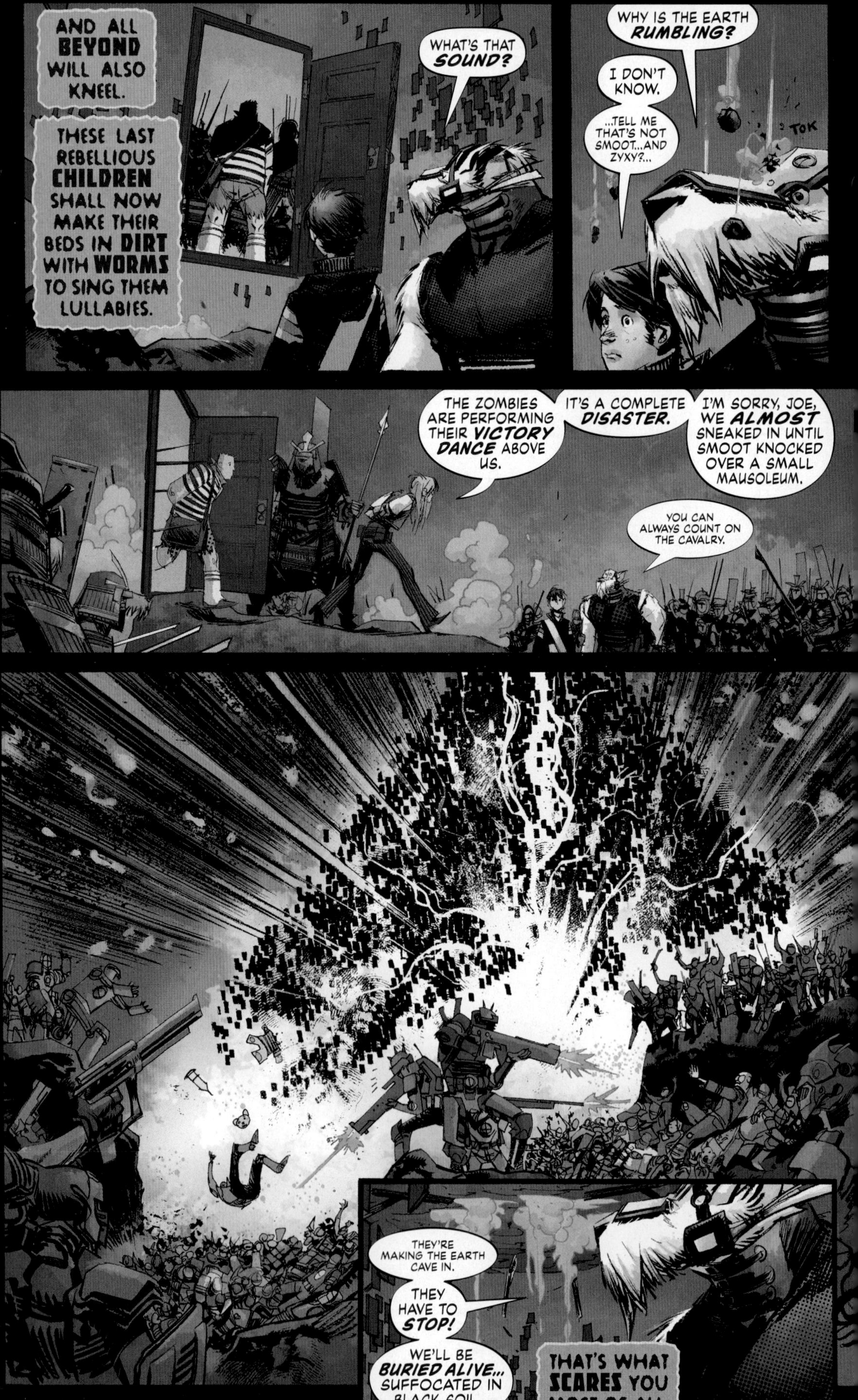
AND ALL BEYOND WILL ALSO KNEEL.
THESE LAST REBELLIOUS CHILDREN SHALL NOW MAKE THEIR BEDS IN DIRT WITH WORMS TO SING THEM LULLABIES.
WHAT'S THAT SOUND?
WHY IS THE EARTH RUMBLING?
I DON'T KNOW.
...TELL ME THAT'S NOT SMOOT...AND ZYXY?...
TOK
THE ZOMBIES ARE PERFORMING THEIR VICTORY DANCE ABOVE US.
IT'S A COMPLETE DISASTER.
I'M SORRY, JOE, WE ALMOST SNEAKED IN UNTIL SMOOT KNOCKED OVER A SMALL MAUSOLEUM.
YOU CAN ALWAYS COUNT ON THE CAVALRY.
THEY'RE MAKING THE EARTH CAVE IN.
THEY HAVE TO STOP!
WE'LL BE BURIED ALIVE... SUFFOCATED IN BLACK SOIL...
THAT'S WHAT SCARES YOU MOST OF ALL.

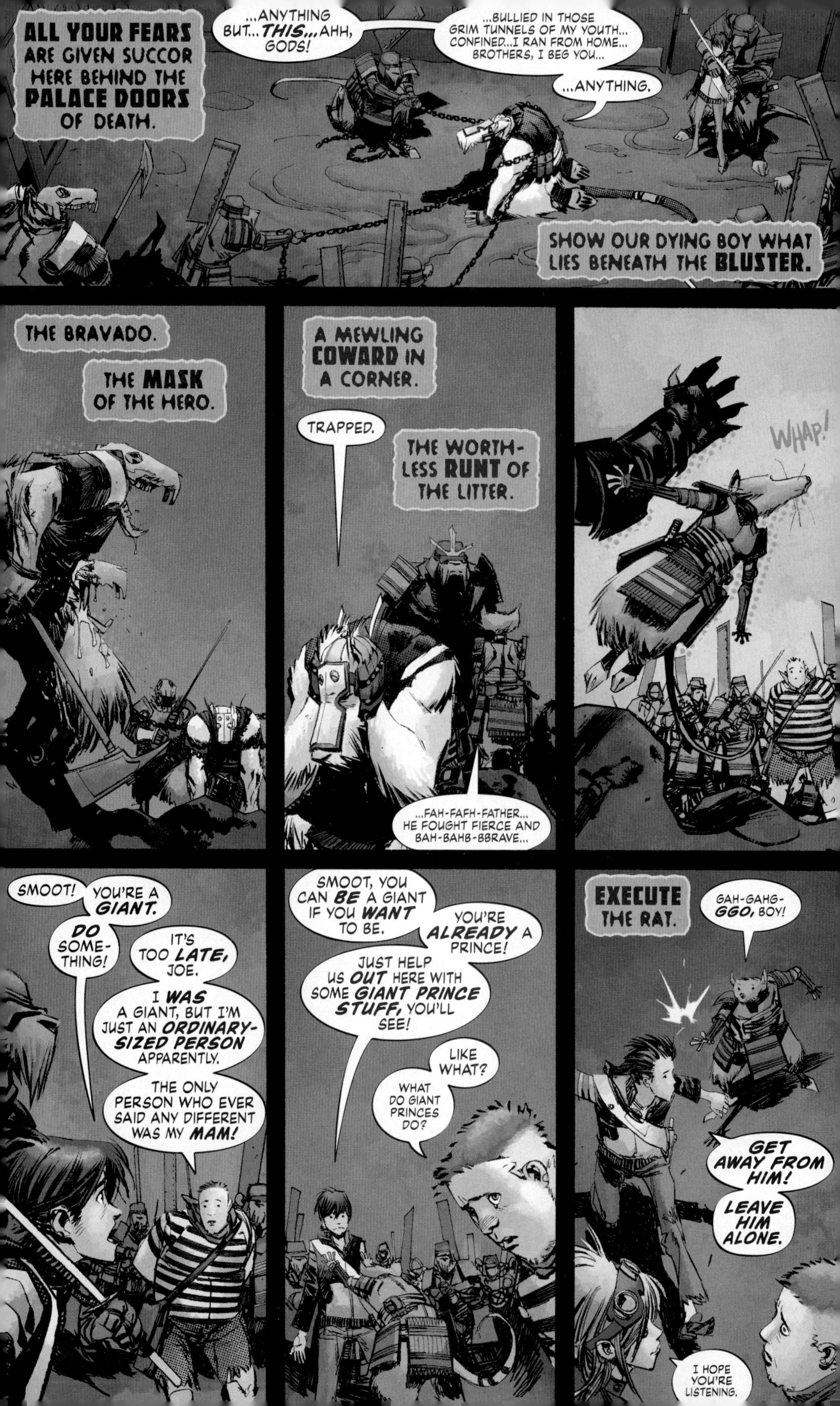
ALL YOUR FEARS ARE GIVEN SUCCOR HERE BEHIND THE PALACE DOORS OF DEATH.
...ANYTHING BUT... THIS... AHH, GODS!
...BULLIED IN THOSE GRIM TUNNELS OF MY YOUTH... CONFINED...I RAN FROM HOME... BROTHERS, I BEG YOU...
...ANYTHING.
SHOW OUR DYING BOY WHAT LIES BENEATH THE BLUSTER.
THE BRAVADO.
THE MASK OF THE HERO.
A MEWLING COWARD IN A CORNER.
TRAPPED.
THE WORTH-LESS RUNT OF THE LITTER.
...FAH-FAFH-FATHER... HE FOUGHT FIERCE AND BAH-BAHB-BBRAVE...
WHAP!
SMOOT!
YOU'RE A GIANT.
DO SOME-THING!
IT'S TOO LATE, JOE.
I WAS A GIANT, BUT I'M JUST AN ORDINARY-SIZED PERSON APPARENTLY.
THE ONLY PERSON WHO EVER SAID ANY DIFFERENT WAS MY MAM!
SMOOT, YOU CAN BE A GIANT IF YOU WANT TO BE.
YOU'RE ALREADY A PRINCE!
JUST HELP US OUT HERE WITH SOME GIANT PRINCE STUFF, YOU'LL SEE!
LIKE WHAT?
WHAT DO GIANT PRINCES DO?
EXECUTE THE RAT.
GAH-GAHG-GGO, BOY!
GET AWAY FROM HIM!
LEAVE HIM ALONE.
I HOPE YOU'RE LISTENING.

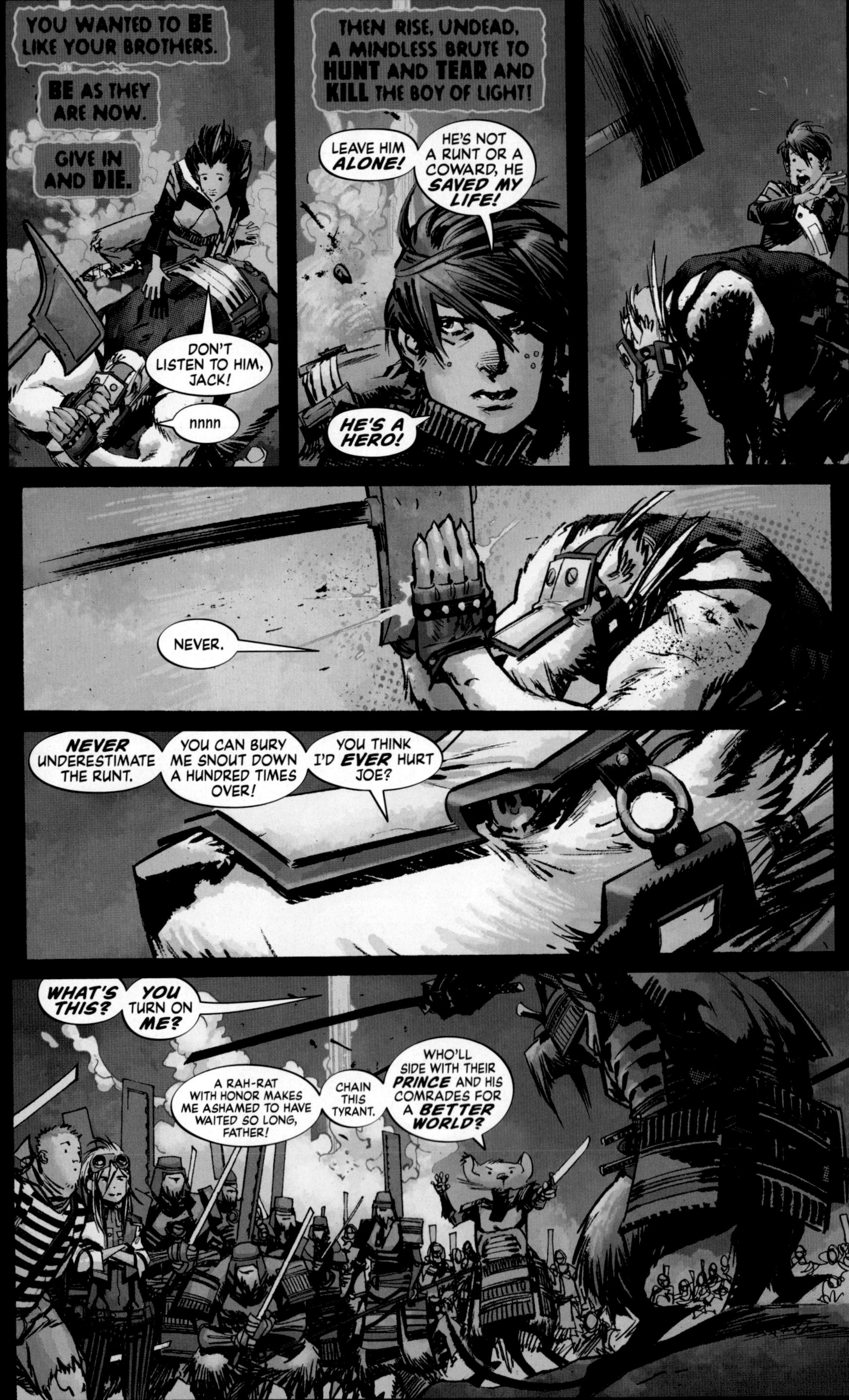
YOU WANTED TO BE LIKE YOUR BROTHERS.
BE AS THEY ARE NOW.
GIVE IN AND DIE.
DON'T LISTEN TO HIM, JACK!
nnnn
THEN RISE, UNDEAD, A MINDLESS BRUTE TO HUNT AND TEAR AND KILL THE BOY OF LIGHT!
LEAVE HIM ALONE!
HE'S NOT A RUNT OR A COWARD, HE SAVED MY LIFE!
HE'S A HERO!
NEVER.
NEVER UNDERESTIMATE THE RUNT.
YOU CAN BURY ME SNOUT DOWN A HUNDRED TIMES OVER!
YOU THINK I'D EVER HURT JOE?
WHAT'S THIS?
YOU TURN ON ME?
A RAH-RAT WITH HONOR MAKES ME ASHAMED TO HAVE WAITED SO LONG, FATHER!
CHAIN THIS TYRANT.
WHO'LL SIDE WITH THEIR PRINCE AND HIS COMRADES FOR A BETTER WORLD?

RAARGH!

REVOLUTION!

HAK!

YOU'LL ALL **REGRET** THIS!

YOU **FOLLOWED** ME? YOU'RE **CRAZY!**

HOW IS THAT **POSSIBLE?**

YOU DROPPED **THIS.**

WHICH IS **ONLY** THE LOST MAP OF **HYPOGEA.**

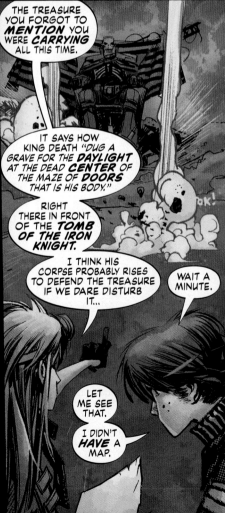

THE TREASURE YOU FORGOT TO **MENTION** YOU WERE **CARRYING** ALL THIS TIME.

IT SAYS HOW KING DEATH "DUG A GRAVE FOR THE **DAYLIGHT** AT THE DEAD **CENTER** OF THE MAZE OF **DOORS** THAT IS HIS BODY."

RIGHT THERE IN FRONT OF THE **TOMB** OF THE **IRON KNIGHT.**

I THINK HIS **CORPSE** PROBABLY RISES TO DEFEND THE TREASURE IF WE DARE DISTURB IT...

TOK!

WAIT A MINUTE.

LET ME SEE THAT.

I DIDN'T **HAVE** A MAP.

WAIT!

LEAVE THAT BE!

SMOOT, BE CAREFUL!

JOE WAS :UNNGH: **RIGHT** AFTER ALL.

ONLY A **GIANT PRINCE** COULD OPEN

THIS!

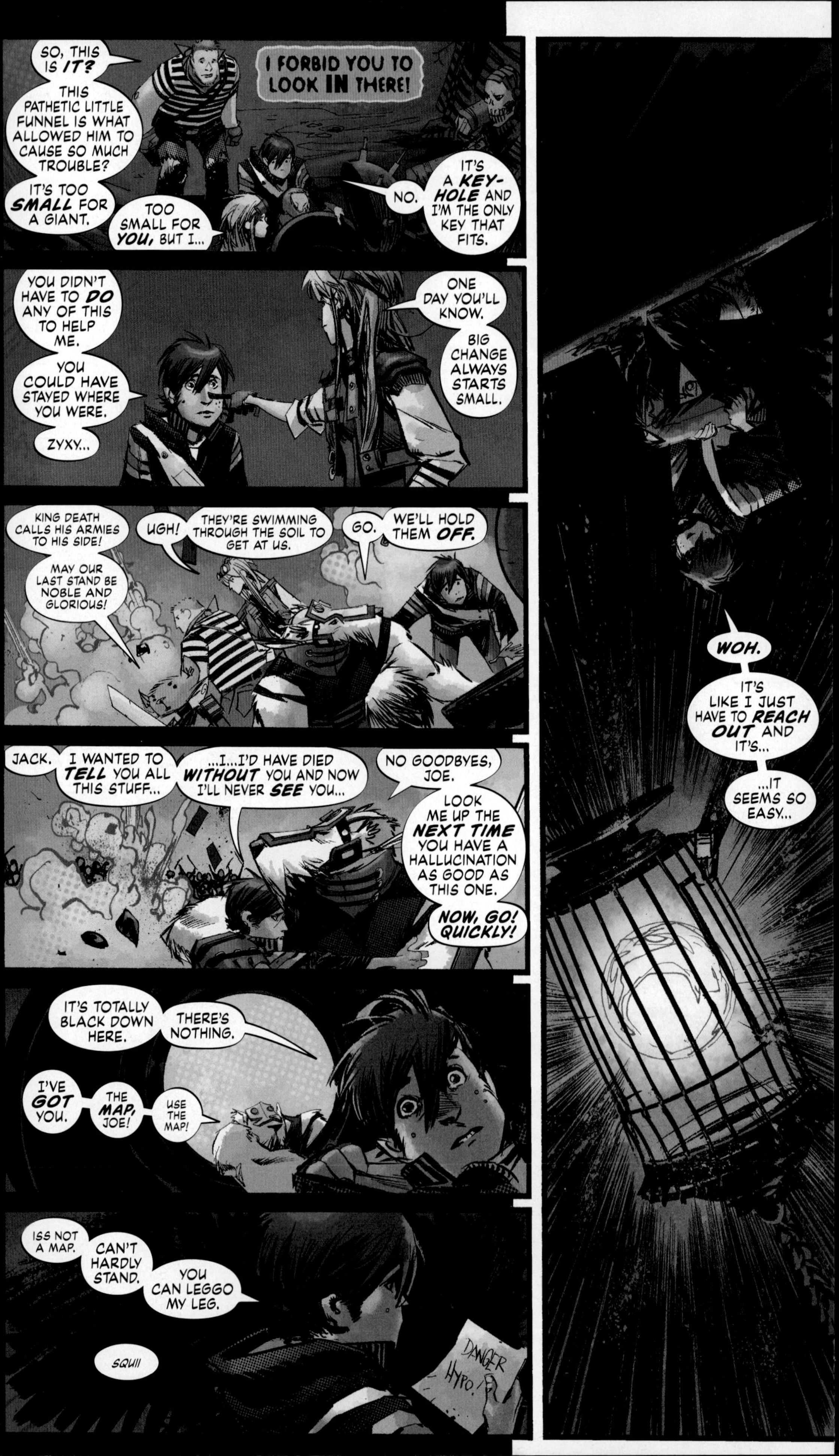
SO, THIS IS IT?
THIS PATHETIC LITTLE FUNNEL IS WHAT ALLOWED HIM TO CAUSE SO MUCH TROUBLE?
IT'S TOO SMALL FOR A GIANT.
I FORBID YOU TO LOOK IN THERE!
TOO SMALL FOR YOU, BUT I...
NO.
IT'S A KEY-HOLE AND I'M THE ONLY KEY THAT FITS.
YOU DIDN'T HAVE TO DO ANY OF THIS TO HELP ME.
YOU COULD HAVE STAYED WHERE YOU WERE.
ZYXY...
ONE DAY YOU'LL KNOW.
BIG CHANGE ALWAYS STARTS SMALL.
KING DEATH CALLS HIS ARMIES TO HIS SIDE!
MAY OUR LAST STAND BE NOBLE AND GLORIOUS!
UGH!
THEY'RE SWIMMING THROUGH THE SOIL TO GET AT US.
GO.
WE'LL HOLD THEM OFF.
JACK.
I WANTED TO TELL YOU ALL THIS STUFF...
...I...I'D HAVE DIED WITHOUT YOU AND NOW I'LL NEVER SEE YOU...
NO GOODBYES, JOE.
LOOK ME UP THE NEXT TIME YOU HAVE A HALLUCINATION AS GOOD AS THIS ONE.
NOW, GO! QUICKLY!
IT'S TOTALLY BLACK DOWN HERE.
THERE'S NOTHING.
I'VE GOT YOU.
THE MAP, JOE!
USE THE MAP!
ISS NOT A MAP.
CAN'T HARDLY STAND.
YOU CAN LEGGO MY LEG.
SQUII
DANGER HYPO!
WOH.
IT'S LIKE I JUST HAVE TO REACH OUT AND IT'S...
...IT SEEMS SO EASY...

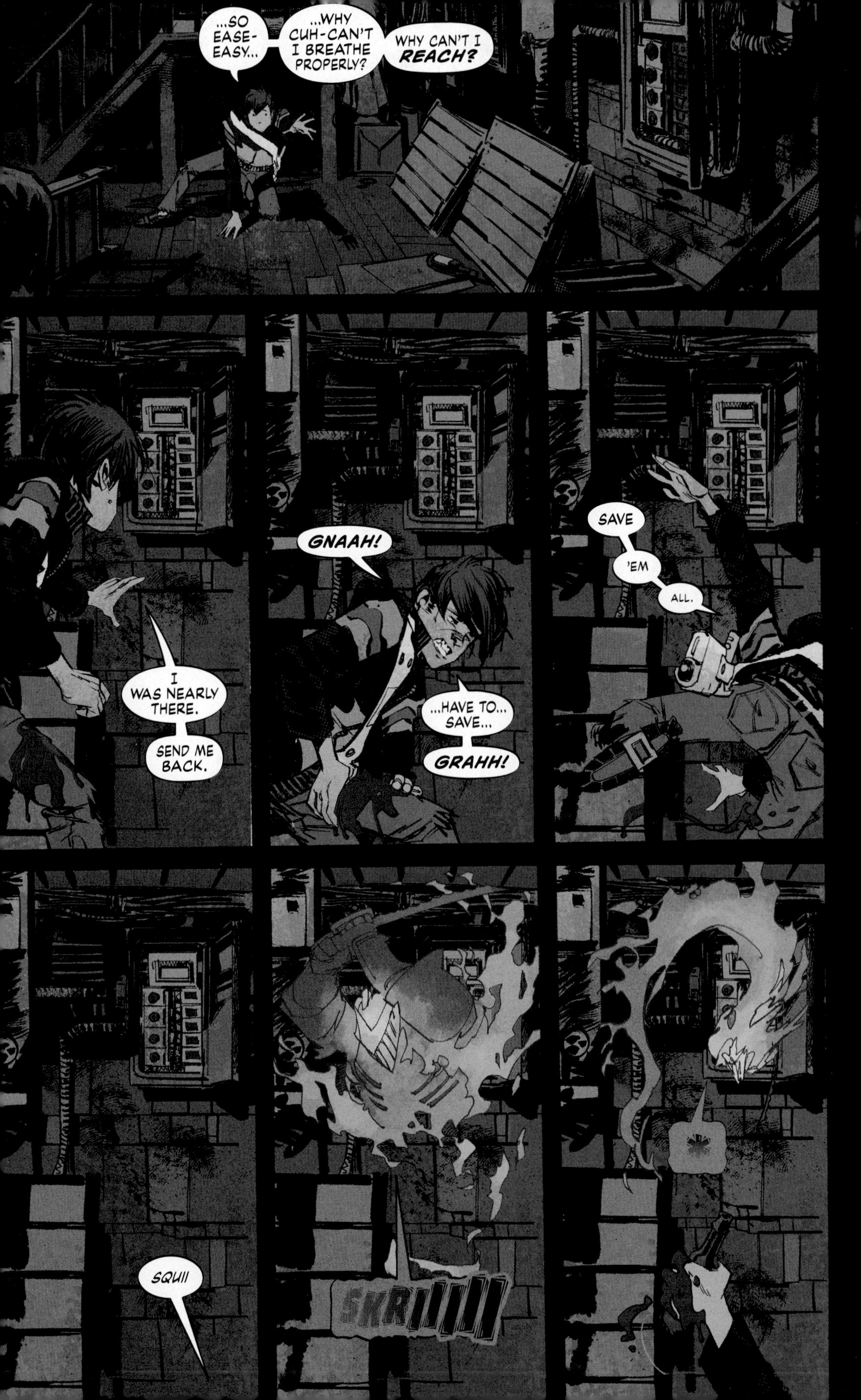
...SO EASE-EASY...
...WHY CUH-CAN'T I BREATHE PROPERLY?
WHY CAN'T I REACH?
I WAS NEARLY THERE.
SEND ME BACK.
GNAAH!
...HAVE TO... SAVE...
GRAHH!
SAVE
'EM
ALL.
SQUII
SKRIIIII

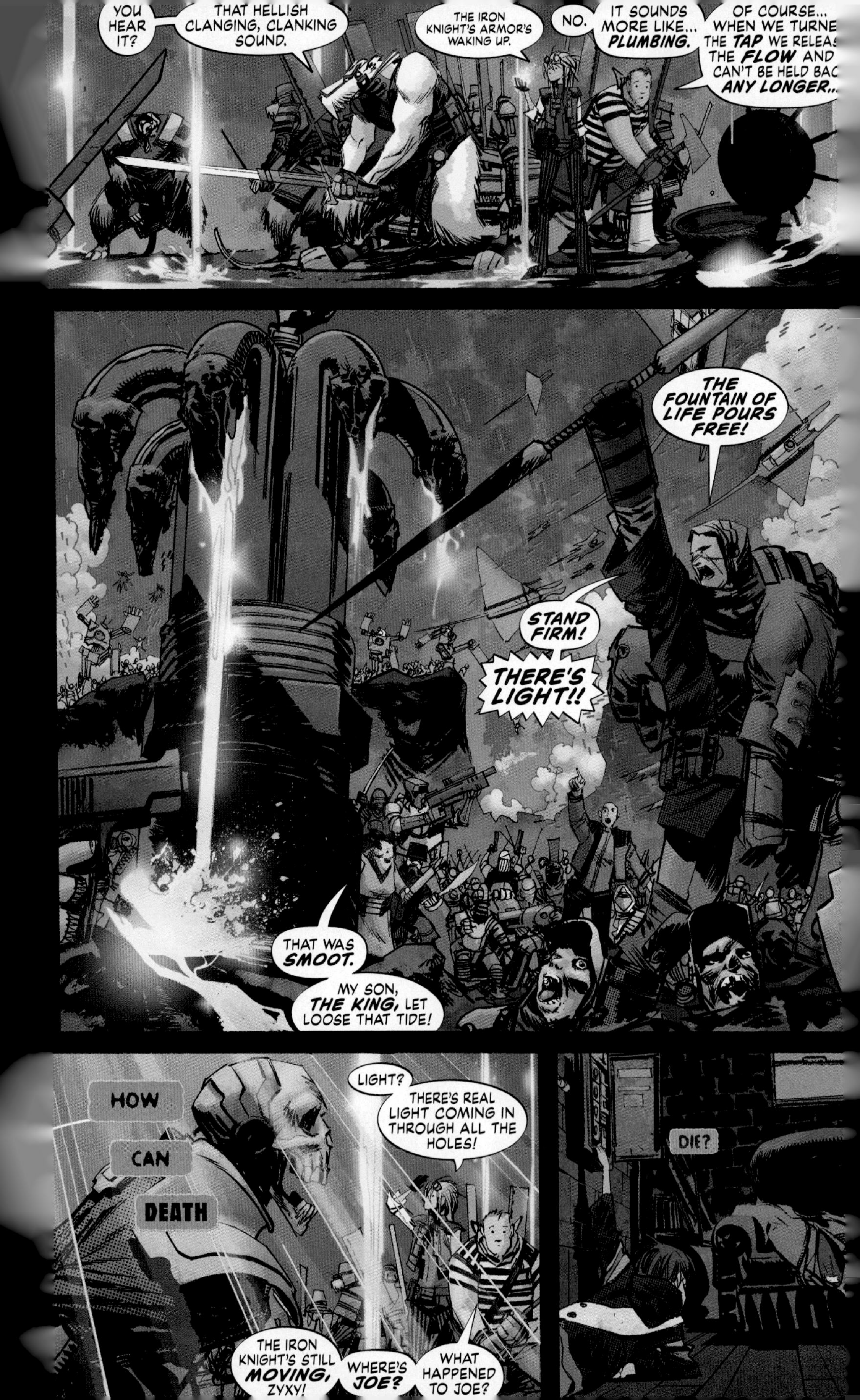
YOU HEAR IT?
THAT HELLISH CLANGING, CLANKING SOUND.
THE IRON KNIGHT'S ARMOR'S WAKING UP.
NO.
IT SOUNDS MORE LIKE... PLUMBING.
OF COURSE... WHEN WE TURNE THE TAP WE RELEAS THE FLOW AND CAN'T BE HELD BAC ANY LONGER...
THE FOUNTAIN OF LIFE POURS FREE!
STAND FIRM!
THERE'S LIGHT!!
THAT WAS SMOOT.
MY SON, THE KING, LET LOOSE THAT TIDE!
HOW
CAN
DEATH
LIGHT?
THERE'S REAL LIGHT COMING IN THROUGH ALL THE HOLES!
THE IRON KNIGHT'S STILL MOVING, ZYXY!
WHERE'S JOE?
WHAT HAPPENED TO JOE?
DIE?

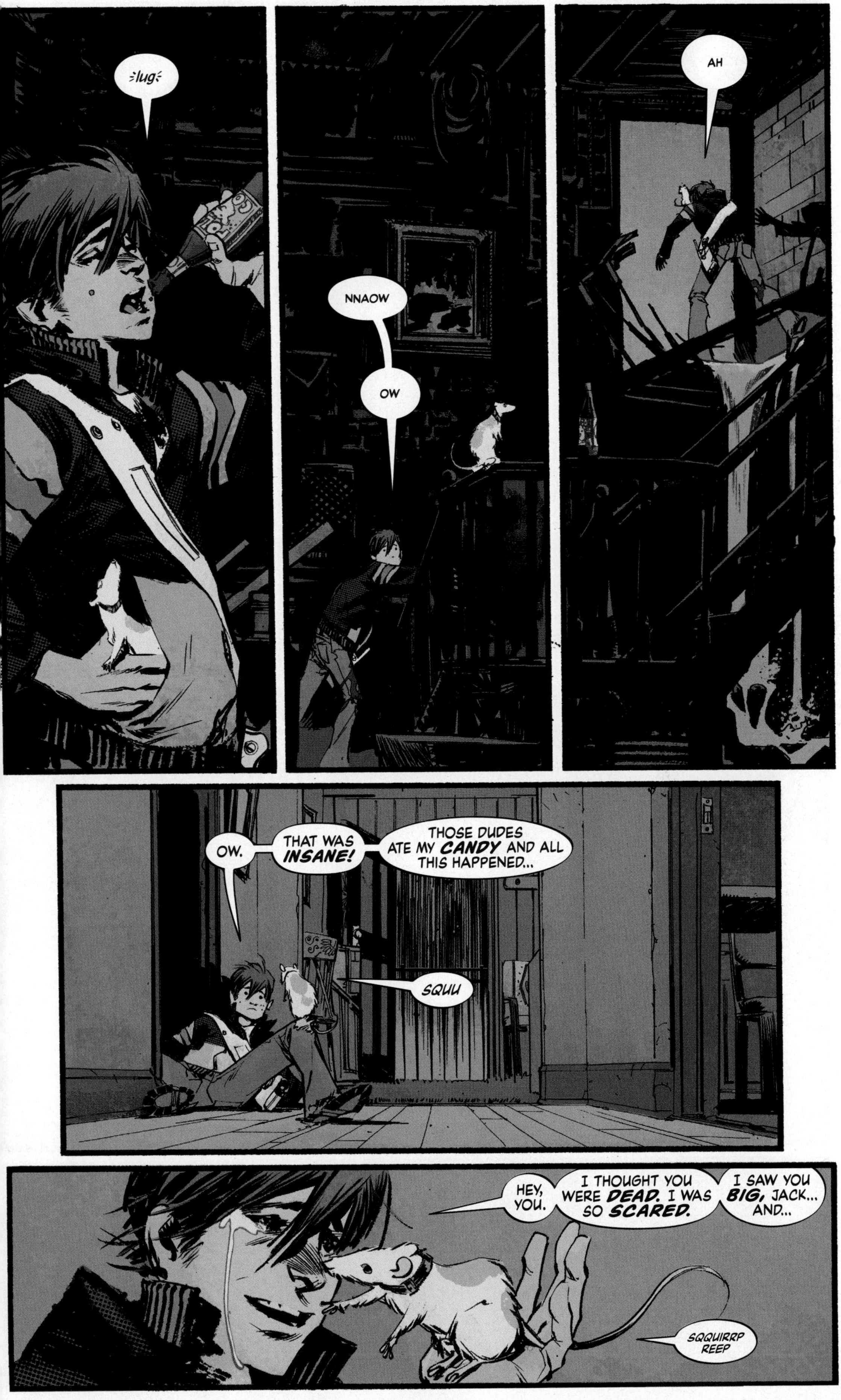
lug
NNAOW
OW
AH
OW.
THAT WAS INSANE!
THOSE DUDES ATE MY CANDY AND ALL THIS HAPPENED...
SQUU
HEY, YOU.
I THOUGHT YOU WERE DEAD. I WAS SO SCARED.
I SAW YOU BIG, JACK... AND...
SQQUIRRP REEP

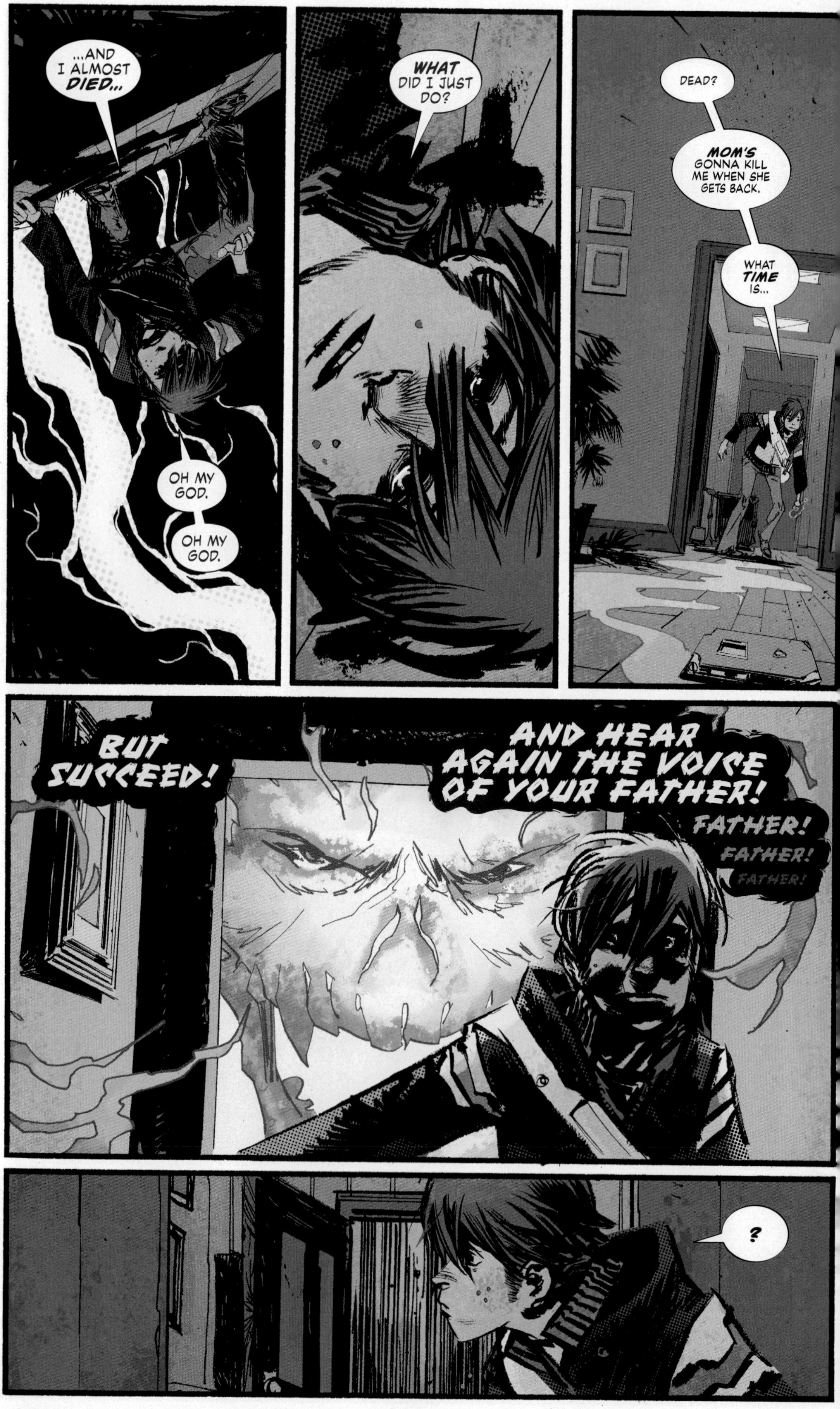
...AND I ALMOST DIED...
OH MY GOD.
OH MY GOD.
WHAT DID I JUST DO?
DEAD?
MOM'S GONNA KILL ME WHEN SHE GETS BACK.
WHAT TIME IS...
BUT SUCCEED!
AND HEAR AGAIN THE VOICE OF YOUR FATHER!
FATHER!
FATHER!
FATHER!
?

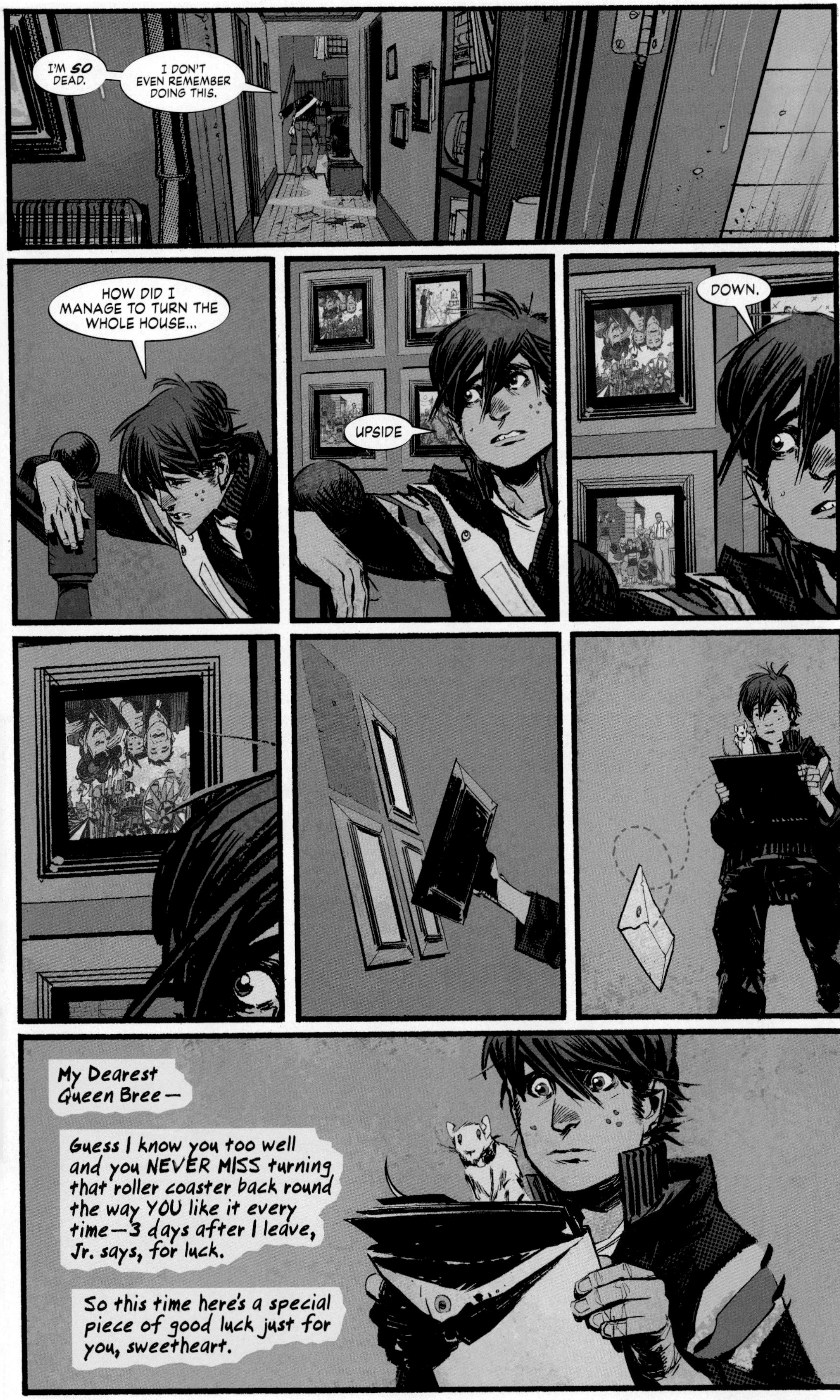

I'M SO DEAD.
I DON'T EVEN REMEMBER DOING THIS.
HOW DID I MANAGE TO TURN THE WHOLE HOUSE...
UPSIDE
DOWN.
My Dearest Queen Bree—
Guess I know you too well and you NEVER MISS turning that roller coaster back round the way YOU like it every time—3 days after I leave, Jr. says, for luck.
So this time here's a special piece of good luck just for you, sweetheart.

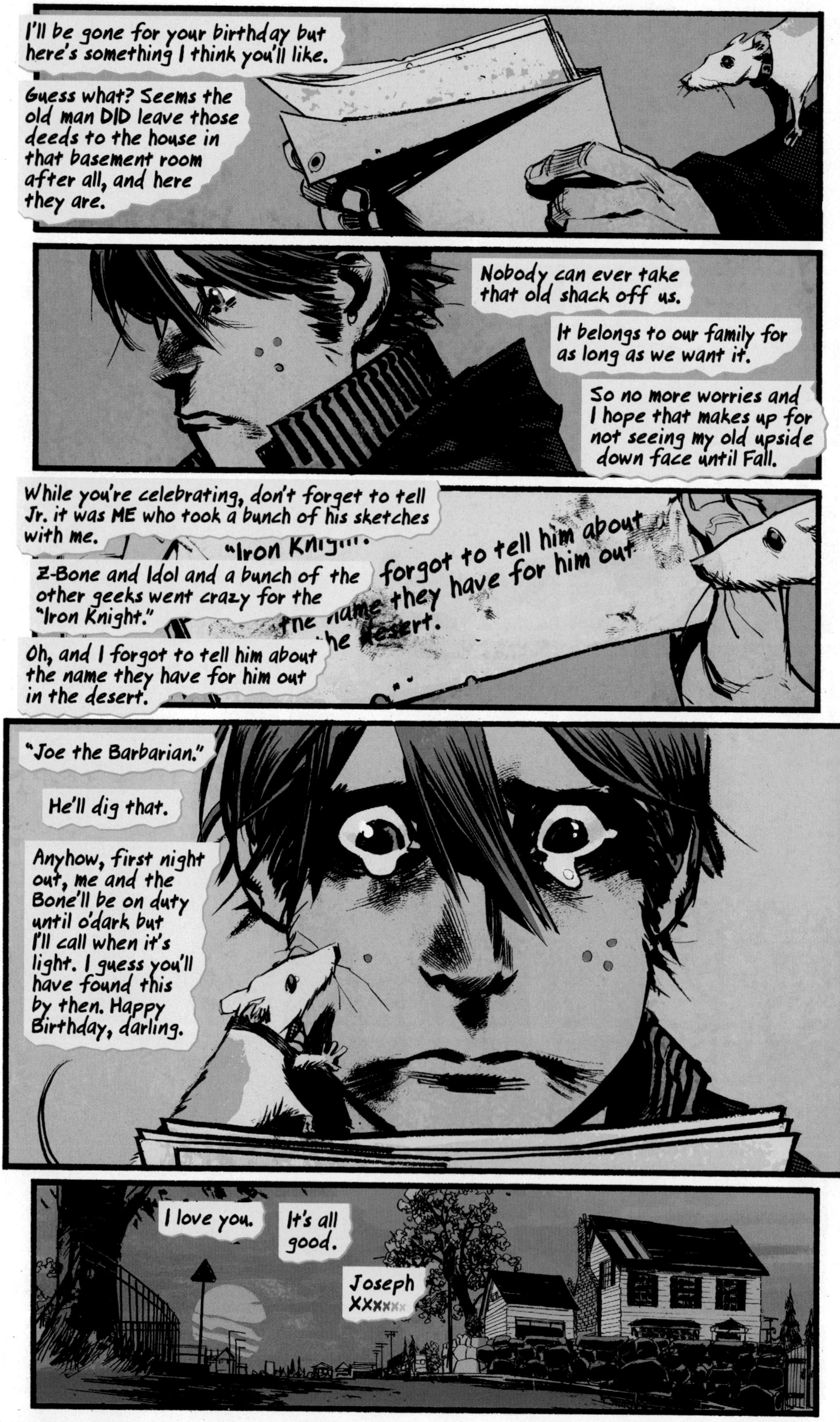
I'll be gone for your birthday but here's something I think you'll like.
Guess what? Seems the old man DID leave those deeds to the house in that basement room after all, and here they are.
Nobody can ever take that old shack off us.
It belongs to our family for as long as we want it.
So no more worries and I hope that makes up for not seeing my old upside down face until Fall.
While you're celebrating, don't forget to tell Jr. it was ME who took a bunch of his sketches with me.
Z-Bone and Idol and a bunch of the other geeks went crazy for the "Iron Knight."
Oh, and I forgot to tell him about the name they have for him out in the desert.
"Joe the Barbarian."
He'll dig that.
Anyhow, first night out, me and the Bone'll be on duty until o'dark but I'll call when it's light. I guess you'll have found this by then. Happy Birthday, darling.
I love you.
It's all good.
Joseph XXXXXX

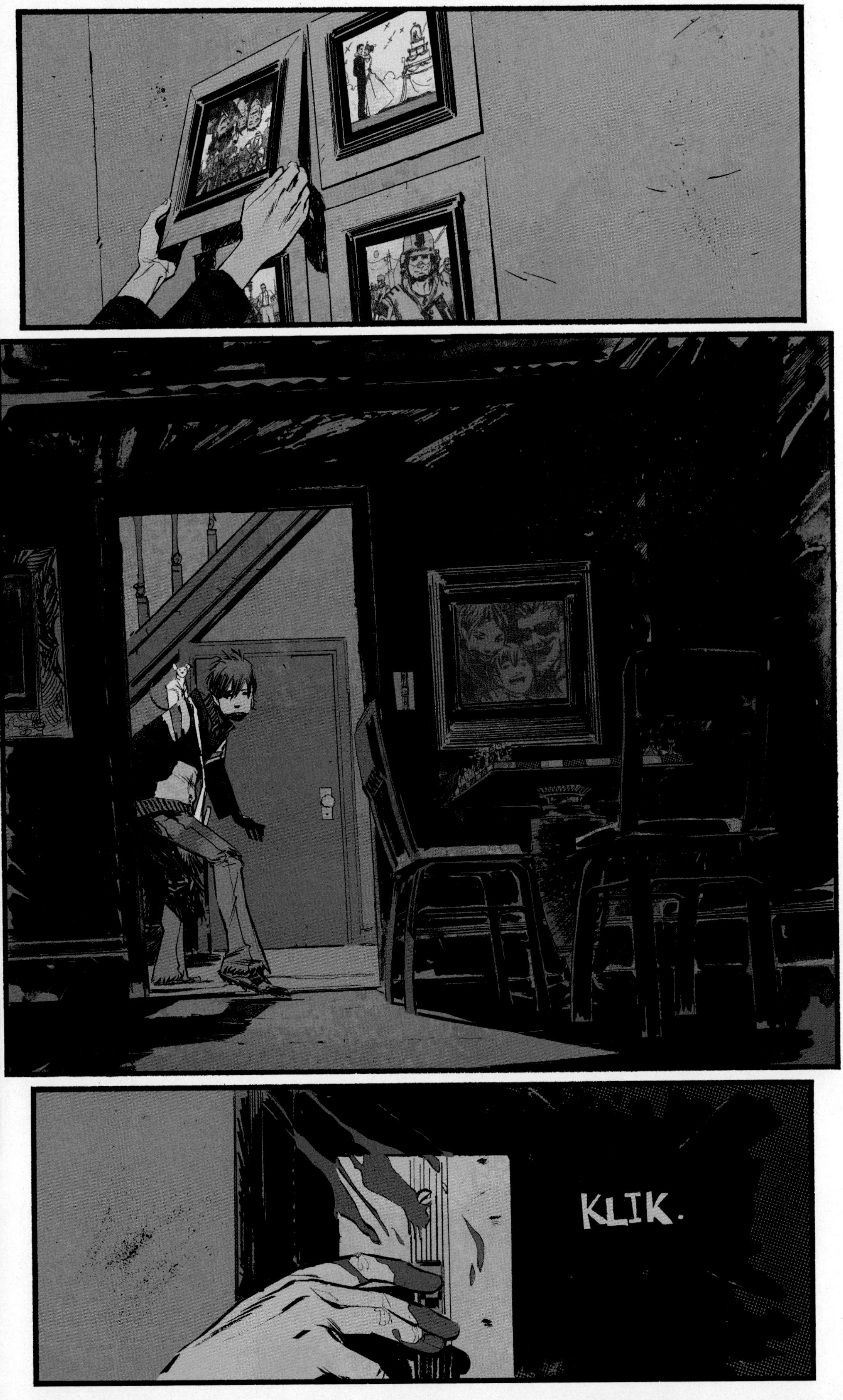
KLIK.

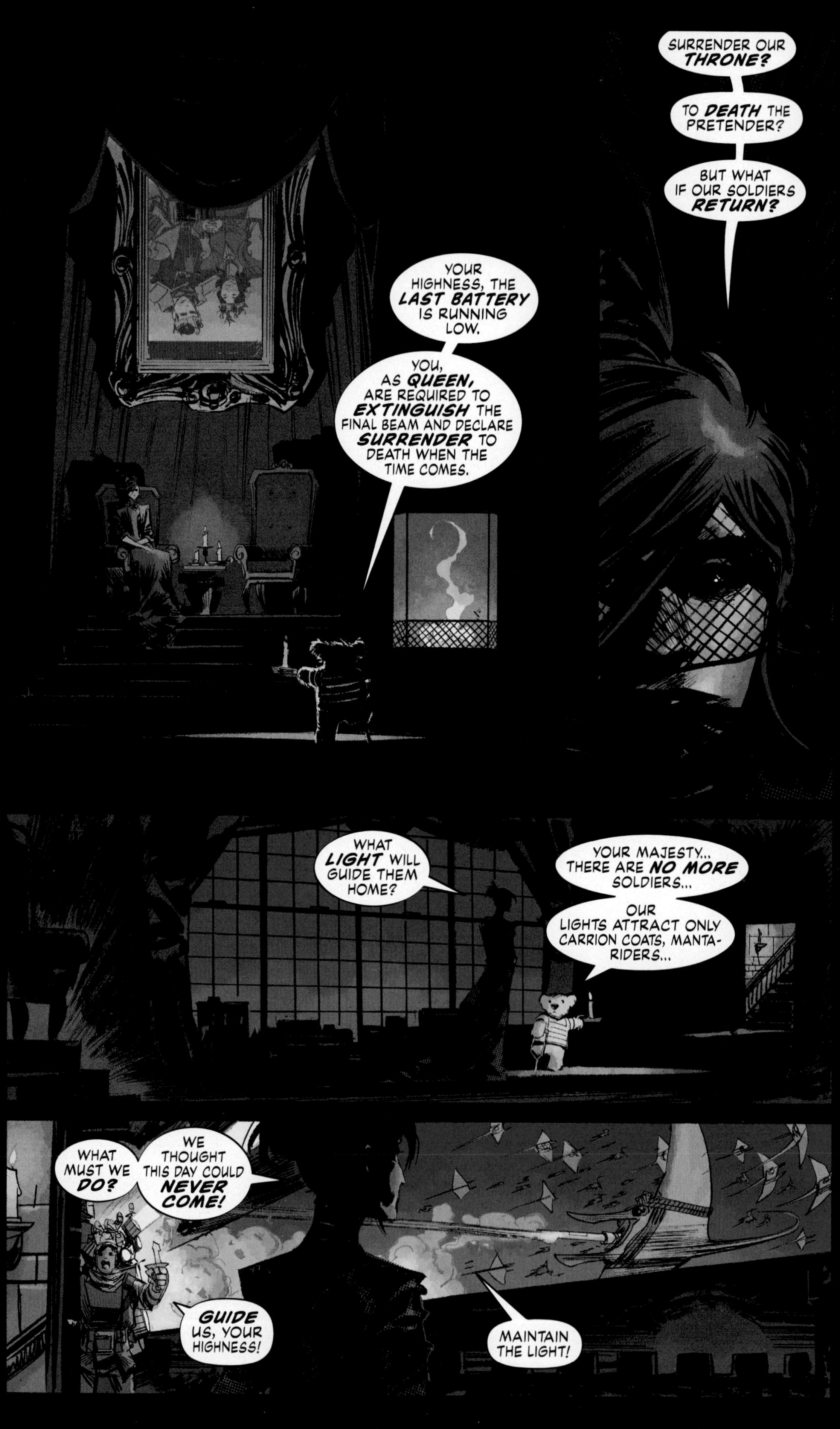
SURRENDER OUR THRONE?
TO DEATH THE PRETENDER?
BUT WHAT IF OUR SOLDIERS RETURN?
YOUR HIGHNESS, THE LAST BATTERY IS RUNNING LOW.
YOU, AS QUEEN, ARE REQUIRED TO EXTINGUISH THE FINAL BEAM AND DECLARE SURRENDER TO DEATH WHEN THE TIME COMES.
WHAT LIGHT WILL GUIDE THEM HOME?
YOUR MAJESTY... THERE ARE NO MORE SOLDIERS...
OUR LIGHTS ATTRACT ONLY CARRION COATS, MANTA-RIDERS...
WHAT MUST WE DO?
WE THOUGHT THIS DAY COULD NEVER COME!
GUIDE US, YOUR HIGHNESS!
MAINTAIN THE LIGHT!

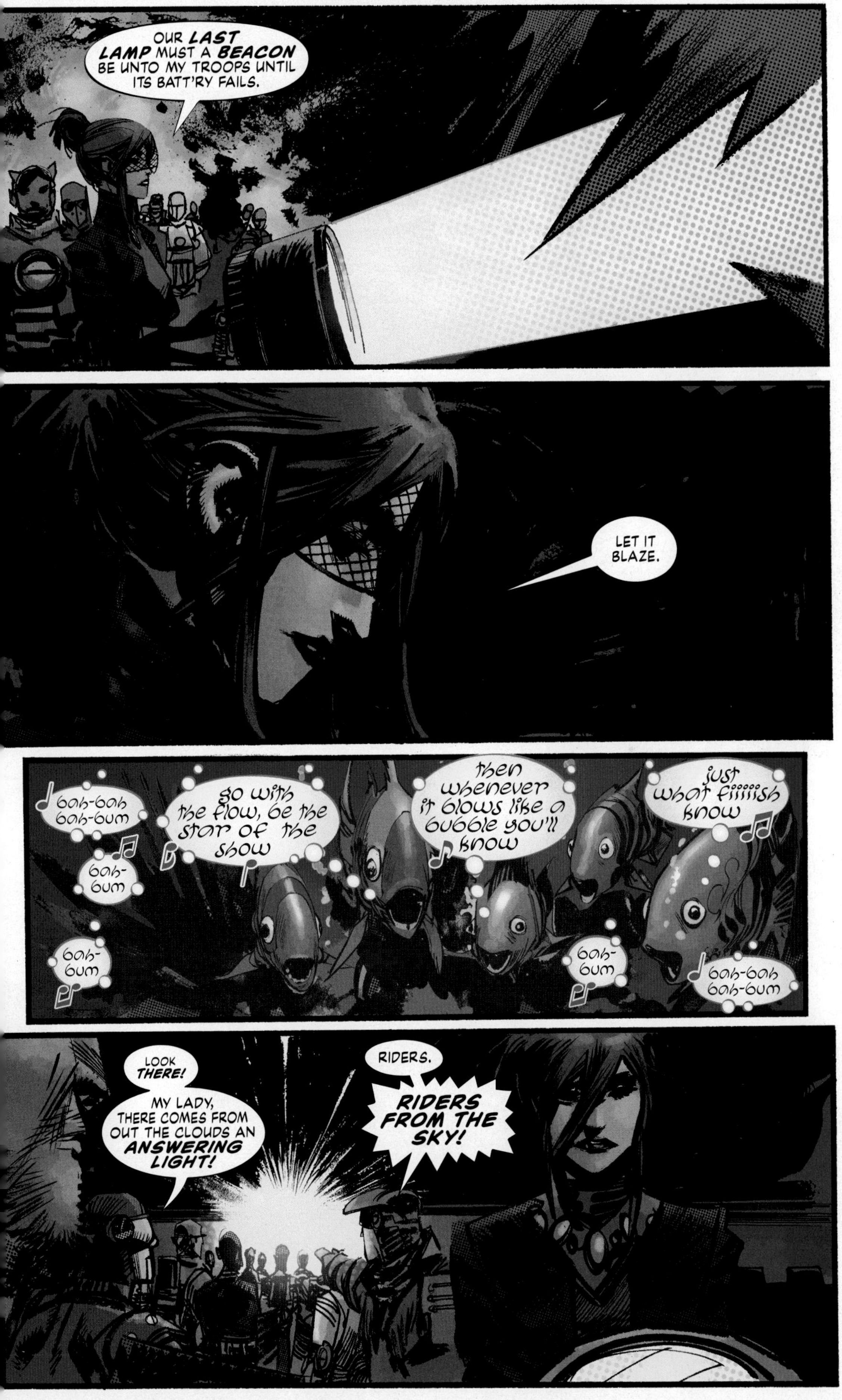
OUR LAST LAMP MUST A BEACON BE UNTO MY TROOPS UNTIL ITS BATT'RY FAILS.
LET IT BLAZE.
bah-bah bah-bum
bah-bum
bah-bum
go with the flow, be the star of the show
then whenever it blows like a bubble you'll know
just what fiiiiiish know
bah-bum
bah-bah bah-bum
LOOK THERE!
MY LADY, THERE COMES FROM OUT THE CLOUDS AN ANSWERING LIGHT!
RIDERS.
RIDERS FROM THE SKY!

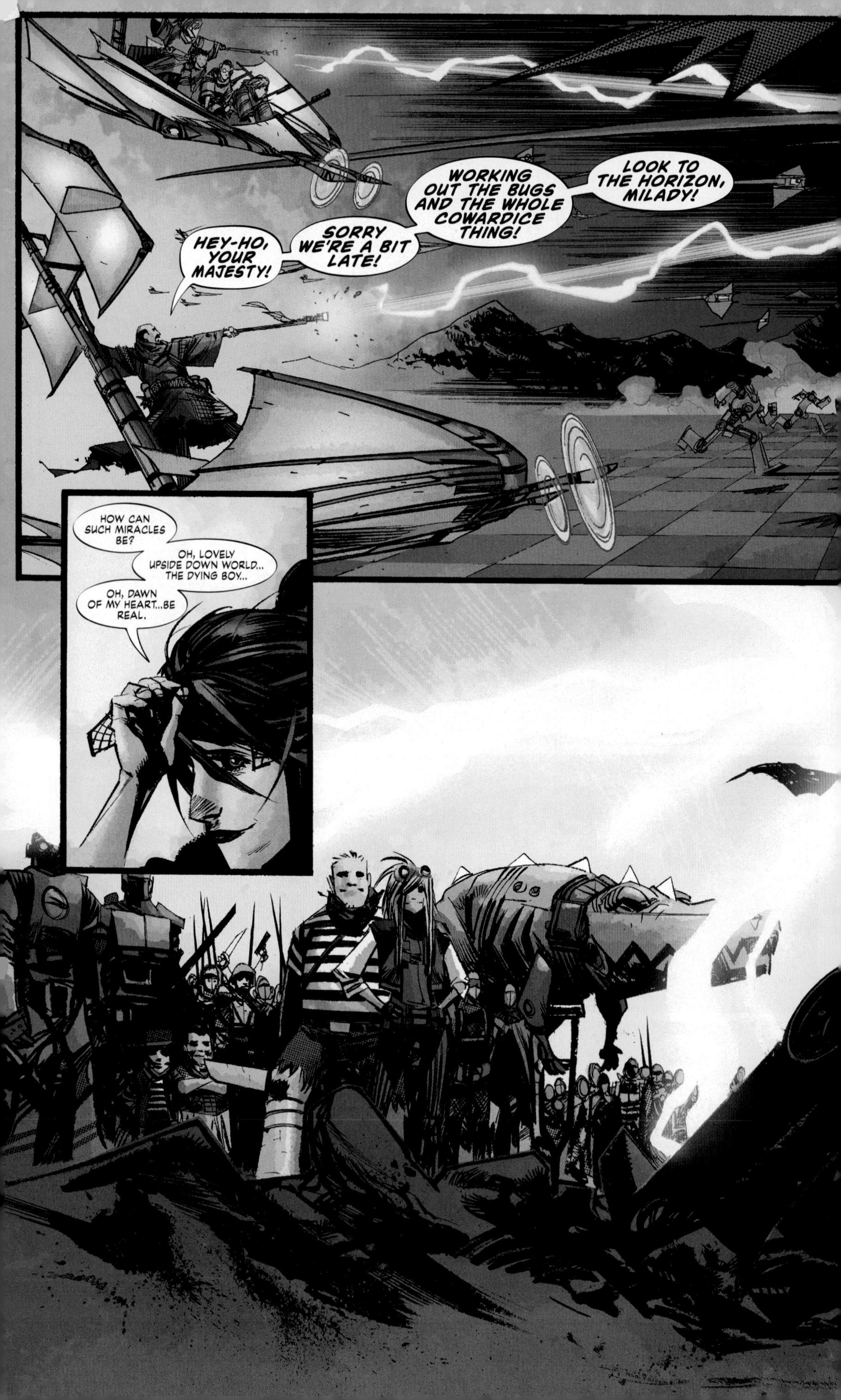
HEY-HO, YOUR MAJESTY!
SORRY WE'RE A BIT LATE!
WORKING OUT THE BUGS AND THE WHOLE COWARDICE THING!
LOOK TO THE HORIZON, MILADY!
HOW CAN SUCH MIRACLES BE?
OH, LOVELY UPSIDE DOWN WORLD... THE DYING BOY...
OH, DAWN OF MY HEART...BE REAL.

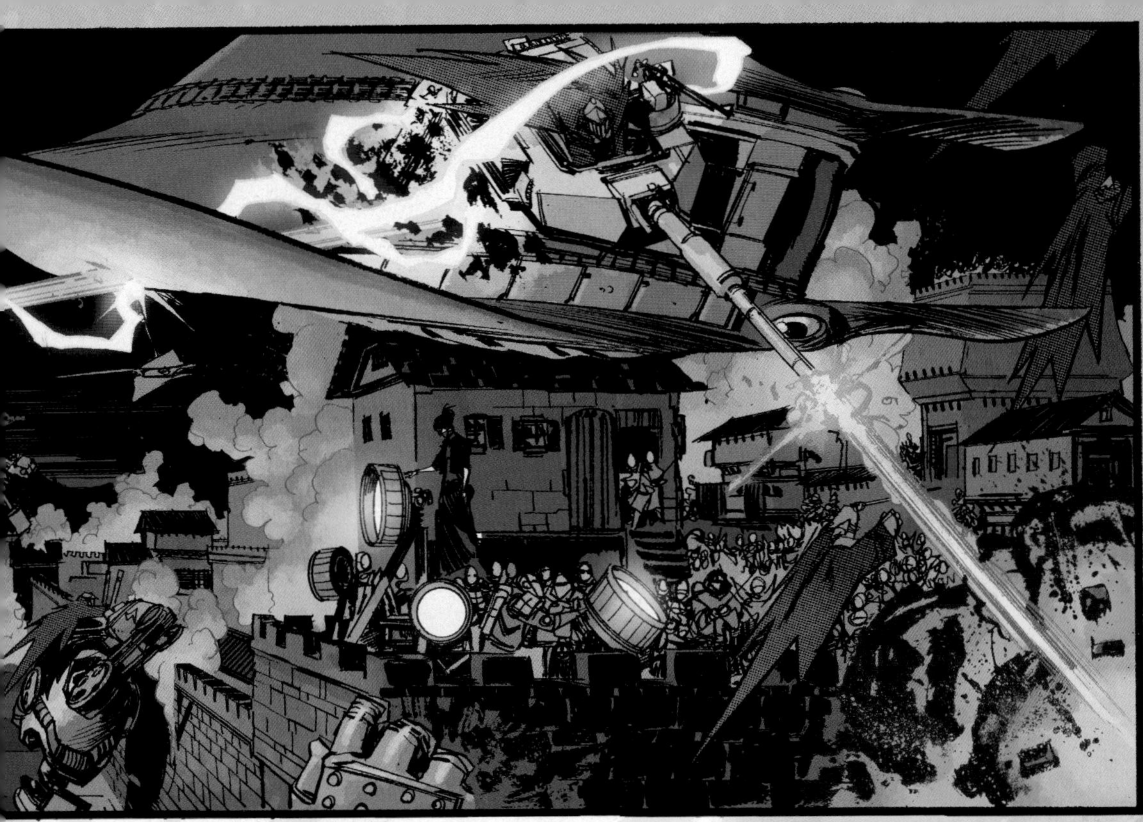

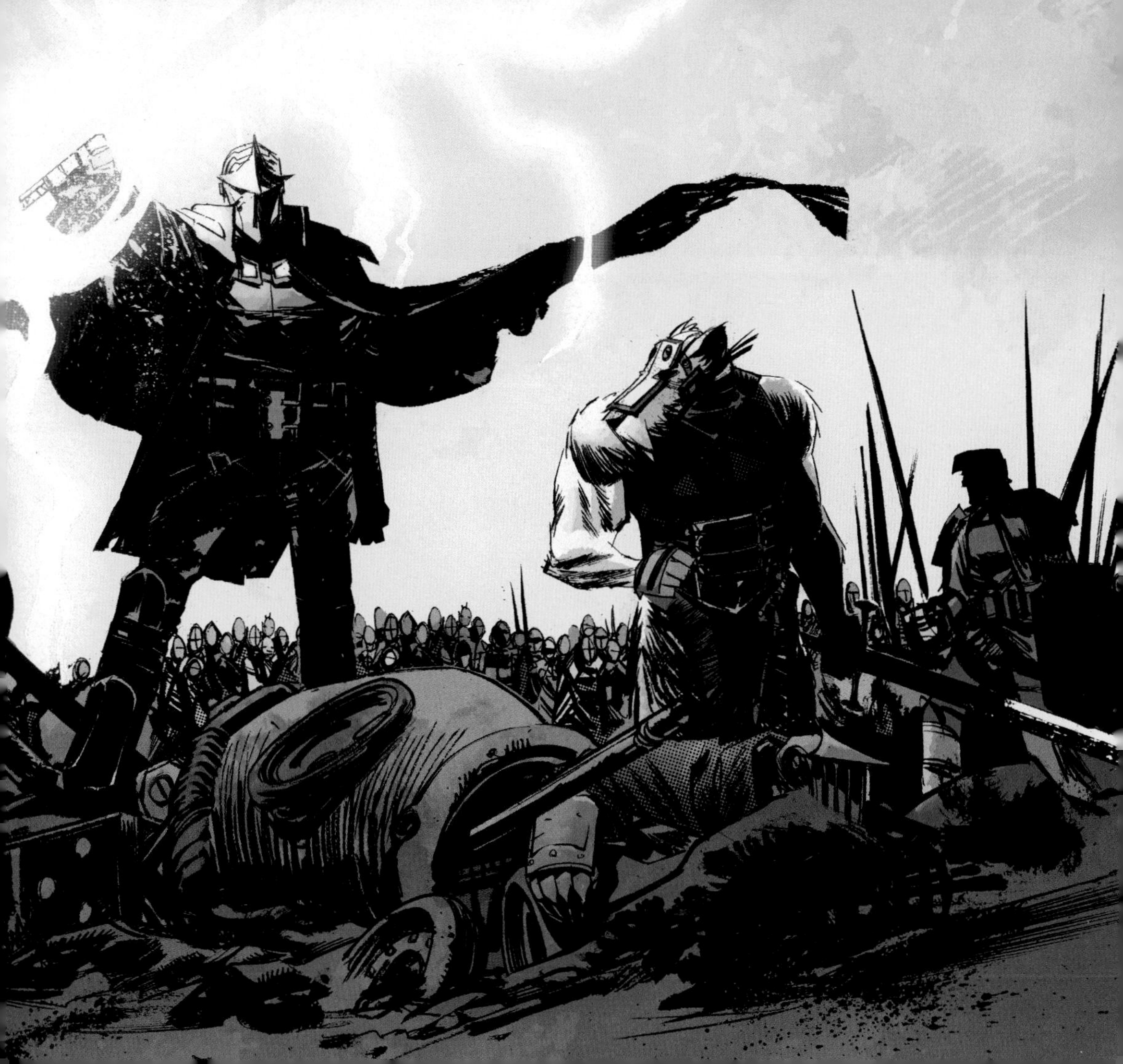

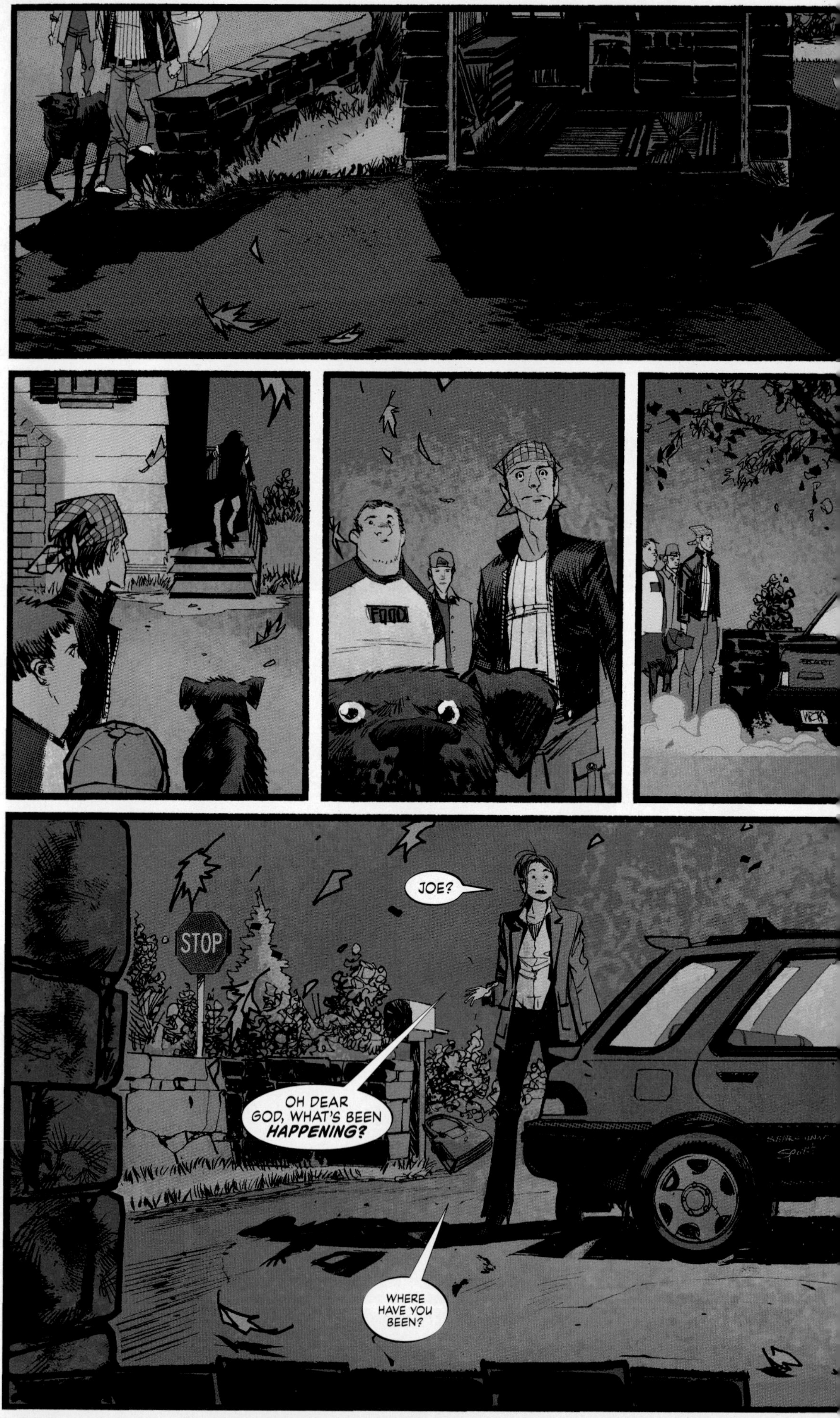
FOOD
STOP
JOE?
OH DEAR GOD, WHAT'S BEEN *HAPPENING?*
WHERE HAVE YOU BEEN?

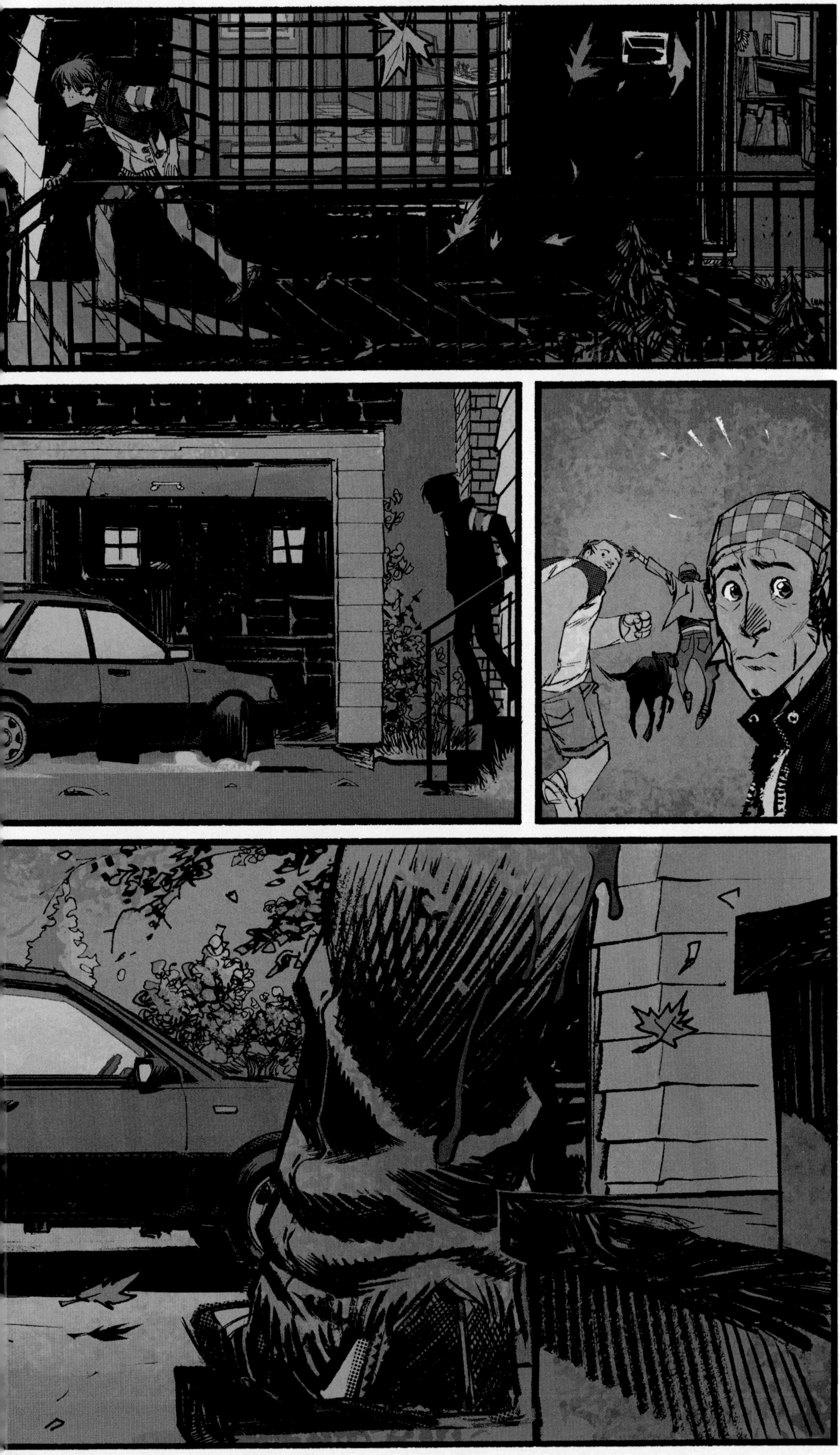

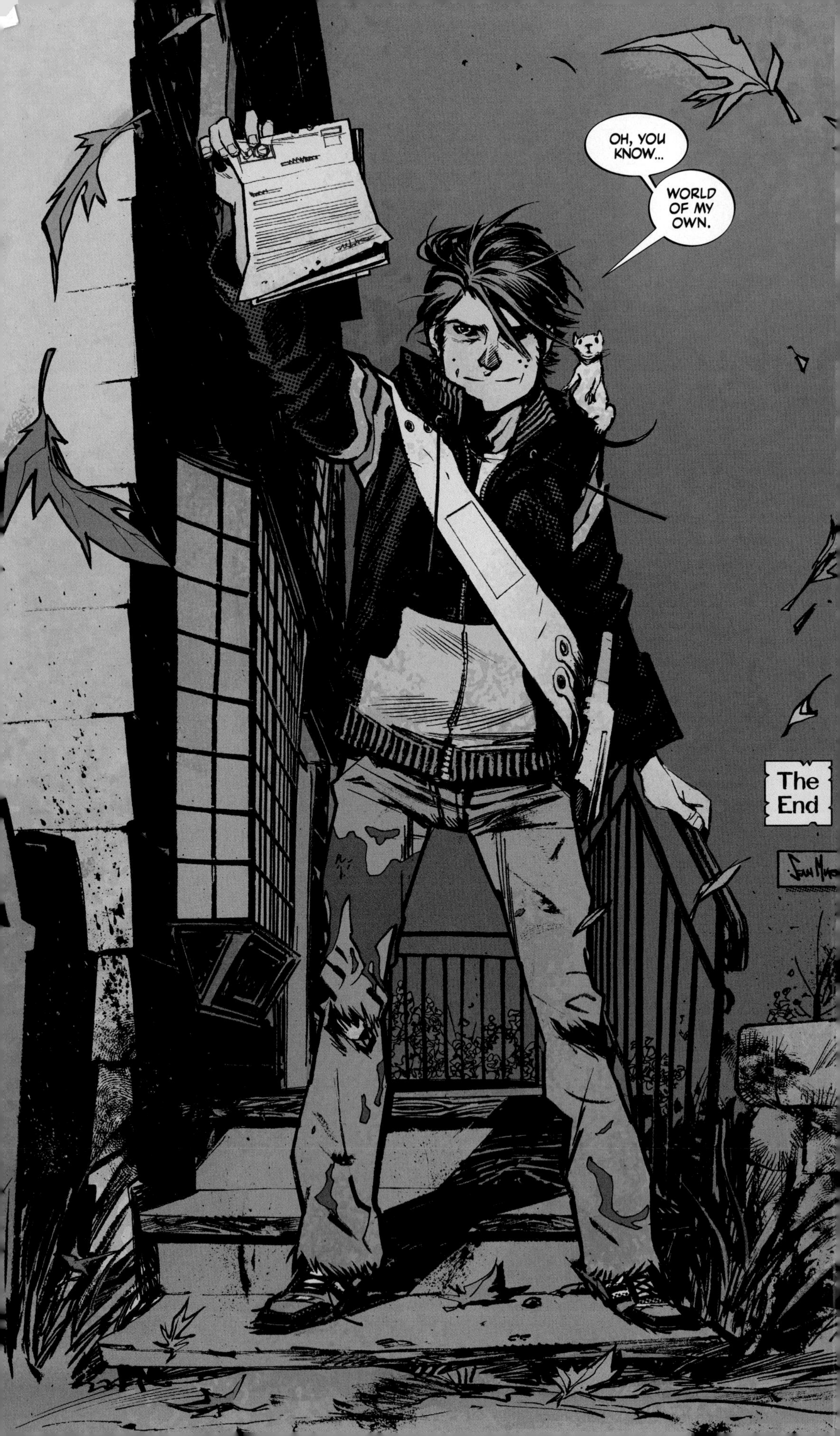
OH, YOU KNOW...
WORLD OF MY OWN.
The End

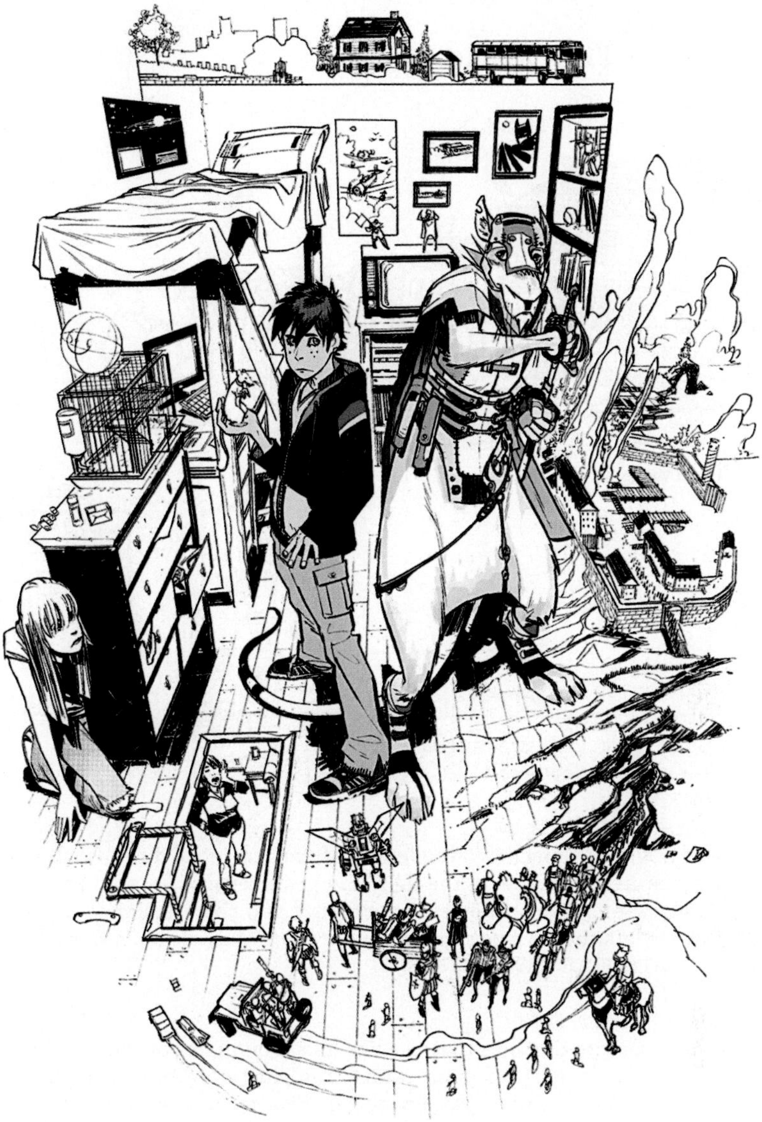

FROM HYPOGLYCEMIC TO HYPOGEA

Drawing up the Iron Kingdom

with GRANT MORRISON *and* SEAN MURPHY

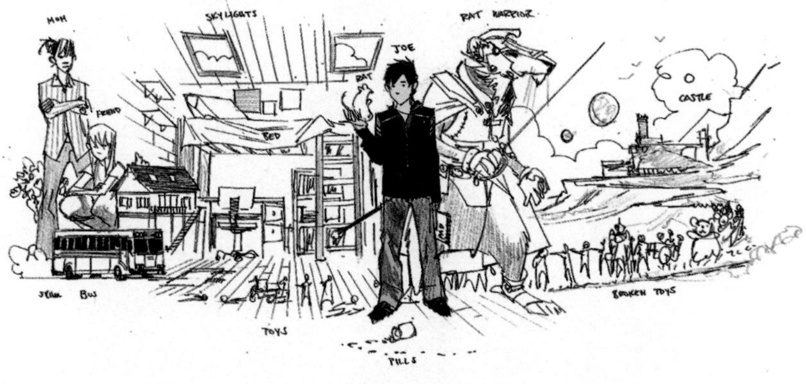
MOM
SKYLIGHTS
RAT WARRIOR
JOE
RAT
FRIEND
BED
CASTLE
JENNA
BUS
TOYS
PILLS
BROKEN TOYS

Initial sketch and final art for a promotional image by Sean Murphy displayed at the 2009 Comic-Con International in San Diego.

The House & The World

JOE'S HOUSE
TOWN
MAIN STREET

Sean Murphy's design an floor plan for Joe's hous

LEVEL 1
LEVEL 2
Attic

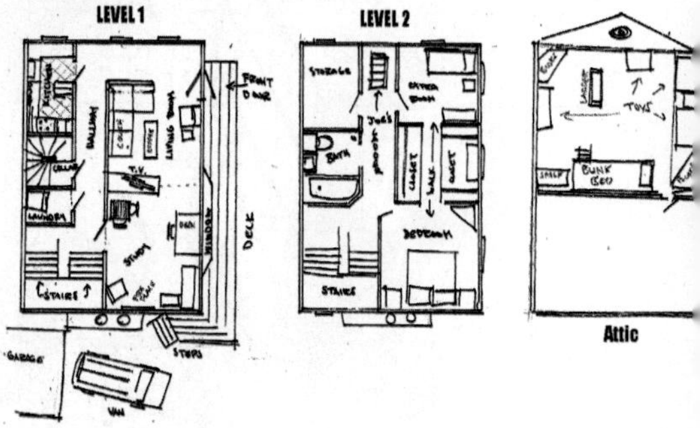

JOE THE BARBARIAN *issue 1*

PAGE 15

Frame 1 — Close up on Jack gnawing the bars of his cage.

Frame 2 — Close up on Joe's sweating face — eyes look down now.

Joe: *JACK?*

Joe: *WHAT WAS THAT?*

Frame 3 — Joe POV — looking down the length of the bed — the duvet is bunched up like hills in miniature landscape. In the lightning glare beyond, we see toys on the shelf at the fa wall, casting wild shadows. Above them a star chart is pinned to the wall. Next to them on the left, there's a peg with a couple of Joe's jackets hung there.

Joe: *DID SOMEBODY SAY SOMETHING.*

Joe: *MOM?*

Joe: *WHAT TIME IS IT?*

Frame 4 — Go closer into the folds that rise like hills around us now, growing in scale and wrappin around us in 360° surround sound. The glow from beyond is like fire... the star char become part of a night sky. Phosgene spots on Joe's retinae, still bright in the darknes after the lightning flash struck tiny flares of the reflective surfaces of the polished toy on the shelf, remain as points of light in the sky, constellations in the shape of the toy — the Car, the Soldier, the X-Box. The Tie-Fighter, etc.

PAGE 16

Frame 1 — Full-page pic as Joe goes into a hallucinatory state. He's standing in mid-distance, facin away from us on a winding road that descends through the jumbled duvet cover, whicl has now become a looming landscape of embroidered hills that rise on either side... dus bunnies — like tumbleweeds as big as sheep but made of stray threads and fluff — blov across the road in a little flock, fleeing from something.

SKY ISLAND
TOYTOWN/CLOUD QUAY
FEATHER FOREST
CRATER FJORDS
STORY TAKES PLACE ON THIS HALF
KINGDOM ISLAND
SPLIT DOWN CENTRE
shape something like this
DOOR TO UNDERGROUND KINGDOM of DEATH (HYPOGEA)
HEARTH CASTLE

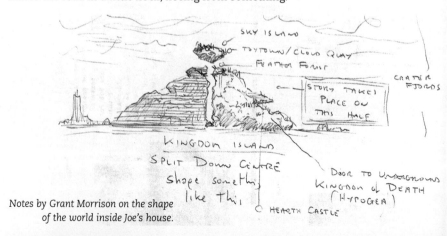

Notes by Grant Morrison on the shape of the world inside Joe's house.

BEACH
Bridge
forest
It's a HUGE ISLAND.
as big as a
COUNTRY
Feathers
Forest
sort of natural
'bowl' at the top
with fjords
Cutaway shot of it
(it's closed in
as above)
Island geography is arranged
on a series of plateaux
like the storeys of the
house

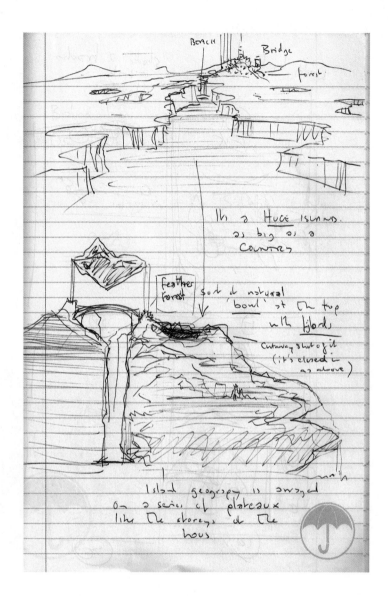

OE THE BARBARIAN *issue 2*

AGE 1 The first-page panel arrangement is the same as in issue 1 — and we'll keep it consistent throughout the series so that the chapter titles and credits are always in the same place. So, as before, we have four panels in the centre of the page with one smaller one in the lower right corner next to the credits. These panels are inserts on 'white page' behind.

This time, drawings appear on the background white in this first panel — a MAP begins to be sketched out. It's like one of those Tolkien maps at the back of fantasy books and we see a new section of it in the first panel of every issue.

Here, we can see the FLOATING ISLAND in the top left and a little dotted trail leading down from the hills to TOYTOWN — which is arranged around the harbour area of CLOUD QUAY where huge sky-faring vessels shaped like cumulonimbus clouds are docked. From Cloud Quay, the dotted trail plummets DOWN to the much bigger island of the KINGDOM and a place called FEATHER FOREST next to BACKBONE BRIDGE (the island continent of the Kingdom is split mysteriously in two — like a giant human brain with its two hemispheres).

Our story takes place on one half of the island, leaving the other for any future sequels. The two halves of the Kingdom were once united by an incredible Kingdom Brunel-meets-Gaudi span called Backbone Bridge, which has been broken since the terrible Battle of Backbone Bridge generations ago.

Character Designs

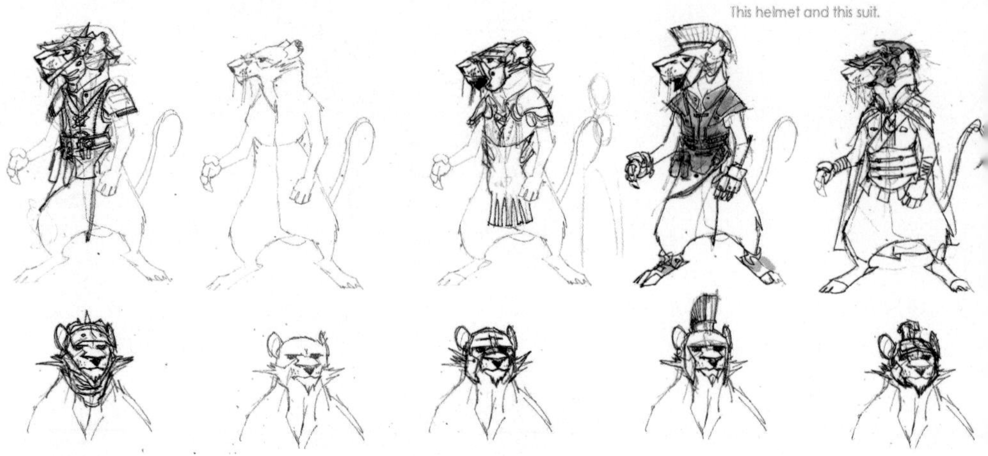
This helmet and this suit.

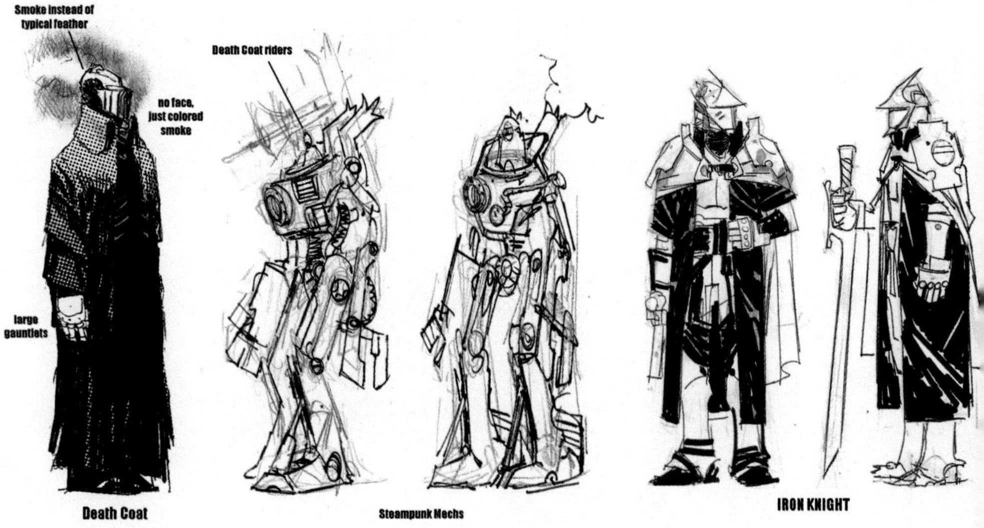
Smoke instead of typical feather
no face, just colored smoke
large gauntlets
Death Coat
Death Coat riders
Steampunk Mechs
IRON KNIGHT

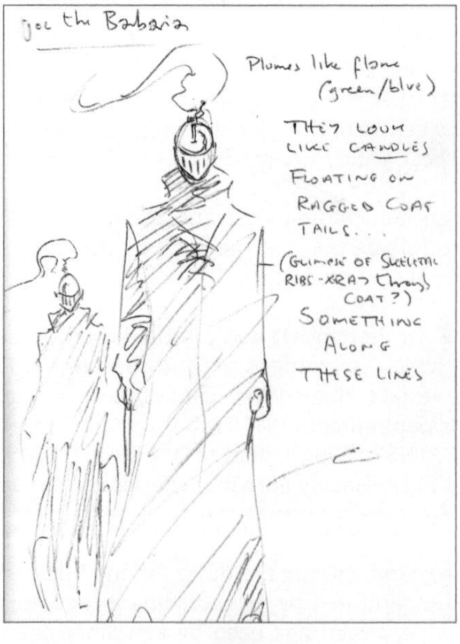
Joe the Barbarian
Plumes like flame (green/blue)
THEY LOOK LIKE CANDLES
FLOATING ON RAGGED COAT TAILS...
(GLIMPSE OF SKELETAL RIBS-XRAY through COAT?)
SOMETHING ALONG THESE LINES

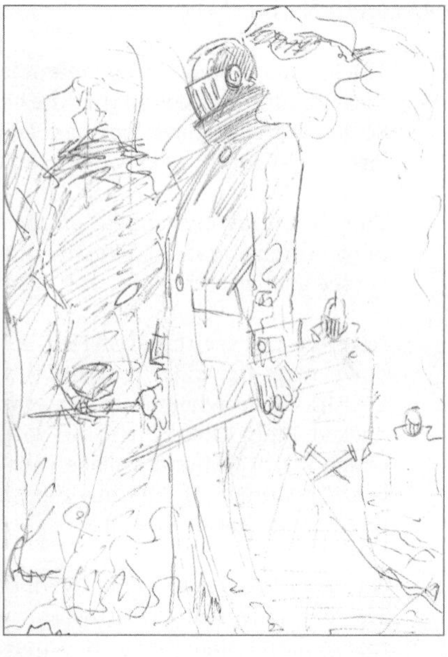

My favorite. If Joe is an introvert then I'm in favor of his hair covering his face a bit. And pale skin reflects someone whose mother is protective and doesn't want him playing outside. Fragile.

Too Harry Potter? Does Joe go to a private school or a public?

My favorite. Something about the blonde hair feels right. Maybe because Joe's world is so dark that she provides some light.

Young Poison Ivy? Haha.

JOE the BARBARIAN — mortar board with TV aerial antlers   ①

WIZARDS of INVENTORIA

Bird or horse skull mask

pushing ceremonial vacuum cleaner

ring of Keys

'OWL' goggles

WING MIRRORS

cloak

floshlight of rank

cloak made from strips of rubber, carpet, telephone wire etc.

each finger on his LEFT hand has a different SWISS army tool

trailing telephone cables

SLIPPERS

PINSTRIPE PANTS

ZEDALUS head sorcerer —

Any others we see follow the same model with detail changes —
Zyxy his apprentice wears a single aerial on a flying helmet —

for Sean Murphy

Thumbnails

Sean Murphy's complete layouts for issue #5.

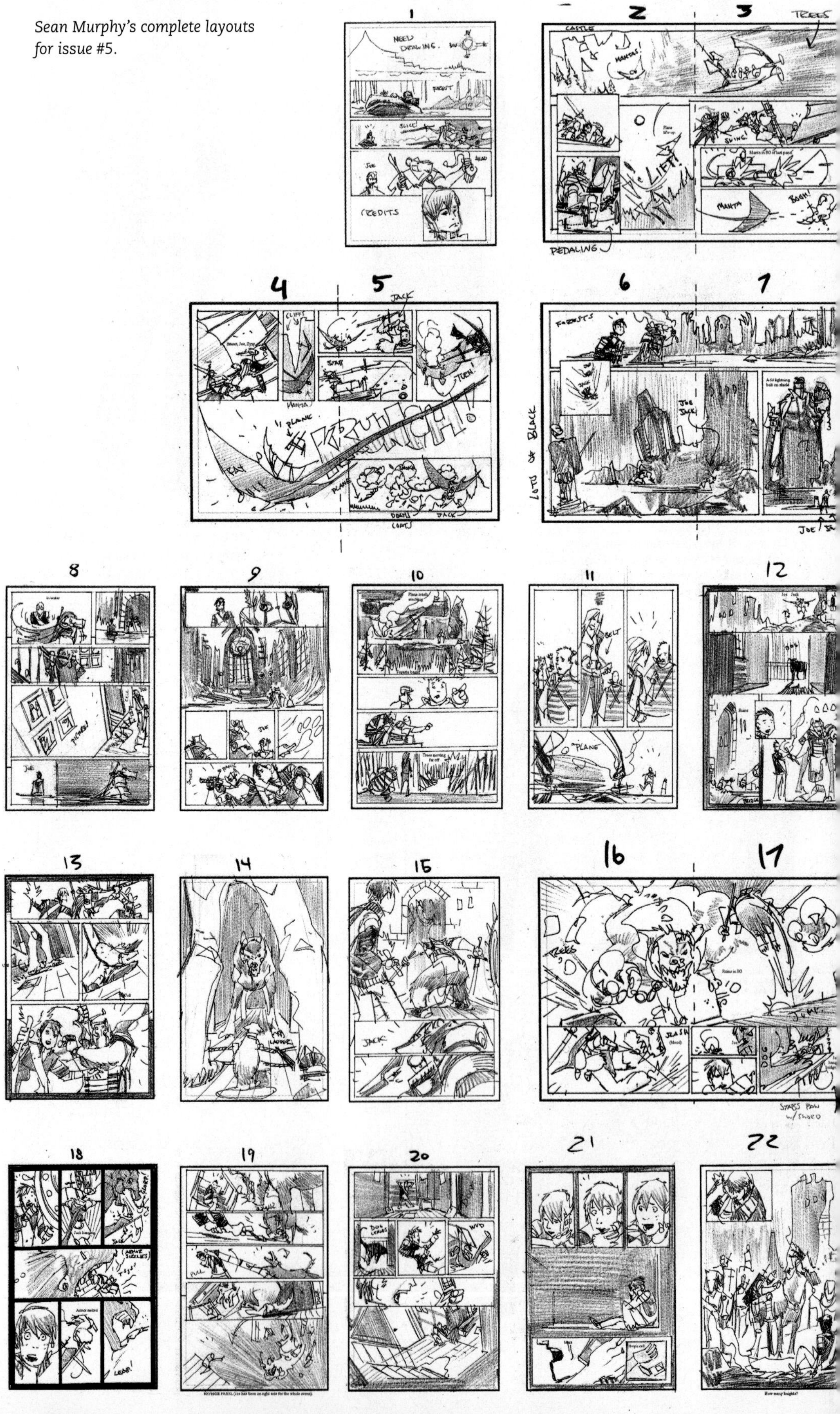
1
NEED DRAWING.
FIRST
SLICE!
JOE
HEAD
CREDITS
2
3
CASTLE
TREES
MANTAS!
LIFT!
SWING
MANTA
BOSH!
PEDALING
4
5
CLIFFS
JACK
STAB
TURN!
MANTA
PLANE
KRUNCH!
RAY
DEATH
JACK
6
7
FORESTS
LOTS OF BLACK
JOE
8
9
10
11
BELT
PLANE
12
13
14
LADDER
15
JACK
16
17
TREES
JUMP
18
LEAP!
19
20
21
22

Storytelling Breakdown

by Sean Murphy

ant's original script for issue #1 called for a silent sequence of Joe walking through his empty •use. Because the details of the house were such an important part of the story, Grant wanted be sure that the layout and room designs were clearly presented to the reader. Once Joe started allucinating, each room design would present certain landscape elements for Joe to experience on s journey through each issue. Because the scene was running silent, I wanted to be sure that the t was interesting enough to hold the scene alone. Originally I thought that readers would think this quence was boring, but to my surprise these pages turned out to be the ones applauded most by tics. Here are a few notes to help explain what I did and why.

• • • • •

The decor of the house wasn't specified, so I was able to run with a lot of ideas of my own that adn't seen done in comics before. The first choice I made was to decorate the house with bad)s and '80s decor, something that I thought would really stand out to readers — especially those no were my age and had the unfortunate experience of growing up with horrible things like plaid uches, shag carpeting and hideous Navajo-style chairs.

The layout for panel one I kept very simple. I didn't want the reader to feel like anything too unusual as happening yet. As the panels progressed, however, I wanted to shift the camera to different angles give readers a sense of eeriness. putting the camera on the ceiling panel two, I felt it helped disrupt e sense of balance in panel one. I ose to not show Joe's face because feel that a character is in more nger when he's not noticing his rroundings.

I love pushing the blacks as much I can, so a shot from the shadowy sement was a must. (While I dn't envision JOE as a dark book, hink it eventually turned into one cause of how much I was playing th blacks.) This also allowed me to ame Joe as he looks warily toward e shadowy basement. If you en't aware that something eerie is ppening yet, this is the panel that akes it clearest.

A nice fish-eye effect really helped is shot. There are a hundred fferent ways to draw someone alking down a hallway where the ader will get bored. I was aiming find the angles that got the reader terested in a scene that normally ould have been dull. My goal was have people thinking, "This is st a stupid scene of a kid walking rough his house! So why can't I op staring at these panels?"

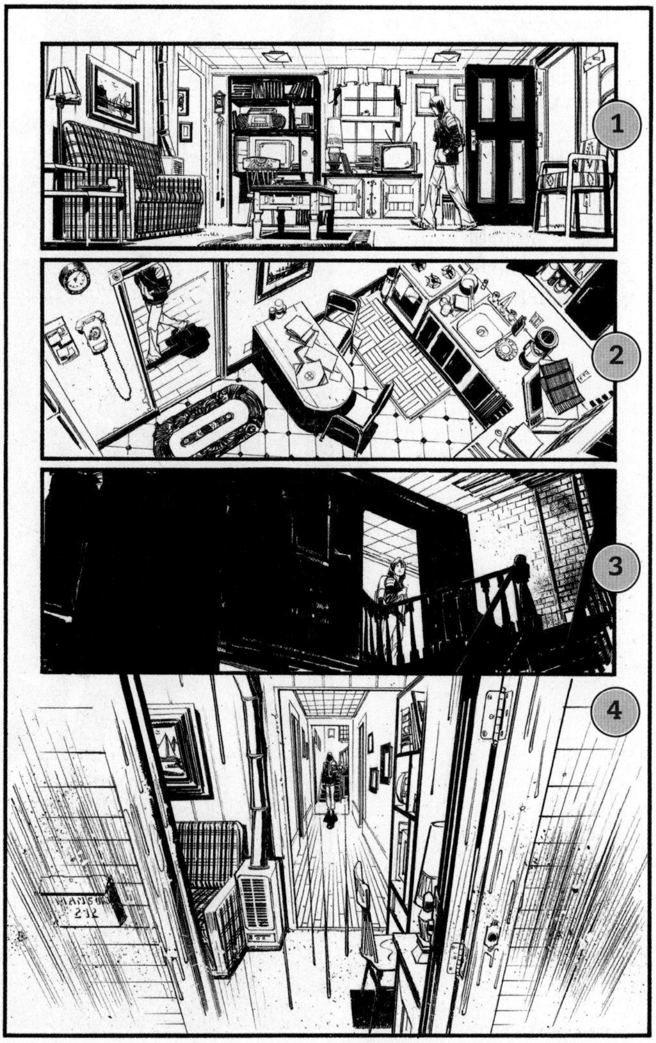
1
2
3
4

1. Grant was clear about the photographs on the wall and about the staircase. I'm not sure if th script called for plants at the bottom of the stairs, but he eventually incorporated them into the serie I often felt that Grant was holding back on writing the script until he saw what I ended up drawin then in each new script he would work around the details I'd added to the previous one. It was sort like an improv performance: each artist working off what the other one did.

2. Again, this panel offered the chance to draw a lot of black — although I probably should have bee more careful about the black at the bottom of the panel and how it blends in the with bleed pan underneath it.

3. This might be one of my favorite shots from the book. I decided to make the staircase twist arou because it was more interesting — in reality, I doubt that a massive staircase like this would ever b built into such a small house, but in a comic book it makes for a great shot (even if an architect wou shake his head).

4. I love tiny panels with small actions happening. Grant wanted to make it clear that Joe had dropp his bag. I believe that this was scripted as a four-panel page, to which I added a fifth panel specifical to show Joe dropping the bag. I hear that not only do most artists never add panels, but some of the even reduce the number of panels from what is listed in the script — something I would never do ended up adding panels every few pages to the entire script because I wanted the storytelling to be ve clear. In a book where a lot of things are happening (toys coming to life, fantasy worlds, hallucinations, etc.), I was afraid that readers might get confused — so I made a point of trying to be as clear as possible with the art.

5. The best way to draw a chess board is from the side. That way you don't have to draw each annoying little piece in perspective.

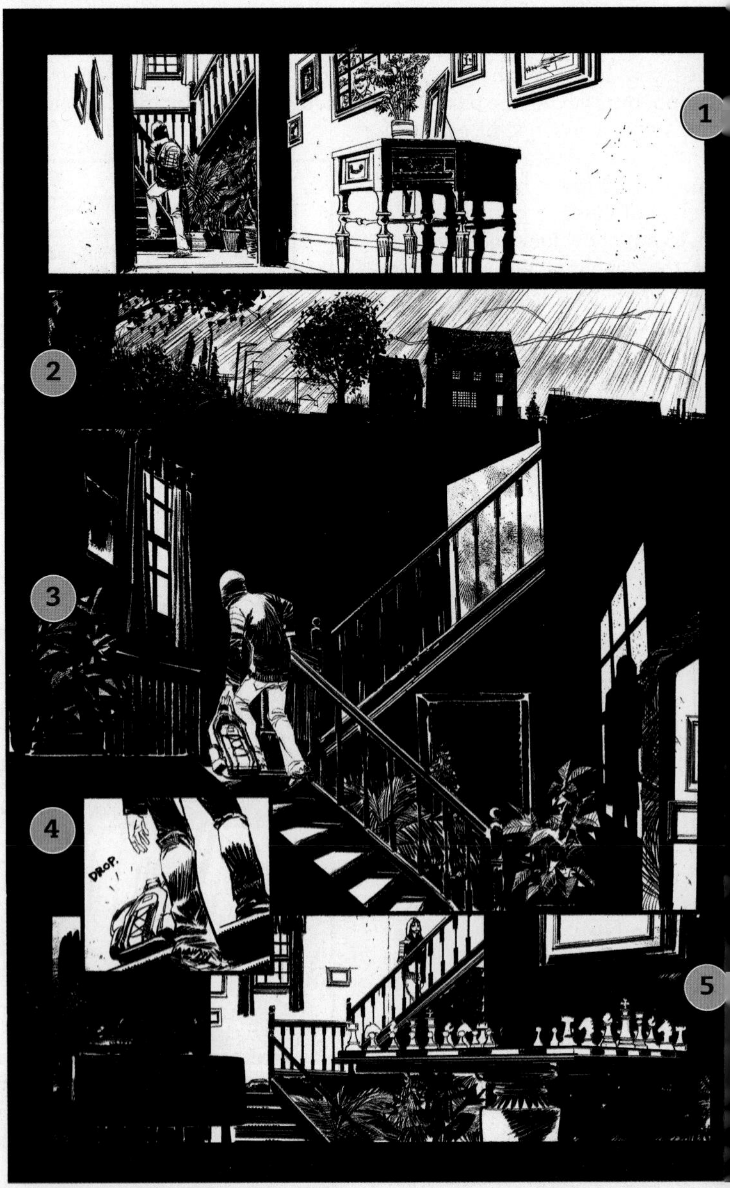
1
2
3
4
DROP.
5

Vhen I sit down to lay out a story, my biggest concern is always clarity. I would rather have something e boring and clear than exciting and confusing. (The goal, of course, is to have it be clear and exciting.) shot drawn in one-point perspective is usually clear, but it can also be boring. For this page I went vith three one-point drawings, which is unusual for me. The reason I chanced it was because of all the etails that I knew were going into the page. Even though Grant suggested things like soldiers, teddy ears and blocks, I couldn't resist drawing more specific toys from the '70s and '80s — stuff that I used o play with. Not only did this make the toys more interesting to draw, but it also became a selling point or a lot of readers. To this day, JOE THE BARBARIAN is described as "that book where the kid's toys all ome to life." If I had gone with generic toys, I'm pretty sure the book would be tagged differently.

. We start with a risky one-point perspective drawing. It's super symmetrical — another layout hoice that can bite you in the ass — but because there are other panels helping to frame the shot, m more likely to get away with it.

. Overlapping panels are tricky because if you overuse them they disrupt the storytelling. On Joe I ried to use them sparingly and with purpose. Because I wanted to draw attention to the bathroom something clearly written into the script), I have panel two floating below the bathroom door o readers won't miss it. This panel also counts as one of those mini "one-action" panels that I ove so much.

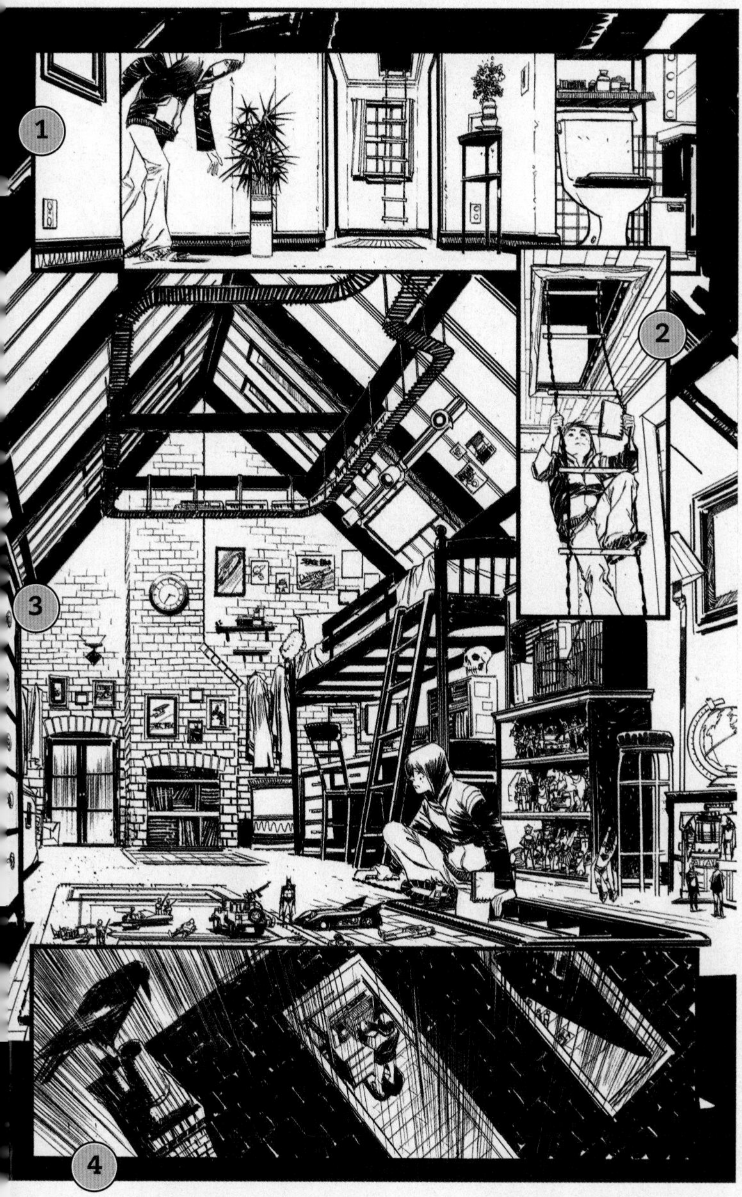

1
2
3
4

3. I'm not going to lie — this is the room I always wanted as a kid. I pretty much just glanced at the script and thought, "I don't even need to read this because I know exactly the type of room Joe should have!"

4. This shot was tough to figure out. The script called for a crow and I assumed it would take on some significance later on. But it never did. I think Grant threw in the crow just to mess with me. It did end up creating a very nice shot, though.

1. Any awesome bedroom of the '80s has to have a bunk bed. I picture Joe sitting up there on a rair day, playing old-school video games with his pet rat scurrying off to the side.

2. I love drawing rain. I hate when artists leave rain to the colorist. For this shot I referenced the wa Bill Watterson did rain in Calvin and Hobbes. With all the spotted blacks and rain textures, this pan ended up being a home run — and believe me, I'm not very secure in my work. Usually I dislike wha I draw and lose sleep over it. So when something comes out okay at the end of the day, I'm thrille because I know I'll sleep well. Drawing loose is fun, but because you're shooting from the hip wit messy inks you're bound to screw up or get something you didn't plan on.

3. After the work that went into these pages, I felt a lot like Joe in this panel: I wanted to take a na This was actually a snap to draw because, in my mind, I was on top of that bunk bed and lookir through the rainy skylight. Even now it's making me feel a bit drowsy. I can actually hear the rain.

4. I draw for black and white, so it's hard for me to leave anything for the colorist. Here I've left the jc of color-holding that lightning bolt to the great Dave Stewart. Dave deserves a special shout-out fc this entire scene. I don't usually give him a lot of color notes, but I loaded him up for this sequence. H probably thought I'd lost my mind when I started sending him horrible, yellowed pictures of broker down '70s decor.